Practical Data Sc

Practical Data Science with R

NINA ZUMEL
JOHN MOUNT

MANNING
Published by:
dreamtech
PRESS

This edition has been published by arrangement with the **Manning Publications Co., USA.** and published in India by **Dreamtech Press, 19-A, Ansari Road, Daryaganj, New Delhi-110002.**

ISBN: 978-93-5119-437-8

Reprint Edition: 2016

Printed at: *Radha Offset, Delhi*

To our parents
Olive and Paul Zumel
Peggy and David Mount

brief contents

contents

foreword

If you're a beginning data scientist, or want to be one, *Practical Data Science with R (PDSwR)* is the place to start. If you're already doing data science, *PDSwR* will fill in gaps in your knowledge and even give you a fresh look at tools you use on a daily basis—it did for me.

While there are many excellent books on statistics and modeling with R, and a few good management books on applying data science in your organization, this book is unique in that it combines solid technical content with practical, down-to-earth advice on how to practice the craft. I would expect no less from Nina and John.

I first met John when he presented at an early Bay Area R Users Group about his joys and frustrations with R. Since then, Nina, John, and I have collaborated on a couple of projects for my former employer. And John has presented early ideas from *PDSwR*—both to the "big" group and our Berkeley R-Beginners meetup. Based on his experience as a practicing data scientist, John is outspoken and has strong views about how to do things. *PDSwR* reflects Nina and John's definite views on how to do data science—what tools to use, the process to follow, the important methods, and the importance of interpersonal communications. There are no ambiguities in *PDSwR*.

This, as far as I'm concerned, is perfectly fine, especially since I agree with 98% of their views. (My only quibble is around SQL—but that's more an issue of my upbringing than of disagreement.) What their unambiguous writing means is that you can focus on the craft and art of data science and not be distracted by choices of which tools and methods to use. This precision is what makes *PDSwR* practical. Let's look at some specifics.

Practical tool set: R is a given. In addition, RStudio is the IDE of choice; I've been using RStudio since it came out. It has evolved into a remarkable tool—integrated debugging is in the latest version. The third major tool choice in *PDSwR* is Hadley Wickham's `ggplot2`. While R has traditionally included excellent graphics and visualization tools, `ggplot2` takes R visualization to the next level. (My practical hint: take a close look at any of Hadley's R packages, or those of his students.) In addition to those main tools, *PDSwR* introduces necessary secondary tools: a proper SQL DBMS for larger datasets; Git and GitHub for source code version control; and knitr for documentation generation.

Practical datasets: The only way to learn data science is by doing it. There's a big leap from the typical teaching datasets to the real world. *PDSwR* strikes a good balance between the need for a practical (simple) dataset for learning and the messiness of the real world. *PDSwR* walks you through how to explore a new dataset to find problems in the data, cleaning and transforming when necessary.

Practical human relations: Data science is all about solving real-world problems for your client—either as a consultant or within your organization. In either case, you'll work with a multifaceted group of people, each with their own motivations, skills, and responsibilities. As practicing consultants, Nina and John understand this well. *PDSwR* is unique in stressing the importance of understanding these roles while working through your data science project.

Practical modeling: The bulk of *PDSwR* is about modeling, starting with an excellent overview of the modeling process, including how to pick the modeling method to use and, when done, gauge the model's quality. The book walks you through the most practical modeling methods you're likely to need. The theory behind each method is intuitively explained. A specific example is worked through—the code and data are available on the authors' GitHub site. Most importantly, tricks and traps are covered. Each section ends with practical takeaways.

In short, *Practical Data Science with R* is a unique and important addition to any data scientist's library.

JIM PORZAK
SENIOR DATA SCIENTIST AND
COFOUNDER OF THE BAY AREA R USERS GROUP

preface

This is the book we wish we'd had when we were teaching ourselves that collection of subjects and skills that has come to be referred to as *data science*. It's the book that we'd like to hand out to our clients and peers. Its purpose is to explain the relevant parts of statistics, computer science, and machine learning that are crucial to data science.

Data science draws on tools from the empirical sciences, statistics, reporting, analytics, visualization, business intelligence, expert systems, machine learning, databases, data warehousing, data mining, and big data. It's because we have so many tools that we need a discipline that covers them all. What distinguishes data science itself from the tools and techniques is the central goal of deploying effective decision-making models to a production environment.

Our goal is to present data science from a pragmatic, practice-oriented viewpoint. We've tried to achieve this by concentrating on fully worked exercises on real data—altogether, this book works through over 10 significant datasets. We feel that this approach allows us to illustrate what we really want to teach and to demonstrate all the preparatory steps necessary to any real-world project.

Throughout our text, we discuss useful statistical and machine learning concepts, include concrete code examples, and explore partnering with and presenting to nonspecialists. We hope if you don't find one of these topics novel, that we're able to shine a light on one or two other topics that you may not have thought about recently.

acknowledgments

We wish to thank all the many reviewers, colleagues, and others who have read and commented on our early chapter drafts, especially Aaron Colcord, Aaron Schumacher, Ambikesh Jayal, Bryce Darling, Dwight Barry, Fred Rahmanian, Hans Donner, Jeelani Basha, Justin Fister, Dr. Kostas Passadis, Leo Polovets, Marius Butuc, Nathanael Adams, Nezih Yigitbasi, Pablo Vaselli, Peter Rabinovitch, Ravishankar Rajagopalan, Rodrigo Abreu, Romit Singhai, Sampath Chaparala, and Zekai Otles. Their comments, questions, and corrections have greatly improved this book. Special thanks to George Gaines for his thorough technical review of the manuscript shortly before it went into production.

We especially would like to thank our development editor, Cynthia Kane, for all her advice and patience as she shepherded us through the writing process. The same thanks go to Benjamin Berg, Katie Tennant, Kevin Sullivan, and all the other editors at Manning who worked hard to smooth out the rough patches and technical glitches in our text.

In addition, we'd like to thank our colleague David Steier, Professors Anno Saxenian and Doug Tygar from UC Berkeley's School of Information Science, as well as all the other faculty and instructors who have reached out to us about the possibility of using this book as a teaching text.

We'd also like to thank Jim Porzak for inviting one of us (John Mount) to speak at the Bay Area R Users Group, for being an enthusiastic advocate of our book, and for contributing the foreword. On days when we were tired and discouraged and wondered why we had set ourselves to this task, his interest helped remind us that there's a need for what we're offering and for the way that we're offering it. Without his encouragement, completing this book would have been much harder.

about this book

This book is about data science: a field that uses results from statistics, machine learning, and computer science to create predictive models. Because of the broad nature of data science, it's important to discuss it a bit and to outline the approach we take in this book.

What is data science?

The statistician William S. Cleveland defined data science as an interdisciplinary field larger than statistics itself. We define data science as managing the process that can transform hypotheses and data into actionable predictions. Typical predictive analytic goals include predicting who will win an election, what products will sell well together, which loans will default, or which advertisements will be clicked on. The data scientist is responsible for acquiring the data, managing the data, choosing the modeling technique, writing the code, and verifying the results.

Because data science draws on so many disciplines, it's often a "second calling." Many of the best data scientists we meet started as programmers, statisticians, business intelligence analysts, or scientists. By adding a few more techniques to their repertoire, they became excellent data scientists. That observation drives this book: we introduce the practical skills needed by the data scientist by concretely working through all of the common project steps on real data. Some steps you'll know better than we do, some you'll pick up quickly, and some you may need to research further.

Much of the theoretical basis of data science comes from statistics. But data science as we know it is strongly influenced by technology and software engineering methodologies, and has largely evolved in groups that are driven by computer science and information technology. We can call out some of the engineering flavor of data science by listing some famous examples:

- Amazon's product recommendation systems
- Google's advertisement valuation systems
- LinkedIn's contact recommendation system
- Twitter's trending topics
- Walmart's consumer demand projection systems

These systems share a lot of features:

- All of these systems are built off large datasets. That's not to say they're all in the realm of big data. But none of them could've been successful if they'd only used small datasets. To manage the data, these systems require concepts from computer science: database theory, parallel programming theory, streaming data techniques, and data warehousing.
- Most of these systems are online or live. Rather than producing a single report or analysis, the data science team deploys a decision procedure or scoring procedure to either directly make decisions or directly show results to a large number of end users. The production deployment is the last chance to get things right, as the data scientist can't always be around to explain defects.
- All of these systems are allowed to make mistakes at some non-negotiable rate.
- None of these systems are concerned with cause. They're successful when they find useful correlations and are not held to correctly sorting cause from effect.

This book teaches the principles and tools needed to build systems like these. We teach the common tasks, steps, and tools used to successfully deliver such projects. Our emphasis is on the whole process—project management, working with others, and presenting results to nonspecialists.

Roadmap

This book covers the following:

- Managing the data science process itself. The data scientist must have the ability to measure and track their own project.
- Applying many of the most powerful statistical and machine learning techniques used in data science projects. Think of this book as a series of explicitly worked exercises in using the programming language R to perform actual data science work.
- Preparing presentations for the various stakeholders: management, users, deployment team, and so on. You must be able to explain your work in concrete terms to mixed audiences with words in their common usage, not in whatever technical definition is insisted on in a given field. You can't get away with just throwing data science project results over the fence.

We've arranged the book topics in an order that we feel increases understanding. The material is organized as follows.

Part 1 describes the basic goals and techniques of the data science process, emphasizing collaboration and data.

Chapter 1 discusses how to work as a data scientist, and chapter 2 works through loading data into R and shows how to start working with R.

Chapter 3 teaches what to first look for in data and the important steps in characterizing and understanding data. Data must be prepared for analysis, and data issues will need to be corrected, so chapter 4 demonstrates how to handle those things.

Part 2 moves from characterizing data to building effective predictive models. Chapter 5 supplies a starting dictionary mapping business needs to technical evaluation and modeling techniques.

Chapter 6 teaches how to build models that rely on memorizing training data. Memorization models are conceptually simple and can be very effective. Chapter 7 moves on to models that have an explicit additive structure. Such functional structure adds the ability to usefully interpolate and extrapolate situations and to identify important variables and effects.

Chapter 8 shows what to do in projects where there is no labeled training data available. Advanced modeling methods that increase prediction performance and fix specific modeling issues are introduced in chapter 9.

Part 3 moves away from modeling and back to process. We show how to deliver results. Chapter 10 demonstrates how to manage, document, and deploy your models. You'll learn how to create effective presentations for different audiences in chapter 11.

The appendixes include additional technical details about R, statistics, and more tools that are available. Appendix A shows how to install R, get started working, and work with other tools (such as SQL). Appendix B is a refresher on a few key statistical ideas. Appendix C discusses additional tools and research ideas. The bibliography supplies references and opportunities for further study.

The material is organized in terms of goals and tasks, bringing in tools as they're needed. The topics in each chapter are discussed in the context of a representative project with an associated dataset. You'll work through 10 substantial projects over the course of this book. All the datasets referred to in this book are at the book's GitHub repository, https://github.com/WinVector/zmPDSwR. You can download the entire repository as a single zip file (one of GitHub's services), clone the repository to your machine, or copy individual files as needed.

Audience

To work the examples in this book, you'll need some familiarity with R, statistics, and (for some examples) SQL databases. We recommend you have some good introductory texts on hand. You don't need to be an expert in R, statistics, and SQL before starting the book, but you should be comfortable tutoring yourself on topics that we mention but can't cover completely in our book.

For R, we recommend *R in Action, Second Edition,* by Robert Kabacoff (www.manning.com/kabacoff2/), along with the text's associated website, Quick-R (www.statmethods.net). For statistics, we recommend *Statistics, Fourth Edition* by David Freedman, Robert Pisani, and Roger Purves. For SQL, we recommend *SQL for Smarties, Fourth Edition* by Joe Celko.

In general, here's what we expect from our ideal reader:

- *An interest in working examples.* By working through the examples, you'll learn at least one way to perform all steps of a project. You must be willing to attempt simple scripting and programming to get the full value of this book. For each example we work, you should try variations and expect both some failures (where your variations don't work) and some successes (where your variations outperform our example analyses).
- *Some familiarity with the R statistical system and the will to write short scripts and programs in R.* In addition to Kabacoff, we recommend a few good books in the bibliography. We work specific problems in R; to understand what's going on, you'll need to run the examples and read additional documentation to understand variations of the commands we didn't demonstrate.
- *Some experience with basic statistical concepts such as probabilities, means, standard deviations, and significance.* We introduce these concepts as needed, but you may need to read additional references as we work through examples. We define some terms and refer to some topic references and blogs where appropriate. But we expect you will have to perform some of your own internet searches on certain topics.
- *A computer (OS X, Linux, or Windows) to install R and other tools on, as well as internet access to download tools and datasets.* We strongly suggest working through the examples, examining R `help()` on various methods, and following up some of the additional references.

What is not in this book?

This book is not an R manual. We use R to concretely demonstrate the important steps of data science projects. We teach enough R for you to work through the examples, but a reader unfamiliar with R will want to refer to appendix A as well as to the many excellent R books and tutorials already available.

This book is not a set of case studies. We emphasize methodology and technique. Example data and code is given only to make sure we're giving concrete usable advice.

This book is not a big data book. We feel most significant data science occurs at a database or file manageable scale (often larger than memory, but still small enough to be easy to manage). Valuable data that maps measured conditions to dependent outcomes tends to be expensive to produce, and that tends to bound its size. For some report generation, data mining, and natural language processing, you'll have to move into the area of big data.

This is not a theoretical book. We don't emphasize the absolute rigorous theory of any one technique. The goal of data science is to be flexible, have a number of good techniques available, and be willing to research a technique more deeply if it appears to apply to the problem at hand. We prefer R code notation over beautifully typeset equations even in our text, as the R code can be directly used.

This is not a machine learning tinkerer's book. We emphasize methods that are already implemented in R. For each method, we work through the theory of operation and show where the method excels. We usually don't discuss how to implement them (even when implementation is easy), as that information is readily available.

Code conventions and downloads

This book is example driven. We supply prepared example data at the GitHub repository (https://github.com/WinVector/zmPDSwR), with R code and links back to original sources. You can explore this repository online or clone it onto your own machine. We also supply the code to produce all results and almost all graphs found in the book as a zip file (https://github.com/WinVector/zmPDSwR/raw/master/CodeExamples.zip), since copying code from the zip file can be easier than copying and pasting from the book. You can also download the code from the publisher's website at www.manning.com/PracticalDataSciencewithR.

We encourage you to try the example R code as you read the text; even when we discuss fairly abstract aspects of data science, we illustrate examples with concrete data and code. Every chapter includes links to the specific dataset(s) that it references.

In this book, code is set with a `fixed-width font like this` to distinguish it from regular text. Concrete variables and values are formatted similarly, whereas abstract math will be in *italic font like this*. R is a mathematical language, so many phrases read correctly in either font. In our examples, any prompts such as > and $ are to be ignored. Inline results may be prefixed by R's comment character #.

Software and hardware requirements

To work through our examples, you'll need some sort of computer (Linux, OS X, or Windows) with software installed (installation described in appendix A). All of the software we recommend is fully cross-platform (Linux, OS X, or Windows), freely available, and usually open source.

We suggest installing at least the following:

- R itself: http://cran.r-project.org.
- Various packages from CRAN (installed by R itself using the `install.packages()` command and activated using the `library()` command).
- Git for version control: http://git-scm.com.
- RStudio for an integrated editor, execution and graphing environment—http://www.rstudio.com.
- A bash shell for system commands. This is built-in for Linux and OS X, and can be added to Windows by installing Cygwin (http://www.cygwin.com). We don't

write any scripts, so an experienced Windows shell user can skip installing Cygwin if they're able to translate our bash commands into the appropriate Windows commands.

Author Online

The purchase of *Practical Data Science with R* includes free access to a private web forum run by Manning Publications, where you can make comments about the book, ask technical questions, and receive help from the authors and from other users. To access the forum and subscribe to it, point your web browser to www.manning.com/PracticalDataSciencewithR. This page provides information on how to get on the forum once you are registered, what kind of help is available, and the rules of conduct on the forum.

Manning's commitment to our readers is to provide a venue where a meaningful dialogue between individual readers and between readers and the authors can take place. It is not a commitment to any specific amount of participation on the part of the authors, whose contribution to the forum remains voluntary (and unpaid). We suggest you try asking the authors some challenging questions lest their interest stray!

The Author Online forum and the archives of previous discussions will be accessible from the publisher's website as long as the book is in print.

About the authors

NINA ZUMEL has worked as a scientist at SRI International, an independent, nonprofit research institute. She has worked as chief scientist of a price optimization company and founded a contract research company. Nina is now a principal consultant at Win-Vector LLC. She can be reached at nzumel@win-vector.com.

JOHN MOUNT has worked as a computational scientist in biotechnology and as a stock trading algorithm designer, and has managed a research team for Shopping.com. He is now a principal consultant at Win-Vector LLC. John can be reached at jmount@win-vector.com.

about the cover illustration

The figure on the cover of *Practical Data Science with R* is captioned "Habit of a Lady of China in 1703." The illustration is taken from Thomas Jefferys' *A Collection of the Dresses of Different Nations, Ancient and Modern* (four volumes), London, published between 1757 and 1772. The title page states that these are hand-colored copperplate engravings, heightened with gum arabic. Thomas Jefferys (1719–1771) was called "Geographer to King George III." He was an English cartographer who was the leading map supplier of his day. He engraved and printed maps for government and other official bodies and produced a wide range of commercial maps and atlases, especially of North America. His work as a mapmaker sparked an interest in local dress customs of the lands he surveyed and mapped; they are brilliantly displayed in this four-volume collection.

Fascination with faraway lands and travel for pleasure were relatively new phenomena in the eighteenth century, and collections such as this one were popular, introducing both the tourist as well as the armchair traveler to the inhabitants of other countries. The diversity of the drawings in Jeffreys' volumes speaks vividly of the uniqueness and individuality of the world's nations centuries ago. Dress codes have changed, and the diversity by region and country, so rich at that time, has faded away. It is now often hard to tell the inhabitant of one continent from another. Perhaps, trying to view it optimistically, we have traded a cultural and visual diversity for a more varied personal life—or a more varied and interesting intellectual and technical life.

At a time when it is hard to tell one computer book from another, Manning celebrates the inventiveness and initiative of the computer business with book covers based on the rich diversity of national costumes three centuries ago, brought back to life by Jeffreys' pictures.

Part 1

Introduction to data science

In part 1, we concentrate on the most essential tasks in data science: working with your partners, defining your problem, and examining your data.

Chapter 1 covers the lifecycle of a typical data science project. We look at the different roles and responsibilities of project team members, the different stages of a typical project, and how to define goals and set project expectations. This chapter serves as an overview of the material that we cover in the rest of the book and is organized in the same order as the topics that we present.

Chapter 2 dives into the details of loading data into R from various external formats and transforming the data into a format suitable for analysis. It also discusses the most important R data structure for a data scientist: the data frame. More details about the R programming language are covered in appendix A.

Chapters 3 and 4 cover the data exploration and treatment that you should do before proceeding to the modeling stage. In chapter 3, we discuss some of the typical problems and issues that you'll encounter with your data and how to use summary statistics and visualization to detect those issues. In chapter 4, we discuss data treatments that will help you deal with the problems and issues in your data. We also recommend some habits and procedures that will help you better manage the data throughout the different stages of the project.

On completing part 1, you'll understand how to define a data science project, and you'll know how to load data into R and prepare it for modeling and analysis.

1 The data science process

This chapter covers

- Defining data science project roles
- Understanding the stages of a data science project
- Setting expectations for a new data science project

The data scientist is responsible for guiding a data science project from start to finish. Success in a data science project comes not from access to any one exotic tool, but from having quantifiable goals, good methodology, cross-discipline interactions, and a repeatable workflow.

This chapter walks you through what a typical data science project looks like: the kinds of problems you encounter, the types of goals you should have, the tasks that you're likely to handle, and what sort of results are expected.

1.1 The roles in a data science project

Data science is not performed in a vacuum. It's a collaborative effort that draws on a number of roles, skills, and tools. Before we talk about the process itself, let's look at the roles that must be filled in a successful project. Project management has been a central concern of software engineering for a long time, so we can look there for guidance. In defining the roles here, we've borrowed some ideas from Fredrick Brooks's *The Mythical Man-Month: Essays on Software Engineering* (Addison-Wesley, 1995) "surgical team" perspective on software development and also from the agile software development paradigm.

1.1.1 Project roles

Let's look at a few recurring roles in a data science project in table 1.1.

Table 1.1 Data science project roles and responsibilities

Role	Responsibilities
Project sponsor	Represents the business interests; champions the project
Client	Represents end users' interests; domain expert
Data scientist	Sets and executes analytic strategy; communicates with sponsor and client
Data architect	Manages data and data storage; sometimes manages data collection
Operations	Manages infrastructure; deploys final project results

Sometimes these roles may overlap. Some roles—in particular client, data architect, and operations—are often filled by people who aren't on the data science project team, but are key collaborators.

PROJECT SPONSOR

The most important role in a data science project is the project sponsor. The sponsor is the person who wants the data science result; generally they represent the business interests. The sponsor is responsible for deciding whether the project is a success or failure. The data scientist may fill the sponsor role for their own project if they feel they know and can represent the business needs, but that's not the optimal arrangement. The ideal sponsor meets the following condition: if they're satisfied with the project outcome, then the project is by definition a success. *Getting sponsor sign-off becomes the central organizing goal of a data science project.*

> **KEEP THE SPONSOR INFORMED AND INVOLVED** It's critical to keep the sponsor informed and involved. Show them plans, progress, and intermediate successes or failures in terms they can understand. A good way to guarantee project failure is to keep the sponsor in the dark.

To ensure sponsor sign-off, you must get clear goals from them through directed interviews. You attempt to capture the sponsor's expressed goals as quantitative statements. An example goal might be "Identify 90% of accounts that will go into default at least two months before the first missed payment with a false positive rate of no more than 25%." This is a precise goal that allows you to check in parallel if meeting the goal is actually going to make business sense and whether you have data and tools of sufficient quality to achieve the goal.

CLIENT

While the sponsor is the role that represents the business interest, the client is the role that represents the model's end users' interests. Sometimes the sponsor and client roles may be filled by the same person. Again, the data scientist may fill the client role if they can weight business trade-offs, but this isn't ideal.

The client is more hands-on than the sponsor; they're the interface between the technical details of building a good model and the day-to-day work process into which the model will be deployed. They aren't necessarily mathematically or statistically sophisticated, but are familiar with the relevant business processes and serve as the domain expert on the team. In the loan application example that we discuss later in this chapter, the client may be a loan officer or someone who represents the interests of loan officers.

As with the sponsor, you should keep the client informed and involved. Ideally you'd like to have regular meetings with them to keep your efforts aligned with the needs of the end users. Generally the client belongs to a different group in the organization and has other responsibilities beyond your project. Keep meetings focused, present results and progress in terms they can understand, and take their critiques to heart. If the end users can't or won't use your model, then the project isn't a success, in the long run.

DATA SCIENTIST

The next role in a data science project is the data scientist, who's responsible for taking all necessary steps to make the project succeed, including setting the project strategy and keeping the client informed. They design the project steps, pick the data sources, and pick the tools to be used. Since they pick the techniques that will be tried, they have to be well informed about statistics and machine learning. They're also responsible for project planning and tracking, though they may do this with a project management partner.

At a more technical level, the data scientist also looks at the data, performs statistical tests and procedures, applies machine learning models, and evaluates results—the science portion of data science.

DATA ARCHITECT

The data architect is responsible for all of the data and its storage. Often this role is filled by someone outside of the data science group, such as a database administrator or architect. Data architects often manage data warehouses for many different projects, and they may only be available for quick consultation.

OPERATIONS

The operations role is critical both in acquiring data and delivering the final results. The person filling this role usually has operational responsibilities outside of the data science group. For example, if you're deploying a data science result that affects how products are sorted on an online shopping site, then the person responsible for running the site will have a lot to say about how such a thing can be deployed. This person will likely have constraints on response time, programming language, or data size that you need to respect in deployment. The person in the operations role may already be supporting your sponsor or your client, so they're often easy to find (though their time may be already very much in demand).

1.2 Stages of a data science project

The ideal data science environment is one that encourages feedback and iteration between the data scientist and all other stakeholders. This is reflected in the lifecycle of a data science project. Even though this book, like any other discussions of the data science process, breaks up the cycle into distinct stages, in reality the boundaries between the stages are fluid, and the activities of one stage will often overlap those of other stages. Often, you'll loop back and forth between two or more stages before moving forward in the overall process. This is shown in figure 1.1.

Even after you complete a project and deploy a model, new issues and questions can arise from seeing that model in action. The end of one project may lead into a follow-up project.

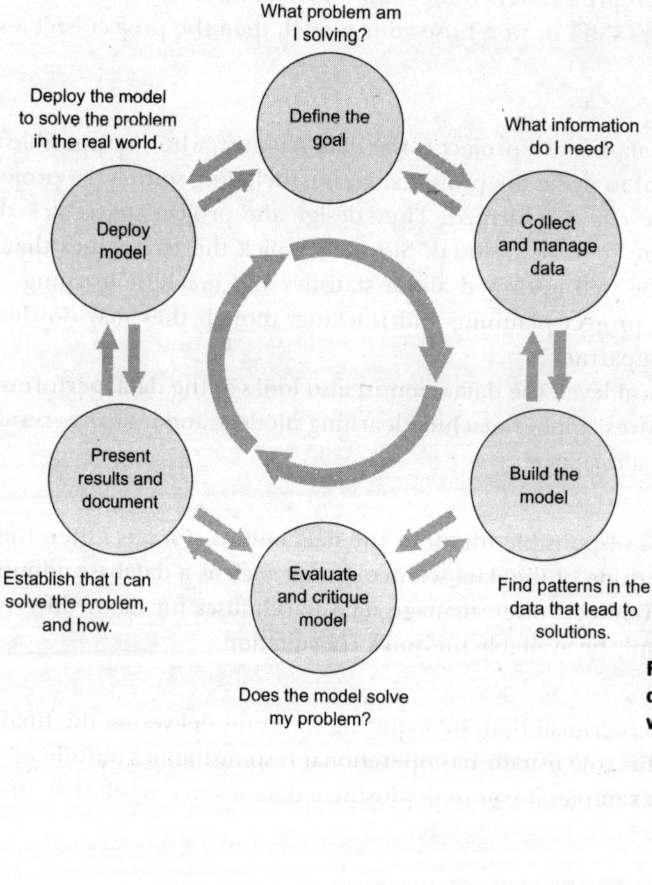

Figure 1.1 The lifecycle of a data science project: loops within loops

Let's look at the different stages shown in figure 1.1. As a real-world example, suppose you're working for a German bank.[1] The bank feels that it's losing too much money to bad loans and wants to reduce its losses. This is where your data science team comes in.

1.2.1 Defining the goal

The first task in a data science project is to define a measurable and quantifiable goal. At this stage, learn all that you can about the context of your project:

- Why do the sponsors want the project in the first place? What do they lack, and what do they need?
- What are they doing to solve the problem now, and why isn't that good enough?
- What resources will you need: what kind of data and how much staff? Will you have domain experts to collaborate with, and what are the computational resources?
- How do the project sponsors plan to deploy your results? What are the constraints that have to be met for successful deployment?

Let's come back to our loan application example. The ultimate business goal is to reduce the bank's losses due to bad loans. Your project sponsor envisions a tool to help loan officers more accurately score loan applicants, and so reduce the number of bad loans made. At the same time, it's important that the loan officers feel that they have final discretion on loan approvals.

Once you and the project sponsor and other stakeholders have established preliminary answers to these questions, you and they can start defining the precise goal of the project. The goal should be specific and measurable, not "We want to get better at finding bad loans," but instead, "We want to reduce our rate of loan charge-offs by at least 10%, using a model that predicts which loan applicants are likely to default."

A concrete goal begets concrete stopping conditions and concrete acceptance criteria. The less specific the goal, the likelier that the project will go unbounded, because no result will be "good enough." If you don't know what you want to achieve, you don't know when to stop trying—or even what to try. When the project eventually terminates—because either time or resources run out—no one will be happy with the outcome.

This doesn't mean that more exploratory projects aren't needed at times: "Is there something in the data that correlates to higher defaults?" or "Should we think about reducing the kinds of loans we give out? Which types might we eliminate?" In this situation, you can still scope the project with concrete stopping conditions, such as a time

---

[1] For this chapter, we use a credit dataset donated by Professor Dr. Hans Hofmann to the UCI Machine Learning Repository in 1994. We've simplified some of the column names for clarity. The dataset can be found at http://archive.ics.uci.edu/ml/datasets/Statlog+(German+Credit+Data). We show how to load this data and prepare it for analysis in chapter 2. Note that the German currency at the time of data collection was the deutsch mark (DM).

limit. The goal is then to come up with candidate hypotheses. These hypotheses can then be turned into concrete questions or goals for a full-scale modeling project.

Once you have a good idea of the project's goals, you can focus on collecting data to meet those goals.

1.2.2 Data collection and management

This step encompasses identifying the data you need, exploring it, and conditioning it to be suitable for analysis. This stage is often the most time-consuming step in the process. It's also one of the most important:

- What data is available to me?
- Will it help me solve the problem?
- Is it enough?
- Is the data quality good enough?

Imagine that for your loan application problem, you've collected a sample of representative loans from the last decade (excluding home loans). Some of the loans have defaulted; most of them (about 70%) have not. You've collected a variety of attributes about each loan application, as listed in table 1.2.

Table 1.2 Loan data attributes

`Status.of.existing.checking.account` *(at time of application)*
`Duration.in.month` *(loan length)*
`Credit.history`
`Purpose` *(car loan, student loan, etc.)*
`Credit.amount` *(loan amount)*
`Savings.Account.or.bonds` *(balance/amount)*
`Present.employment.since`
`Installment.rate.in.percentage.of.disposable.income`
`Personal.status.and.sex`
`Cosigners`
`Present.residence.since`
`Collateral` *(car, property, etc.)*
`Age.in.years`
`Other.installment.plans` *(other loans/lines of credit—the type)*
`Housing` *(own, rent, etc.)*
`Number.of.existing.credits.at.this.bank`
`Job` *(employment type)*
`Number.of.dependents`
`Telephone` *(do they have one)*
`Good.Loan` *(dependent variable)*

In your data, `Good.Loan` takes on two possible values: `GoodLoan` and `BadLoan`. For the purposes of this discussion, assume that a `GoodLoan` was paid off, and a `BadLoan` defaulted.

As much as possible, try to use information that can be directly measured, rather than information that is inferred from another measurement. For example, you might be tempted to use income as a variable, reasoning that a lower income implies more difficulty paying off a loan. The ability to pay off a loan is more directly measured by considering the size of the loan payments relative to the borrower's disposable income. This information is more useful than income alone; you have it in your data as the variable `Installment.rate.in.percentage.of.disposable.income`.

This is the stage where you conduct initial exploration and visualization of the data. You'll also clean the data: repair data errors and transform variables, as needed. In the process of exploring and cleaning the data, you may discover that it isn't suitable for your problem, or that you need other types of information as well. You may discover things in the data that raise issues more important than the one you originally planned to address. For example, the data in figure 1.2 seems counterintuitive.

Why would some of the seemingly safe applicants (those who repaid all credits to the bank) default at a higher rate than seemingly riskier ones (those who had been delinquent in the past)? After looking more carefully at the data and sharing puzzling findings with other stakeholders and domain experts, you realize that this sample is inherently biased: *you only have loans that were actually made (and therefore already*

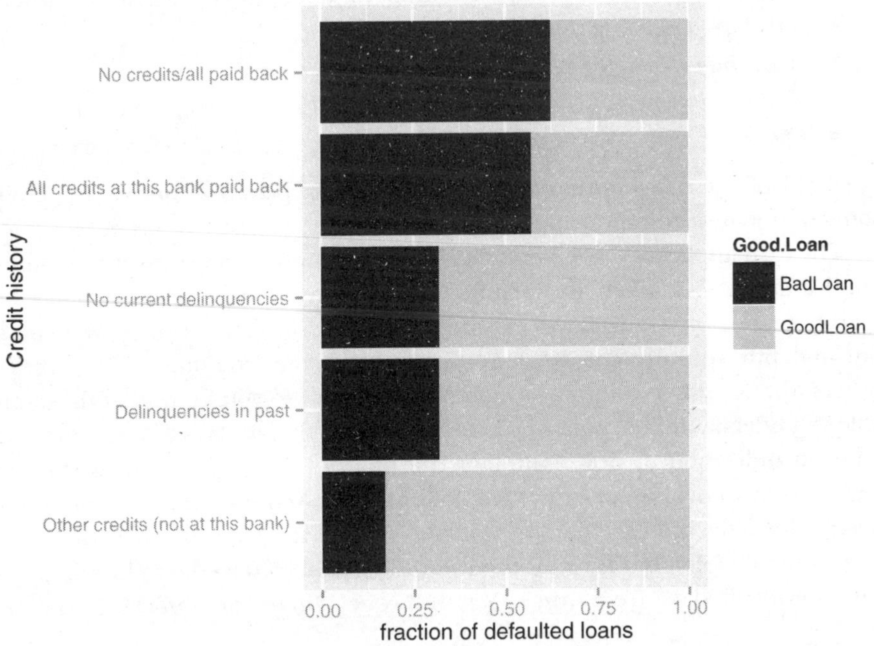

Figure 1.2 The fraction of defaulting loans by credit history category. The dark region of each bar represents the fraction of loans in that category that defaulted.

accepted). Overall, there are fewer risky-looking loans than safe-looking ones in the data. The probable story is that risky-looking loans were approved after a much stricter vetting process, a process that perhaps the safe-looking loan applications could bypass. This suggests that if your model is to be used downstream of the current application approval process, credit history is no longer a useful variable. It also suggests that even seemingly safe loan applications should be more carefully scrutinized.

Discoveries like this may lead you and other stakeholders to change or refine the project goals. In this case, you may decide to concentrate on the seemingly safe loan applications. It's common to cycle back and forth between this stage and the previous one, as well as between this stage and the modeling stage, as you discover things in the data. We'll cover data exploration and management in depth in chapters 3 and 4.

1.2.3 Modeling

You finally get to statistics and machine learning during the modeling, or analysis, stage. Here is where you try to extract useful insights from the data in order to achieve your goals. Since many modeling procedures make specific assumptions about data distribution and relationships, there will be overlap and back-and-forth between the modeling stage and the data cleaning stage as you try to find the best way to represent the data and the best form in which to model it.

The most common data science modeling tasks are these:

- *Classification—Deciding* if something belongs to one category or another
- *Scoring—Predicting* or *estimating* a numeric value, such as a price or probability
- *Ranking*—Learning to *order items* by preferences
- *Clustering—Grouping items* into most-similar groups
- *Finding relations—Finding correlations* or potential causes of effects seen in the data
- *Characterization*—Very general *plotting* and *report generation* from data

For each of these tasks, there are several different possible approaches. We'll cover some of the most common approaches to the different tasks in this book.

The loan application problem is a classification problem: you want to identify loan applicants who are likely to default. Three common approaches in such cases are logistic regression, Naive Bayes classifiers, and decision trees (we'll cover these methods in-depth in future chapters). You've been in conversation with loan officers and others who would be using your model in the field, so you know that they want to be able to understand the chain of reasoning behind the model's classification, and they want an indication of how confident the model is in its decision: is this applicant highly likely to default, or only somewhat likely? Given the preceding desiderata, you decide that a decision tree is most suitable. We'll cover decision trees more extensively in a future chapter, but for now the call in R is as shown in the following listing (you can download data from https://github.com/WinVector/zmPDSwR/tree/master/Statlog).[2]

[2] In this chapter, for clarity of illustration we deliberately fit a small and shallow tree.

Listing 1.1 Building a decision tree

```
library('rpart')
load('GCDData.RData')
model <- rpart(Good.Loan ~
   Duration.in.month +
   Installment.rate.in.percentage.of.disposable.income +
   Credit.amount +
   Other.installment.plans,
   data=d,
   control=rpart.control(maxdepth=4),
   method="class")
```

Let's suppose that you discover the model shown in figure 1.3.

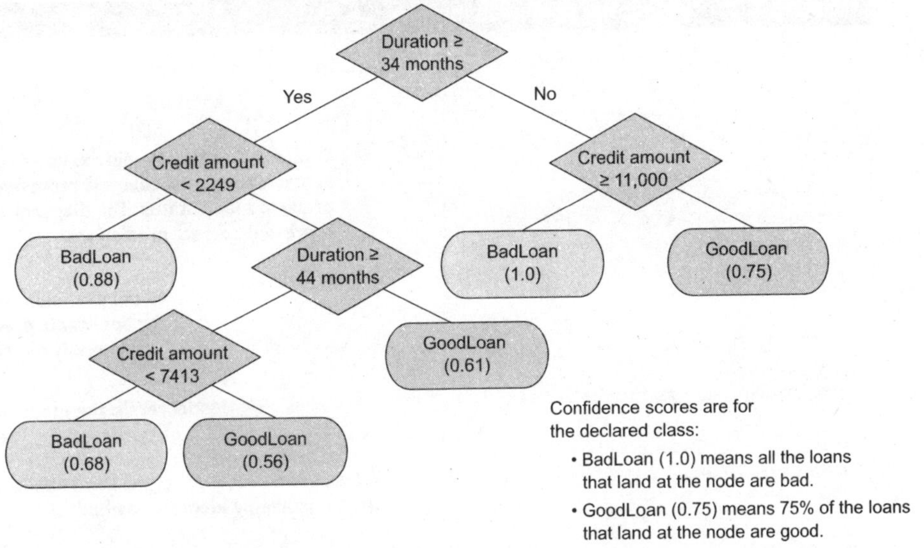

Figure 1.3 A decision tree model for finding bad loan applications, with confidence scores

We'll discuss general modeling strategies in chapter 5 and go into details of specific modeling algorithms in part 2.

1.2.4 Model evaluation and critique

Once you have a model, you need to determine if it meets your goals:

- Is it accurate enough for your needs? Does it generalize well?
- Does it perform better than "the obvious guess"? Better than whatever estimate you currently use?
- Do the results of the model (coefficients, clusters, rules) make sense in the context of the problem domain?

If you've answered "no" to any of these questions, it's time to loop back to the modeling step—or decide that the data doesn't support the goal you're trying to achieve. No one likes negative results, but understanding when you can't meet your success criteria with current resources will save you fruitless effort. Your energy will be better spent on crafting success. This might mean defining more realistic goals or gathering the additional data or other resources that you need to achieve your original goals.

Returning to the loan application example, the first thing to check is that the rules that the model discovered make sense. Looking at figure 1.3, you don't notice any obviously strange rules, so you can go ahead and evaluate the model's accuracy. A good summary of classifier accuracy is the *confusion matrix,* which tabulates actual classifications against predicted ones.[3]

Listing 1.2 Plotting the confusion matrix

```
> resultframe <- data.frame(Good.Loan=creditdata$Good.Loan,
                    pred=predict(model, type="class"))
> rtab <- table(resultframe)
> rtab
          pred
Good.Loan  BadLoan GoodLoan
  BadLoan       41      259
  GoodLoan      13      687
> sum(diag(rtab))/sum(rtab)
[1] 0.728
> sum(rtab[1,1])/sum(rtab[,1])
[1] 0.7592593
> sum(rtab[1,1])/sum(rtab[1,])
[1] 0.1366667
> sum(rtab[2,1])/sum(rtab[2,])
[1] 0.01857143
```

Create the confusion matrix. Rows represent actual loan status; columns represent predicted loan status. The diagonal entries represent correct predictions.

Overall model accuracy: 73% of the predictions were correct.

Model precision: 76% of the applicants predicted as bad really did default.

Model recall: the model found 14% of the defaulting loans.

False positive rate: 2% of the good applicants were mistakenly identified as bad.

The model predicted loan status correctly 73% of the time—better than chance (50%). In the original dataset, 30% of the loans were bad, so guessing `GoodLoan` all the time would be 70% accurate (though not very useful). So you know that the model does better than random and somewhat better than obvious guessing.

Overall accuracy is not enough. You want to know what kinds of mistakes are being made. Is the model missing too many bad loans, or is it marking too many good loans as bad? *Recall* measures how many of the bad loans the model can actually find. *Precision* measures how many of the loans identified as bad really are bad. *False positive rate* measures how many of the good loans are mistakenly identified as bad. Ideally, you want the recall and the precision to be high, and the false positive rate to be low. What constitutes "high enough" and "low enough" is a decision that you make together with

[3] Normally, we'd evaluate the model against a test set (data that wasn't used to build the model). In this example, for simplicity, we evaluate the model against the training data (data that was used to build the model).

the other stakeholders. Often, the right balance requires some trade-off between recall and precision.

There are other measures of accuracy and other measures of the quality of a model, as well. We'll talk about model evaluation in chapter 5.

1.2.5 Presentation and documentation

Once you have a model that meets your success criteria, you'll present your results to your project sponsor and other stakeholders. You must also document the model for those in the organization who are responsible for using, running, and maintaining the model once it has been deployed.

Different audiences require different kinds of information. Business-oriented audiences want to understand the impact of your findings in terms of business metrics. In our loan example, the most important thing to present to business audiences is how your loan application model will reduce charge-offs (the money that the bank loses to bad loans). Suppose your model identified a set of bad loans that amounted to 22% of the total money lost to defaults. Then your presentation or executive summary should emphasize that the model can potentially reduce the bank's losses by that amount, as shown in figure 1.4.

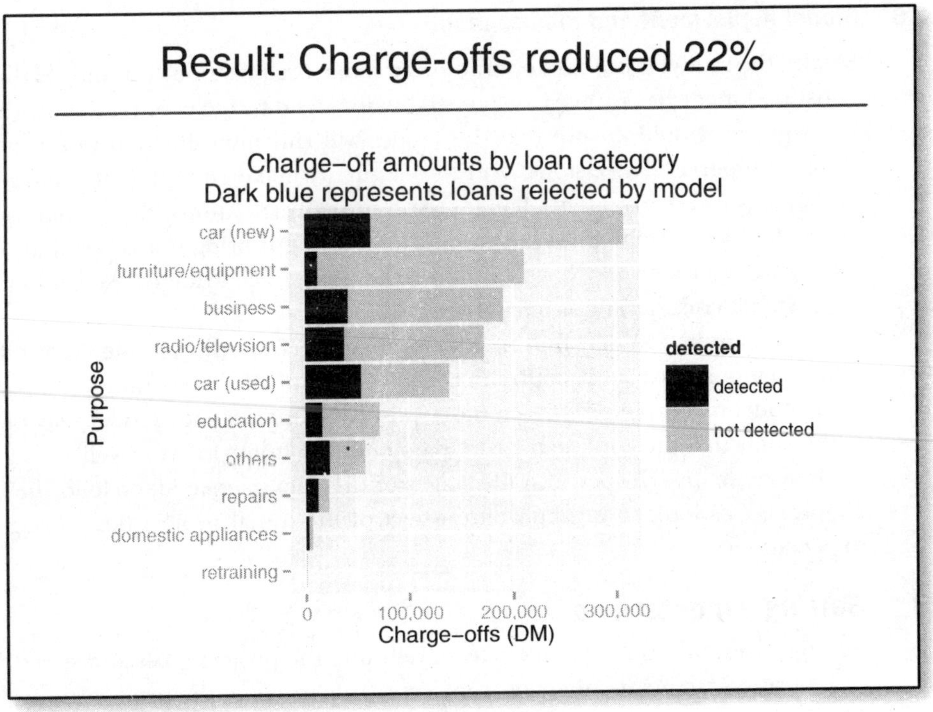

Figure 1.4 Notional slide from an executive presentation

You also want to give this audience your most interesting findings or recommendations, such as that new car loans are much riskier than used car loans, or that most losses are tied to bad car loans and bad equipment loans (assuming that the audience didn't already know these facts). Technical details of the model won't be as interesting to this audience, and you should skip them or only present them at a high level.

A presentation for the model's end users (the loan officers) would instead emphasize how the model will help them do their job better:

- How should they interpret the model?
- What does the model output look like?
- If the model provides a trace of which rules in the decision tree executed, how do they read that?
- If the model provides a confidence score in addition to a classification, how should they use the confidence score?
- When might they potentially overrule the model?

Presentations or documentation for operations staff should emphasize the impact of your model on the resources that they're responsible for.

We'll talk about the structure of presentations and documentation for various audiences in part 3.

1.2.6 Model deployment and maintenance

Finally, the model is put into operation. In many organizations this means the data scientist no longer has primary responsibility for the day-to-day operation of the model. But you still should ensure that the model will run smoothly and won't make disastrous unsupervised decisions. You also want to make sure that the model can be updated as its environment changes. And in many situations, the model will initially be deployed in a small pilot program. The test might bring out issues that you didn't anticipate, and you may have to adjust the model accordingly. We'll discuss model deployment considerations in chapter 10.

For example, you may find that loan officers frequently override the model in certain situations because it contradicts their intuition. Is their intuition wrong? Or is your model incomplete? Or, in a more positive scenario, your model may perform so successfully that the bank wants you to extend it to home loans as well.

Before we dive deeper into the stages of the data science lifecycle in the following chapters, let's look at an important aspect of the initial project design stage: setting expectations.

1.3 Setting expectations

Setting expectations is a crucial part of defining the project goals and success criteria. The business-facing members of your team (in particular, the project sponsor) probably already have an idea of the performance required to meet business goals: for example, the bank wants to reduce their losses from bad loans by at least 10%. Before you get too deep into a project, you should make sure that the resources you have are enough for you to meet the business goals.

In this section, we discuss ways to estimate whether the data you have available is good enough to potentially meet desired accuracy goals. This is an example of the fluidity of the project lifecycle stages. You get to know the data better during the exploration and cleaning phase; after you have a sense of the data, you can get a sense of whether the data is good enough to meet desired performance thresholds. If it's not, then you'll have to revisit the project design and goal-setting stage.

1.3.1 Determining lower and upper bounds on model performance

Understanding how well a model *should* do for acceptable performance and how well it *can* do given the available data are both important when defining acceptance criteria.

THE NULL MODEL: A LOWER BOUND ON PERFORMANCE

You can think of the *null model* as being "the obvious guess" that your model must do better than. In situations where there's a working model or solution already in place that you're trying to improve, the null model is the existing solution. In situations where there's no existing model or solution, the null model is the simplest possible model (for example, always guessing `GoodLoan`, or always predicting the mean value of the output, when you're trying to predict a numerical value). The null model represents the lower bound on model performance that you should strive for.

In our loan application example, 70% of the loan applications in the dataset turned out to be good loans. A model that labels all loans as `GoodLoan` (in effect, using only the existing process to classify loans) would be correct 70% of the time. So you know that any actual model that you fit to the data should be better than 70% accurate to be useful. Since this is the simplest possible model, its error rate is called the *base error rate*.

How much better than 70% should you be? In statistics there's a procedure called *hypothesis testing*, or *significance testing*, that tests whether your model is equivalent to a null model (in this case, whether a new model is basically only as accurate as guessing `GoodLoan` all the time). You want your model's accuracy to be "significantly better"—in statistical terms—than 70%. We'll cover the details of significance testing in chapter 5.

Accuracy is not the only (or even the best) performance metric. In our example, the null model would have zero recall in identifying bad loans, which obviously is not what you want. Generally if there is an existing model or process in place, you'd like to have an idea of its precision, recall, and false positive rates; if the purpose of your project is to improve the existing process, then the current model must be unsatisfactory for at least one of these metrics. This also helps you determine lower bounds on desired performance.

THE BAYES RATE: AN UPPER BOUND ON MODEL PERFORMANCE

The business-dictated performance goals will of course be higher than the lower bounds discussed here. You should try to make sure as early as possible that you have the data to meet your goals.

One thing to look at is what statisticians call the *unexplainable variance*: how much of the variation in your output can't be explained by your input variables. Let's take a very simple example: suppose you want to use the rule of thumb that loans that equal more than 15% of the borrower's disposable income will default; otherwise, loans are good. You want to know if this rule alone will meet your goal of predicting bad loans with at least 85% accuracy. Let's consider the two populations next.

Listing 1.3 Plotting the relation between disposable income and loan outcome

```
> tab1
                               loan.quality.pop1
loan.as.pct.disposable.income goodloan badloan
                      LT.15pct       50       0
                      GT.15pct        6      44
> sum(diag(tab1))/sum(tab1)
[1] 0.94
>
> tab2
                               loan.quality.pop2
loan.as.pct.disposable.income goodloan badloan
                      LT.15pct       34      16
                      GT.15pct       18      32
> sum(diag(tab2))/sum(tab2)
[1] 0.66
```

The count of correct predictions is on the diagonal of tab1. In this first population, all the loans that were less than 15% of disposable income were good loans, and all but six of the loans that were greater than 15% of disposable income defaulted. So you know that loan.as.pct.disposable.income models loan quality well in this population. Or as statisticians might say, loan.as.pct.disposable.income "explains" the output (loan quality).

In fact, it's 94% accurate.

In the second population, about a third of the loans that were less than 15% of disposable income defaulted, and over half of the loans that were greater than 15% of disposable income were good. So you know that loan.as.pct.disposable.income doesn't model loan quality well in this population.

The rule of thumb is only 66% accurate.

For the second population, you know that you can't meet your goals using only loan.as.pct.disposable.income. To build a more accurate model, you'll need additional input variables.

The limit on prediction accuracy due to unexplainable variance is known as the *Bayes rate*. You can think of the Bayes rate as describing the best accuracy you can achieve given your data. If the Bayes rate doesn't meet your business-dictated performance goals, then you shouldn't start the project without revisiting your goals or finding additional data to improve your model.[4]

Exactly finding the Bayes rate is not always possible—if you could always find the best possible model, then your job would already be done. If all your variables are discrete (and you have a lot of data), you can find the Bayes rate by building a lookup table for all possible variable combinations. In other situations, a nearest-neighbor classifier (we'll discuss them in chapter 8) can give you a good estimate of the Bayes rate, even though a nearest-neighbor classifier may not be practical to deploy as an actual production model. In any case, you should try to get some idea of the

[4] The Bayes rate gives the best possible accuracy, but the most accurate model doesn't always have the best possible precision or recall (though it may represent the best trade-off of the two).

limitations of your data early in the process, so you know whether it's adequate to meet your goals.

1.4 Summary

The data science process involves a lot of back-and-forth—between the data scientist and other project stakeholders, and between the different stages of the process. Along the way, you'll encounter surprises and stumbling blocks; this book will teach you procedures for overcoming some of these hurdles. It's important to keep all the stakeholders informed and involved; when the project ends, no one connected with it should be surprised by the final results.

In the next chapters, we'll look at the stages that follow project design: loading, exploring, and managing the data. Chapter 2 covers a few basic ways to load the data into R, in a format that's convenient for analysis.

Key takeaways

- A successful data science project involves more than just statistics. It also requires a variety of roles to represent business and client interests, as well as operational concerns.
- Make sure you have a clear, verifiable, quantifiable goal.
- Make sure you've set realistic expectations for all stakeholders.

2 Loading data into R

This chapter covers

- Understanding R's data frame structure
- Loading data into R from files and from relational databases
- Transforming data for analysis

If your experience has been like ours, many of your data science projects start when someone points you toward a bunch of data and you're left to make sense of it. Your first thought may be to use shell tools or spreadsheets to sort through it, but you quickly realize that you're taking more time tinkering with the tools than actually analyzing the data. Luckily, there's a better way. In this chapter, we'll demonstrate how to quickly load and start working with data using R. Using R to transform data is easy because R's main data type (the data frame) is ideal for working with structured data, and R has adapters that read data from many common data formats. In this chapter, we'll start with small example datasets found in files and then move to datasets from relational databases. By the end of the chapter, you'll be able to confidently use R to extract, transform, and load data for analysis.[1]

For our first example, let's start with some example datasets from files.

[1] We'll demonstrate and comment on the R commands necessary to prepare the data, but if you're unfamiliar with programming in R, we recommend at least skimming appendix A or consulting a good book on R such as *R in Action, Second Edition* (Robert Kabacoff, Manning Publications (2014), http://mng.bz/ybS4). All the tools you need are freely available and we provide instructions how to download and start working with them in appendix A.

2.1 Working with data from files

The most common ready-to-go data format is a family of tabular formats called *structured values.* Most of the data you find will be in (or nearly in) one of these formats. When you can read such files into R, you can analyze data from an incredible range of public and private data sources. In this section, we'll work on two examples of loading data from structured files, and one example of loading data directly from a relational database. The point is to get data quickly into R so we can then use R to perform interesting analyses.

2.1.1 Working with well-structured data from files or URLs

The easiest data format to read is table-structured data with headers. As shown in figure 2.1, this data is arranged in rows and columns where the first row gives the column names. Each column represents a different fact or measurement; each row represents an instance or datum about which we know the set of facts. A lot of public data is in this format, so being able to read it opens up a lot of opportunities.

Before we load the German credit data that we used in the previous chapter, let's demonstrate the basic loading commands with a simple data file from the University of California Irvine Machine Learning Repository (http://archive.ics.uci.edu/ml/). The UCI data files tend to come without headers, so to save steps (and to keep it very basic, at this point) we've pre-prepared our first data example from the UCI car dataset: http://archive.ics.uci.edu/ml/machine-learning-databases/car/. Our pre-prepared file is at http://win-vector.com/dfiles/car.data.csv and looks like the following (details found at https://github.com/WinVector/zmPDSwR/tree/master/UCICar):

```
buying,maint,doors,persons,lug_boot,safety,rating
vhigh,vhigh,2,2,small,low,unacc
vhigh,vhigh,2,2,small,med,unacc
vhigh,vhigh,2,2,small,high,unacc
vhigh,vhigh,2,2,med,low,unacc
...
```

The header row contains the names of the data columns, in this case separated by commas. When the separators are commas, the format is called comma-separated values, or .csv.

The data rows are in the same format as the header row, but each row contains actual data values. In this case, the first row represents the set of name/value pairs: buying=vhigh, maintenance=vhigh, doors=2, persons=2, and so on.

◇	A	B	C	D	E	F	G
1	buying	maint	doors	persons	lug_boot	safety	rating
2	vhigh	vhigh	2	2	small	low	unacc
3	vhigh	vhigh	2	2	small	med	unacc
4	vhigh	vhigh	2	2	small	high	unacc
5	vhigh	vhigh	2	2	med	low	unacc
6	vhigh	vhigh	2	2	med	med	unacc

Figure 2.1 Car data viewed as a table

> **AVOID "BY HAND" STEPS** We strongly encourage you to avoid performing any steps "by hand" when importing data. It's tempting to use an editor to add a header line to a file, as we did in our example. A better strategy is to write a script either outside R (using shell tools) or inside R to perform any necessary reformatting. Automating these steps greatly reduces the amount of trauma and work during the inevitable data refresh.

Notice that this file is already structured like a spreadsheet with easy-to-identify rows and columns. The data shown here is claimed to be the details about recommendations on cars, but is in fact made-up examples used to test some machine-learning theories. Each (nonheader) row represents a review of a different model of car. The columns represent facts about each car model. Most of the columns are objective measurements (purchase cost, maintenance cost, number of doors, and so on) and the final column "rating" is marked with the overall rating (`vgood`, `good`, `acc`, and `unacc`). These sorts of explanations can't be found in the data but must be extracted from the documentation found with the original data.

LOADING WELL-STRUCTURED DATA FROM FILES OR URLS

Loading data of this type into R is a one-liner: we use the R command `read.table()` and we're done. If data were always in this format, we'd meet all of the goals of this section and be ready to move on to modeling with just the following code.

Listing 2.1 Reading the UCI car data

```
uciCar <- read.table(
   'http://www.win-vector.com/dfiles/car.data.csv',
   sep=',',
   header=T
   )
```

- Filename or URL to get the data from. (`'http://www.win-vector.com/dfiles/car.data.csv'`)
- Specify the column or field separator as a comma. (`sep=','`)
- Command to read from a file or URL and store the result in a new data frame object called uciCar.
- Tell R to expect a header line that defines the data column names. (`header=T`)

This loads the data and stores it in a new R data frame object called `uciCar`. Data frames are R's primary way of representing data and are well worth learning to work with (as we discuss in our appendixes). The `read.table()` command is powerful and flexible; it can accept many different types of data separators (commas, tabs, spaces, pipes, and others) and it has many options for controlling quoting and escaping data. `read.table()` can read from local files or remote URLs. If a resource name ends with the *.gz* suffix, `read.table()` assumes the file has been compressed in gzip style and will automatically decompress it while reading.

EXAMINING OUR DATA

Once we've loaded the data into R, we'll want to examine it. The commands to always try first are these:

- `class()`—Tells you what type of R object you have. In our case, `class(uciCar)` tells us the object `uciCar` is of class `data.frame`.
- `help()`—Gives you the documentation for a class. In particular try `help(class(uciCar))` or `help("data.frame")`.

- `summary()`—Gives you a summary of almost any R object. `summary(uciCar)` shows us a lot about the distribution of the UCI car data.

For data frames, the command `dim()` is also important, as it shows you how many rows and columns are in the data. We show the results of a few of these steps next (steps are prefixed by > and R results are shown after each step).

Listing 2.2 Exploring the car data

```
> class(uciCar)
[1] "data.frame"
> summary(uciCar)
   buying       maint        doors
 high :432   high :432   2    :432
 low  :432   low  :432   3    :432
 med  :432   med  :432   4    :432
 vhigh:432   vhigh:432   5more:432

 persons    lug_boot    safety
 2   :576   big  :576   high:576
 4   :576   med  :576   low :576
 more:576   small:576   med :576

   rating
 acc  : 384
 good :  69
 unacc:1210
 vgood:  65

> dim(uciCar)
[1] 1728    7
```

The loaded object uciCar is of type data.frame.

The [1] is just an output sequence marker. The actual information is this: uciCar has 1728 rows and 7 columns. Always try to confirm you got a good parse by at least checking that the number of rows is exactly one fewer than the number of lines of text in the original file. The difference of one is because the column header counts as a line, but not as a data row.

The `summary()` command shows us the distribution of each variable in the dataset. For example, we know each car in the dataset was declared to seat `2`, `4` or `more` persons, and we know there were 576 two-seater cars in the dataset. Already we've learned a lot about our data, without having to spend a lot of time setting pivot tables as we would have to in a spreadsheet.

WORKING WITH OTHER DATA FORMATS

.csv is not the only common data file format you'll encounter. Other formats include .tsv (tab-separated values), pipe-separated files, Microsoft Excel workbooks, JSON data, and XML. R's built-in `read.table()` command can be made to read most separated value formats. Many of the deeper data formats have corresponding R packages:

- *XLS/XLSX*—http://cran.r-project.org/doc/manuals/R-data.html#Reading-Excel-spreadsheets
- *JSON*—http://cran.r-project.org/web/packages/rjson/index.html
- *XML*—http://cran.r-project.org/web/packages/XML/index.html
- *MongoDB*—http://cran.r-project.org/web/packages/rmongodb/index.html
- *SQL*—http://cran.r-project.org/web/packages/DBI/index.html

2.1.2 Using R on less-structured data

Data isn't always available in a ready-to-go format. Data curators often stop just short of producing a ready-to-go machine-readable format. The German bank credit dataset discussed in chapter 1 is an example of this. This data is stored as tabular data without headers; it uses a cryptic encoding of values that requires the dataset's accompanying documentation to untangle. This isn't uncommon and is often due to habits or limitations of other tools that commonly work with the data. Instead of reformatting the data before we bring it into R, as we did in the last example, we'll now show how to reformat the data using R. This is a much better practice, as we can save and reuse the R commands needed to prepare the data.

Details of the German bank credit dataset can be found at http://mng.bz/mZbu. We'll show how to transform this data into something meaningful using R. After these steps, you can perform the analysis already demonstrated in chapter 1. As we can see in our file excerpt, the data is an incomprehensible block of codes with no meaningful explanations:

```
A11 6 A34 A43 1169 A65 A75 4 A93 A101 4 ...
A12 48 A32 A43 5951 A61 A73 2 A92 A101 2 ...
A14 12 A34 A46 2096 A61 A74 2 A93 A101 3 ...
   ...
```

TRANSFORMING DATA IN R

Data often needs a bit of transformation before it makes any sense. In order to decrypt troublesome data, you need what's called the *schema documentation* or a *data dictionary*. In this case, the included dataset description says the data is 20 input columns followed by one result column. In this example, there's no header in the data file. The column definitions and the meaning of the cryptic A-* codes are all in the accompanying data documentation. Let's start by loading the raw data into R. We can either save the data to a file or let R load the data directly from the URL. Start a copy of R or RStudio (see appendix A) and type in the commands in the following listing.

Listing 2.3 Loading the credit dataset

```
d <- read.table(paste('http://archive.ics.uci.edu/ml/',
   'machine-learning-databases/statlog/german/german.data',sep=''),
   stringsAsFactors=F,header=F)
print(d[1:3,])
```

Notice that this prints out the exact same three rows we saw in the raw file with the addition of column names V1 through V21. We can change the column names to something meaningful with the command in the following listing.

Listing 2.4 Setting column names

```
colnames(d) <- c('Status.of.existing.checking.account',
   'Duration.in.month',  'Credit.history', 'Purpose',
   'Credit.amount', 'Savings account/bonds',
   'Present.employment.since',
```

```
    'Installment.rate.in.percentage.of.disposable.income',
    'Personal.status.and.sex', 'Other.debtors/guarantors',
    'Present.residence.since', 'Property', 'Age.in.years',
    'Other.installment.plans', 'Housing',
    'Number.of.existing.credits.at.this.bank', 'Job',
    'Number.of.people.being.liable.to.provide.maintenance.for',
    'Telephone', 'foreign.worker', 'Good.Loan')
d$Good.Loan <- as.factor(ifelse(d$Good.Loan==1,'GoodLoan','BadLoan'))
print(d[1:3,])
```

The `c()` command is R's method to construct a vector. We copied the names directly from the dataset documentation. By assigning our vector of names into the data frame's `colnames()` slot, we've reset the data frame's column names to something sensible. We can find what slots and commands our data frame `d` has available by typing `help(class(d))`.

The data documentation further tells us the column names, and also has a dictionary of the meanings of all of the cryptic A-* codes. For example, it says in column 4 (now called *Purpose*, meaning the purpose of the loan) that the code A40 is a new car loan, A41 is a used car loan, and so on. We copied 56 such codes into an R list that looks like the next listing.

Listing 2.5 Building a map to interpret loan use codes

```
mapping <- list(
    'A40'='car (new)',
    'A41'='car (used)',
    'A42'='furniture/equipment',
    'A43'='radio/television',
    'A44'='domestic appliances',
    ...
  )
```

LISTS ARE R'S MAP STRUCTURES Lists are R's map structures. They can map strings to arbitrary objects. The important list operations `[]` and `%in%` are *vectorized*. This means that, when applied to a vector of values, they return a vector of results by performing one lookup per entry.

With the mapping list defined, we can then use the following for loop to convert values in each column that was of type `character` from the original cryptic A-* codes into short level descriptions taken directly from the data documentation. We, of course, skip any such transform for columns that contain numeric data.

Listing 2.6 Transforming the car data

```
for(i in 1:(dim(d))[2]) {
  if(class(d[,i])=='character') {
    d[,i] <- as.factor(as.character(mapping[d[,i]]))
  }
}
```

(dim(d))[2] is the number of columns in the data frame d.

Note that the indexing operator [] is vectorized. Each step in the for loop remaps an entire column of data through our list.

We share the complete set of column preparations for this dataset here: https://github.com/WinVector/zmPDSwR/tree/master/Statlog/. We encourage readers to download the data and try these steps themselves.

EXAMINING OUR NEW DATA

We can now easily examine the purpose of the first three loans with the command `print(d[1:3,'Purpose'])`. We can look at the distribution of loan purpose with `summary(d$Purpose)` and even start to investigate the relation of loan type to loan outcome, as shown in the next listing.

Listing 2.7 Summary of `Good.Loan` and `Purpose`

```
> table(d$Purpose,d$Good.Loan)

                      BadLoan GoodLoan
  business                 34       63
  car (new)                89      145
  car (used)               17       86
  domestic appliances       4        8
  education                22       28
  furniture/equipment      58      123
  others                    5        7
  radio/television         62      218
  repairs                   8       14
  retraining                1        8
```

You should now be able to load data from files. But a lot of data you want to work with isn't in files; it's in databases. So it's important that we work through how to load data from databases directly into R.

2.2 Working with relational databases

In many production environments, the data you want lives in a relational or SQL database, not in files. Public data is often in files (as they are easier to share), but your most important client data is often in databases. Relational databases scale easily to the millions of records and supply important production features such as parallelism, consistency, transactions, logging, and audits. When you're working with transaction data, you're likely to find it already stored in a relational database, as relational databases excel at online transaction processing (OLTP).

Often you can export the data into a structured file and use the methods of our previous sections to then transfer the data into R. But this is generally not the right way to do things. Exporting from databases to files is often unreliable and idiosyncratic due to variations in database tools and the typically poor job these tools do when quoting and escaping characters that are confused with field separators. Data in a database is often stored in what is called a *normalized form*, which requires relational preparations called *joins* before the data is ready for analysis. Also, you often don't want a dump of the entire database, but instead wish to freely specify which columns and aggregations you need during analysis.

The right way to work with data found in databases is to connect R directly to the database, which is what we'll demonstrate in this section.

As a step of the demonstration, we'll show how to load data into a database. Knowing how to load data into a database is useful for problems that need more sophisticated preparation than we've so far discussed. Relational databases are the right place for transformations such as joins or sampling. Let's start working with data in a database for our next example.

2.2.1 A production-size example

For our production-size example we'll use the United States Census 2011 national PUMS American Community Survey data found at www.census.gov/acs/www/data_documentation/pums_data/. This is a remarkable set of data involving around 3 million individuals and 1.5 million households. Each row contains over 200 facts about each individual or household (income, employment, education, number of rooms, and so on). The data has household cross-reference IDs so individuals can be joined to the household they're in. The size of the dataset is interesting: a few gigabytes when zipped up. So it's small enough to store on a good network or thumb drive, but larger than is convenient to work with on a laptop with R alone (which is more comfortable when working in the range of hundreds of thousands of rows).

This size—millions of rows—is the sweet spot for relational database or SQL-assisted analysis on a single machine. We're not yet forced to move into a MapReduce or database cluster to do our work, but we do want to use a database for some of the initial data handling. We'll work through all of the steps for acquiring this data and preparing it for analysis in R.

CURATING THE DATA

A hard rule of data science is that you must be able to reproduce your results. At the very least, be able to repeat your own successful work through your recorded steps and without depending on a stash of intermediate results. Everything must either have directions on how to produce it or clear documentation on where it came from. We call this the "no alien artifacts" discipline. For example, when we said we're using PUMS American Community Survey data, this statement isn't precise enough for anybody to know what data we specifically mean. Our actual notebook entry (which we keep online, so we can search it) on the PUMS data is as shown in the next listing.

Listing 2.8 PUMS data provenance documentation

```
3-12-2013
PUMS Data set from:
  http://www.census.gov/acs/www/data_documentation/pums_data/
  select "2011 ACS 1-year PUMS"
```

Where we found the data documentation. This is important to record as many data files don't contain links back to the documentation. Census PUMS does in fact contain embedded documentation, but not every source is so careful. (annotates the URL line)

How we navigated from the documentation site to the actual data files. It may be necessary to record this if the data supplier requires any sort of click-through license to get to the actual data. (annotates the select line)

```
select "2011 ACS 1-year Public Use Microdata Samples\
(PUMS) - CSV format"
download "United States Population Records" and
"United States Housing Unit Records"
  http://www2.census.gov/acs2011_1yr/pums/csv_pus.zip
  http://www2.census.gov/acs2011_1yr/pums/csv_hus.zip
downloaded file details:
  $ ls -lh *.zip
    239M Oct 15 13:17 csv_hus.zip
    580M Mar  4 06:31 csv_pus.zip
  $ shasum *.zip
    cdfdfb326956e202fdb560ee34471339ac8abd6c  csv_hus.zip
    aa0f4add21e327b96d9898b850e618aeca10f6d0  csv_pus.zip
```

The actual files we downloaded.

The sizes of the files after we downloaded them.

Cryptographic hashes of the file contents we downloaded. These are very short summaries (called hashes) that are very unlikely to have the same value for different files. These summaries can later help us determine if another researcher in our organization is using the same data distribution or not.

KEEP NOTES A big part of being a data scientist is being able to defend your results and repeat your work. We strongly advise keeping a notebook. We also strongly advise keeping all of your scripts and code under version control, as we discuss in appendix A. You absolutely need to be able to answer exactly what code and which data were used to build the results you presented last week.

STAGING THE DATA INTO A DATABASE

Structured data at a scale of millions of rows is best handled in a database. You can try to work with text-processing tools, but a database is much better at representing the fact that your data is arranged in both rows and columns (not just lines of text).

We'll use three database tools in this example: the serverless database engine H2, the database loading tool SQL Screwdriver, and the database browser SQuirreL SQL. All of these are Java-based, run on many platforms, and are open source. We describe how to download and start working with all of them in appendix A.[2]

If you have a database such as MySQL or PostgreSQL already available, we recommend using one of them instead of using H2.[3] To use your own database, you'll need to know enough of your database driver and connection information to build a JDBC connection. If using H2, you'll only need to download the H2 driver as described in appendix A, pick a file path to store your results, and pick a username and password (both are set on first use, so there are no administrative steps). H2 is a serverless zero-install relational database that supports queries in SQL. It's powerful enough to work on PUMS data and easy to use. We show how to get H2 running in appendix A.

[2] Other easy ways to use SQL in R include the sqldf and RSQLite packages.

[3] If you have access to a parallelized SQL database such as Greenplum, we strongly suggest using it to perform aggregation and preparation steps on your big data. Being able to write standard SQL queries and have them finish quickly at big data scale can be game-changing.

We'll use the Java-based tool SQL Screwdriver to load the PUMS data into our database. We first copy our database credentials into a Java properties XML file.

Listing 2.9 SQL Screwdriver XML configuration file

```
<?xml version="1.0" encoding="UTF-8"?>
<!DOCTYPE properties SYSTEM "http://java.sun.com/dtd/properties.dtd">
<properties>
  <comment>testdb</comment>
  <entry key="user">u</entry>
  <entry key="password">u</entry>
  <entry key="driver">org.h2.Driver</entry>
  <entry key="url">jdbc:h2:H2DB \
    ;LOG=0;CACHE_SIZE=65536;LOCK_MODE=0;UNDO_LOG=0</entry>
</properties>
```

- Username to use for database connection. (user entry)
- Password to use for database connection. (password entry)
- Java classname of the database driver. SQL Screwdriver used JDBC, which is a broad database application programming interface layer. You could use another database such as PostgreSQL by specifying a different driver name, such as org.postgresql.Driver. (driver entry)
- URL specifying database. For H2, it's just jdbc:h2: followed by the file prefix you wish to use to store data. The items after the semicolon are performance options. For PostgreSQL, it would be something more like jdbc:postgresql://host:5432/db. The descriptions of the URL format and drivers should be part of your database documentation, and you can use SQuirreL SQL to confirm you have them right. (url entry)

We'll then use Java at the command line to load the data. To load the four files containing the two tables, run the commands in the following listing.

Listing 2.10 Loading data with SQL Screwdriver

```
java -classpath SQLScrewdriver.jar:h2-1.3.170.jar \
  com.winvector.db.LoadFiles \
  file:dbDef.xml \
  , \
  hus \
  file:csv_hus/ss11husa.csv file:csv_hus/ss11husb.csv
java -classpath SQLScrewdriver.jar:h2-1.3.170.jar \
  com.winvector.db.LoadFiles \
  file:dbDef.xml , pus \
  file:csv_pus/ss11pusa.csv file:csv_pus/ss11pusb.csv
```

- Java command and required JARs. The JARs in this case are SQL Screwdriver and the required database driver. (java -classpath line)
- Class to run: LoadFiles, the meat of SQL Screwdriver. (com.winvector.db.LoadFiles)
- URL pointing to database credentials. (file:dbDef.xml)
- Separator to expect in input file (use t for tab). (,)
- Name of table to create. (hus)
- List of comma-separated files to load into table. (file:csv_hus/...)
- Same load pattern for personal information table. (second java command)

SQL Screwdriver infers data types by scanning the file and creates new tables in your database. It then populates these tables with the data. SQL Screwdriver also adds four additional "provenance" columns when loading your data. These columns are ORIGINSERTTIME, ORIGFILENAME, ORIGFILEROWNUMBER, and ORIGRANDGROUP. The first three fields record when you ran the data load, what filename the row came from, and what line the row came from. The ORIGRANDGROUP is a pseudo-random integer distributed uniformly from 0 through 999, designed to make repeatable sampling plans easy to implement. You should get in the habit of having annotations and keeping notes at each step of the process.

We can now use a database browser like SQuirreL SQL to examine this data. We start up SQuirreL SQL and copy the connection details from our XML file into a database alias, as shown in appendix A. We're then ready to type SQL commands into the

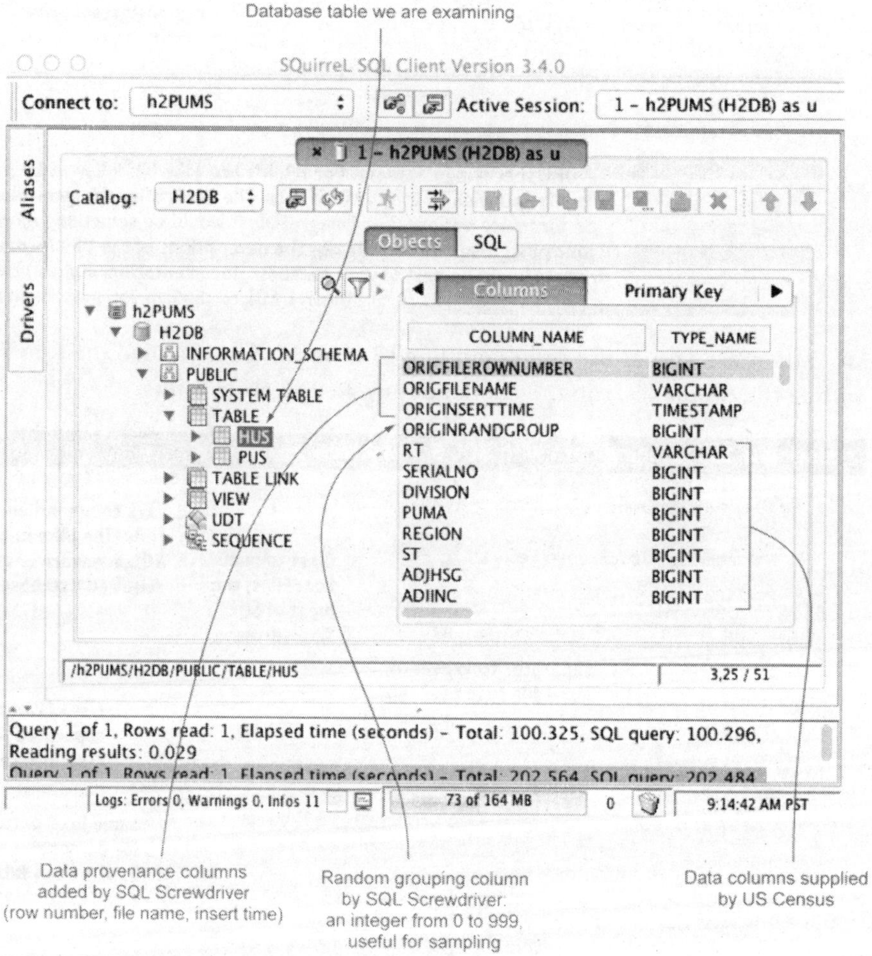

Figure 2.2 SQuirreL SQL table explorer

execution window. A couple of commands you can try are `SELECT COUNT(1) FROM hus` and `SELECT COUNT(1) FROM pus`, which will tell you that the `hus` table has 1,485,292 rows and the `pus` table has 3,112,017 rows. Each of the tables has over 200 columns, and there are over a billion cells of data in these two tables. We can actually do a lot more. In addition to the SQL execution panel, SQuirreL SQL has an Objects panel that allows graphical exploration of database table definitions. Figure 2.2 shows some of the columns in the `hus` table.

Now we can view our data as a table (as we would in a spreadsheet). We can now examine, aggregate, and summarize our data using the SQuirreL SQL database browser. Figure 2.3 shows a few example rows and columns from the household data table.

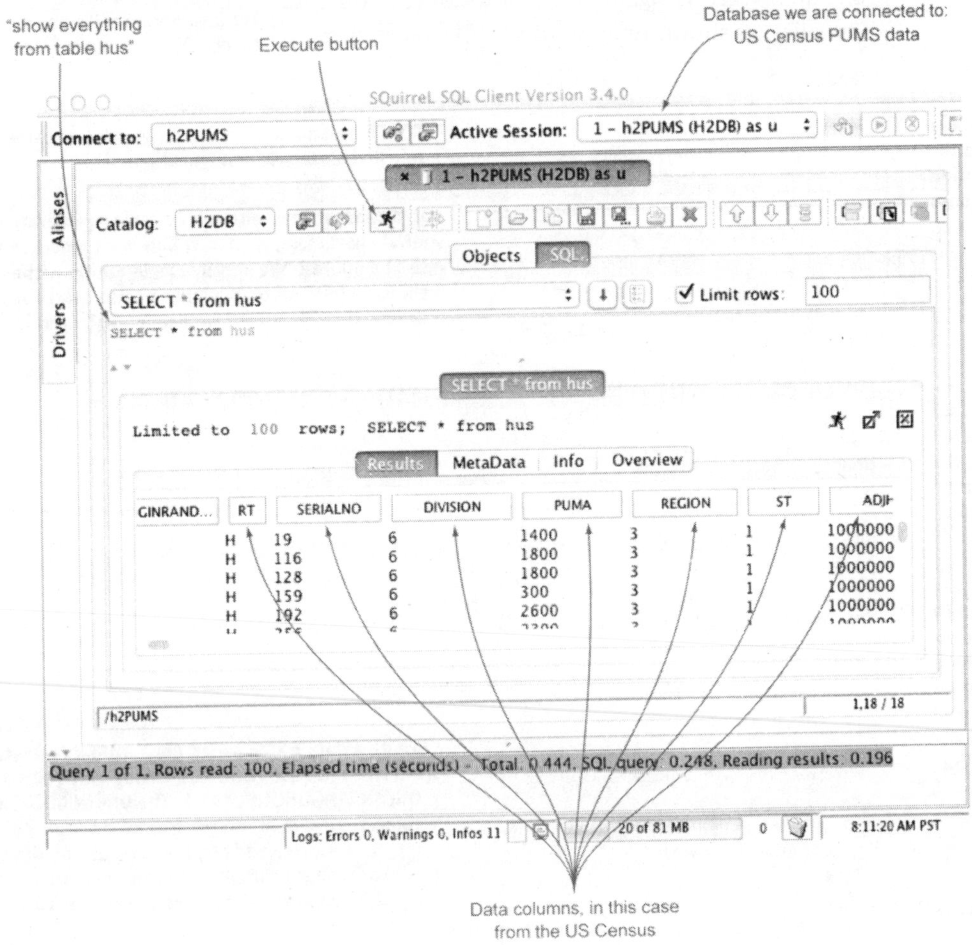

Figure 2.3 Browsing PUMS data using SQuirreL SQL

2.2.2 Loading data from a database into R

To load data from a database, we use a database connector. Then we can directly issue SQL queries from R. SQL is the most common database query language and allows us to specify arbitrary joins and aggregations. SQL is called a *declarative* language (as opposed to a *procedural* language) because in SQL we specify what relations we would like our data sample to have, not how to compute them. For our example, we load a sample of the household data from the hus table and the rows from the person table (pus) that are associated with those households.[4]

Listing 2.11 Loading data into R from a relational database

```
options( java.parameters = "-Xmx2g" )
library(RJDBC)
drv <- JDBC("org.h2.Driver",
   "h2-1.3.170.jar",
   identifier.quote="'")
options<-";LOG=0;CACHE_SIZE=65536;LOCK_MODE=0;UNDO_LOG=0"
conn <- dbConnect(drv,paste("jdbc:h2:H2DB",options,sep=''),"u","u")
dhus <- dbGetQuery(conn,"SELECT * FROM hus WHERE ORIGRANDGROUP<=1")
dpus <- dbGetQuery(conn,"SELECT pus.* FROM pus WHERE pus.SERIALNO IN \
   (SELECT DISTINCT hus.SERIALNO FROM hus \
   WHERE hus.ORIGRANDGROUP<=1)")
dbDisconnect(conn)
save(dhus,dpus,file='phsample.RData')
```

Set Java option for extra memory before DB drivers are loaded.

Specify where to find the implementation of the database driver.

Specify the name of the database driver, same as in our XML database configuration.

SQL column names with mixed-case capitalization, special characters, or that collide with reserved words must be quoted. We specify single-quote as the quote we'll use when quoting column names, which may be different than the quote we use for SQL literals.

Create a data frame called dpus from the database table pus, taking only records that have a household ID in the set of household IDs we selected from households table hus.

Create a data frame called dhus from * (everything) from the database table hus, taking only rows where ORGINRANGGROUP <= 1. The ORGINRANDGROUP column is a random integer from 0 through 999 that SQL Screwdriver adds to the rows during data load to facilitate sampling. In this case, we're taking 2/1000 of the data rows to get a small sample.

Disconnect for the database.

Save the two data frames into a file named phsample.RData, which can be read in with load(). Try help("save") or help("load") for more details.

[4] Producing composite records that represent matches between one or more tables (in our case hus and pus) is usually done with what is called a *join*. For this example, we use an even more efficient pattern called a subselect that uses the keyword in.

And we're in business; the data has been unpacked from the Census-supplied .csv files into our database and a useful sample has been loaded into R for analysis. We have actually accomplished a lot. Generating, as we have, a uniform sample of households and matching people would be tedious using shell tools. It's exactly what SQL databases are designed to do well.

> **DON'T BE TOO PROUD TO SAMPLE** Many data scientists spend too much time adapting algorithms to work directly with big data. Often this is wasted effort, as for many model types you would get almost exactly the same results on a reasonably sized data sample. You only need to work with "all of your data" when what you're modeling isn't well served by sampling, such as when characterizing rare events or performing bulk calculations over social networks.

Note that this data is still in some sense large (out of the range where using spreadsheets is actually reasonable). Using `dim(dhus)` and `dim(dpus)`, we see that our household sample has 2,982 rows and 210 columns, and the people sample has 6,279 rows and 288 columns. All of these columns are defined in the Census documentation.

2.2.3 Working with the PUMS data

Remember that the whole point of loading data (even from a database) into R is to facilitate modeling and analysis. Data analysts should always have their "hands in the data" and always take a quick look at their data after loading it. If you're not willing to work with the data, you shouldn't bother loading it into R. To emphasize analysis, we'll demonstrate how to perform a quick examination of the PUMS data.

LOADING AND CONDITIONING THE PUMS DATA

Each row of PUMS data represents a single anonymized person or household. Personal data recorded includes occupation, level of education, personal income, and many other demographics variables. To load our prepared data frame, download `phsample.Rdata` from https://github.com/WinVector/zmPDSwR/tree/master/PUMS and run the following command in R: `load('phsample.RData')`.

Our example problem will be to predict income (represented in US dollars in the field `PINCP`) using the following variables:

- *Age*—An integer found in column `AGEP`.
- *Employment class*—Examples: for-profit company, nonprofit company, ... found in column `COW`.
- *Education level*—Examples: no high school diploma, high school, college, and so on, found in column `SCHL`.
- *Sex of worker*—Found in column `SEX`.

We don't want to concentrate too much on this data; our goal is only to illustrate the modeling procedure. Conclusions are very dependent on choices of data conditioning (what subset of the data you use) and data coding (how you map records to informative symbols). This is why empirical scientific papers have a mandatory "materials and methods" section describing how data was chosen and prepared. Our data treatment is to select a subset of "typical full-time workers" by restricting the subset to data that meets all of the following conditions:

- Workers self-described as full-time employees
- Workers reporting at least 40 hours a week of activity
- Workers 20–50 years of age
- Workers with an annual income between $1,000 and $250,000 dollars

The following listing shows the code to limit to our desired subset of the data.

Listing 2.12 Selecting a subset of the Census data

```
psub = subset(dpus,with(dpus,(PINCP>1000)&(ESR==1)&
   (PINCP<=250000)&(PERNP>1000)&(PERNP<=250000)&
   (WKHP>=40)&(AGEP>=20)&(AGEP<=50)&
   (PWGTP1>0)&(COW %in% (1:7))&(SCHL %in% (1:24))))
```

Subset of data rows matching detailed employment conditions

RECODING THE DATA

Before we work with the data, we'll recode some of the variables for readability. In particular, we want to recode variables that are enumerated integers into meaningful factor-level names, but for readability and to prevent accidentally treating such variables as mere numeric values. Listing 2.13 shows the typical steps needed to perform a useful recoding.

Listing 2.13 Recoding variables

```
psub$SEX = as.factor(ifelse(psub$SEX==1,'M','F'))
psub$SEX = relevel(psub$SEX,'M')
cowmap <- c("Employee of a private for-profit",
   "Private not-for-profit employee",
   "Local government employee",
   "State government employee",
   "Federal government employee",
   "Self-employed not incorporated",
   "Self-employed incorporated")
psub$COW = as.factor(cowmap[psub$COW])
psub$COW = relevel(psub$COW,cowmap[1])
schlmap = c(
   rep("no high school diploma",15),
  "Regular high school diploma",
  "GED or alternative credential",
  "some college credit, no degree",
  "some college credit, no degree",
  "Associate's degree",
  "Bachelor's degree",
```

Reencode sex from 1/2 to M/F.

Make the reference sex M, so F encodes a difference from M in models.

Reencode class of worker info into a more readable form.

Reencode education info into a more readable form and fewer levels (merge all levels below high school into same encoding).

```
  "Master's degree",
  "Professional degree",
  "Doctorate degree")
psub$SCHL = as.factor(schlmap[psub$SCHL])
psub$SCHL = relevel(psub$SCHL,schlmap[1])
dtrain = subset(psub,ORIGRANDGROUP >= 500)
dtest = subset(psub,ORIGRANDGROUP < 500)
```

Subset of data rows used for model training.

Subset of data rows used for model testing.

The data preparation is making use of R's vectorized lookup operator `[]`. For details on this or any other R commands, we suggest using the R `help()` command and appendix A (for help with `[]`, type `help('[')`).

The standard trick to work with variables that take on a small number of string values is to reencode them into what's called a *factor* as we've done with the `as.factor()` command. A factor is a list of all possible values of the variable (possible values are called *levels*), and each level works (under the covers) as an *indicator variable.* An indicator is a variable with a value of `1` (one) when a condition we're interested in is true, and `0` (zero) otherwise. Indicators are a useful encoding trick. For example, `SCHL` is reencoded as 8 indicators with the names shown in figure 7.6 in chapter 7, plus the undisplayed level "no high school diploma." Each indicator takes a value of `0`, except when the `SCHL` variable has a value equal to the indicator's name. When the `SCHL` variable matches the indicator name, the indicator is set to `1` to indicate the match. Figure 2.4 illustrates the process. `SEX` and `COW` underwent similar transformations.

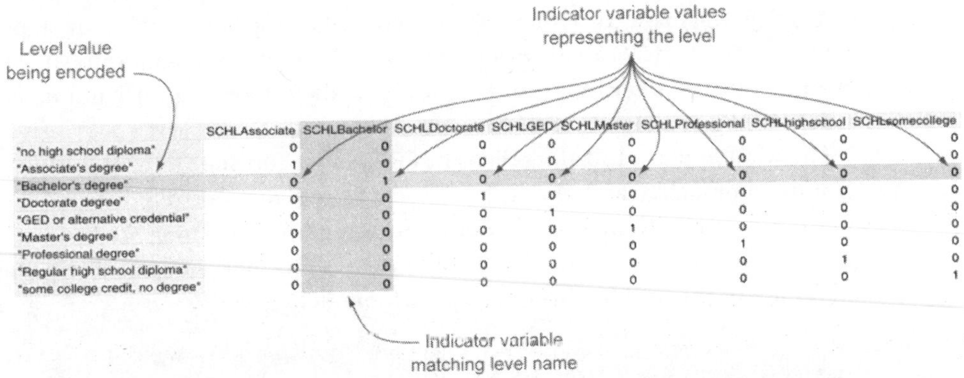

Figure 2.4 Strings encoded as indicators

EXAMINING THE PUMS DATA

At this point, we're ready to do some science, or at least start looking at the data. For example, we can quickly tabulate the distribution of category of work.

Listing 2.14 Summarizing the classifications of work

```
> summary(dtrain$COW)
Employee of a private for-profit        Federal government employee
                             423                                 21
       Local government employee  Private not-for-profit employee
                              39                                 55
     Self-employed incorporated   Self-employed not incorporated
                              17                                 16
       State government employee
                              24
```

WATCH OUT FOR NAS R's representation for blank or missing data is `NA`. Unfortunately a lot of R commands quietly skip `NA`s without warning. The command `table(dpus$COW,useNA='always')` will show `NA`s much like `summary(dpus$COW)` does.

We'll return to the Census example and demonstrate more sophisticated modeling techniques in chapter 7.

2.3 Summary

In this chapter, we've shown how to extract, transform, and load data for analysis. For smaller datasets we perform the transformations in R, and for larger datasets we advise using a SQL database. In either case we save *all* of the transformation steps as code (either in SQL or in R) that can be reused in the event of a data refresh. The whole purpose of this chapter is to prepare for the actual interesting work in our next chapters: exploring, managing, and correcting data.

The whole point of loading data into R is so we can start to work with it: explore, examine, summarize, and plot it. In chapter 3, we'll demonstrate how to characterize your data through summaries, exploration, and graphing. These are key steps early in any modeling effort because it is through these steps that you learn the actual details and nature of the problem you're hoping to model.

Key takeaways

- Data frames are your friend.
- Use `read_table()` to load small, structured datasets into R.
- You can use a package like `RJDBC` to load data into R from relational databases, and to transform or aggregate the data before loading using SQL.
- Always document data provenance.

3 Exploring data

This chapter covers

- Using summary statistics to explore data
- Exploring data using visualization
- Finding problems and issues during data exploration

In the last two chapters, you learned how to set the scope and goal of a data science project, and how to load your data into R. In this chapter, we'll start to get our hands into the data.

Suppose your goal is to build a model to predict which of your customers don't have health insurance; perhaps you want to market inexpensive health insurance packages to them. You've collected a dataset of customers whose health insurance status you know. You've also identified some customer properties that you believe help predict the probability of insurance coverage: age, employment status, income, information about residence and vehicles, and so on. You've put all your data into a single data frame called *custdata* that you've input into R.[1] Now you're ready to start building the model to identify the customers you're interested in.

1 We have a copy of this synthetic dataset available for download from https://github.com/WinVector/zmPDSwR/tree/master/Custdata, and once saved, you can load it into R with the command `custdata <- read.table('custdata.tsv',header=T,sep='\t')`.

It's tempting to dive right into the modeling step without looking very hard at the dataset first, especially when you have a lot of data. Resist the temptation. No dataset is perfect: you'll be missing information about some of your customers, and you'll have incorrect data about others. Some data fields will be dirty and inconsistent. If you don't take the time to examine the data before you start to model, you may find yourself redoing your work repeatedly as you discover bad data fields or variables that need to be transformed before modeling. In the worst case, you'll build a model that returns incorrect predictions—and you won't be sure why. By addressing data issues early, you can save yourself some unnecessary work, and a lot of headaches!

You'd also like to get a sense of who your customers are: Are they young, middle-aged, or seniors? How affluent are they? Where do they live? Knowing the answers to these questions can help you build a better model, because you'll have a more specific idea of what information predicts the probability of insurance coverage more accurately.

In this chapter, we'll demonstrate some ways to get to know your data, and discuss some of the potential issues that you're looking for as you explore. Data exploration uses a combination of *summary statistics*—means and medians, variances, and counts—and *visualization*, or graphs of the data. You can spot some problems just by using summary statistics; other problems are easier to find visually.

> **Organizing data for analysis**
>
> For most of this book, we'll assume that the data you're analyzing is in a single data frame. This is not how that data is usually stored. In a database, for example, data is usually stored in *normalized form* to reduce redundancy: information about a single customer is spread across many small tables. In log data, data about a single customer can be spread across many log entries, or sessions. These formats make it easy to add (or in the case of a database, modify) data, but are not optimal for analysis. You can often join all the data you need into a single table in the database using SQL, but in appendix A we'll discuss commands like `join` that you can use within R to further consolidate data.

3.1 Using summary statistics to spot problems

In R, you'll typically use the `summary` command to take your first look at the data.

Listing 3.1 The `summary()` command

```
> summary(custdata)
custid          sex
Min.   :   2068   F:440
1st Qu.: 345667   M:560
Median : 693403
Mean   : 698500
3rd Qu.:1044606
Max.   :1414286
```

```
is.employed         income
Mode :logical    Min.   : -8700
FALSE:73         1st Qu.: 14600
TRUE :599        Median : 35000
NA's :328        Mean   : 53505
                 3rd Qu.: 67000
                 Max.   :615000
```

The variable is.employed is missing for about a third of the data. The variable income has negative values, which are potentially invalid.

```
marital.stat
Divorced/Separated:155
Married           :516
Never Married     :233
Widowed           : 96

health.ins
Mode :logical
FALSE:159
TRUE :841
NA's :0
```

About 84% of the customers have health insurance.

```
housing.type
Homeowner free and clear    :157
Homeowner with mortgage/loan:412
Occupied with no rent       : 11
Rented                      :364
NA's                        : 56
```

The variables housing.type, recent.move, and num.vehicles are each missing 56 values.

```
recent.move        num.vehicles
Mode :logical    Min.   :0.000
FALSE:820        1st Qu.:1.000
TRUE :124        Median :2.000
NA's :56         Mean   :1.916
                 3rd Qu.:2.000
                 Max.   :6.000
                 NA's   :56

age                 state.of.res
Min.   :  0.0    California  :100
1st Qu.: 38.0    New York    : 71
Median : 50.0    Pennsylvania: 70
Mean   : 51.7    Texas       : 56
3rd Qu.: 64.0    Michigan    : 52
Max.   :146.7    Ohio        : 51
                 (Other)     :600
```

The average value of the variable age seems plausible, but the minimum and maximum values seem unlikely. The variable state.of.res is a categorical variable; summary() reports how many customers are in each state (for the first few states).

The summary command on a data frame reports a variety of summary statistics on the numerical columns of the data frame, and count statistics on any categorical columns (if the categorical columns have already been read in as factors[2]). You can also ask for summary statistics on specific numerical columns by using the commands `mean`, `variance`, `median`, `min`, `max`, and `quantile` (which will return the quartiles of the data by default).

---

[2] Categorical variables are of class `factor` in R. They can be represented as strings (class `character`), and some analytical functions will automatically convert string variables to factor variables. To get a summary of a variable, it needs to be a factor.

As you see from listing 3.1, the summary of the data helps you quickly spot potential problems, like missing data or unlikely values. You also get a rough idea of how categorical data is distributed. Let's go into more detail about the typical problems that you can spot using the summary.

3.1.1 Typical problems revealed by data summaries

At this stage, you're looking for several common issues: missing values, invalid values and outliers, and data ranges that are too wide or too narrow. Let's address each of these issues in detail.

MISSING VALUES

A few missing values may not really be a problem, but if a particular data field is largely unpopulated, it shouldn't be used as an input without some repair (as we'll discuss in chapter 4, section 4.1.1). In R, for example, many modeling algorithms will, by default, quietly drop rows with missing values. As you see in listing 3.2, all the missing values in the `is.employed` variable could cause R to quietly ignore nearly a third of the data.

Listing 3.2 · Will the variable `is.employed` be useful for modeling?

```
is.employed
  Mode :logical
 FALSE:73
 TRUE :599
 NA's :328
```

The variable is.employed is missing for about a third of the data. Why? Is employment status unknown? Did the company start collecting employment data only recently? Does NA mean "not in the active workforce" (for example, students or stay-at-home parents)?

```
                    housing.type
  Homeowner free and clear    :157
 Homeowner with mortgage/loan:412
 Occupied with no rent       : 11
 Rented                      :364
 NA's                        : 56
```

The variables housing.type, recent.move, and num.vehicles are only missing a few values. It's probably safe to just drop the rows that are missing values—especially if the missing values are all the same 56 rows.

```
 recent.move       num.vehicles
 Mode :logical   Min.   :0.000
 FALSE:820       1st Qu.:1.000
 TRUE :124       Median :2.000
 NA's :56        Mean   :1.916
                 3rd Qu.:2.000
                 Max.   :6.000
                 NA's   :56
```

If a particular data field is largely unpopulated, it's worth trying to determine why; sometimes the fact that a value is missing is informative in and of itself. For example, why is the `is.employed` variable missing so many values? There are many possible reasons, as we noted in listing 3.2.

Whatever the reason for missing data, you must decide on the most appropriate action. Do you include a variable with missing values in your model, or not? If you decide to include it, do you drop all the rows where this field is missing, or do you convert the missing values to `0` or to an additional category? We'll discuss ways to treat missing data in chapter 4. In this example, you might decide to drop the data rows where you're missing data about housing or vehicles, since there aren't many of them. You probably don't want to throw out the data where you're missing employment information, but instead treat the `NA`s as a third employment category. You will likely encounter missing values when model scoring, so you should deal with them during model training.

INVALID VALUES AND OUTLIERS

Even when a column or variable isn't missing any values, you still want to check that the values that you do have make sense. Do you have any invalid values or outliers? Examples of invalid values include negative values in what should be a non-negative numeric data field (like age or income), or text where you expect numbers. Outliers are data points that fall well out of the range of where you expect the data to be. Can you spot the outliers and invalid values in listing 3.3?

Listing 3.3 Examples of invalid values and outliers

```
> summary(custdata$income)
   Min. 1st Qu.  Median    Mean 3rd Qu.
  -8700   14600   35000   53500   67000
    Max.
 615000
```

Negative values for income could indicate bad data. They might also have a special meaning, like "amount of debt."

Either way, you should check how prevalent the issue is, and decide what to do: Do you drop the data with negative income? Do you convert negative values to zero?

```
> summary(custdata$age)
   Min. 1st Qu.  Median    Mean 3rd Qu.
    0.0    38.0    50.0    51.7    64.0
    Max.
  146.7
```

Customers of age zero, or customers of an age greater than about 110 are outliers. They fall out of the range of expected customer values.

Outliers could be data input errors. They could be special sentinel values: zero might mean "age unknown" or "refuse to state." And some of your customers might be especially long-lived.

Often, invalid values are simply bad data input. Negative numbers in a field like `age`, however, could be a *sentinel value* to designate "unknown." Outliers might also be data errors or sentinel values. Or they might be valid but unusual data points—people do occasionally live past 100.

As with missing values, you must decide the most appropriate action: drop the data field, drop the data points where this field is bad, or convert the bad data to a useful value. Even if you feel certain outliers are valid data, you might still want to omit them from model construction (and also collar allowed prediction range), since the usual achievable goal of modeling is to predict the typical case correctly.

DATA RANGE

You also want to pay attention to how much the values in the data vary. If you believe that age or income helps to predict the probability of health insurance coverage, then you should make sure there is enough variation in the age and income of your customers for you to see the relationships. Let's look at income again, in listing 3.4. Is the data range wide? Is it narrow?

Listing 3.4 Looking at the data range of a variable

```
> summary(custdata$income)
   Min. 1st Qu.  Median    Mean 3rd Qu.
  -8700   14600   35000   53500   67000
   Max.
 615000
```

Income ranges from zero to over half a million dollars; a very wide range.

Even ignoring negative income, the `income` variable in listing 3.4 ranges from zero to over half a million dollars. That's pretty wide (though typical for income). Data that ranges over several orders of magnitude like this can be a problem for some modeling methods. We'll talk about mitigating data range issues when we talk about logarithmic transformations in chapter 4.

Data can be too narrow, too. Suppose all your customers are between the ages of 50 and 55. It's a good bet that age range wouldn't be a very good predictor of the probability of health insurance coverage for that population, since it doesn't vary much at all.

How narrow is "too narrow" a data range?

Of course, the term *narrow* is relative. If we were predicting the ability to read for children between the ages of 5 and 10, then age probably is a useful variable as-is. For data including adult ages, you may want to transform or bin ages in some way, as you don't expect a significant change in reading ability between ages 40 and 50. You should rely on information about the problem domain to judge if the data range is narrow, but a rough rule of thumb is the ratio of the standard deviation to the mean. If that ratio is very small, then the data isn't varying much.

We'll revisit data range in section 3.2, when we talk about examining data graphically.

One factor that determines apparent data range is the unit of measurement. To take a nontechnical example, we measure the ages of babies and toddlers in weeks or in months, because developmental changes happen at that time scale for very young children. Suppose we measured babies' ages in years. It might appear numerically that there isn't much difference between a one-year-old and a two-year-old. In reality, there's a dramatic difference, as any parent can tell you! Units can present potential issues in a dataset for another reason, as well.

UNITS

Does the income data in listing 3.5 represent hourly wages, or yearly wages in units of \$1000? As a matter of fact, it's the latter, but what if you thought it was the former? You might not notice the error during the modeling stage, but down the line someone will start inputting hourly wage data into the model and get back bad predictions in return.

Listing 3.5 Checking units can prevent inaccurate results later

```
> summary(Income)
   Min. 1st Qu.  Median    Mean 3rd Qu.    Max.
   -8.7    14.6    35.0    53.5    67.0   615.0
```

The variable Income is defined as Income = custdata$income/1000. But suppose you didn't know that. Looking only at the summary, the values could plausibly be interpreted to mean either "hourly wage" or "yearly income in units of $1000."

Are time intervals measured in days, hours, minutes, or milliseconds? Are speeds in kilometers per second, miles per hour, or knots? Are monetary amounts in dollars, thousands of dollars, or 1/100 of a penny (a customary practice in finance, where calculations are often done in fixed-point arithmetic)? This is actually something that you'll catch by checking data definitions in data dictionaries or documentation, rather than in the summary statistics; the difference between hourly wage data and annual salary in units of $1000 may not look that obvious at a casual glance. But it's still something to keep in mind while looking over the value ranges of your variables, because often you can spot when measurements are in unexpected units. Automobile speeds in knots look a lot different than they do in miles per hour.

3.2 Spotting problems using graphics and visualization

As you've seen, you can spot plenty of problems just by looking over the data summaries. For other properties of the data, pictures are better than text.

> *We cannot expect a small number of numerical values [summary statistics] to consistently convey the wealth of information that exists in data. Numerical reduction methods do not retain the information in the data.*
>
> —William Cleveland
> *The Elements of Graphing Data*

Figure 3.1 shows a plot of how customer ages are distributed. We'll talk about what the y-axis of the graph means later; for right now, just know that the height of the graph corresponds to how many customers in the population are of that age. As you can see, information like the peak age of the distribution, the existence of subpopulations, and the presence of outliers is easier to absorb visually than it is to determine textually.

The use of graphics to examine data is called *visualization*. We try to follow William Cleveland's principles for scientific visualization. Details of specific plots aside, the key points of Cleveland's philosophy are these:

- A graphic should display as much information as it can, with the lowest possible cognitive strain to the viewer.
- Strive for clarity. Make the data stand out. Specific tips for increasing clarity include
  - Avoid too many superimposed elements, such as too many curves in the same graphing space.

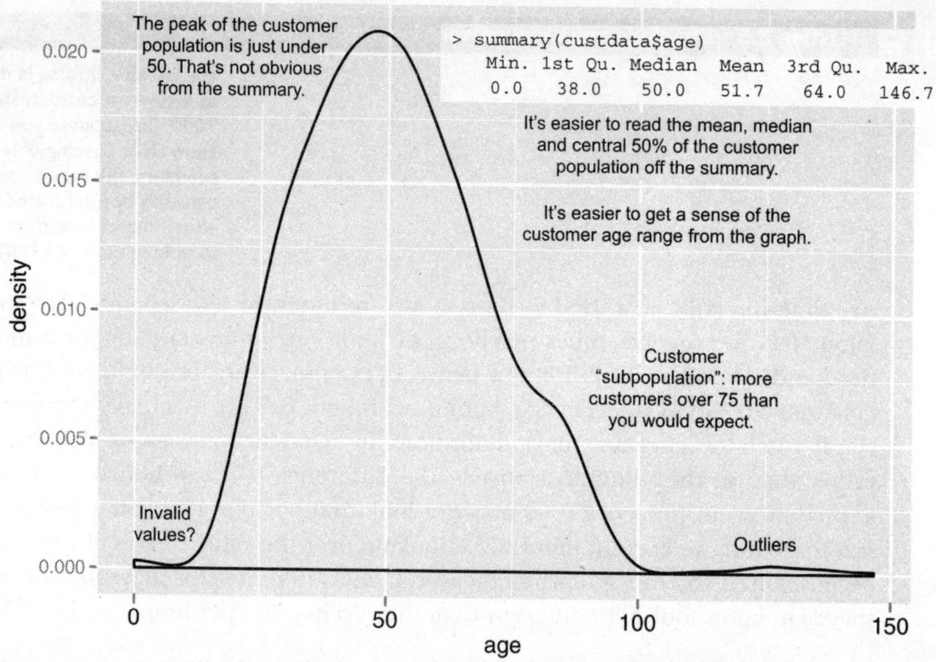

Figure 3.1 Some information is easier to read from a graph, and some from a summary.

- Find the right aspect ratio and scaling to properly bring out the details of the data.
- Avoid having the data all skewed to one side or the other of your graph.

- Visualization is an iterative process. Its purpose is to answer questions about the data.

During the visualization stage, you graph the data, learn what you can, and then regraph the data to answer the questions that arise from your previous graphic. Different graphics are best suited for answering different questions. We'll look at some of them in this section.

In this book, we use `ggplot2` to demonstrate the visualizations and graphics; of course, other R visualization packages can produce similar graphics.

A note on ggplot2

The theme of this section is how to use visualization to explore your data, not how to use `ggplot2`. We chose `ggplot2` because it excels at combining multiple graphical elements together, but its syntax can take some getting used to. The key points to understand when looking at our code snippets are these:

- Graphs in `ggplot2` can only be defined on data frames. The variables in a graph—the *x* variable, the *y* variable, the variables that define the color or the size of the points—are called *aesthetics*, and are declared by using the `aes` function.

- The `ggplot()` function declares the graph object. The arguments to `ggplot()` can include the data frame of interest and the aesthetics. The `ggplot()` function doesn't of itself produce a visualization; visualizations are produced by *layers*.
- Layers produce the plots and plot transformations and are added to a given graph object using the + operator. Each layer can also take a data frame and aesthetics as arguments, in addition to plot-specific parameters. Examples of layers are `geom_point` (for a scatter plot) or `geom_line` (for a line plot).

This syntax will become clearer in the examples that follow. For more information, we recommend Hadley Wickham's reference site http://ggplot2.org, which has pointers to online documentation, as well as to Dr. Wickham's *ggplot2: Elegant Graphics for Data Analysis (Use R!)* (Springer, 2009).

In the next two sections, we'll show how to use pictures and graphs to identify data characteristics and issues. In section 3.2.2, we'll look at visualizations for two variables. But let's start by looking at visualizations for single variables.

3.2.1 Visually checking distributions for a single variable

The visualizations in this section help you answer questions like these:

- What is the peak value of the distribution?
- How many peaks are there in the distribution (unimodality versus bimodality)?
- How normal (or lognormal) is the data? We'll discuss normal and lognormal distributions in appendix B.
- How much does the data vary? Is it concentrated in a certain interval or in a certain category?

One of the things that's easier to grasp visually is the shape of the data distribution. Except for the blip to the right, the graph in figure 3.1 (which we've reproduced as the gray curve in figure 3.2) is almost shaped like the normal distribution (see appendix B). As that appendix explains, many summary statistics assume that the data is approximately normal in distribution (at least for continuous variables), so you want to verify whether this is the case.

You can also see that the gray curve in figure 3.2 has only one peak, or that it's *unimodal.* This is another property that you want to check in your data.

Why? Because (roughly speaking), a unimodal distribution corresponds to one population of subjects. For the gray curve in figure 3.2, the mean customer age is about 52, and 50% of the customers are between 38 and 64 (the first and third quartiles). So you can say that a "typical" customer is middle-aged and probably possesses many of the demographic qualities of a middle-aged person—though of course you have to verify that with your actual customer information.

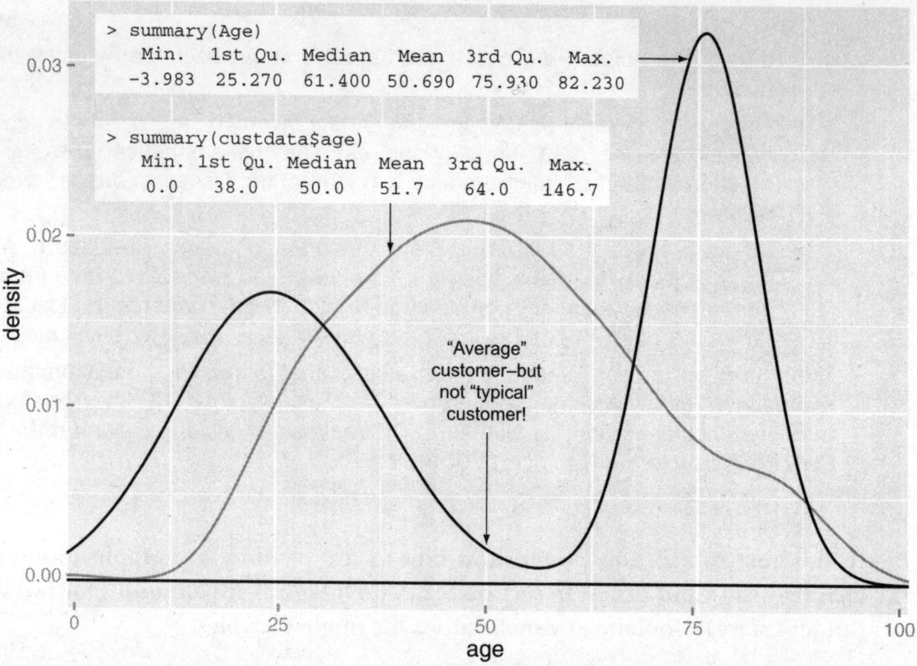

Figure 3.2 A unimodal distribution (gray) can usually be modeled as coming from a single population of users. With a bimodal distribution (black), your data often comes from two populations of users.

The black curve in figure 3.2 shows what can happen when you have two peaks, or a *bimodal distribution*. (A distribution with more than two peaks is *multimodal*.) This set of customers has about the same mean age as the customers represented by the gray curve—but a 50-year-old is hardly a "typical" customer! This (admittedly exaggerated) example corresponds to two populations of customers: a fairly young population mostly in their 20s and 30s, and an older population mostly in their 70s. These two populations probably have very different behavior patterns, and if you want to model whether a customer probably has health insurance or not, it wouldn't be a bad idea to model the two populations separately—especially if you're using linear or logistic regression.

The histogram and the density plot are two visualizations that help you quickly examine the distribution of a numerical variable. Figures 3.1 and 3.2 are density plots. Whether you use histograms or density plots is largely a matter of taste. We tend to prefer density plots, but histograms are easier to explain to less quantitatively-minded audiences.

HISTOGRAMS

A basic histogram bins a variable into fixed-width buckets and returns the number of data points that falls into each bucket. For example, you could group your customers by age range, in intervals of five years: 20–25, 25–30, 30–35, and so on. Customers at a

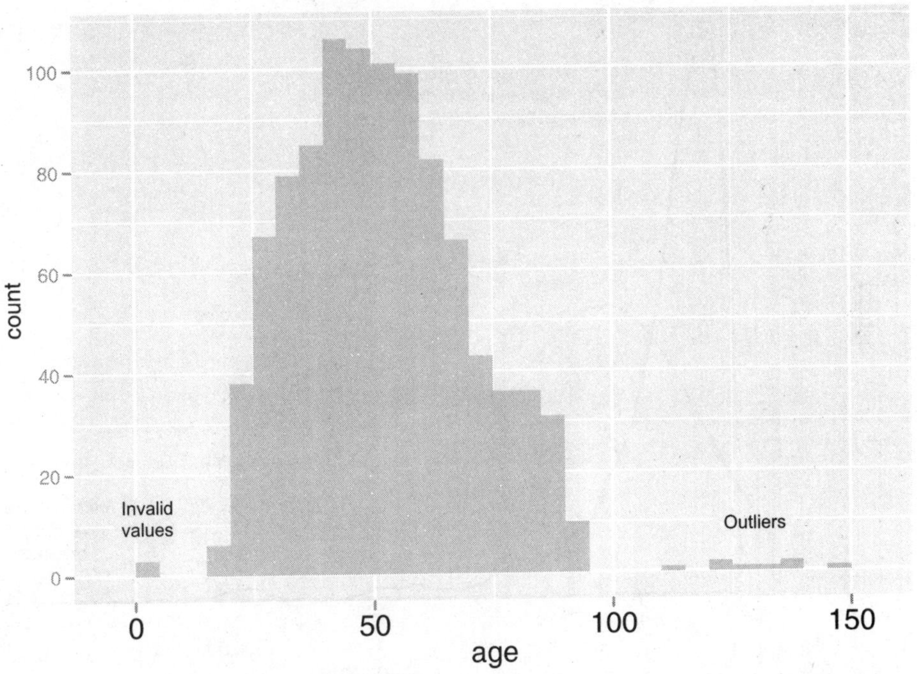

Figure 3.3 A histogram tells you where your data is concentrated. It also visually highlights outliers and anomalies.

boundary age would go into the higher bucket: 25-year-olds go into the 25–30 bucket. For each bucket, you then count how many customers are in that bucket. The resulting histogram is shown in figure 3.3.

You create the histogram in figure 3.3 in `ggplot2` with the `geom_histogram` layer.

Listing 3.6 Plotting a histogram

```
library(ggplot2)

ggplot(custdata) +
  geom_histogram(aes(x=age),
  binwidth=5, fill="gray")
```

Load the ggplot2 library, if you haven't already done so.

The binwidth parameter tells the geom_histogram call how to make bins of five-year intervals (default is datarange/30). The fill parameter specifies the color of the histogram bars (default: black).

The primary disadvantage of histograms is that you must decide ahead of time how wide the buckets are. If the buckets are too wide, you can lose information about the shape of the distribution. If the buckets are too narrow, the histogram can look too noisy to read easily. An alternative visualization is the density plot.

DENSITY PLOTS

You can think of a *density plot* as a "continuous histogram" of a variable, except the area under the density plot is equal to 1. A point on a density plot corresponds to the

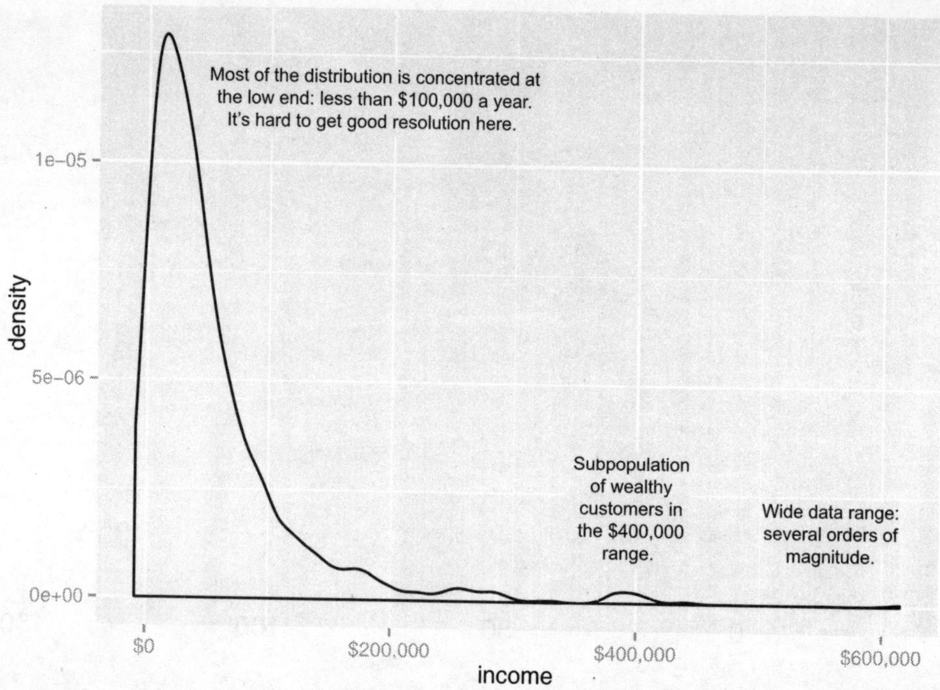

Figure 3.4 Density plots show where data is concentrated. This plot also highlights a population of higher-income customers.

fraction of data (or the percentage of data, divided by 100) that takes on a particular value. This fraction is usually very small. When you look at a density plot, you're more interested in the overall shape of the curve than in the actual values on the y-axis. You've seen the density plot of age; figure 3.4 shows the density plot of income. You produce figure 3.4 with the `geom_density` layer, as shown in the following listing.

Listing 3.7 Producing a density plot

```
library(scales)                                        <-- The scales package brings in
                                                           the dollar scale notation.
ggplot(custdata) + geom_density(aes(x=income)) +
   scale_x_continuous(labels=dollar)                   <-- Set the x-axis labels to dollars.
```

When the data range is very wide and the mass of the distribution is heavily concentrated to one side, like the distribution in figure 3.4, it's difficult to see the details of its shape. For instance, it's hard to tell the exact value where the income distribution has its peak. If the data is non-negative, then one way to bring out more detail is to plot the distribution on a logarithmic scale, as shown in figure 3.5. This is equivalent to plotting the density plot of `log10(income)`.

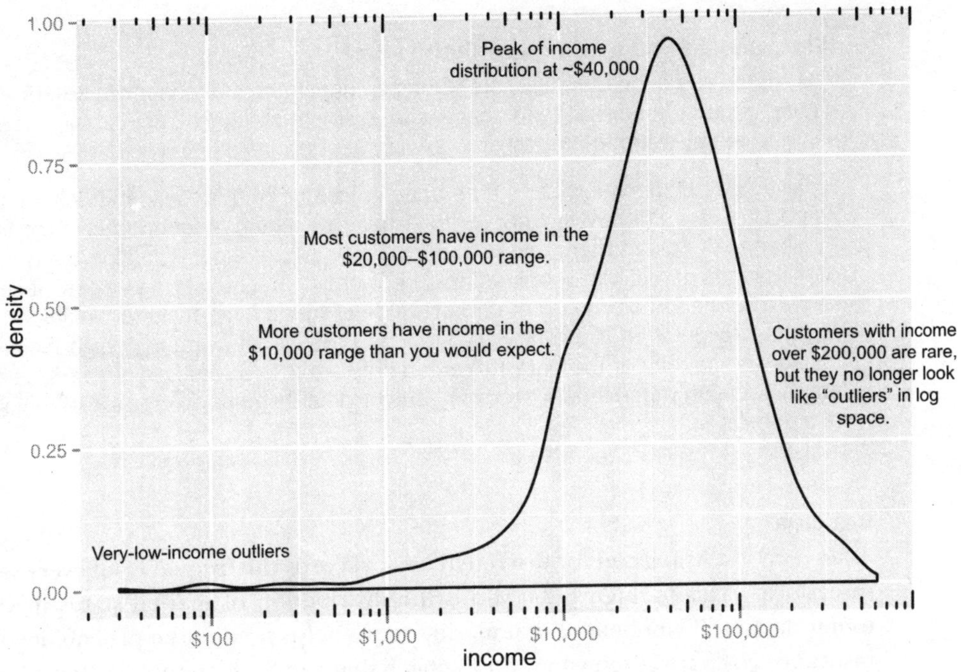

Figure 3.5 The density plot of income on a log10 scale highlights details of the income distribution that are harder to see in a regular density plot.

In ggplot2, you can plot figure 3.5 with the geom_density and scale_x_log10 layers, such as in the next listing.

Listing 3.8 Creating a log-scaled density plot

```
ggplot(custdata) + geom_density(aes(x=income)) +
   scale_x_log10(breaks=c(100,1000,10000,100000), labels=dollar) +
   annotation_logticks(sides="bt")
```

Set the x-axis to be in log10 scale, with manually set tick points and labels as dollars.

Add log-scaled tick marks to the top and bottom of the graph.

When you issued the preceding command, you also got back a warning message:

```
Warning messages:
1: In scale$trans$trans(x) : NaNs produced
2: Removed 79 rows containing non-finite values (stat_density).
```

This tells you that ggplot2 ignored the zero- and negative-valued rows (since log(0) = Infinity), and that there were 79 such rows. Keep that in mind when evaluating the graph.

In log space, income is distributed as something that looks like a "normalish" distribution, as will be discussed in appendix B. It's not exactly a normal distribution (in fact, it appears to be at least two normal distributions mixed together).

When should you use a logarithmic scale?

You should use a logarithmic scale when percent change, or change in orders of magnitude, is more important than changes in absolute units. You should also use a log scale to better visualize data that is heavily skewed.

For example, in income data, a difference in income of five thousand dollars means something very different in a population where the incomes tend to fall in the tens of thousands of dollars than it does in populations where income falls in the hundreds of thousands or millions of dollars. In other words, what constitutes a "significant difference" depends on the order of magnitude of the incomes you're looking at. Similarly, in a population like that in figure 3.5, a few people with very high income will cause the majority of the data to be compressed into a relatively small area of the graph. For both those reasons, plotting the income distribution on a logarithmic scale is a good idea.

BAR CHARTS

A *bar chart* is a histogram for discrete data: it records the frequency of every value of a categorical variable. Figure 3.6 shows the distribution of marital status in your customer dataset. If you believe that marital status helps predict the probability of health insurance coverage, then you want to check that you have enough customers with different marital statuses to help you discover the relationship between being married (or not) and having health insurance.

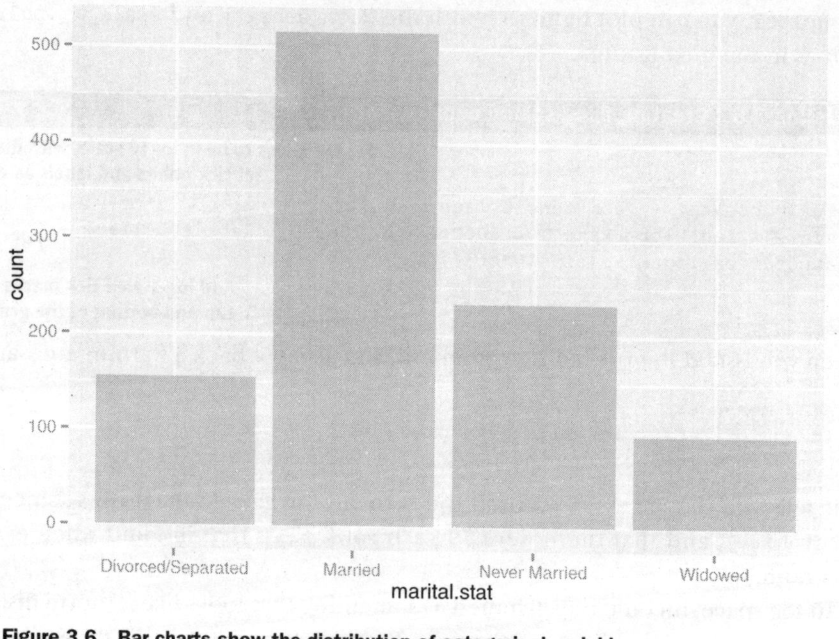

Figure 3.6 Bar charts show the distribution of categorical variables.

The ggplot2 command to produce figure 3.6 uses geom_bar:

```
ggplot(custdata) + geom_bar(aes(x=marital.stat), fill="gray")
```

This graph doesn't really show any more information than summary(custdata$marital.stat) would show, although some people find the graph easier to absorb than the text. Bar charts are most useful when the number of possible values is fairly large, like state of residence. In this situation, we often find that a horizontal graph is more legible than a vertical graph.

The ggplot2 command to produce figure 3.7 is shown in the next listing.

Listing 3.9 Producing a horizontal bar chart

```
ggplot(custdata) +
   geom_bar(aes(x=state.of.res), fill="gray") +
   coord_flip() +
   theme(axis.text.y=element_text(size=rel(0.8)))
```

Plot bar chart as before: state.of.res is on x axis, count is on y-axis.

Flip the x and y axes: state.of.res is now on the y-axis.

Reduce the size of the y-axis tick labels to 80% of default size for legibility.

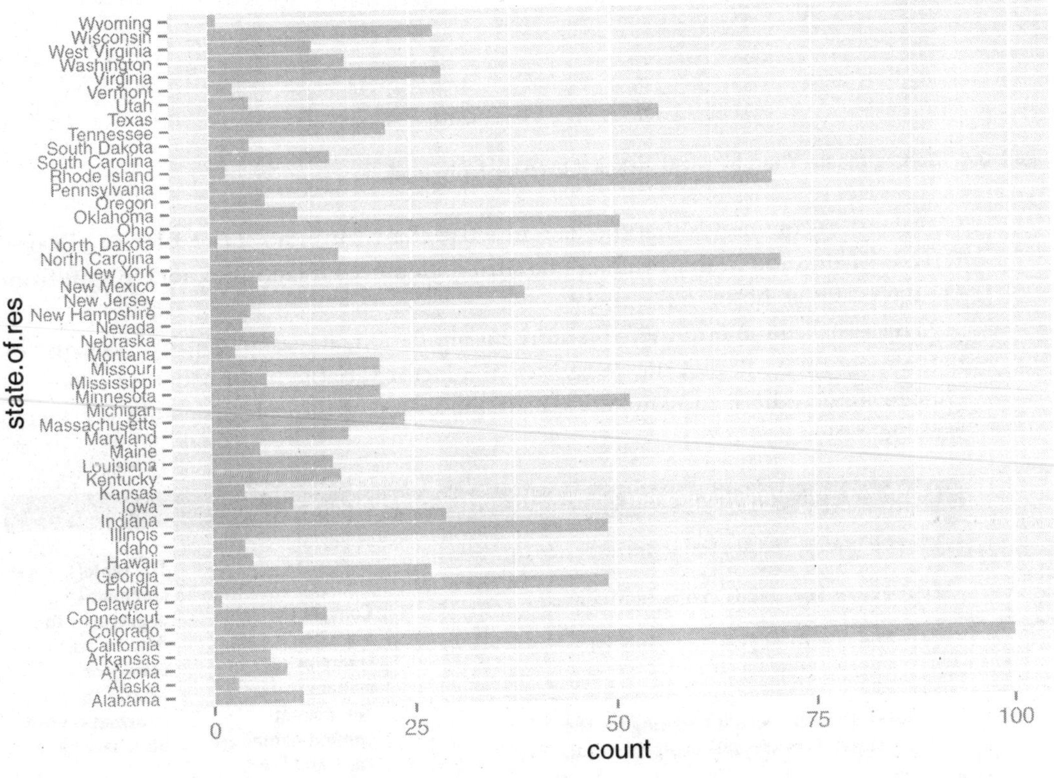

Figure 3.7 A horizontal bar chart can be easier to read when there are several categories with long names.

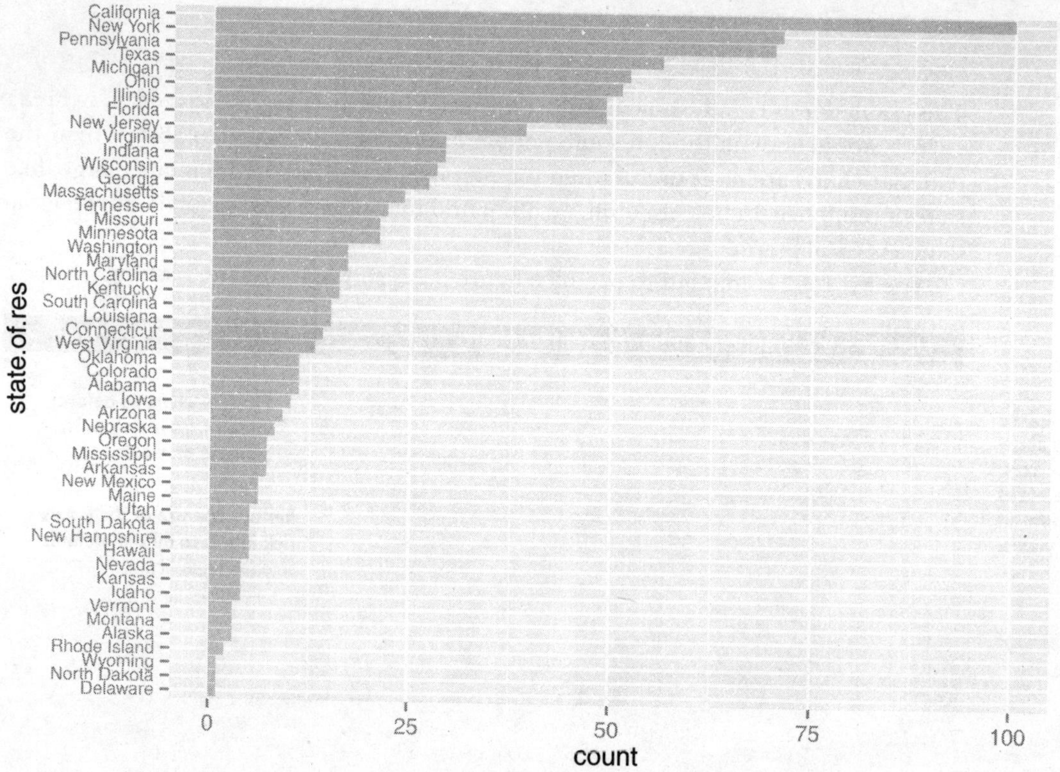

Figure 3.8 Sorting the bar chart by count makes it even easier to read.

Cleveland[3] recommends that the data in a bar chart (or in a *dot plot,* Cleveland's preferred visualization in this instance) be sorted, to more efficiently extract insight from the data. This is shown in figure 3.8.

This visualization requires a bit more manipulation, at least in `ggplot2`, because by default, `ggplot2` will plot the categories of a factor variable in alphabetical order. To change this, we have to manually specify the order of the categories—in the factor variable, not in `ggplot2`.

Listing 3.10 Producing a bar chart with sorted categories

```
> statesums <- table(custdata$state.of.res)

> statef <- as.data.frame(statesums)

> colnames(statef)<-c("state.of.res", "count")

> summary(statef)
```

The table() command aggregates the data by state of residence—exactly the information the bar chart plots.

Convert the table object to a data frame using as.data.frame(). The default column names are Var1 and Freq.

Rename the columns for readability.

Notice that the default ordering for the state.of.res variable is alphabetical.

[3] See William S. Cleveland, *The Elements of Graphing Data,* Hobart Press, 1994.

```
state.of.res      count
Alabama    : 1    Min.   :  1.00
Alaska     : 1    1st Qu.:  5.00
Arizona    : 1    Median : 12.00
Arkansas   : 1    Mean   : 20.00
California: 1     3rd Qu.: 26.25
Colorado   : 1    Max.   :100.00
(Other)    :44
> statef <- transform(statef,
 state.of.res=reorder(state.of.res, count))
> summary(statef)
 state.of.res      count
Delaware      : 1    Min.   :  1.00
North Dakota: 1      1st Qu.:  5.00
Wyoming       : 1    Median : 12.00
Rhode Island: 1      Mean   : 20.00
Alaska        : 1    3rd Qu.: 26.25
Montana       : 1    Max.   :100.00
(Other)       :44
> ggplot(statef)+ geom_bar(aes(x=state.of.res,y=count),
 stat="identity",
 fill="gray") +
 coord_flip() +
 theme(axis.text.y=element_text(size=rel(0.8)))
```

Use the reorder() function to set the state.of.res variable to be count ordered. Use the transform() function to apply the transformation to the state.of.res data frame.

The state.of.res variable is now count ordered.

Since the data is being passed to geom_bar pre-aggregated, specify both the x and y variables, and use stat="identity" to plot the data exactly as given.

Flip the axes and reduce the size of the label text as before.

Before we move on to visualizations for two variables, in table 3.1 we'll summarize the visualizations that we've discussed in this section.

Table 3.1 Visualizations for one variable

Graph type	Uses
Histogram or density plot	Examines data range Checks number of modes Checks if distribution is normal/lognormal Checks for anomalies and outliers
Bar chart	Compares relative or absolute frequencies of the values of a categorical variable

3.2.2 *Visually checking relationships between two variables*

In addition to examining variables in isolation, you'll often want to look at the relationship between two variables. For example, you might want to answer questions like these:

- Is there a relationship between the two inputs *age* and *income* in my data?
- What kind of relationship, and how strong?
- Is there a relationship between the input *marital status* and the output *health insurance*? How strong?

You'll precisely quantify these relationships during the modeling phase, but exploring them now gives you a feel for the data and helps you determine which variables are the best candidates to include in a model.

First, let's consider the relationship between two continuous variables. The most obvious way (though not always the best) is the line plot.

LINE PLOTS

Line plots work best when the relationship between two variables is relatively clean: each *x* value has a unique (or nearly unique) *y* value, as in figure 3.9. You plot figure 3.9 with `geom_line`.

Listing 3.11 Producing a line plot

```
x <- runif(100)
y <- x^2 + 0.2*x
ggplot(data.frame(x=x,y=y), aes(x=x,y=y)) + geom_line()
```

First, generate the data for this example. The x variable is uniformly randomly distributed between 0 and 1.

The y variable is a quadratic function of x.

Plot the line plot.

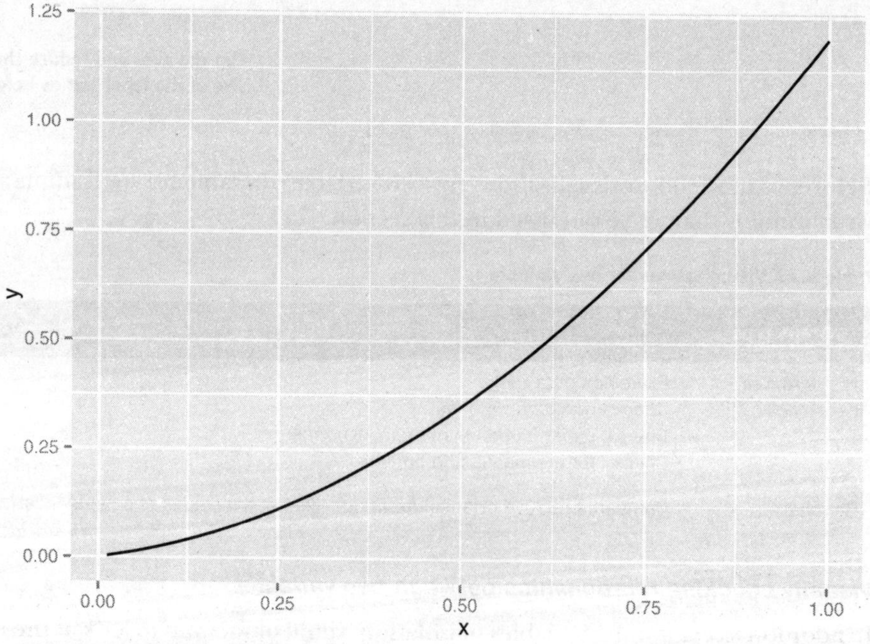

Figure 3.9 Example of a line plot

When the data is not so cleanly related, line plots aren't as useful; you'll want to use the scatter plot instead, as you'll see in the next section.

SCATTER PLOTS AND SMOOTHING CURVES

You'd expect there to be a relationship between age and health insurance, and also a relationship between income and health insurance. But what is the relationship between age and income? If they track each other perfectly, then you might not want to use both variables in a model for health insurance. The appropriate summary statistic is the correlation, which we compute on a safe subset of our data.

Listing 3.12 Examining the correlation between age and income

```
custdata2 <- subset(custdata,
   (custdata$age > 0 & custdata$age < 100
   & custdata$income > 0))

cor(custdata2$age, custdata2$income)

[1] -0.02240845
```

- Only consider a subset of data with reasonable age and income values.
- Get correlation of age and income.
- Resulting correlation.

The negative correlation is surprising, since you'd expect that income should increase as people get older. A visualization gives you more insight into what's going on than a single number can. Let's try a scatter plot first; you plot figure 3.10 with `geom_point`:

```
ggplot(custdata2, aes(x=age, y=income)) +
   geom_point() + ylim(0, 200000)
```

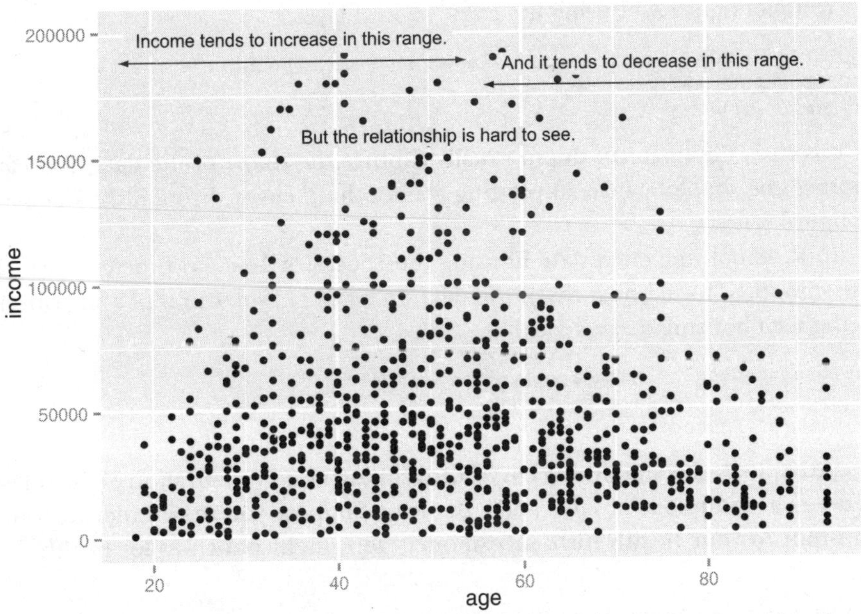

Figure 3.10 A scatter plot of income versus age

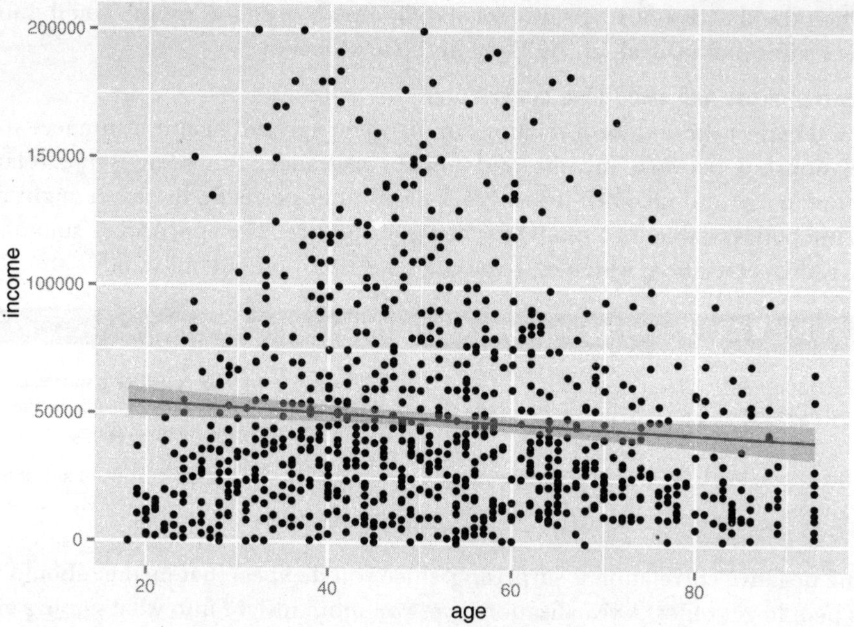

Figure 3.11 A scatter plot of income versus age, with a linear fit

The relationship between age and income isn't easy to see. You can try to make the relationship clearer by also plotting a linear fit through the data, as shown in figure 3.11.

You plot figure 3.11 using the `stat_smooth` layer:[4]

```
ggplot(custdata2, aes(x=age, y=income)) + geom_point() +
  stat_smooth(method="lm") +
  ylim(0, 200000)
```

In this case, the linear fit doesn't really capture the shape of the data. You can better capture the shape by instead plotting a smoothing curve through the data, as shown in figure 3.12.

In R, smoothing curves are fit using the `loess` (or `lowess`) functions, which calculate smoothed local linear fits of the data. In `ggplot2`, you can plot a smoothing curve to the data by using `geom_smooth`:

```
ggplot(custdata2, aes(x=age, y=income)) +
   geom_point() + geom_smooth() +
   ylim(0, 200000)
```

A scatter plot with a smoothing curve also makes a good visualization of the relationship between a continuous variable and a Boolean. Suppose you're considering using age as an input to your health insurance model. You might want to plot health insurance

---

[4] The *stat* layers in `ggplot2` are the layers that perform transformations on the data. They're usually called under the covers by the *geom* layers. Sometimes you have to call them directly, to access parameters that aren't accessible from the geom layers. In this case, the default smoothing curve used `geom_smooth`, which is a loess curve, as you'll see shortly. To plot a linear fit we must call `stat_smooth` directly.

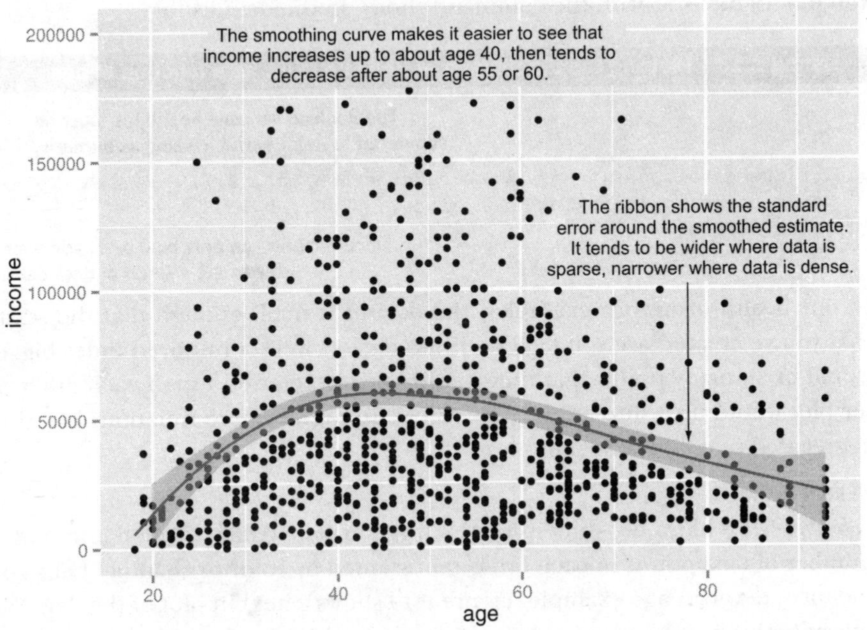

Figure 3.12 A scatter plot of income versus age, with a smoothing curve

coverage as a function of age, as shown in figure 3.13. This will show you that the probability of having health insurance increases as customer age increases.

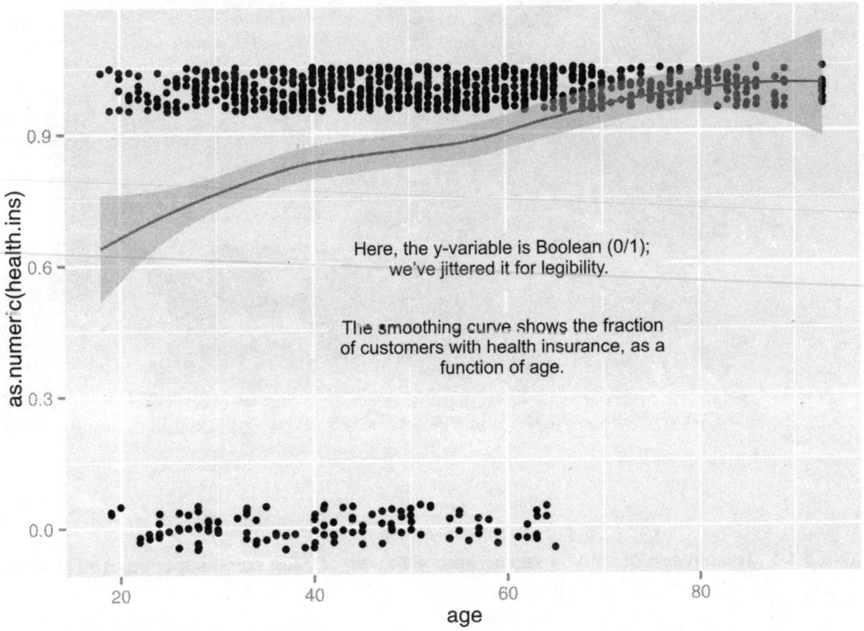

Figure 3.13 Distribution of customers with health insurance, as a function of age

You plot figure 3.13 with the command shown in the next listing.

Listing 3.13 Plotting the distribution of health.ins as a function of age

```
ggplot(custdata2, aes(x=age, y=as.numeric(health.ins))) +
    geom_point(position=position_jitter(w=0.05, h=0.05)) +
    geom_smooth()
```

- The Boolean variable health.ins must be converted to a 0/1 variable using as.numeric.
- Since y values can only be 0 or 1, add a small jitter to get a sense of data density.
- Add smoothing curve.

In our health insurance examples, the dataset is small enough that the scatter plots that you've created are still legible. If the dataset were a hundred times bigger, there would be so many points that they would begin to plot on top of each other; the scatter plot would turn into an illegible smear. In high-volume situations like this, try an aggregated plot, like a hexbin plot.

HEXBIN PLOTS

A *hexbin plot* is like a two-dimensional histogram. The data is divided into bins, and the number of data points in each bin is represented by color or shading. Let's go back to the income versus age example. Figure 3.14 shows a hexbin plot of the data. Note how the smoothing curve traces out the shape formed by the densest region of data.

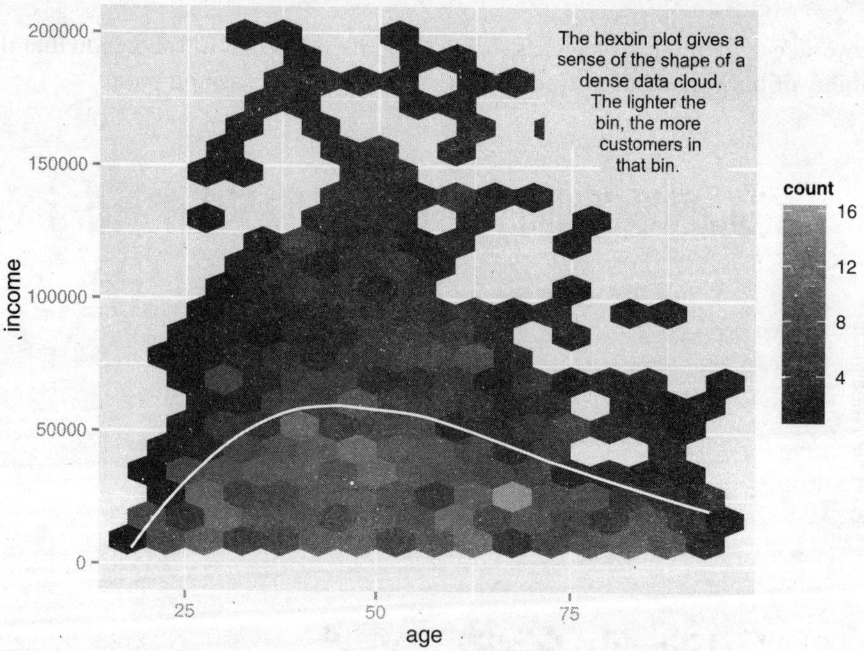

Figure 3.14 Hexbin plot of income versus age, with a smoothing curve superimposed in white

To make a hexbin plot in R, you must have the `hexbin` package installed. We'll discuss how to install R packages in appendix A. Once `hexbin` is installed and the library loaded, you create the plots using the `geom_hex` layer.

Listing 3.14 Producing a `hexbin` plot

```
library(hexbin)                                  <— Load hexbin library.

ggplot(custdata2, aes(x=age, y=income)) +
   geom_hex(binwidth=c(5, 10000)) +              <— Create hexbin with age binned into 5-year increments, income in increments of $10,000.
   geom_smooth(color="white", se=F) +            <— Add smoothing curve in white; suppress standard error ribbon (se=F).
   ylim(0,200000)
```

In this section and the previous section, we've looked at plots where at least one of the variables is numerical. But in our health insurance example, the output is categorical, and so are many of the input variables. Next we'll look at ways to visualize the relationship between two categorical variables.

Bar charts for two categorical variables

Let's examine the relationship between marital status and the probability of health insurance coverage. The most straightforward way to visualize this is with a *stacked bar chart*, as shown in figure 3.15.

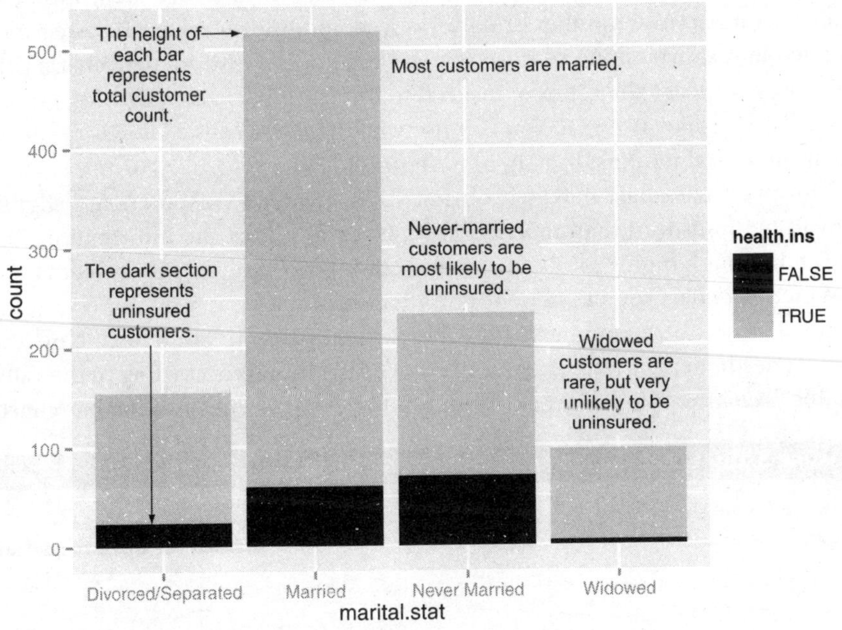

Figure 3.15 Health insurance versus marital status: stacked bar chart

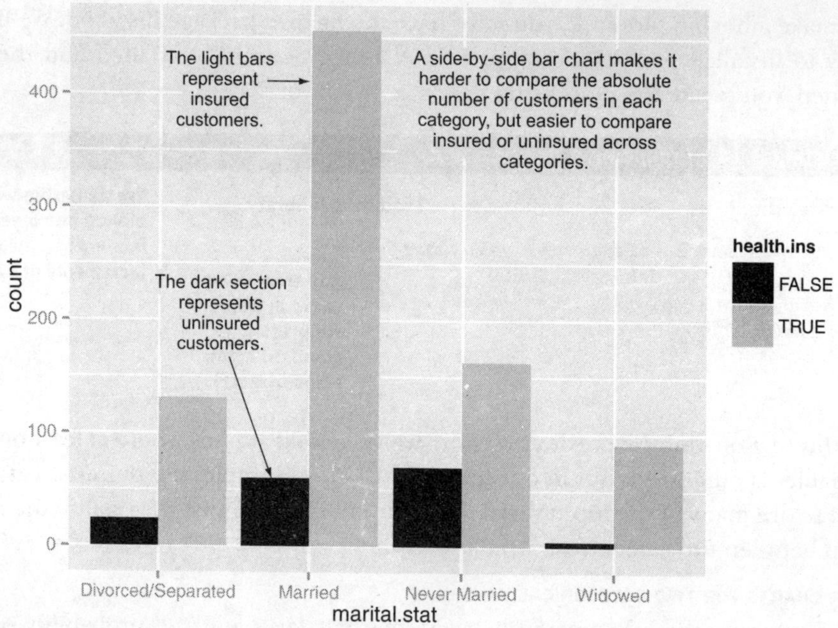

Figure 3.16 Health insurance versus marital status: side-by-side bar chart

Some people prefer the side-by-side bar chart, shown in figure 3.16, which makes it easier to compare the number of both insured and uninsured across categories.

The main shortcoming of both the stacked and side-by-side bar charts is that you can't easily compare the ratios of insured to uninsured across categories, especially for rare categories like *Widowed.* You can use what `ggplot2` calls a *filled bar chart* to plot a visualization of the ratios directly, as in figure 3.17.

The filled bar chart makes it obvious that divorced customers are slightly more likely to be uninsured than married ones. But you've lost the information that being widowed, though highly predictive of insurance coverage, is a rare category.

Which bar chart you use depends on what information is most important for you to convey. The `ggplot2` commands for each of these plots are given next. Note the use of the `fill` aesthetic; this tells `ggplot2` to color (fill) the bars according to the value of the variable *health.ins.* The `position` argument to `geom_bar` specifies the bar chart style.

Listing 3.15 Specifying different styles of bar chart

```
ggplot(custdata) + geom_bar(aes(x=marital.stat,
   fill=health.ins))                          <— Stacked bar chart, the default

ggplot(custdata) + geom_bar(aes(x=marital.stat,
   fill=health.ins),
   position="dodge")                          <— Side-by-side bar chart

ggplot(custdata) + geom_bar(aes(x=marital.stat,
   fill=health.ins),
   position="fill")                 <— Filled bar chart
```

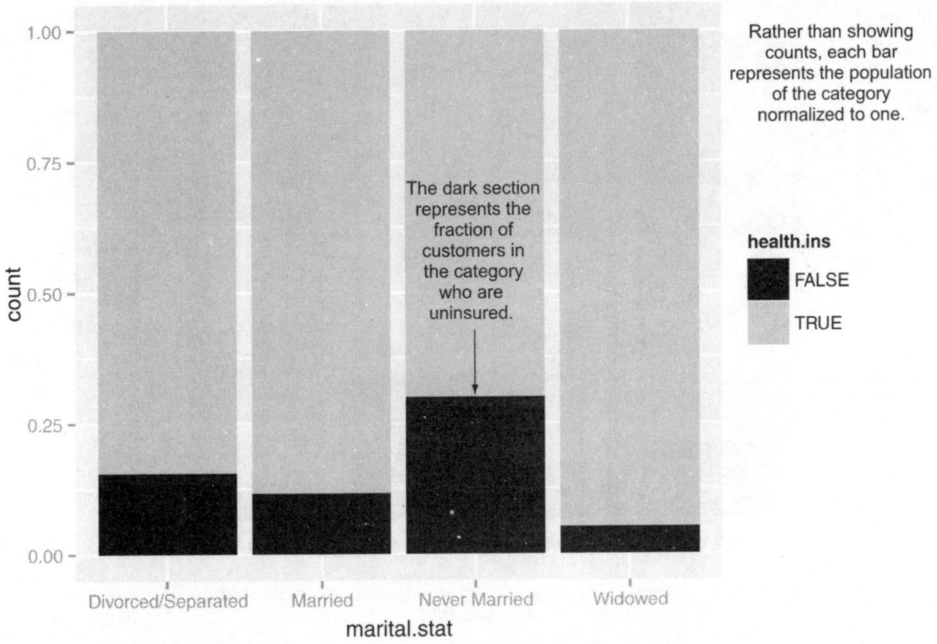

Figure 3.17 Health insurance versus marital status: filled bar chart

To get a simultaneous sense of both the population in each category and the ratio of insured to uninsured, you can add what's called a *rug* to the filled bar chart. A rug is a series of ticks or points on the x-axis, one tick per datum. The rug is dense where you have a lot of data, and sparse where you have little data. This is shown in figure 3.18. You generate this graph by adding a `geom_point` layer to the graph.

Listing 3.16 Plotting data with a rug

```
ggplot(custdata, aes(x=marital.stat)) +
   geom_bar(aes(fill=health.ins), position="fill") +
   geom_point(aes(y=-0.05), size=0.75, alpha=0.3,
   position=position_jitter(h=0.01))
```

Set the points just under the y-axis, three-quarters of default size, and make them slightly transparent with the alpha parameter.

Jitter the points slightly for legibility.

In the preceding examples, one of the variables was binary; the same plots can be applied to two variables that each have several categories, but the results are harder to read. Suppose you're interested in the distribution of marriage status across housing types. Some find the side-by-side bar chart easiest to read in this situation, but it's not perfect, as you see in figure 3.19.

A graph like figure 3.19 gets cluttered if either of the variables has a large number of categories. A better alternative is to break the distributions into different graphs, one for each housing type. In `ggplot2` this is called *faceting* the graph, and you use the `facet_wrap` layer. The result is in figure 3.20.

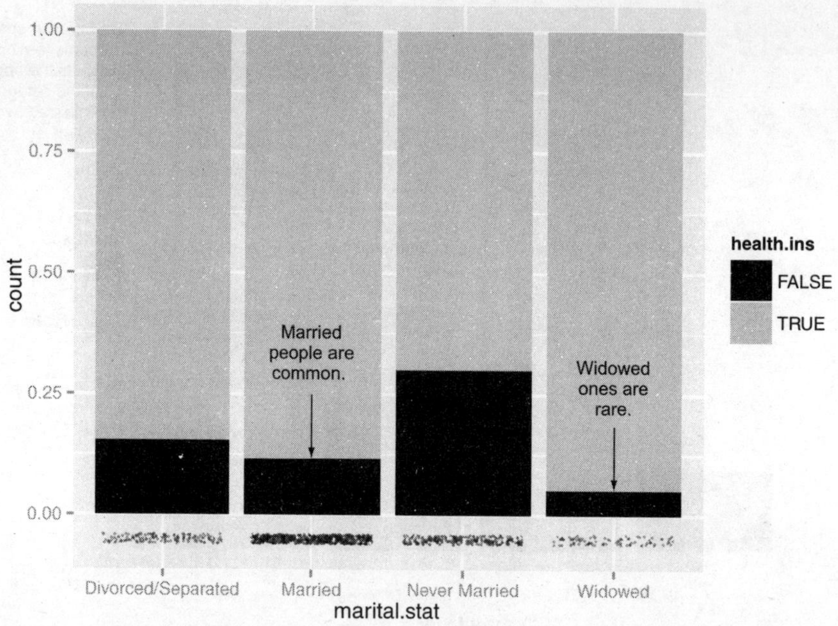

Figure 3.18 Health insurance versus marital status: filled bar chart with rug

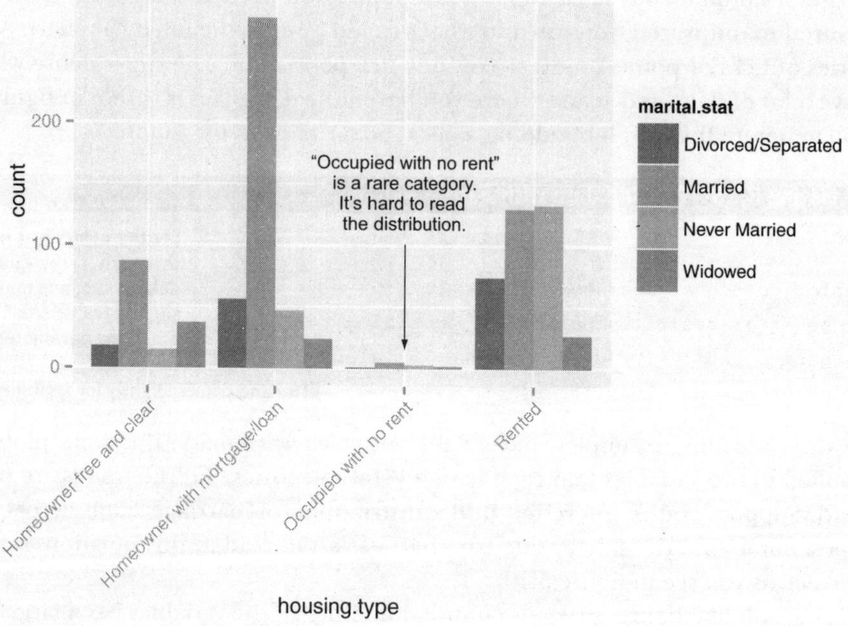

Figure 3.19 Distribution of marital status by housing type: side-by-side bar chart

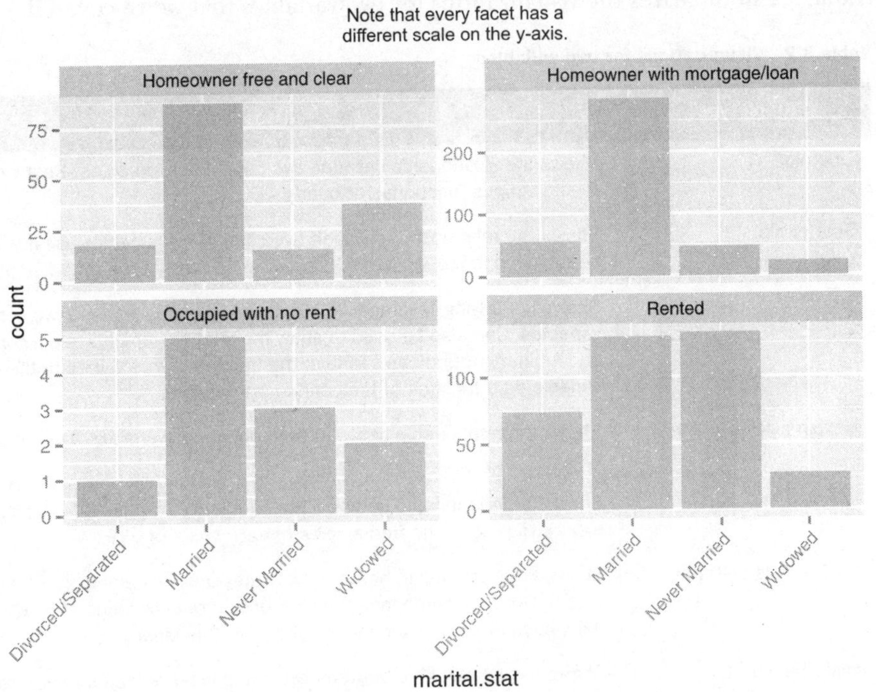

Figure 3.20 Distribution of marital status by housing type: faceted side-by-side bar chart

The code for figures 3.19 and 3.20 looks like the next listing.

Listing 3.17 Plotting a bar chart with and without facets

```
ggplot(custdata2) +
   geom_bar(aes(x=housing.type, fill=marital.stat ),
      position="dodge") +
   theme(axis.text.x = element_text(angle = 45, hjust = 1))

ggplot(custdata2) +
   geom_bar(aes(x=marital.stat), position="dodge",
      fill="darkgray") +
   facet_wrap(~housing.type, scales="free_y") +
   theme(axis.text.x = element_text(angle = 45, hjust = 1))
```

Side-by-side bar chart. (first `ggplot` call)

Tilt the x-axis labels so they don't overlap. You can also use coord_flip() to rotate the graph, as we saw previously. Some prefer coord_flip() because the theme() layer is complicated to use.

The faceted bar chart. (second `ggplot` call)

Facet the graph by housing.type. The scales="free_y" argument specifies that each facet has an independently scaled y-axis (the default is that all facets have the same scales on both axes). The argument free_x would free the x-axis scaling, and the argument free frees both axes.

As of this writing, facet_wrap is incompatible with coord_flip, so we have to tilt the x-axis labels.

Table 3.2 summarizes the visualizations for two variables that we've covered.

Table 3.2 Visualizations for two variables

Graph type	Uses
Line plot	Shows the relationship between two continuous variables. Best when that relationship is functional, or nearly so.
Scatter plot	Shows the relationship between two continuous variables. Best when the relationship is too loose or cloud-like to be easily seen on a line plot.
Smoothing curve	Shows underlying "average" relationship, or trend, between two continuous variables. Can also be used to show the relationship between a continuous and a binary or Boolean variable: the fraction of *true* values of the discrete variable as a function of the continuous variable.
Hexbin plot	Shows the relationship between two continuous variables when the data is very dense.
Stacked bar chart	Shows the relationship between two categorical variables (`var1` and `var2`). Highlights the frequencies of each value of `var1`.
Side-by-side bar chart	Shows the relationship between two categorical variables (`var1` and `var2`). Good for comparing the frequencies of each value of `var2` across the values of `var1`. Works best when `var2` is binary.
Filled bar chart	Shows the relationship between two categorical variables (`var1` and `var2`). Good for comparing the relative frequencies of each value of `var2` within each value of `var1`. Works best when `var2` is binary.
Bar chart with faceting	Shows the relationship between two categorical variables (`var1` and `var2`). Best for comparing the relative frequencies of each value of `var2` within each value of `var1` when `var2` takes on more than two values.

There are many other variations and visualizations you could use to explore the data; the preceding set covers some of the most useful and basic graphs. You should try different kinds of graphs to get different insights from the data. It's an interactive process. One graph will raise questions that you can try to answer by replotting the data again, with a different visualization.

Eventually, you'll explore your data enough to get a sense of it and to spot most major problems and issues. In the next chapter, we'll discuss some ways to address common problems that you may discover in the data.

3.3 Summary

At this point, you've gotten a feel for your data. You've explored it through summaries and visualizations; you now have a sense of the quality of your data, and of the relationships among your variables. You've caught and are ready to correct several kinds of data issues—although you'll likely run into more issues as you progress.

Maybe some of the things you've discovered have led you to reevaluate the question you're trying to answer, or to modify your goals. Maybe you've decided that you need more or different types of data to achieve your goals. This is all good. As we mentioned in the previous chapter, the data science process is made of loops within loops. The data exploration and data cleaning stages (we'll discuss cleaning in the next chapter) are two of the more time-consuming—and also the most important—stages of the process. Without good data, you can't build good models. Time you spend here is time you don't waste elsewhere.

In the next chapter, we'll talk about fixing the issues that you've discovered in the data.

Key takeaways

- Take the time to examine your data before diving into the modeling.
- The `summary` command helps you spot issues with data range, units, data type, and missing or invalid values.
- Visualization additionally gives you a sense of data distribution and relationships among variables.
- Visualization is an iterative process and helps answer questions about the data. Time spent here is time not wasted during the modeling process.

4 Managing data

This chapter covers

- Fixing data quality problems
- Organizing your data for the modeling process

In chapter 3, you learned how to explore your data and to identify common data issues. In this chapter, you'll see how to fix the data issues that you've discovered. After that, we'll talk about organizing the data for the modeling process.[1]

4.1 Cleaning data

In this section, we'll address issues that you discovered during the data exploration/visualization phase. First you'll see how to treat missing values. Then we'll discuss some common data transformations and when they're appropriate: converting continuous variables to discrete; normalization and rescaling; and logarithmic transformations.

[1] For all of the examples in this chapter, we'll use synthetic customer data (mostly derived from US Census data) with specifically introduced flaws. The data can be loaded by saving the file exampleData.rData from https://github.com/WinVector/zmPDSwR/tree/master/Custdata and then running `load("exampleData.rData")` in R.

4.1.1 *Treating missing values (NAs)*

Let's take another look at some of the variables with missing values in our customer dataset from the previous chapter. We've reproduced the summary in figure 4.1.

Fundamentally, there are two things you can do with these variables: drop the rows with missing values, or convert the missing values to a meaningful value.

TO DROP OR NOT TO DROP?

Remember that we have a dataset of 1,000 customers; 56 missing values represents about 6% of the data. That's not trivial, but it's not huge, either. The fact that three variables are all missing exactly 56 values suggests that it's the same 56 customers in each case. That's easy enough to check.

Listing 4.1 Checking locations of missing data

```
> summary(custdata[is.na(custdata$housing.type),
                   c("recent.move","num.vehicles")])

 recent.move       num.vehicles
 Mode:logical     Min.    : NA
 NA's:56          1st Qu.: NA
                  Median : NA
                  Mean    :NaN
                  3rd Qu.: NA
                  Max.    : NA
                  NA's    :56
```

Restrict to the rows where housing.type is NA.

Look only at the columns recent.move and num.vehicles.

The output: all NAs. All the missing data comes from the same rows.

Because the missing data represents a fairly small fraction of the dataset, it's probably safe just to drop these customers from your analysis. But what about the variable

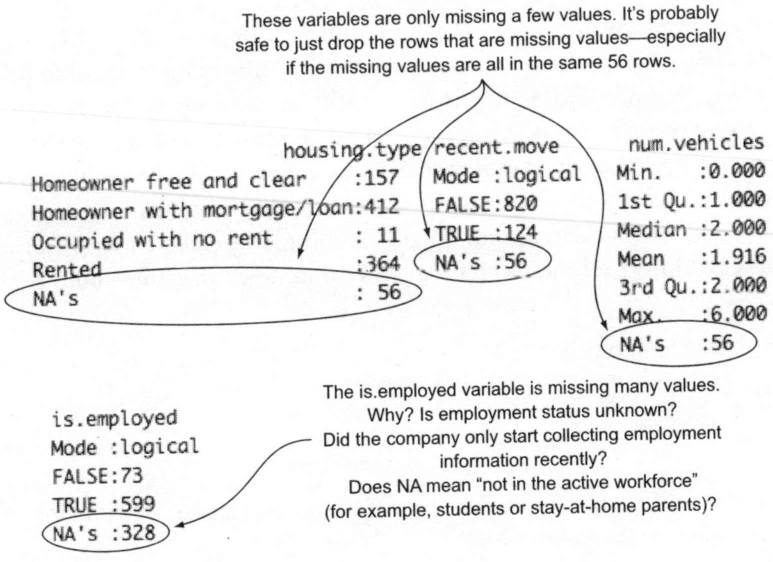

Figure 4.1 Variables with missing values

is.employed? Here you're missing data from a third of the customers. What do you do then?

MISSING DATA IN CATEGORICAL VARIABLES

The most straightforward solution is just to create a new category for the variable, called *missing*.

Listing 4.2 Remapping NA to a level

```
> custdata$is.employed.fix <- ifelse(is.na(custdata$is.employed),
                                     "missing",
                                     ifelse(custdata$is.employed==T,
                                            "employed",
                                            "not employed"))
```

If is.employed value is missing... ...assign the value "missing". Otherwise... ...if is.employed==TRUE, assign the value "employed"... ...or the value "not employed".

```
> summary(as.factor(custdata$is.employed.fix))

employed      missing not employed
     599          328           73
```

The transformation has turned the variable type from factor to string. You can change it back with the as.factor() function.

Practically speaking, this is exactly equivalent to what we had before; but remember that most analysis functions in R (and in a great many other statistical languages and packages) will, by default, drop rows with missing data. Changing each NA (which is R's code for missing values) to the token missing (which is people-code for missing values) will prevent that.

The preceding fix will get the job done, but as a data scientist, you ought to be interested in *why* so many customers are missing this information. It could just be bad record-keeping, but it could be semantic, as well. In this case, the format of the data (using the same row type for all customers) hints that the NA actually encodes that the customer is not in the active workforce: they are a homemaker, a student, retired, or otherwise not seeking paid employment. Assuming that you don't want to differentiate between retirees, students, and so on, naming the category appropriately will make it easier to interpret the model that you build down the line—both for you and for others:

```
custdata$is.employed.fix <- ifelse(is.na(custdata$is.employed),
                      "not in active workforce",
                       ifelse(custdata$is.employed==T,
                                    "employed",
                                     "not employed"))
```

If you *did* want to differentiate retirees from students and so on, you'd need additional data to make the correct assignments.

> **Why a new variable?**
>
> You'll notice that we created a new variable called `is.employed.fix`, rather than simply replacing `is.employed`. This is a matter of taste. We prefer to have the original variable on hand, in case we second-guess our data cleaning and want to redo it. This is mostly a problem when the data cleaning involves a complicated transformation, like determining which customers are retirees and which ones are students. On the other hand, having two variables about employment in your data frame leaves you open to accidentally using the wrong one. Both choices have advantages and disadvantages.

Missing values in categorical variables are a relatively straightforward case to work through. What about numeric data?

MISSING VALUES IN NUMERIC DATA

Suppose your income variable is missing substantial data:

```
> summary(custdata$Income)

 Min. 1st Qu.  Median    Mean 3rd Qu.    Max.    NA's
    0   25000   45000   66200   82000  615000     328
```

You believe that income is still an important predictor of the probability of health insurance coverage, so you still want to use the variable. What do you do?

WHEN VALUES ARE MISSING RANDOMLY

You might believe that the data is missing because of a *faulty sensor*—in other words, the data collection failed at random. In this case, you can replace the missing values with the expected, or mean, income:

```
> meanIncome <- mean(custdata$Income, na.rm=T)
> Income.fix <- ifelse(is.na(custdata$Income),
                       meanIncome,
                       custdata$Income)
> summary(Income.fix)

 Min. 1st Qu.  Median    Mean 3rd Qu.    Max.
    0   35000   66200   66200   66200  615000
```

Don't forget the argument "na.rm=T"! Otherwise, the mean() function will include the NAs by default, and meanIncome will be NA.

Assuming that the customers with missing income are distributed the same way as the others, this estimate will be correct on average, and you'll be about as likely to have overestimated customer income as underestimated it. It's also an easy fix to implement.

This estimate can be improved when you remember that income is related to other variables in your data—for instance, you know from your data exploration in the previous chapter that there's a relationship between age and income. There might be a relationship between state of residence or marital status and income, as well. If you have this information, you can use it.

Note that the method of imputing a missing value of an input variable based on the other input variables can be applied to categorical data, as well. The text *R in*

Action, Second Edition (Robert Kabacoff, 2014, http://mng.bz/ybS4) includes an extensive discussion of several methods available in R.

It's important to remember that replacing missing values by the mean, as well as many more sophisticated methods for imputing missing values, assumes that the customers with missing income are in some sense random (the "faulty sensor" situation). It's possible that the customers with missing income data are *systematically* different from the others. For instance, it could be the case that the customers with missing income information truly have no income—because they're not in the active workforce. If this is so, then "filling in" their income information by using one of the preceding methods is the wrong thing to do. In this situation, there are two transformations you can try.

WHEN VALUES ARE MISSING SYSTEMATICALLY

One thing you can do is to convert the numeric data into categorical data, and then use the methods that we discussed previously. In this case, you would divide the income into some income categories of interest, such as "below $10,000," or "from $100,000 to $250,000" using the `cut()` function, and then treat the NAs as we did when working with missing categorical values.

Listing 4.3 Converting missing numeric data to a level

Select some income ranges of interest. To use the cut() function, the upper and lower bounds should encompass the full income range of the data.

```
> breaks <-c(0, 10000, 50000, 100000, 250000, 1000000)
```

Cut the data into income ranges. The include.lowest=T argument makes sure that zero income data is included in the lowest income range category. By default it would be excluded.

```
> Income.groups <-
     cut(custdata$Income,
                   breaks=breaks, include.lowest=T)
> summary(Income.groups)

 [0,1e+04] (1e+04,5e+04] (5e+04,1e+05] (1e+05,2.5e+05] (2.5e+05,1e+06]
        63           312           178              98              21
      NA's
       328
```

The cut() function produces factor variables. Note the NAs are preserved.

To preserve the category names before adding a new category, convert the variables to strings.

```
> Income.groups <- as.character(Income.groups)
```

Add the "no income" category to replace the NAs.

```
> Income.groups <- ifelse(is.na(Income.groups),
                   "no income", Income.groups)
> summary(as.factor(Income.groups))

 (1e+04,5e+04] (1e+05,2.5e+05] (2.5e+05,1e+06]  (5e+04,1e+05]    [0,1e+04]
           312              98              21            178           63
     no income
           328
```

This grouping approach can work well, especially if the relationship between income and insurance is nonmonotonic (the likelihood of having insurance doesn't strictly increase or decrease with income). It does require that you select good cuts, and it's a less concise representation of income than a numeric variable.

You could also replace all the NAs with zero income—but the data already has customers with zero income. Those zeros could be from the same mechanism as the NAs (customers not in the active workforce), or they could come from another mechanism—for example, customers who have been unemployed the entire year. A trick that has worked well for us is to replace the NAs with zeros and add an additional variable (we call it a *masking variable*) to keep track of which data points have been altered.

Listing 4.4 Tracking original NAs with an extra categorical variable

The missingIncome variable lets you differentiate the two kinds of zeros in the data: the ones that you are about to add, and the ones that were already there.

```
missingIncome <- is.na(custdata$Income)
Income.fix <- ifelse(is.na(custdata$Income), 0, custdata$Income)
```

Replace the NAs with zeros.

You give both variables, `missingIncome` and `Income.fix`, to the modeling algorithm, and it can determine how to best use the information to make predictions. Note that if the missing values really are missing randomly, then the masking variable will basically pick up the variable's mean value (at least in regression models).

In summary, to properly handle missing data you need to know why the data is missing in the first place. If you don't know whether the missing values are random or systematic, we recommend assuming that the difference is systematic, rather than trying to impute values to the variables based on the faulty sensor assumption.

In addition to fixing missing data, there are other ways that you can transform the data to address issues that you found during the exploration phase. In the next section, we'll examine some common transformations.

4.1.2 Data transformations

The purpose of data transformation is to make data easier to model—and easier to understand. For example, the cost of living will vary from state to state, so what would be a high salary in one region could be barely enough to scrape by in another. If you want to use income as an input to your insurance model, it might be more meaningful to normalize a customer's income by the typical income in the area where they live. The next listing is an example of a relatively simple (and common) transformation.

Listing 4.5 Normalizing income by state

```
> summary(medianincome)

     State      Median.Income
        : 1    Min.    :37427
```

Suppose medianincome is a data frame of median income by state.

```
  Alabama    : 1   1st Qu.:47483
  Alaska     : 1   Median :52274
  Arizona    : 1   Mean   :52655
  Arkansas   : 1   3rd Qu.:57195
  California: 1    Max.   :68187
  (Other)    :46

> custdata <- merge(custdata, medianincome,
                by.x="state.of.res", by.y="State")

> summary(custdata[,c("state.of.res", "income", "Median.Income")])

        state.of.res       income           Median.Income
  California  :100    Min.   :  -8700    Min.   :37427
  New York    : 71    1st Qu.: 14600     1st Qu.:44819
  Pennsylvania: 70    Median : 35000     Median :50977
  Texas       : 56    Mean   : 53505     Mean   :51161
  Michigan    : 52    3rd Qu.: 67000     3rd Qu.:55559
  Ohio        : 51    Max.   :615000     Max.   :68187
  (Other)     :600

> custdata$income.norm <- with(custdata, income/Median.Income)

> summary(custdata$income.norm)

   Min. 1st Qu.  Median    Mean 3rd Qu.    Max.
-0.1791  0.2729  0.6992  1.0820  1.3120 11.6600
```

Merge median income information into the custdata data frame by matching the column custdata$state.of.res to the column medianincome$State.

Median.Income is now part of custdata.

Normalize income by Median.Income.

The need for data transformation can also depend on which modeling method you plan to use. For linear and logistic regression, for example, you ideally want to make sure that the relationship between input variables and output variable is approximately linear, and that the output variable is constant variance (the variance of the output variable is independent of the input variables). You may need to transform some of your input variables to better meet these assumptions.

In this section, we'll look at some useful data transformations and when to use them: converting continuous variables to discrete; normalizing variables; and log transformations.

CONVERTING CONTINUOUS VARIABLES TO DISCRETE

For some continuous variables, their exact value matters less than whether they fall into a certain range. For example, you may notice that customers with incomes less than $20,000 have different health insurance patterns than customers with higher incomes. Or you may notice that customers younger than 25 and older than 65 have high probabilities of insurance coverage, because they tend to be on their parents' coverage or on a retirement plan, respectively, whereas customers between those ages have a different pattern.

In these cases, you might want to convert the continuous `age` and `income` variables into ranges, or discrete variables. Discretizing continuous variables is useful when the relationship between input and output isn't linear, but you're using a modeling technique that assumes it is, like regression (see figure 4.2).

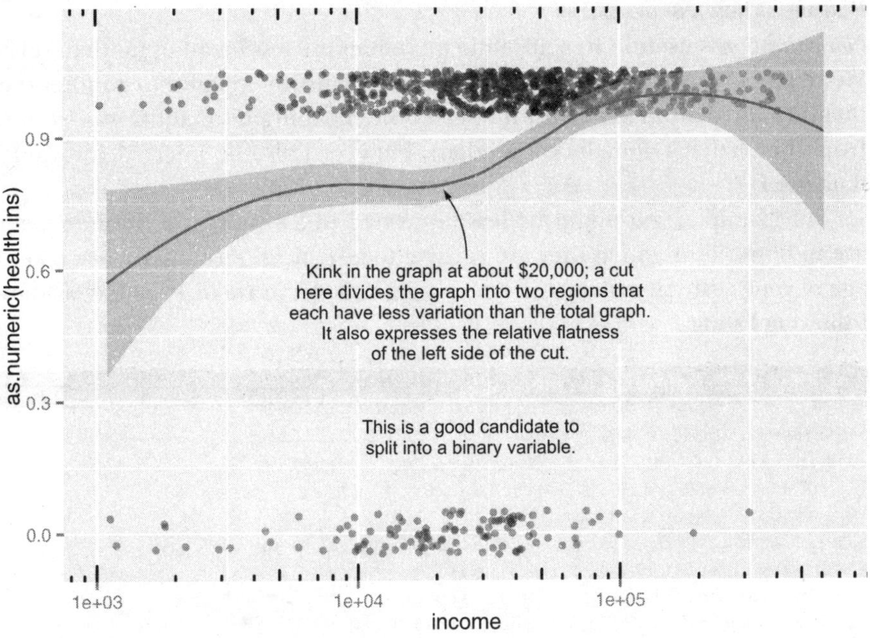

Figure 4.2 Health insurance coverage versus income (log10 scale)

Looking at figure 4.2, you see that you can replace the `income` variable with a Boolean variable that indicates whether income is less than $20,000:

```
> custdata$income.lt.20K <- custdata$income < 20000
> summary(custdata$income.lt.20K)
   Mode   FALSE    TRUE    NA's
logical     678     322       0
```

If you want more than a simple threshold (as in the age example), you can use the `cut()` function, as you saw in the section "When values are missing systematically."

Listing 4.6 Converting age into ranges

```
> brks <- c(0, 25, 65, Inf)
> custdata$age.range <- cut(custdata$age,
  breaks=brks, include.lowest=T)
> summary(custdata$age.range)
  [0,25]  (25,65] (65,Inf]
      56      732      212
```

Select the age ranges of interest. The upper and lower bounds should encompass the full range of the data.

Cut the data into age ranges. The include.lowest=T argument makes sure that zero age data is included in the lowest age range category. By default it would be excluded.

The output of cut() is a factor variable.

Even when you do decide not to discretize a numeric variable, you may still need to transform it to better bring out the relationship between it and other variables. You saw this in the example that introduced this section, where we normalized income by the regional median income. In the next section, we'll talk about normalization and rescaling.

NORMALIZATION AND RESCALING

Normalization is useful when absolute quantities are less meaningful than relative ones. We've already seen an example of normalizing income relative to another meaningful quantity (median income). In that case, the meaningful quantity was external (came from the analyst's domain knowledge); but it can also be internal (derived from the data itself).

For example, you might be less interested in a customer's absolute age than you are in how old or young they are relative to a "typical" customer. Let's take the mean age of your customers to be the typical age. You can normalize by that, as shown in the following listing.

Listing 4.7 Centering on mean age

```
> summary(custdata$age)
   Min. 1st Qu.  Median    Mean 3rd Qu.    Max.
    0.0    38.0    50.0    51.7    64.0   146.7
> meanage <- mean(custdata$age)
> custdata$age.normalized <- custdata$age/meanage
> summary(custdata$age.normalized)
   Min. 1st Qu.  Median    Mean 3rd Qu.    Max.
 0.0000  0.7350  0.9671  1.0000  1.2380  2.8370
```

A value for `age.normalized` that is much less than `1` signifies an unusually young customer; much greater than `1` signifies an unusually old customer. But what constitutes "much less" or "much greater" than `1`? That depends on how wide an age spread your customers tend to have. See figure 4.3 for an example.

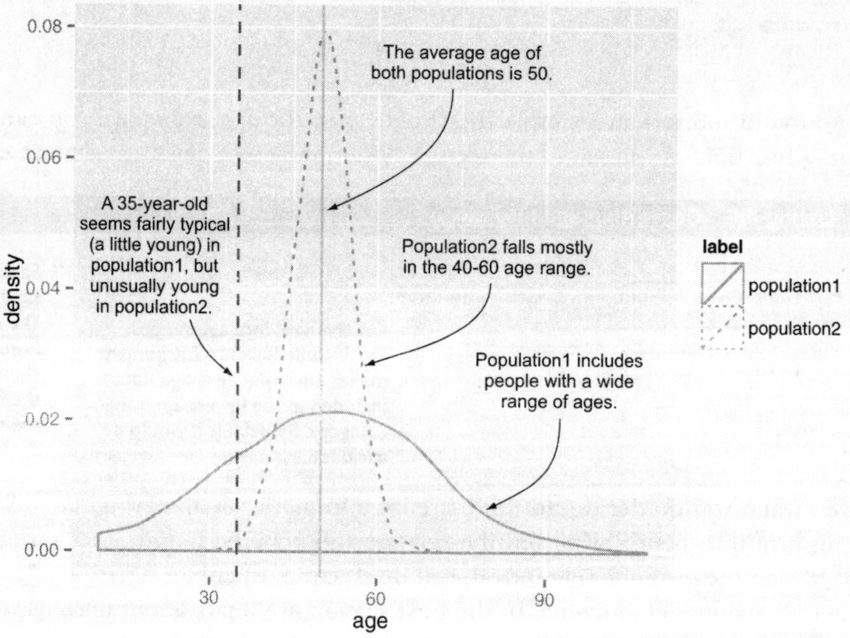

Figure 4.3 Is a 35-year-old young?

The typical age spread of your customers is summarized in the standard deviation. You can *rescale* your data by using the standard deviation as a unit of distance. A customer who is within one standard deviation of the mean is not much older or younger than typical. A customer who is more than one or two standard deviations from the mean can be considered much older, or much younger.

Listing 4.8 Summarizing age

```
> summary(custdata$age)
   Min. 1st Qu.  Median    Mean 3rd Qu.    Max.
    0.0    38.0    50.0    51.7    64.0   146.7
> meanage <- mean(custdata$age)
> stdage <- sd(custdata$age)
> meanage
[1] 51.69981
> stdage
[1] 18.86343
> custdata$age.normalized <- (custdata$age-meanage)/stdage
> summary(custdata$age.normalized)
    Min.  1st Qu.   Median     Mean  3rd Qu.     Max.
-2.74100 -0.72630 -0.09011  0.00000  0.65210  5.03500
```

Take the mean.

Take the standard deviation.

Use the mean value as the origin (or reference point) and rescale the distance from the mean by the standard deviation.

Now, values less than `-1` signify customers younger than typical; values greater than `1` signify customers older than typical.

Normalizing by mean and standard deviation is most meaningful when the data distribution is roughly symmetric. Next, we'll look at a transformation that can make some distributions more symmetric.

LOG TRANSFORMATIONS FOR SKEWED AND WIDE DISTRIBUTIONS

Monetary amounts—incomes, customer value, account, or purchase sizes—are some of the most commonly encountered sources of skewed distributions in data science applications. In fact, as we discuss in appendix B, monetary amounts are often lognormally distributed—the log of the data is normally distributed. This leads us to the idea that taking the log of the data can restore symmetry to it. We demonstrate this in figure 4.4.

For the purposes of modeling, *which* logarithm you use—natural logarithm, log base 10, or log base 2—is generally not critical. In regression, for example, the choice of logarithm affects the

> **A technicality**
>
> The common interpretation of standard deviation as a unit of distance implicitly assumes that the data is distributed normally. For a normal distribution, roughly two-thirds of the data (about 68%) is within plus/minus one standard deviation from the mean. About 95% of the data is within plus/minus two standard deviations from the mean. In figure 4.3, a 35-year-old is (just barely) within one standard deviation from the mean in `population1`, but more than two standard deviations from the mean in `population2`.
>
> You can still use this transformation if the data isn't normally distributed, but the standard deviation is most meaningful as a unit of distance if the data is unimodal and roughly symmetric around the mean.

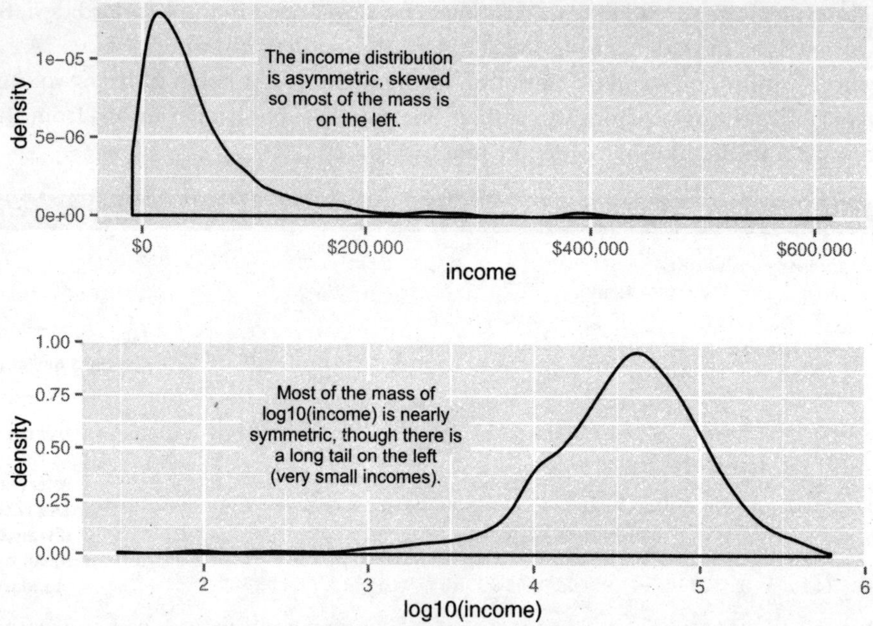

Figure 4.4 A nearly lognormal distribution and its log

magnitude of the coefficient that corresponds to the logged variable, but it doesn't affect the value of the outcome. We like to use log base 10 for monetary amounts, because orders of ten seem natural for money: $100, $1000, $10,000, and so on. The transformed data is easy to read.

AN ASIDE ON GRAPHING Notice that the bottom panel of figure 4.4 has the same shape as figure 3.5. The difference between using the `ggplot` layer `scale_x_log10` on a density plot of *income* and plotting a density plot of *log10(income)* is primarily axis labeling. Using `scale_x_log10` will label the x-axis in dollars amounts, rather than in logs.

It's also generally a good idea to log transform data with values that range over several orders of magnitude—first, because modeling techniques often have a difficult time with very wide data ranges; and second, because such data often comes from multiplicative processes, so log units are in some sense more natural.

For example, when you're studying weight loss, the natural unit is often pounds or kilograms. If you weigh 150 pounds and your friend weighs 200, you're both equally active, and you both go on the exact same restricted-calorie diet, then you'll probably both lose about the same number of pounds—in other words, how much weight you lose doesn't (to first order) depend on how much you weighed in the first place, only on calorie intake. This is an *additive* process.

On the other hand, if management gives everyone in the department a raise, it probably isn't giving everyone $5,000 extra. Instead, everyone gets a 2% raise: how much extra money ends up in your paycheck depends on your initial salary. This is a *multiplicative* process, and the natural unit of measurement is percentage, not absolute dollars. Other examples of multiplicative processes: a change to an online retail site increases conversion (purchases) for each item by 2% (not by exactly two purchases); a change to a restaurant menu increases patronage every night by 5% (not by exactly five customers every night). When the process is multiplicative, log transforming the process data can make modeling easier.

Of course, taking the logarithm only works if the data is non-negative. There are other transforms, such as *arcsinh*, that you can use to decrease data range if you have zero or negative values. We don't always use arcsinh, because we don't find the values of the transformed data to be meaningful. In applications where the skewed data is monetary (like account balances or customer value), we instead use what we call a *signed logarithm.* A signed logarithm takes the logarithm of the absolute value of the variable and multiplies by the appropriate sign. Values strictly between `-1` and `1` are mapped to zero. The difference between log and signed log is shown in figure 4.5.

Here's how to calculate signed log base 10, in R:

```
signedlog10 <- function(x) {
  ifelse(abs(x) <= 1, 0, sign(x)*log10(abs(x)))
}
```

Clearly this isn't useful if values below unit magnitude are important. But with many monetary variables (in US currency), values less than a dollar aren't much different

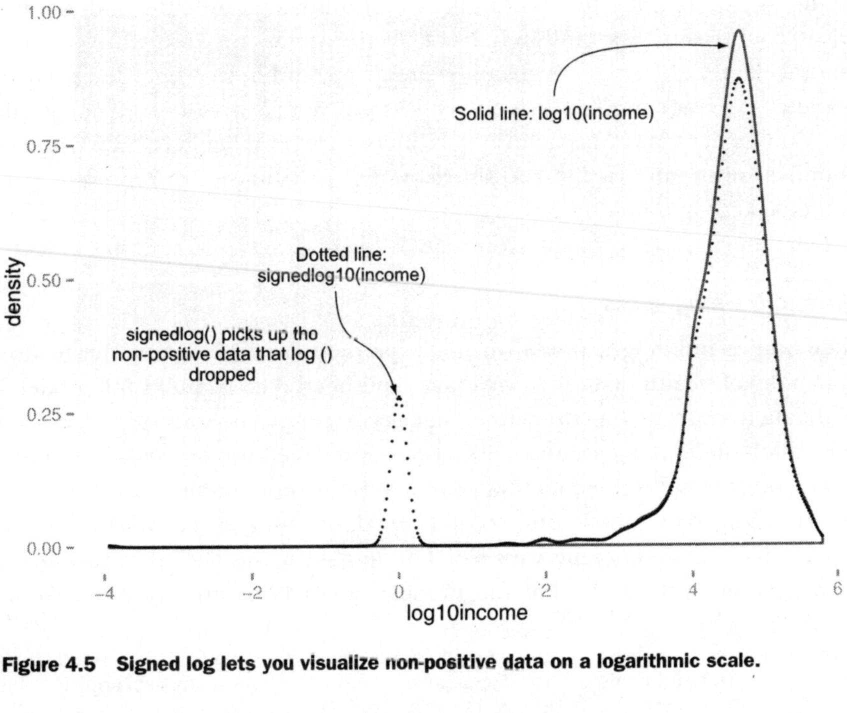

Figure 4.5 Signed log lets you visualize non-positive data on a logarithmic scale.

from zero (or one), for all practical purposes. So, for example, mapping account balances that are less than or equal to $1 (the equivalent of every account always having a minimum balance of one dollar) is probably okay.[2]

Once you've got the data suitably cleaned and transformed, you're almost ready to start the modeling stage. Before we get there, we have one more step.

4.2 Sampling for modeling and validation

Sampling is the process of selecting a subset of a population to represent the whole, during analysis and modeling. In the current era of big datasets, some people argue that computational power and modern algorithms let us analyze the entire large dataset without the need to sample.

We can certainly analyze larger datasets than we could before, but sampling is a necessary task for other reasons. When you're in the middle of developing or refining a modeling procedure, it's easier to test and debug the code on small subsamples before training the model on the entire dataset. Visualization can be easier with a subsample of the data; `ggplot` runs faster on smaller datasets, and too much data will often obscure the patterns in a graph, as we mentioned in chapter 3. And often it's not feasible to use your entire customer base to train a model.

It's important that the dataset that you do use is an accurate representation of your population as a whole. For example, your customers might come from all over the United States. When you collect your `custdata` dataset, it might be tempting to use all the customers from one state, say Connecticut, to train the model. But if you plan to use the model to make predictions about customers all over the country, it's a good idea to pick customers randomly from all the states, because what predicts health insurance coverage for Texas customers might be different from what predicts health insurance coverage in Connecticut. This might not always be possible (perhaps only your Connecticut and Massachusetts branches currently collect the customer health insurance information), but the shortcomings of using a nonrepresentative dataset should be kept in mind.

The other reason to sample your data is to create test and training splits.

4.2.1 Test and training splits

When you're building a model to make predictions, like our model to predict the probability of health insurance coverage, you need data to build the model. You also need data to test whether the model makes correct predictions on new data. The first set is called the *training set*, and the second set is called the *test (or hold-out) set.*

The training set is the data that you feed to the model-building algorithm—regression, decision trees, and so on—so that the algorithm can set the correct parameters to best predict the outcome variable. The test set is the data that you feed into the resulting model, to verify that the model's predictions are accurate. We'll go into

[2] There are methods other than capping to deal with signed logarithms, such as the arcsinh function (see http://mng.bz/ZWQa), but they also distort data near zero and make almost any data appear to be bimodal.

detail about the kinds of modeling issues that you can detect by using hold-out data in chapter 5. For now, we'll just get our data ready for doing hold-out experiments at a later stage.

Many writers recommend train/calibration/test splits, which is also good advice. Our philosophy is this: split the data into train/test early, don't look at test until final evaluation, and if you need calibration data, resplit it from your training subset.

4.2.2 Creating a sample group column

A convenient way to manage random sampling is to add a sample group column to the data frame. The sample group column contains a number generated uniformly from zero to one, using the `runif` function. You can draw a random sample of arbitrary size from the data frame by using the appropriate threshold on the sample group column.

For example, once you've labeled all the rows of your data frame with your sample group column (let's call it `gp`), then the set of all rows such that `gp` < 0.4 will be about four-tenths, or 40%, of the data. The set of all rows where `gp` is between 0.55 and 0.70 is about 15% of the data (`0.7 - 0.55 = 0.15`). So you can repeatably generate a random sample of the data of any size by using `gp`.

Listing 4.9 Splitting into test and training using a random group mark

```
> custdata$gp <- runif(dim(custdata)[1])
> testSet <- subset(custdata, custdata$gp <= 0.1)
> trainingSet <- subset(custdata, custdata$gp > 0.1)
> dim(testSet)[1]
[1] 93
> dim(trainingSet)[1]
[1] 907
```

dim(custdata) returns the number of rows and columns of the data frame as a vector, so dim(custdata)[1] returns the number of rows.

Here we generate a test set of about 10% of the data (93 customers—a little over 9%, actually) and train on the remaining 90%.

Here we generate a training using the remaining data.

R also has a function called `sample` that draws a random sample (a uniform random sample, by default) from a data frame. Why not just use `sample` to draw training and test sets? You could, but using a sample group column guarantees that you'll draw the same sample group every time. This reproducible sampling is convenient when you're debugging code. In many cases, code will crash because of a corner case that you forgot to guard against. This corner case might show up in your random sample. If you're using a different random input sample every time you run the code, you won't know if you will tickle the bug again. This makes it hard to track down and fix errors.

You also want repeatable input samples for what software engineers call *regression testing* (not to be confused with statistical regression). In other words, when you make changes to a model or to your data treatment, you want to make sure you don't break what was already working. If model version 1 was giving "the right answer" for a certain input set, you want to make sure that model version 2 does so also.

> **REPRODUCIBLE SAMPLING IS NOT JUST A TRICK FOR R** If your data is in a database or other external store, and you only want to pull a subset of the data into R for analysis, you can draw a reproducible random sample by generating a sample group column in an appropriate table in the database, using the SQL command `RAND`.

4.2.3 *Record grouping*

One caveat is that the preceding trick works if every object of interest (every customer, in this case) corresponds to a unique row. But what if you're interested less in which customers don't have health insurance, and more about which *households* have uninsured members? If you're modeling a question at the household level rather than the customer level, then *every member of a household should be in the same group (test or training)*. In other words, the random sampling also has to be at the household level.

	household_id	cust_id	income
Household 1	hh1	cust1	30200
Household 2	hh2	cust1	24800
	hh2	cust2	134800
Household 3	hh3	cust1	299000
	hh3	cust2	65000
	hh3	cust3	95000
Household 4	hh4	cust1	38800
	hh4	cust2	0
Household 5	hh5	cust1	100300
	hh5	cust2	27000

Figure 4.6 Example of dataset with customers and households

Suppose your customers are marked both by a household ID and a customer ID (so the unique ID for a customer is the combination `(household_id, cust_id)`. This is shown in figure 4.6. We want to split the households into a training set and a test set. The next listing shows one way to generate an appropriate sample group column.

Listing 4.10 Ensuring test/train split doesn't split inside a household

```
hh <- unique(hhdata$household_id)

households <- data.frame(household_id = hh, gp = runif(length(hh)))

hhdata <- merge(hhdata, households, by="household_id")
```

Get all unique household IDs from your data frame.

Create a temporary data frame of household IDs and a uniformly random number from 0 to 1.

Merge new random sample group column back into original data frame.

The resulting sample group column is shown in figure 4.7. Now we can generate the test and training sets as before. This time, however, the threshold 0.1 doesn't represent 10% of the data rows, but 10% of the households (which may be more or less than 10% of the data, depending on the sizes of the households).

4.2.4 *Data provenance*

You'll also want to add a column (or columns) to record data provenance: when your dataset was collected, perhaps what version of your data cleaning procedure was used

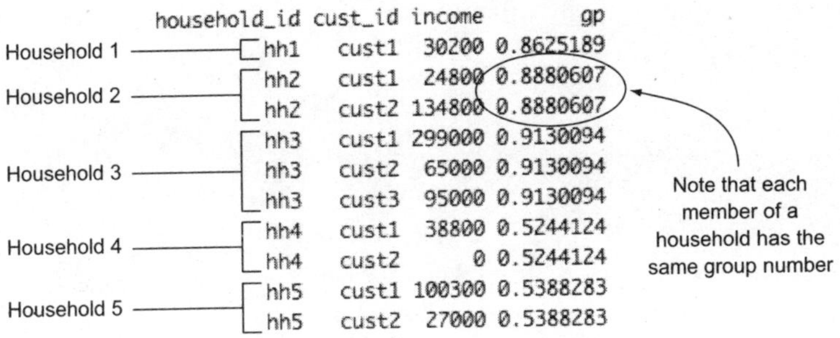

Figure 4.7 Example of dataset with customers and households

on the data before modeling, and so on. This is akin to version control for data. It's handy information to have, to make sure that you're comparing apples to apples when you're in the process of improving your model, or comparing different models or different versions of a model.

4.3 Summary

At some point, you'll have data quality that is as good as you can make it. You've fixed problems with missing data and performed any needed transformations. You're ready to go on to the modeling stage.

Remember, though, that data science is an iterative process. You may discover during the modeling process that you have to do additional data cleaning or transformation. You may have to go back even further and collect different types of data. That's why we recommend adding columns for sample groups and data provenance to your datasets (and later, to the models and model output), so you can keep track of the data management steps as the data and the models evolve.

In the part 2 of the book, we'll talk about the process of building and evaluating models to meet your stated objectives.

Key takeaways

- What you do with missing values depends on how many there are, and whether they're missing randomly or systematically.
- When in doubt, assume that missing values are missing systematically.
- Appropriate data transformations can make the data easier to understand and easier to model.
- Normalization and rescaling are important when relative changes are more important than absolute ones.
- Data provenance records help reduce errors as you iterate over data collection, data treatment, and modeling.

Part 2

Modeling methods

In part 1, we discussed the initial stages of a data science project. After you've defined more precisely the questions you want to answer and the scope of the problem you want to solve, it's time to analyze the data and find the answers. In part 2, we work with powerful modeling methods from statistics and machine learning.

Chapter 5 covers how to identify appropriate modeling methods to address your specific business problem. It also discusses how to evaluate the quality and effectiveness of models that you or others have discovered. The remaining chapters in part 2 cover specific modeling techniques.

Chapter 6 covers what we call *memorization-based* techniques. These methods make predictions based primarily on summary statistics of your data. We cover lookup tables, nearest-neighbor methods, Naive Bayes classification, and decision trees. Chapter 7 covers methods that fit simple functions with additive functional structure: linear and logistic regression. These two methods not only make predictions, but also provide you with information about the relationship between the input variables and the outcome.

Chapter 8 covers unsupervised methods: clustering and association rule mining. Unsupervised methods don't make explicit outcome predictions; they discover relationships and hidden structure in the data. Chapter 9 touches on some more advanced modeling algorithms. We discuss bagged decision trees and random forests, generalized additive models, kernels, and support vector machines.

We work through every method that we cover with a specific data science problem, and a nontrivial dataset. In each chapter, we also discuss additional model evaluation procedures that are specific to the methods that we cover.

On completing part 2, you'll be familiar with the most popular modeling methods, and you'll have a sense of which methods are most appropriate for answering different types of questions.

Choosing and evaluating models

This chapter covers

- Mapping business problems to machine learning tasks
- Evaluating model quality
- Validating model soundness

As a data scientist, your ultimate goal is to solve a concrete business problem: increase look-to-buy ratio, identify fraudulent transactions, predict and manage the losses of a loan portfolio, and so on. Many different statistical modeling methods can be used to solve any given problem. Each statistical method will have its advantages and disadvantages for a given business goal and business constraints. This chapter presents an outline of the most common machine learning and statistical methods used in data science.

To make progress, you must be able to measure model quality during training and also ensure that your model will work as well in the production environment as it did on your training data. In general, we'll call these two tasks model *evaluation* and model *validation*. To prepare for these statistical tests, we always split our data into training data and test data, as illustrated in figure 5.1.

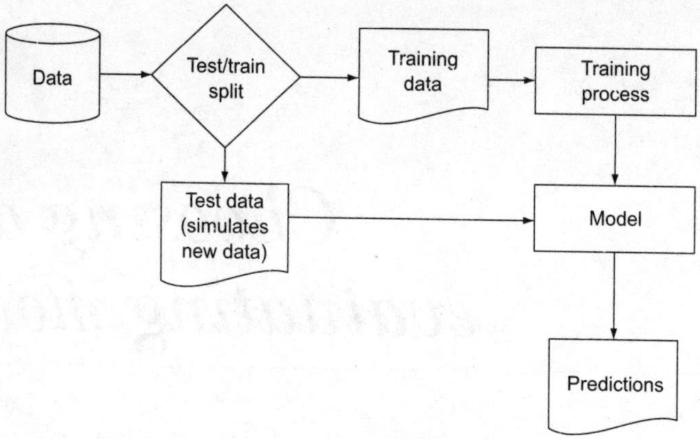

Figure 5.1 Schematic model construction and evaluation

We define model evaluation as quantifying the performance of a model. To do this we must find a measure of model performance that's appropriate to both the original business goal and the chosen modeling technique. For example, if we're predicting who would default on loans, we have a classification task, and measures like precision and recall are appropriate. If we instead are predicting revenue lost to defaulting loans, we have a scoring task, and measures like root mean square error (RMSE) are appropriate. The point is this: there are a number of measures the data scientist should be familiar with.

We define model validation as the generation of an assurance that the model will work in production as well as it worked during training. It is a disaster to build a model that works great on the original training data and then performs poorly when used in production. The biggest cause of model validation failures is not having enough training data to represent the variety of what may later be encountered in production. For example, training a loan default model only on people who repaid their loans might score well on a simple evaluation ("predicts no defaults and is 100% accurate!") but would obviously not be a good model to put into production. Validation techniques attempt to quantify this type of risk before you put a model into production.

5.1 Mapping problems to machine learning tasks

Your task is to map a business problem to a good machine learning method. To use a real-world situation, let's suppose that you're a data scientist at an online retail company. There are a number of business problems that your team might be called on to address:

- Predicting what customers might buy, based on past transactions
- Identifying fraudulent transactions
- Determining price elasticity (the rate at which a price increase will decrease sales, and vice versa) of various products or product classes
- Determining the best way to present product listings when a customer searches for an item

- Customer segmentation: grouping customers with similar purchasing behavior
- AdWord valuation: how much the company should spend to buy certain AdWords on search engines
- Evaluating marketing campaigns
- Organizing new products into a product catalog

Your intended uses of the model have a big influence on what methods you should use. If you want to know how small variations in input variables affect outcome, then you likely want to use a regression method. If you want to know what single variable drives most of a categorization, then decision trees might be a good choice. Also, each business problem suggests a statistical approach to try. If you're trying to predict scores, some sort of regression is likely a good choice; if you're trying to predict categories, then something like random forests is probably a good choice.

5.1.1 Solving classification problems

Suppose your task is to automate the assignment of new products to your company's product categories, as shown in figure 5.2. This can be more complicated than it sounds. Products that come from different sources may have their own product classification that doesn't coincide with the one that you use on your retail site, or they may come without any classification at all. Many large online retailers use teams of human taggers to hand-categorize their products. This is not only labor-intensive, but inconsistent and error-prone. Automation is an attractive option; it's labor-saving, and can improve the quality of the retail site.

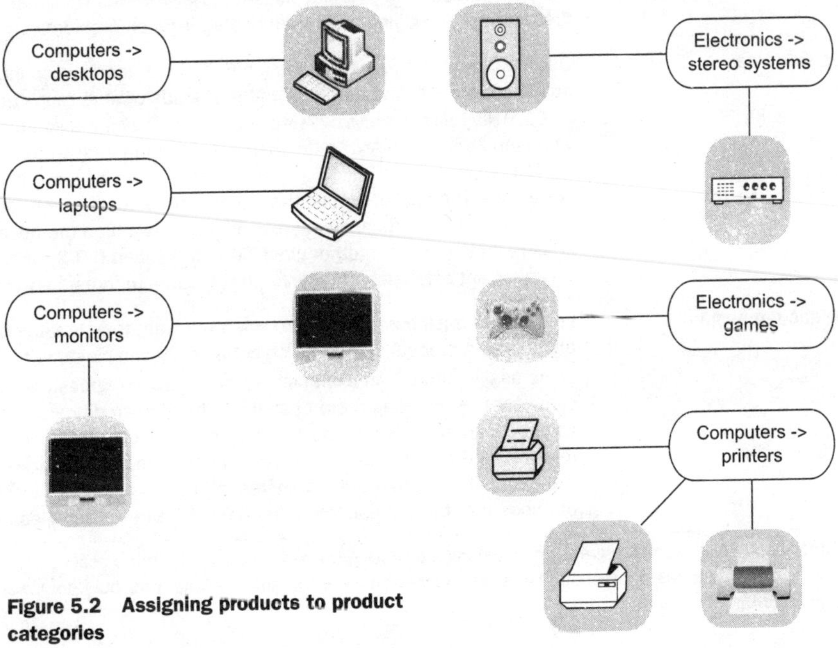

Figure 5.2 Assigning products to product categories

Product categorization based on product attributes and/or text descriptions of the product is an example of *classification*: deciding how to assign (known) labels to an object. Classification itself is an example of what is called *supervised learning*: in order to learn how to classify objects, you need a dataset of objects that have already been classified (called the *training set*). Building training data is the major expense for most classification tasks, especially text-related ones. Table 5.1 lists some of the more common effective classification methods.

> **Multicategory vs. two-category classification**
> Product classification is an example of *multicategory* or *multinomial* classification. Most classification problems and most classification algorithms are specialized for two-category, or binomial, classification. There are tricks to using binary classifiers to solve multicategory problems (for example, building one classifier for each category, called a "one versus rest" classifier). But in most cases it's worth the effort to find a suitable multiple-category implementation, as they tend to work better than multiple binary classifiers (for example, using the package `mlogit` instead of the base method `glm()` for logistic regression).

Table 5.1 Some common classification methods

Method	Description
Naive Bayes	Naive Bayes classifiers are especially useful for problems with many input variables, categorical input variables with a very large number of possible values, and text classification. Naive Bayes would be a good first attempt at solving the product categorization problem.
Decision trees	Decision trees (discussed in section 6.3.2) are useful when input variables interact with the output in "if-then" kinds of ways (such as IF `age > 65`, THEN `has.health.insurance=T`). They are also suitable when inputs have an AND relationship to each other (such as IF `age < 25` AND `student=T`, THEN...) or when input variables are redundant or correlated. The decision rules that come from a decision tree are in principle easier for nontechnical users to understand than the decision processes that come from other classifiers. In section 6.3.2, we'll discuss an important extension of decision trees: random forests.
Logistic regression	Logistic regression is appropriate when you want to estimate class probabilities (the probability that an object is in a given class) in addition to class assignments.[a] An example use of a logistic regression–based classifier is estimating the probability of fraud in credit card purchases. Logistic regression is also a good choice when you want an idea of the relative impact of different input variables on the output. For example, you might find out that a $100 increase in transaction size increases the odds that the transaction is fraud by 2%, all else being equal.

a. Strictly speaking, logistic regression is scoring (covered in the next section). To turn a scoring algorithm into a classifier requires a threshold. For scores higher than the threshold, assign one label; for lower scores, assign an alternative label.

Table 5.1 Some common classification methods *(continued)*

Method	Description
Support vector machines	Support vector machines (SVMs) are useful when there are very many input variables or when input variables interact with the outcome or with each other in complicated (nonlinear) ways. SVMs make fewer assumptions about variable distribution than do many other methods, which makes them especially useful when the training data isn't completely representative of the way the data is distributed in production.

5.1.2 *Solving scoring problems*

For a scoring example, suppose that your task is to help evaluate how different marketing campaigns can increase valuable traffic to the website. The goal is not only to bring more people to the site, but to bring more people who buy. You're looking at a number of different factors: the communication channel (ads on websites, YouTube videos, print media, email, and so on); the traffic source (Facebook, Google, radio stations, and so on); the demographic targeted; the time of year; and so on.

Predicting the increase in sales from a particular marketing campaign is an example of *regression*, or *scoring*. Fraud detection can be considered scoring, too, if you're trying to estimate the probability that a given transaction is a fraudulent one (rather than just returning a yes/no answer). This is shown in figure 5.3. Scoring is also an instance of supervised learning.

COMMON SCORING METHODS

We'll cover the following two general scoring methods in more detail in later chapters.

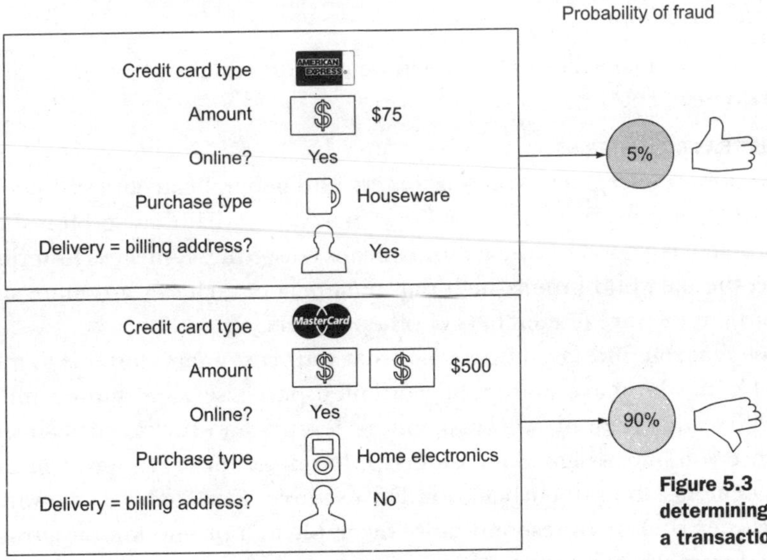

Figure 5.3 Notional example of determining the probability that a transaction is fraudulent

Linear regression

Linear regression builds a model such that the predicted numerical output is a linear additive function of the inputs. This can be a very effective approximation, even when the underlying situation is in fact nonlinear. The resulting model also gives an indication of the relative impact of each input variable on the output. Linear regression is often a good first model to try when trying to predict a numeric value.

Logistic regression

Logistic regression always predicts a value between 0 and 1, making it suitable for predicting probabilities (when the observed outcome is a categorical value) and rates (when the observed outcome is a rate or ratio). As we mentioned, logistic regression is an appropriate approach to the fraud detection problem, if what you want to estimate is the probability that a given transaction is fraudulent or legitimate.

5.1.3 Working without known targets

The preceding methods require that you have a training dataset of situations with known outcomes. In some situations, there's not (yet) a specific outcome that you want to predict. Instead, you may be looking for patterns and relationships in the data that will help you understand your customers or your business better.

These situations correspond to a class of approaches called *unsupervised learning*: rather than predicting outputs based on inputs, the objective of unsupervised learning is to discover similarities and relationships in the data. Some common clustering methods include these:

- K-means clustering
- Apriori algorithm for finding association rules
- Nearest neighbor

But these methods make more sense when we provide some context and explain their use, as we do next.

WHEN TO USE BASIC CLUSTERING

Suppose you want to segment your customers into general categories of people with similar buying patterns. You might not know in advance what these groups should be.

This problem is a good candidate for k-means clustering. K-means clustering is one way to sort the data into groups such that members of a cluster are more similar to each other than they are to members of other clusters.

Suppose that you find (as in figure 5.4) that your customers cluster into those with young children, who make more family-oriented purchases, and those with no children or with adult children, who make more leisure- and social-activity-related purchases. Once you have assigned a customer into one of those clusters, you can make general statements about their behavior. For example, a customer in the with-young-children cluster is likely to respond more favorably to a promotion on attractive but durable glassware than to a promotion on fine crystal wine glasses.

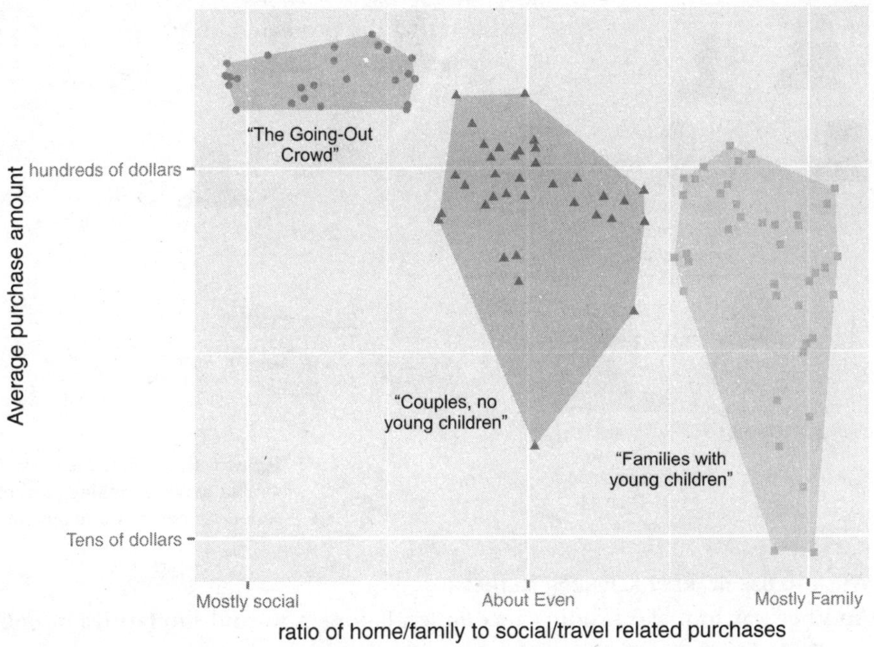

Figure 5.4 Notional example of clustering your customers by purchase pattern and purchase amount

When to use association rules

You might be interested in directly determining which products tend to be purchased together. For example, you might find that bathing suits and sunglasses are frequently purchased at the same time, or that people who purchase certain cult movies, like *Repo Man*, will often buy the movie soundtrack at the same time.

This is a good application for association rules (or even recommendation systems). You can mine useful product recommendations: whenever you observe that someone has put a bathing suit into their shopping cart, you can recommend suntan lotion, as well. This is shown in figure 5.5. We'll cover the Apriori algorithm for discovering association rules in section 8.2.

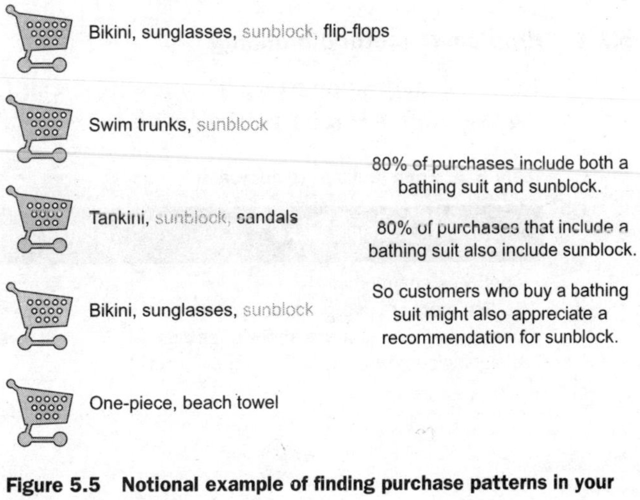

Figure 5.5 Notional example of finding purchase patterns in your data

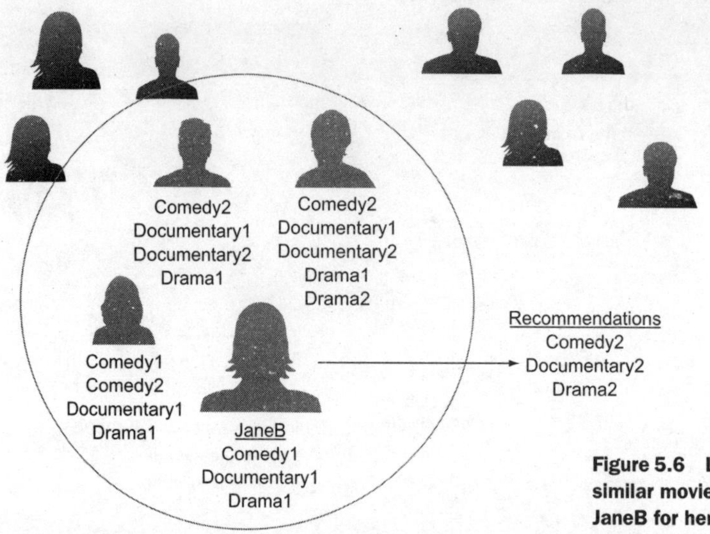

Figure 5.6 Look to the customers with similar movie-watching patterns as JaneB for her movie recommendations.

WHEN TO USE NEAREST NEIGHBOR METHODS

Another way to make product recommendations is to find similarities in people (figure 5.6). For example, to make a movie recommendation to customer *JaneB,* you might look for the three customers whose movie rental histories are the most like hers. Any movies that those three people rented, but JaneB has not, are potentially useful recommendations for her.

This can be solved with *nearest neighbor* (or k-nearest neighbor methods, with $K = 3$). Nearest neighbor algorithms predict something about a data point p (like a customer's future purchases) based on the data point or points that are most similar to p. We'll cover the nearest neighbor approach in section 6.3.3.

5.1.4 *Problem-to-method mapping*

Table 5.2 maps some typical business problems to their corresponding machine learning task, and to some typical algorithms to tackle each task.

Table 5.2 From problem to approach

Example tasks	Machine learning terminology	Typical algorithms
Identifying spam email Sorting products in a product catalog Identifying loans that are about to default Assigning customers to customer clusters	Classification: assigning known labels to objects	Decision trees Naive Bayes Logistic regression (with a threshold) Support vector machines

Table 5.2 From problem to approach *(continued)*

Example tasks	Machine learning terminology	Typical algorithms
Predicting the value of AdWords Estimating the probability that a loan will default Predicting how much a marketing campaign will increase traffic or sales	Regression: predicting or forecasting numerical values	Linear regression Logistic regression
Finding products that are purchased together Identifying web pages that are often visited in the same session Identifying successful (much-clicked) combinations of web pages and AdWords	Association rules: finding objects that tend to appear in the data together	Apriori
Identifying groups of customers with the same buying patterns Identifying groups of products that are popular in the same regions or with the same customer clusters Identifying news items that are all discussing similar events	Clustering: finding groups of objects that are more similar to each other than to objects in other groups	K-means
Making product recommendations for a customer based on the purchases of other similar customers Predicting the final price of an auction item based on the final prices of similar products that have been auctioned in the past	Nearest neighbor: predicting a property of a datum based on the datum or data that are most similar to it	Nearest neighbor

Notice that some problems show up multiple times in the table. Our mapping isn't hard-and-fast; any problem can be approached through a variety of mindsets, with a variety of algorithms. We're merely listing some common mappings and approaches to typical business problems. Generally, these should be among the first approaches to consider for a given problem; if they don't perform well, then you'll want to research other approaches, or get creative with data representation and with variations of common algorithms.

Prediction vs. forecasting

In everyday language, we tend to use the terms *prediction* and *forecasting* interchangeably. Technically, to predict is to pick an outcome, such as "It will rain tomorrow," and to forecast is to assign a probability: "There's an 80% chance it will rain tomorrow." For unbalanced class applications (such as predicting credit default), the difference is important. Consider the case of modeling loan defaults, and assume the overall default rate is 5%. Identifying a group that has a 30% default rate is an inaccurate prediction (you don't know who in the group will default, and most people in the group won't default), but potentially a very useful forecast (this group defaults at six times the overall rate).

5.2 Evaluating models

When building a model, the first thing to check is if the model even works on the data it was trained from. In this section, we do this by introducing quantitative measures of model performance. From an evaluation point of view, we group model types this way:

- Classification
- Scoring
- Probability estimation
- Ranking
- Clustering

For most model evaluations, we just want to compute one or two summary scores that tell us if the model is effective. To decide if a given score is high or low, we have to appeal to a few ideal models: a null model (which tells us what low performance looks like), a Bayes rate model (which tells us what high performance looks like), and the best single-variable model (which tells us what a simple model can achieve). We outline the concepts in table 5.3.

Table 5.3 Ideal models to calibrate against

Ideal model	Purpose
Null model	A null model is the best model of a very simple form you're trying to outperform. The two most typical null model choices are a model that is a single constant (returns the same answer for all situations) or a model that is independent (doesn't record any important relation or interaction between inputs and outputs). We use null models to lower-bound desired performance, so we usually compare to a best null model. For example, in a categorical problem, the null model would always return the most popular category (as this is the easy guess that is least often wrong); for a score model, the null model is often the average of all the outcomes (as this has the least square deviation from all of the outcomes); and so on. The idea is this: if you're not out-performing the null model, you're not delivering value. Note that it can be hard to do as good as the best null model, because even though the null model is simple, it's privileged to know the overall distribution of the items it will be quizzed on. We always assume the null model we're comparing to is the best of all possible null models.
Bayes rate model	A Bayes rate model (also sometimes called a *saturated model*) is a best possible model given the data at hand. The Bayes rate model is the perfect model and it only makes mistakes when there are multiple examples with the exact same set of known facts (same *xs*) but different outcomes (different *ys*). It isn't always practical to construct the Bayes rate model, but we invoke it as an upper bound on a model evaluation score. If we feel our model is performing significantly above the null model rate and is approaching the Bayes rate, then we can stop tuning. When we have a lot of data and very few modeling features, we can estimate the Bayes error rate. Another way to estimate the Bayes rate is to ask several different people to score the same small sample of your data; the found inconsistency rate can be an estimate of the Bayes rate.[a]

Table 5.3 Ideal models to calibrate against *(continued)*

Ideal model	Purpose
Single-variable models	We also suggest comparing any complicated model against the best single-variable model you have available (see section 6.2 for how to convert single variables into single-variable models). A complicated model can't be justified if it doesn't outperform the best single-variable model available from your training data. Also, business analysts have many tools for building effective single-variable models (such as pivot tables), so if your client is an analyst, they're likely looking for performance above this level.

a. There are a few machine learning magic methods that can introduce new synthetic features and in fact alter the Bayes rate. Typically, this is done by adding higher-order terms, interaction terms, or kernelizing.

In this section, we'll present the standard measures of model quality, which are useful in model construction. In all cases, we suggest that in addition to the standard model quality assessments you try to design your own custom "business-oriented loss function" with your project sponsor or client. Usually this is as simple as assigning a notional dollar value to each outcome and then seeing how your model performs under that criterion. Let's start with how to evaluate classification models and then continue from there.

5.2.1 *Evaluating classification models*

A classification model places examples into two or more categories. The most common measure of classifier quality is *accuracy*. For measuring classifier performance, we'll first introduce the incredibly useful tool called the *confusion matrix* and show how it can be used to calculate many important evaluation scores. The first score we'll discuss is accuracy, and then we'll move on to better and more detailed measures such as precision and recall.

Let's use the example of classifying email into spam (email we in no way want) and non-spam (email we want). A ready-to-go example (with a good description) is the *Spambase* dataset (http://mng.bz/e8Rh). Each row of this dataset is a set of features measured for a specific email and an additional column telling whether the mail was spam (unwanted) or non-spam (wanted). We'll quickly build a spam classification model so we have results to evaluate. To do this, download the file Spambase/spamD.tsv from the book's GitHub site (https://github.com/WinVector/zmPDSwR/tree/master/Spambase) and then perform the steps shown in the following listing.

Listing 5.1 Building and applying a logistic regression spam model

```
spamD <- read.table('spamD.tsv',header=T,sep='\t')
spamTrain <- subset(spamD,spamD$rgroup>=10)
spamTest <- subset(spamD,spamD$rgroup<10)
spamVars <- setdiff(colnames(spamD),list('rgroup','spam'))
spamFormula <- as.formula(paste('spam=="spam"',
   paste(spamVars,collapse=' + '),sep=' ~ '))
spamModel <- glm(spamFormula,family=binomial(link='logit'),
```

```
    data=spamTrain)
spamTrain$pred <- predict(spamModel,newdata=spamTrain,
    type='response')
spamTest$pred <- predict(spamModel,newdata=spamTest,
    type='response')
print(with(spamTest,table(y=spam,glmPred=pred>0.5)))
##          glmPred
## y         FALSE TRUE
##   non-spam   264   14
##   spam        22  158
```

A sample of the results of our simple spam classifier is shown in the next listing.

Listing 5.2 Spam classifications

```
> sample <- spamTest[c(7,35,224,327),c('spam','pred')]
> print(sample)
         spam         pred
115      spam 0.9903246227
361      spam 0.4800498077
2300 non-spam 0.0006846551
3428 non-spam 0.0001434345
```

THE CONFUSION MATRIX

The absolute most interesting summary of classifier performance is the confusion matrix. This matrix is just a table that summarizes the classifier's predictions against the actual known data categories.

The confusion matrix is a table counting how often each combination of known outcomes (the truth) occurred in combination with each prediction type. For our email spam example, the confusion matrix is given by the following R command.

Listing 5.3 Spam confusion matrix

```
> cM <- table(truth=spamTest$spam,prediction=spamTest$pred>0.5)
> print(cM)
          prediction
truth      FALSE TRUE
  non-spam   264   14
  spam        22  158
```

Using this summary, we can now start to judge the performance of the model. In a two-by-two confusion matrix, every cell has a special name, as illustrated in table 5.4.

> **CHANGING A SCORE TO A CLASSIFICATION** Note that we converted the numerical prediction score into a decision by checking if the score was above or below 0.5. For some scoring models (like logistic regression) the 0.5 score is likely a high accuracy value. However, accuracy isn't always the end goal, and for unbalanced training data the 0.5 threshold won't be good. Picking thresholds other than 0.5 can allow the data scientist to trade *precision* for *recall* (two terms that we'll define later in this chapter). You can start at 0.5, but consider trying other thresholds and looking at the ROC curve.

Table 5.4 Standard two-by-two confusion matrix

	Prediction=NEGATIVE	Prediction=POSITIVE
Truth mark=NOT IN CATEGORY	True negatives (TN) `cM[1,1]=264`	False positives (FP) `cM[1,2]=14`
Truth mark=IN CATEGORY	False negatives (FN) `cM[2,1]=22`	True positives (TP) `cM[2,2]=158`

Most of the performance measures of a classifier can be read off the entries of this confusion matrix. We start with the most common measure: accuracy.

ACCURACY

Accuracy is by far the most widely known measure of classifier performance. For a classifier, accuracy is defined as the number of items categorized correctly divided by the total number of items. It's simply what fraction of the time the classifier is correct. At the very least, you want a classifier to be accurate. In terms of our confusion matrix, accuracy is `(TP+TN)/(TP+FP+TN+FN)=(cM[1,1]+cM[2,2])/sum(cM)` or 92% accurate. The error of around 8% is unacceptably high for a spam filter, but good for illustrating different sorts of model evaluation criteria.

CATEGORIZATION ACCURACY ISN'T THE SAME AS NUMERIC ACCURACY It's important to not confuse *accuracy* used in a classification sense with *accuracy* used in a numeric sense (as in ISO 5725, which defines score-based accuracy as a numeric quantity that can be decomposed into numeric versions of trueness and precision). These are, unfortunately, two different meanings of the word.

Before we move on, we'd like to share the confusion matrix of a good spam filter. In the next listing we create the confusion matrix for the Akismet comment spam filter from the Win-Vector blog.

Listing 5.4 Entering data by hand

```
> t <- as.table(matrix(data=c(288-1,17,1,13882-17),nrow=2,ncol=2))
> rownames(t) <- rownames(cM)
> colnames(t) <- colnames(cM)
> print(t)
         FALSE  TRUE
non-spam   287     1
spam        17 13865
```

Because the Akismet filter uses link destination clues and determination from other websites (in addition to text features), it achieves a more acceptable accuracy of `(t[1,1]+t[2,2])/sum(t)`, or over 99.87%. More importantly, Akismet seems to have suppressed fewer good comments. Our next section on precision and recall will help quantify this distinction.

ACCURACY IS AN INAPPROPRIATE MEASURE FOR UNBALANCED CLASSES Suppose we have a situation where we have a rare event (say, severe complications during childbirth). If the event we're trying to predict is rare (say, around 1% of the population), the null model—the rare event never happens— is *very* accurate. The null model is in fact more accurate than a useful (but not perfect model) that identifies 5% of the population as being "at risk" and captures all of the bad events in the 5%. This is not any sort of paradox. It's just that accuracy is not a good measure for events that have unbalanced distribution or unbalanced costs (different costs of "type 1" and "type 2" errors).

PRECISION AND RECALL

Another evaluation measure used by machine learning researchers is a pair of numbers called precision and recall. These terms come from the field of information retrieval and are defined as follows. *Precision* is what fraction of the items the classifier flags as being in the class actually *are* in the class. So precision is `TP/(TP+FP)`, which is `cM[2,2]/(cM[2,2]+cM[1,2])`, or about 0.92 (it is only a coincidence that this is so close to the accuracy number we reported earlier). Again, precision is how often a positive indication turns out to be correct. It's important to remember that precision is a function of the combination of the classifier and the dataset. It doesn't make sense to ask how precise a classifier is in isolation; it's only sensible to ask how precise a classifier is for a given dataset.

In our email spam example, 93% precision means 7% of what was flagged as spam was in fact not spam. This is an unacceptable rate for losing possibly important messages. Akismet, on the other hand, had a precision of `t[2,2]/(t[2,2]+t[1,2])`, or over 99.99%, so in addition to having high accuracy, Akismet has even higher precision (very important in a spam filtering application).

The companion score to precision is recall. Recall is what fraction of the things that are in the class are detected by the classifier, or `TP/(TP+FN)=cM[2,2]/(cM[2,2]+cM[2,1])`. For our email spam example this is 88%, and for the Akismet example it is 99.87%. In both cases most spam is in fact tagged (we have high recall) and precision is emphasized over recall (which is appropriate for a spam filtering application).

It's important to remember this: precision is a measure of confirmation (when the classifier indicates positive, how often it is in fact correct), and recall is a measure of utility (how much the classifier finds of what there actually is to find). Precision and recall tend to be relevant to business needs and are good measures to discuss with your project sponsor and client.

F1

The F1 score is a useful combination of precision and recall. If either precision or recall is very small, then F1 is also very small. F1 is defined as `2*precision*recall/(precision+recall)`. So our email spam example with 0.93 precision and 0.88 recall has an F1 score of 0.90. The idea is that a classifier that improves precision or recall by sacrificing a lot of the complementary measure will have a lower F1.

SENSITIVITY AND SPECIFICITY

Scientists and doctors tend to use a pair of measures called sensitivity and specificity.

Sensitivity is also called the *true positive rate* and is exactly equal to recall. *Specificity* is also called the *true negative rate* and is equal to `TN/(TN+FP)=cM[1,1]/(cM[1,1]+cM[1,2])` or about 95%. Both sensitivity and specificity are measures of effect: what fraction of class members are identified as positive and what fraction of non-class members are identified as negative.

An important property of sensitivity and specificity is this: if you flip your labels (switch from *spam* being the class you're trying to identify to *non-spam* being the class you're trying to identify), you just switch sensitivity and specificity. Also, any of the so-called *null classifiers* (classifiers that always say positive or always say negative) always return a zero score on either sensitivity or specificity. So useless classifiers always score poorly on at least one of these measures. Finally, unlike precision and accuracy, sensitivity and specificity each only involve entries from a single row of table 5.4. So they're independent of the population distribution (which means they're good for some applications and poor for others).

COMMON CLASSIFICATION PERFORMANCE MEASURES

Table 5.5 summarizes the behavior of both the email spam example and the Akismet example under the common measures we've discussed.

Table 5.5 Example classifier performance measures

Measure	Formula	Email spam example	Akismet spam example
Accuracy	`(TP+TN)/(TP+FP+TN+FN)`	0.9214	0.9987
Precision	`TP/(TP+FP)`	0.9187	0.9999
Recall	`TP/(TP+FN)`	0.8778	0.9988
Sensitivity	`TP/(TP+FN)`	0.8778	0.9988
Specificity	`TN/(TN+FP)`	0.9496	0.9965

All of these formulas can seem confusing, and the best way to think about them is to shade in various cells in table 5.4. If your denominator cells shade in a column, then you're measuring a confirmation of some sort (how often the classifier's decision is correct). If your denominator cells shade in a row, then you're measuring effectiveness (how much of a given class is detected by a the classifier). The main idea is to use these standard scores and then work with your client and sponsor to see what most models their business needs. For each score, you should ask them if they need that score to be high and then run a quick thought experiment with them to confirm you've gotten their business need. You should then be able to write a project goal in terms of a minimum bound on a pair of these measures. Table 5.6 shows a typical business need and an example follow-up question for each measure.

Table 5.6 Classifier performance measures business stories

Measure	Typical business need	Follow-up question
Accuracy	"We need most of our decisions to be correct."	"Can we tolerate being wrong 5% of the time? And do users see mistakes like spam marked as non-spam or non-spam marked as spam as being equivalent?"
Precision	"Most of what we marked as spam had darn well better be spam."	"That would guarantee that most of what is in the spam folder is in fact spam, but it isn't the best way to measure what fraction of the user's legitimate email is lost. We could cheat on this goal by sending all our users a bunch of easy-to-identify spam that we correctly identify. Maybe we really want good specificity."
Recall	"We want to cut down on the amount of spam a user sees by a factor of 10 (eliminate 90% of the spam)."	"If 10% of the spam gets through, will the user see mostly non-spam mail or mostly spam? Will this result in a good user experience?"
Sensitivity	"We have to cut a lot of spam, otherwise the user won't see a benefit."	"If we cut spam down to 1% of what it is now, would that be a good user experience?"
Specificity	"We must be at least *three nines* on legitimate email; the user must see at least 99.9% of their non-spam email."	"Will the user tolerate missing 0.1% of their legitimate email, and should we keep a spam folder the user can look at?"

One conclusion for this dialogue process on spam classification would be to recommend writing the business goals as maximizing sensitivity while maintaining a specificity of at least 0.999.

5.2.2 Evaluating scoring models

Evaluating models that assign scores can be a somewhat visual task. The main concept is looking at what is called the *residuals* or the difference between our predictions `f(x[i,])` and actual outcomes `y[i]`. Figure 5.7 illustrates the concept.

The data and graph in figure 5.7 were produced by the R commands in the following listing.

Listing 5.5 Plotting residuals

```
d <- data.frame(y=(1:10)^2,x=1:10)
model <- lm(y~x,data=d)
d$prediction <- predict(model,newdata=d)
library('ggplot2')
ggplot(data=d) + geom_point(aes(x=x,y=y)) +
    geom_line(aes(x=x,y=prediction),color='blue') +
    geom_segment(aes(x=x,y=prediction,yend=y,xend=x)) +
    scale_y_continuous('')
```

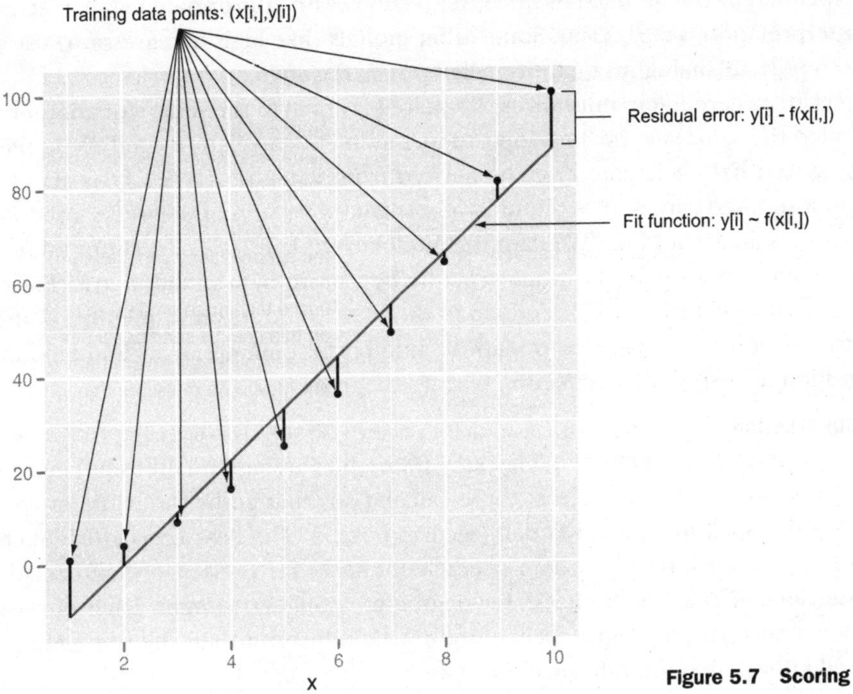

Figure 5.7 Scoring residuals

ROOT MEAN SQUARE ERROR

The most common goodness-of-fit measure is called *root mean square error (RMSE).* This is the square root of the average square of the difference between our prediction and actual values. Think of it as being like a standard deviation: how much your prediction is typically off. In our case, the RMSE is `sqrt(mean((d$prediction-d$y)^2))`, or about 7.27. The RMSE is in the same units as your y-values are, so if your y-units are pounds, your RMSE is in pounds. RMSE is a good measure, because it is often what the fitting algorithms you're using are explicitly trying to minimize. A good RMSE business goal would be "We want the RMSE on account valuation to be under $1,000 per account."

Most RMSE calculations (including ours) don't include any bias correction for sample size or model complexity, though you'll see adjusted RMSE in chapter 7.

R-SQUARED

Another important measure of fit is called R-squared (or R^2, or the coefficient of determination). It's defined as 1.0 minus how much unexplained variance your model leaves (measured relative to a null model of just using the average *y* as a prediction). In our case, the R-squared is `1-sum((d$prediction-d$y)^2)/sum((mean(d$y)-d$y)^2)`, or 0.95. R-squared is dimensionless (it's not the units of what you're trying to predict), and the best possible R-squared is 1.0 (with near-zero or negative R-squared being horrible). R-squared can be thought of as what fraction of the *y* variation is explained by the model. For linear regression (with appropriate bias corrections), this interpretation is fairly clear. Some other models (like logistic regression) use deviance to report an analogous quantity called *pseudo R-squared.*

Under certain circumstances, R-squared is equal to the square of another measure called the *correlation* (or Pearson product-moment correlation coefficient; see http://mng.bz/ndYf). R-squared can be derived from RMSE plus a few facts about the data (so R-squared can be thought of as a normalized version of RMSE). A good R-squared business goal would be "We want the model to explain 70% of account value."

However, R-squared is not always the best business-oriented metric. For example, it's hard to tell what a 10% reduction of RMSE would mean in relation to the Netflix Prize. But it would be easy to map the number of ranking errors and amount of suggestion diversity to actual Netflix business benefits.

CORRELATION

Correlation is very helpful in checking if variables are potentially useful in a model. Be advised that there are at least three calculations that go by the name of correlation: Pearson, Spearman, and Kendall (see `help(cor)`). The Pearson coefficient checks for linear relations, the Spearman coefficient checks for rank or ordered relations, and the Kendall coefficient checks for degree of voting agreement. Each of these coefficients performs a progressively more drastic transform than the one before and has well-known direct significance tests (see `help(cor.test)`).

> **DON'T USE CORRELATION TO EVALUATE MODEL QUALITY IN PRODUCTION** It's tempting to use correlation to measure model quality, but we advise against it. The problem is this: correlation ignores shifts and scaling factors. So correlation is actually computing if there is any shift and rescaling of your predictor that is a good predictor. This isn't a problem for training data (as these predictions tend to not have a systematic bias in shift or scaling by design) but can mask systematic errors that may arise when a model is used in production.

ABSOLUTE ERROR

For many applications (especially those involving predicting monetary amounts), measures such as absolute error (`sum(abs(d$prediction-d$y))`), mean absolute error (`sum(abs(d$prediction-d$y))/length(d$y)`), and relative absolute error (`sum(abs(d$prediction-d$y))/sum(abs(d$y))`) are tempting measures. It does make sense to check and report these measures, but it's usually not advisable to make these measures the project goal or to attempt to directly optimize them. This is because absolute error measures tend not to "get aggregates right" or "roll up reasonably" as most of the squared errors do.

As an example, consider an online advertising company with three advertisement purchases returning \$0, \$0, and \$25 respectively. Suppose our modeling task is as simple as picking a single summary value not too far from the original three prices. The price minimizing absolute error is the median, which is \$0, yielding an absolute error of `sum(abs(c(0,0,25)-20))`, or \$25. The price minimizing square error is the mean, which is $8.33 (which has a worse absolute error of $33.33). However the median price of $0 misleadingly values the entire campaign at $0. One great advantage of the mean is this: aggregating a mean prediction gives an unbiased prediction of the aggregate in question. It is *often* an unstated project need that various totals or roll-ups of the predicted amounts be close to the roll-ups of the unknown values to be predicted. For monetary applications, predicting the totals or aggregates accurately is often more important than getting individual values right. In fact, most statistical modeling techniques are designed for *regression*, which is the unbiased prediction of means or expected values.

5.2.3 Evaluating probability models

Probability models are useful for both classification and scoring tasks. Probability models are models that both decide if an item is in a given class and return an estimated probability (or confidence) of the item being in the class. The modeling techniques of logistic regression and decision trees are fairly famous for being able to return good probability estimates. Such models can be evaluated on their final decisions, as we've already shown in section 5.2.1, but they can also be evaluated in terms of their estimated probabilities. We'll continue the example from section 5.2.1 in this vein. In our opinion, most of the measures for probability models are very technical and very good at comparing the qualities of different models on the same dataset. But these criteria aren't easy to precisely translate into businesses needs. So we recommend tracking them, but not using them with your project sponsor or client.

When thinking about probability models, it's useful to construct a double density plot (illustrated in figure 5.8).

Listing 5.6 Making a double density plot

```
ggplot(data=spamTest) +
   geom_density(aes(x=pred,color=spam,linetype=spam))
```

Figure 5.8 is particularly useful at picking and explaining classifier thresholds. It also illustrates what we're going to try to check when evaluating estimated probability models: examples in the class should mostly have high scores and examples not in the class should mostly have low scores.

THE RECEIVER OPERATING CHARACTERISTIC CURVE

The *receiver operating characteristic curve* (or *ROC curve*) is a popular alternative to the double density plot. For each different classifier we'd get by picking a different score threshold between positive and negative determination, we plot both the true positive rate and the false positive rate. This curve represents every possible trade-off between sensitivity and specificity that is available for this classifier. The steps to produced the ROC plot in figure 5.9 are shown in the next listing. In the last line, we compute the *AUC* or *area under the curve*, which is 1.0 for perfect classifiers and 0.5 for classifiers that do no better than random guesses.

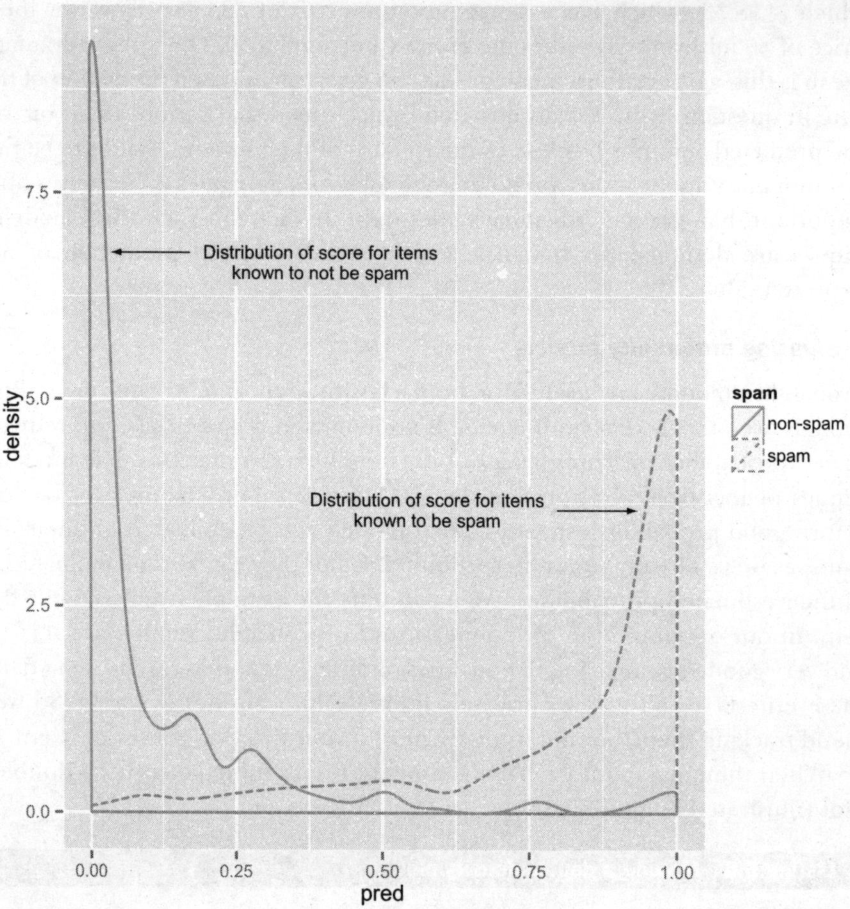

Figure 5.8 Distribution of score broken up by known classes

Listing 5.7 Plotting the receiver operating characteristic curve

```
library('ROCR')
eval <- prediction(spamTest$pred,spamTest$spam)
plot(performance(eval,"tpr","fpr"))
print(attributes(performance(eval,'auc'))$y.values[[1]])
[1] 0.9660072
```

We're not big fans of the AUC; many of its claimed interpretations are either incorrect (see http://mng.bz/Zugx) or not relevant to actual business questions.[1] But working around the ROC curve with your project client is a good way to explore possible project goal trade-offs.

---

1 See D. J. Hand, "Measuring classifier performance: a coherent alternative to the area under the ROC curve," *Machine Learning*, 2009, 77(1), pp. 103-123.

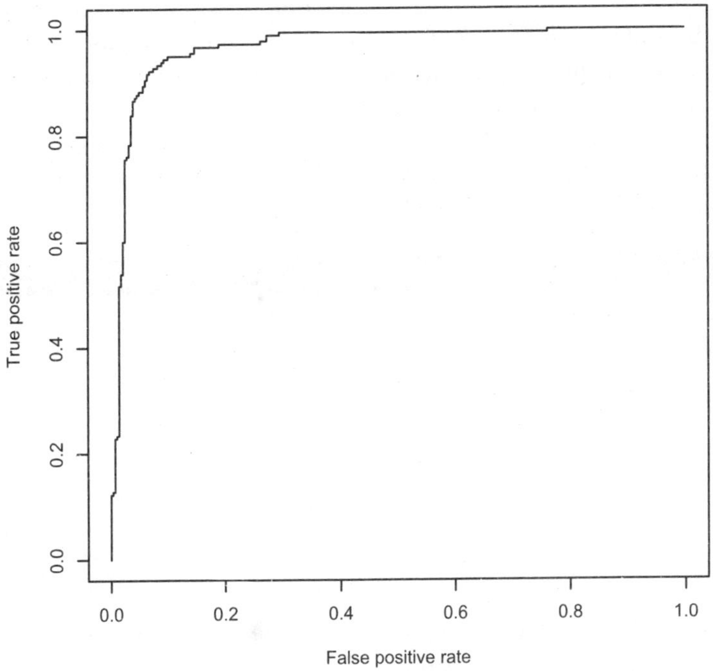

Figure 5.9 ROC curve for the email spam example

LOG LIKELIHOOD

An important evaluation of an estimated probability is the log likelihood. The log likelihood is the logarithm of the product of the probability the model assigned to each example.[2] For a spam email with an estimated likelihood of 0.9 of being spam, the log likelihood is `log(0.9)`; for a non-spam email, the same score of 0.9 is a log likelihood of `log(1-0.9)` (or just the log of 0.1, which was the estimated probability of not being spam). The principle is this: if the model is a good explanation, then the data should look likely (not implausible) under the model. The following listing shows how the log likelihood of our example is derived.

Listing 5.8 Calculating log likelihood

```
> sum(ifelse(spamTest$spam=='spam',
   log(spamTest$pred),
   log(1-spamTest$pred)))
[1] -134.9478
> sum(ifelse(spamTest$spam=='spam',
   log(spamTest$pred),
   log(1-spamTest$pred)))/dim(spamTest)[[1]]
[1] -0.2946458
```

[2] The traditional way of calculating the log likelihood is to compute the sum of the logarithms of the probabilities the model assigns to each example.

The first term (`-134.9478`) is the model log likelihood the model assigns to the test data. This number will always be negative, and is better as we get closer to 0. The second expression is the log likelihood rescaled by the number of data points to give us a rough average surprise per data point. Now a good null model in this case would be always returning the probability of `180/458` (the number of known spam emails over the total number of emails as the best single-number estimate of the chance of spam). This null model gives the log likelihood shown in the next listing.

Listing 5.9 Computing the null model's log likelihood

```
> pNull <- sum(ifelse(spamTest$spam=='spam',1,0))/dim(spamTest)[[1]]
> sum(ifelse(spamTest$spam=='spam',1,0))*log(pNull) +
   sum(ifelse(spamTest$spam=='spam',0,1))*log(1-pNull)
[1] -306.8952
```

The spam model assigns a log likelihood of `-134.9478`, which is much better than the null model's `-306.8952`.

DEVIANCE

Another common measure when fitting probability models is the *deviance*. The deviance is defined as `-2*(logLikelihood-S)`, where `S` is a technical constant called "the log likelihood of the saturated model." The lower the residual deviance, the better the model. In most cases, the saturated model is a perfect model that returns probability 1 for items in the class and probability 0 for items not in the class (so `S=0`). We're most concerned with differences of deviance, such as the difference between the null deviance and the model deviance (and in the case of our example, the Ss cancels out). In our case, this difference is `-2*(-306.8952-S) - -2*(-134.9478-S)=344.9`. With `S=0` the deviance can be used to calculate a pseudo R-squared (see http://mng.bz/j338). Think of the null deviance as how much variation there is to explain, and the model deviance as how much was left unexplained by the model. So in this case, our pseudo R-squared is `1 - (-2*(-134.9478-S))/(-2*(-306.8952-S))=0.56` (good, but not great).

AIC

An important variant of deviance is the *Akaike information criterion* (*AIC*). This is equivalent to `deviance + 2*numberOfParameters` used in the model used to make the prediction. Thus, AIC is deviance penalized for model complexity. A nice trick is to do as the Bayesians do: use *Bayesian information criterion* (*BIC*) (instead of AIC) where an empirical estimate of the model complexity (such as `2*2^entropy`, instead of `2*numberOfParameters`) is used as the penalty. The AIC is useful for comparing models with different measures of complexity and variables with differing number of levels.[3]

ENTROPY

Entropy is a fairly technical measure of information or surprise, and is measured in a unit called *bits*. If p is a vector containing the probability of each possible outcome,

[3] Rigorously balancing model quality and model complexity is a deep problem.

then the entropy of the outcomes is calculated as `sum(-p*log(p,2))` (with the convention that `0*log(0) = 0`). As entropy measures surprise, you want what's called the *conditional entropy* of your model to be appreciably lower than the original entropy. The conditional entropy is a measure that gives an indication of how good the prediction is on different categories, tempered by how often it predicts different categories. In terms of our confusion matrix `cM`, we can calculate the original entropy and conditional (or residual) entropy as shown next.

Listing 5.10 Calculating entropy and conditional entropy

```
> entropy <- function(x) {
    xpos <- x[x>0]
    scaled <- xpos/sum(xpos)
    sum(-scaled*log(scaled,2))
  }

> print(entropy(table(spamTest$spam)))
[1] 0.9667165

> conditionalEntropy <- function(t) {
     (sum(t[,1])*entropy(t[,1]) + sum(t[,2])*entropy(t[,2]))/sum(t)
  }

> print(conditionalEntropy(cM))
[1] 0.3971897
```

- Define function that computes the entropy from list of outcome counts
- Calculate entropy of spam/non-spam distribution
- Function to calculate conditional or remaining entropy of spam distribution (rows) given prediction (columns)
- Calculate conditional or remaining entropy of spam distribution given prediction

We see the initial entropy is `0.9667` bits per example (so a lot of surprise is present), and the conditional entropy is only `0.397` bits per example.

5.2.4 *Evaluating ranking models*

Ranking models are models that, given a set of examples, sort the rows or (equivalently) assign ranks to the rows. Ranking models are often trained by converting groups of examples into many pair-wise decisions (statements like "a is before b"). You can then apply the criteria for evaluating classifiers to quantify the quality of your ranking function. Two other standard measures of a ranking model are Spearman's rank correlation coefficient (treating assigned rank as a numeric score) and the data mining concept of *lift* (treating ranking as sorting; see http://mng.bz/1LBl). Ranking evaluation is well handled by business-driven ad hoc methods, so we won't spend any more time on this issue.

5.2.5 *Evaluating clustering models*

Clustering models are hard to evaluate because they're unsupervised: the clusters that items are assigned to are generated by the modeling procedure, not supplied in a series of annotated examples. Evaluation is largely checking observable summaries about the clustering. As a quick example, we'll demonstrate evaluating division of 100 random points in a plane into five clusters. We generate our example data and proposed k-means-based clustering in the next listing.

Listing 5.11 Clustering random data in the plane

```
set.seed(32297)
d <- data.frame(x=runif(100),y=runif(100))
clus <- kmeans(d,centers=5)
d$cluster <- clus$cluster
```

Because our example is two-dimensional, it's easy to visualize, so we can use the following commands to generate figure 5.10, which we can refer to when thinking about clustering quality.

Listing 5.12 Plotting our clusters

```
library('ggplot2'); library('grDevices')
h <- do.call(rbind,
   lapply(unique(clus$cluster),
      function(c) { f <- subset(d,cluster==c); f[chull(f),]}))
ggplot() +
 geom_text(data=d,aes(label=cluster,x=x,y=y,
   color=cluster),size=3)  +
 geom_polygon(data=h,aes(x=x,y=y,group=cluster,fill=as.factor(cluster)),
   alpha=0.4,linetype=0) +
 theme(legend.position = "none")
```

The first qualitative metrics are how many clusters you have (sometimes chosen by the user, sometimes chosen by the algorithm) and the number of items in each cluster. This is quickly calculated by the `table` command.

Listing 5.13 Calculating the size of each cluster

```
> table(d$cluster)

 1  2  3  4  5
10 27 18 17 28
```

We see we have five clusters, each with 10–28 points. Two things to look out for are *hair clusters* (clusters with very few points) and *waste clusters* (clusters with a very large number of points). Both of these are usually not useful—hair clusters are essentially individual examples, and items in waste clusters usually have little in common.

INTRA-CLUSTER DISTANCES VERSUS CROSS-CLUSTER DISTANCES

A desirable feature in clusters is for them to be compact in whatever distance scheme you used to define them. The traditional measure of this is comparing the typical distance between two items in the same cluster to the typical distance between two items from different clusters. We can produce a table of all these distance facts as shown in the following listing.

Listing 5.14 Calculating the typical distance between items in every pair of clusters

```
> library('reshape2')
> n <- dim(d)[[1]]
> pairs <- data.frame(
```

```
    ca = as.vector(outer(1:n,1:n,function(a,b) d[a,'cluster'])),
    cb = as.vector(outer(1:n,1:n,function(a,b) d[b,'cluster'])),
    dist = as.vector(outer(1:n,1:n,function(a,b)
            sqrt((d[a,'x']-d[b,'x'])^2 + (d[a,'y']-d[b,'y'])^2)))
  )
> dcast(pairs,ca~cb,value.var='dist',mean)
  ca         1         2         3         4         5
1  1 0.1478480 0.6524103 0.3780785 0.4404508 0.7544134
2  2 0.6524103 0.2794181 0.5551967 0.4990632 0.5165320
3  3 0.3780785 0.5551967 0.2031272 0.6122986 0.4656730
4  4 0.4404508 0.4990632 0.6122986 0.2048268 0.8365336
5  5 0.7544134 0.5165320 0.4656730 0.8365336 0.2221314
```

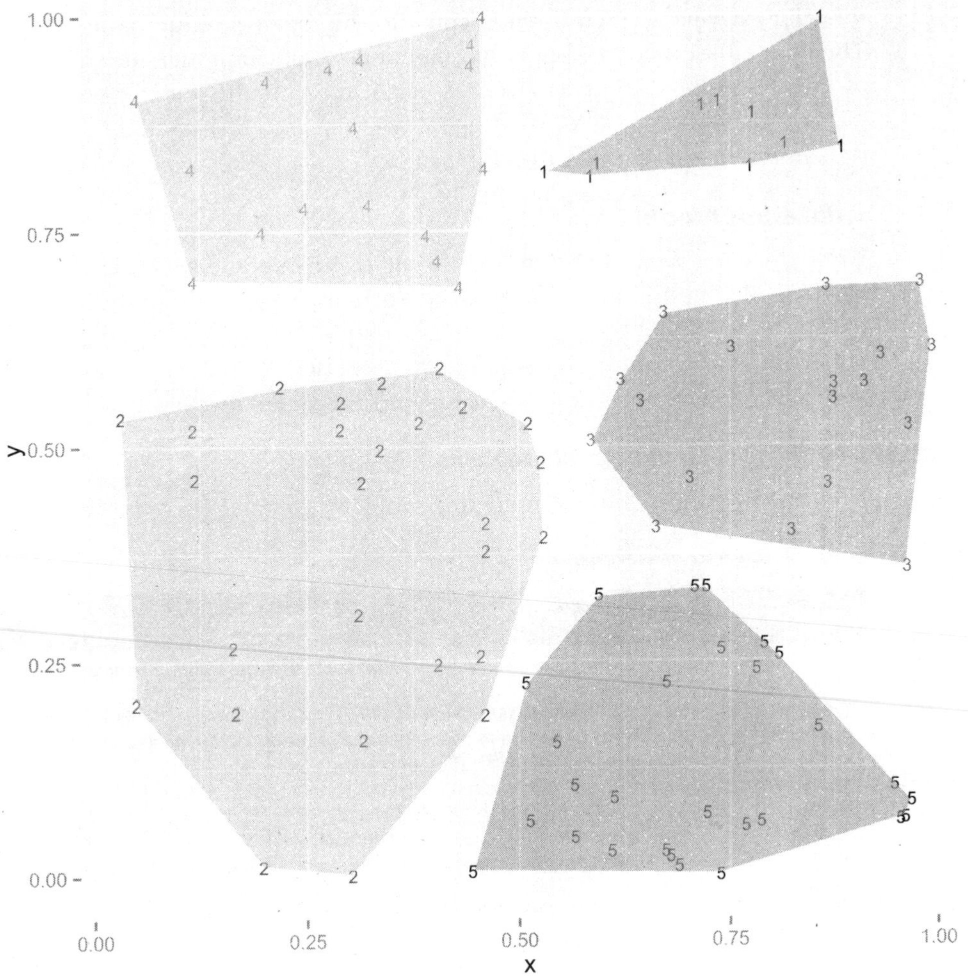

Figure 5.10 Clustering example

The resulting table gives the mean distance from points in one cluster to points in another. For example, the mean distance between points in cluster 3 is given in the `[3,3]` position of the table and is `0.2031272`. What we are looking for is intra-cluster distances (the diagonal elements of the table) to be smaller than inter-cluster distances (the off-diagonal elements of the table).

TREATING CLUSTERS AS CLASSIFICATIONS OR SCORES

Distance metrics are good for checking the performance of clustering algorithms, but they don't always translate to business needs. When sharing a clustering with your project sponsor or client, we advise treating the cluster assignment as if it were a classification. For each cluster label, generate an outcome assigned to the cluster (such as all email in the cluster is marked as spam/non-spam, or all accounts in the cluster are treated as having a revenue value equal to the mean revenue value in the cluster). Then use either the classifier or scoring model evaluation ideas to evaluate the value of the clustering. This scheme works best if the column you're considering *outcome* (such as spam/non-spam or revenue value of the account) was not used as one of the dimensions in constructing the clustering.

5.3 Validating models

We've discussed how to choose a modeling technique and evaluate the performance of the model on training data. At this point your biggest worry should be the validity of your model: will it show similar quality on new data in production? We call the testing of a model on new data (or a simulation of new data from our test set) *model validation.* The following sections discuss the main problems we try to identify.

5.3.1 Identifying common model problems

Table 5.7 lists some common modeling problems you may encounter.

Table 5.7 Common model problems

Problem	Description
Bias	Systematic error in the model, such as always underpredicting.
Variance	Undesirable (but non-systematic) distance between predictions and actual values. Often due to oversensitivity of the model training procedure to small variations in the distribution of training data.
Overfit	Features of the model that arise from relations that are in the training data, but not representative of the general population. Overfit can usually be reduced by acquiring more training data and by techniques like regularization and bagging.
Nonsignificance	A model that appears to show an important relation when in fact the relation may not hold in the general population, or equally good predictions can be made without the relation.

OVERFITTING

A lot of modeling problems are related to overfitting. Looking for signs of overfit is a good first step in diagnosing models.

An overfit model looks great on the training data and performs poorly on new data. A model's prediction error on the data that it trained from is called *training error*. A model's prediction error on new data is called *generalization error*. Usually, training error will be smaller than generalization error (no big surprise). Ideally, though, the two error rates should be close. If generalization error is large, then your model has probably *overfit*—it's memorized the training data instead of discovering generalizable rules or patterns. You want to avoid overfitting by preferring (as long as possible) simpler models, which do in fact tend to generalize better.[4] In this section, we're not just evaluating a single model, we're evaluating your data and work procedures. Figure 5.11 shows the typical appearance of a reasonable model and an overfit model.

An overly complicated and overfit model is bad for at least two reasons. First, an overfit model may be much more complicated than anything useful. For example, the extra wiggles in the overfit part of figure 5.11 could make optimizing with respect to *x* needlessly difficult. Also, as we mentioned, overfit models tend to be less accurate in production than during training, which is embarrassing.

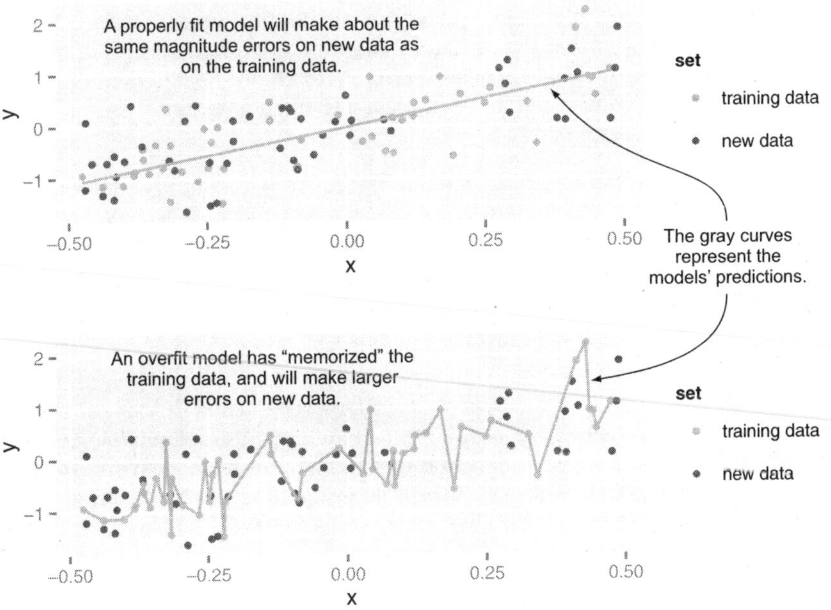

Figure 5.11 A notional illustration of overfitting

4 Other techniques to prevent overfitting include regularization (preferring small effects from model variables) and bagging (averaging different models to reduce variance).

5.3.2 Quantifying model soundness

It's important that you know, quantify, and share how sound your model is. Evaluating a model only on the data used to construct it is favorably biased: models tend to look good on the data they were built from. Also, a single evaluation of model performance gives only a *point estimate* of performance. You need a good characterization of how much potential variation there is in your model production and measurement procedure, and how well your model is likely to perform on future data. We see these questions as being fundamentally *frequentist* concerns because they're questions about how model behavior changes under variations in data. The formal statistical term closest to these business questions is *significance*, and we'll abuse notation and call what we're doing significance testing.[5] In this section, we'll discuss some testing procedures, but postpone demonstrating implementation until later in this book.

Frequentist and Bayesian inference

Following Efron,[6] there are at least two fundamental ways of thinking about inference: frequentist and Bayesian (there are more; for example, Fisherian and information theoretic). In frequentist inference, we assume there is a single unknown *fixed* quantity (be it a parameter, model, or prediction) that we're trying to estimate. The frequentist inference for a given dataset is a *point estimate* that varies as different possible datasets are proposed (yielding a distribution of estimates). In Bayesian inference, we assume that the unknown quantity to be estimated has many plausible values modeled by what's called a *prior distribution*. Bayesian inference is then using data (that is considered as unchanging) to build a tighter posterior distribution for the unknown quantity.

There's a stylish snobbery that Bayesian inference is newer and harder to do than frequentist inference, and therefore more sophisticated. It is true that Bayesian methods model the joint nature of parameters and data more explicitly than frequentist methods. And frequentist methods tend to be much more compact and efficient (which isn't always a plus, as frequentist testing procedures can degenerate into ritual when applied without thought).

In practice, choosing your inference framework isn't a matter of taste, but a direct consequence of what sort of business question you're trying to answer. If you're worried about the sensitivity of your result to variation in data and modeling procedures, you should work in the frequentist framework. If you're worried about the sensitivity of your result to possible variation in the unknown quantity to be modeled, you should work in the Bayesian framework (see http://mng.bz/eHGj).

---

5 A lot of what we're doing is in fact significance testing. We just re-derive it in small steps to make sure we keep our testing strategy linked in an explainable way to our original business goals.

6 See Bradley Efron, "Controversies In The Foundation Of Statistics," *American Mathematical Monthly*, 1978, 85 (4), pp. 231-246.

5.3.3 Ensuring model quality

The standards of scientific presentation are that you should always share how sensitive your conclusions are to variations in your data and procedures. You should never just show a model and its quality statistics. You should also show the likely distribution of the statistics under variations in your modeling procedure or your data. This is why you wouldn't say something like "We have an accuracy of 90% on our training data," but instead you'd run additional experiments so you could say something like "We see an accuracy of 85% on hold-out data." Or even better: "We saw accuracies of at least 80% on all but 5% of our reruns." These distributional statements tell you if you need more modeling features and/or more data.

TESTING ON HELD-OUT DATA

The data used to build a model is not the best data for testing the model's performance. This is because there's an upward measurement *bias* in this data. Because this data was seen during model construction, and model construction is optimizing your performance measure (or at least something related to your performance measure), you tend to get exaggerated measures of performance on your training data. Most standard fitting procedures have some built-in measure for this effect (for example, the "adjusted R-squared" report in linear regression, discussed in section 7.1.5) and the effect tends to diminish as your training data becomes large with respect to the complexity of your model.[7]

The precaution for this optimistic bias we demonstrate throughout this book is this: split your available data into test and training. Perform all of your clever work on the training data alone, and delay measuring your performance with respect to your test data until as late as possible in your project (as all choices you make after seeing your test or hold-out performance introduce a modeling bias). The desire to keep the test data secret for as long as possible is why we often actually split data into training, calibration, and test sets (as we'll demonstrate in section 6.1.1).

K-FOLD CROSS-VALIDATION

Testing on hold-out data, while useful, only gives a single-point estimate of model performance. In practice we want both an unbiased estimate of our model's future performance on new data (simulated by test data) *and* an estimate of the distribution of this estimate under typical variations in data and training procedures. A good method to perform these estimates is *k-fold cross-validation* and the related ideas of empirical resampling and bootstrapping.

The idea behind k-fold cross-validation is to repeat the construction of the model on different subsets of the available training data and then evaluate the model only on data not seen during construction. This is an attempt to simulate the performance of the model on unseen future data. The need to cross-validate is one of the reasons it's critical that model construction be automatable, such as with a script in a language

7 See, for example, "The Unreasonable Effectiveness of Data," Alon Halevy, Peter Norvig, and Fernando Pereira, *IEEE Intelligent Systems*, 2009.

like R, and not depend on manual steps. Assuming you have enough data to cross-validate (not having to worry too much about the statistical efficiency of techniques) is one of the differences between the attitudes of data science and traditional statistics. Section 6.2.3 works through an example of automating k-fold cross-validation.

SIGNIFICANCE TESTING

Statisticians have a powerful idea related to cross-validation called *significance testing*. Significance also goes under the name of *p-value* and you will actually be asked, "What is your p-value?" when presenting.

The idea behind significance testing is that we can believe our model's performance is good if it's very unlikely that a naive model (a *null hypothesis*) could score as well as our model. The standard incantation in that case is "We can reject the null hypothesis." This means our model's measured performance is unlikely for the null model. Null models are always of a simple form: assuming two effects are independent when we're trying to model a relation, or assuming a variable has no effect when we're trying to measure an effect strength.

For example, suppose you've trained a model to predict how much a house will sell for, based on certain variables. You want to know if your model's predictions are better than simply guessing the average selling price of a house in the neighborhood (call this the *null model*). Your new model will mispredict a given house's selling price by a certain average amount, which we'll call `err.model`. The null model will also mispredict a given house's selling price by a different amount, `err.null`. The null hypothesis is that `D = (err.null - err.model) == 0`—on average, the new model performs the same as the null model.

When you evaluate your model over a test set of houses, you will (hopefully) see that `D = (err.null - err.model) > 0` (your model is more accurate). You want to make sure that this positive outcome is genuine, and not just something you observed by chance. The p-value is the probability that you'd see a `D` as large as you observed if the two models actually perform the same.

Our advice is this: always think about p-values as estimates of how often you'd find a relation (between the model and the data) when there actually is none. This is why low p-values are good, as they're estimates of the probabilities of undetected disastrous situations (see http://mng.bz/A3G1). You might also think of the p-value as the probability of your whole modeling result being one big "false positive." So, clearly, you want the p-value (or the significance) to be small, say less than 0.05.

The traditional statistical method of computing significance or p-values is through a Student's t-test or an f-test (depending on what you're testing). For classifiers, there's a particularly good significance test that's run on the confusion matrix called the `fisher.test()`. These tests are built into most model fitters. They have a lot of math behind them that lets a statistician avoid fitting more than one model. These tests also rely on a few assumptions (to make the math work) that may or may not be true about your data and your modeling procedure.

One way to directly simulate a bad modeling situation is by using a *permutation test.* This is when you permute the input (or independent) variables among examples. In this case, there's no real relation between the modeling features (which we have permuted among examples) and the quantity to be predicted, because in our new dataset the modeling features and the result come from different (unrelated) examples. Thus each rerun of the permuted procedure builds something much like a null model. If our actual model isn't much better than the population of permuted models, then we should be suspicious of our actual model. Note that in this case, we're thinking about the uncertainty of our estimates as being a distribution drawn about the null model.

We could modify the code in section 6.2.3 to perform an approximate permutation test by permuting the y-values each time we resplit the training data. Or we could try a package that performs the work and/or brings in convenient formulas for the various probability and significance statements that come out of permutation experiments (for example, http://mng.bz/SvyB).

CONFIDENCE INTERVALS

An important and very technical frequentist statistical concept is the *confidence interval.* To illustrate, a 95% confidence interval is an interval from an estimation procedure such that the *procedure* is thought to have a 95% (or better) chance of catching the true unknown value to be estimated in an interval. It is *not* the case that there is a 95% chance that the unknown true value is actually in the interval at hand (thought it's often misstated as such). The Bayesian alternative to confidence intervals is *credible intervals* (which can be easier to understand, but do require the introduction of a prior distribution).

USING STATISTICAL TERMINOLOGY

The field of statistics has spent the most time formally studying the issues of model correctness and model soundness (probability theory, operations research, theoretical computer science, econometrics, and a few other fields have of course also contributed). Because of their priority, statisticians often insist that the checking of model performance and soundness be *solely* described in traditional statistical terms. But a data scientist must present to many non-statistical audiences, so the reasoning behind a given test is in fact best explicitly presented and discussed. It's not always practical to allow the dictates of a single field to completely style a cross-disciplinary conversation.

5.4 Summary

You now have some solid ideas on how to choose among modeling techniques. You also know how to evaluate the quality of data science work, be it your own or that of others. The remaining chapters of part 2 of the book will go into more detail on how to build, test, and deliver effective predictive models. In the next chapter, we'll actually start building predictive models, using the simplest types of models that essentially memorize and summarize portions of the training data.

Key takeaways

- Always first explore your data, but don't start modeling before designing some measurable goals.
- Divide you model testing into establishing the model's effect (performance on various metrics) and soundness (likelihood of being a correct model versus arising from overfitting).
- Keep a portion of your data out of your modeling work for final testing. You may also want to subdivide your training data into training and calibration and to estimate best values for various modeling parameters.
- Keep many different model metrics in mind, and for a given project try to pick the metrics that best model your intended business goal.

6 Memorization methods

This chapter covers

- Building single-variable models
- Cross-validated variable selection
- Building basic multivariable models
- Starting with decision trees, nearest neighbor, and naive Bayes models

The simplest methods in data science are what we call *memorization methods*. These are methods that generate answers by returning a majority category (in the case of classification) or average value (in the case of scoring) of a subset of the original training data. These methods can vary from models depending on a single variable (similar to the analyst's pivot table), to decision trees (similar to what are called *business rules*), to nearest neighbor and Naive Bayes methods.[1] In this chapter, you'll learn how to use these memorization methods to solve classification problems (though the same techniques also work for scoring problems).

1 Be aware: *memorization methods* are a nonstandard classification of techniques that we're using to organize our discussion.

6.1 KDD and KDD Cup 2009

We'll demonstrate all of the techniques in this chapter on the KDD Cup 2009 dataset as our example dataset. The Conference on Knowledge Discovery and Data Mining (KDD) is the premier conference on machine learning methods. Every year KDD hosts a data mining cup, where teams analyze a dataset and then are ranked against each other. The KDD Cup is a huge deal and the inspiration for the famous Netflix Prize and even Kaggle competitions.

The KDD Cup 2009 provided a dataset about customer relationship management. The contest supplied 230 facts about 50,000 credit card accounts. From these features, the goal was to predict account cancellation (called *churn*), the innate tendency to use new products and services (called *appetency*), and willingness to respond favorably to marketing pitches (called *upselling*).[2] As with many score-based competitions, this contest concentrated on machine learning and deliberately abstracted or skipped over a number of important data science issues, such as cooperatively defining goals, requesting new measurements, collecting data, and quantifying classifier performance in terms of business goals. In fact, for this contest we don't have names or definitions for any of the independent (or input) variables and no real definition of the dependent (or outcome) variables. We have the advantage that the data is already in a ready-to-model format (all input variables and the results arranged in single rows). But we don't know the meaning of any variable (so we can't merge in outside data sources), and we can't use any method that treats time and repetition of events carefully (such as time series methods or survival analysis).

To simulate the data science processes, we'll assume that we can use any column we're given to make predictions (that all of these columns are known prior to needing a prediction[3]), the contest metric (AUC) is the correct one, and the AUC of the top contestant is a good Bayes rate estimate (telling us when to stop tuning).

THE WORST POSSIBLE MODELING OUTCOME The worst possible modeling outcome is not failing to find a good model. The worst possible modeling outcome is thinking you have a good model when you don't. One of the easiest ways to accidentally build such a deficient model is to have an instrumental or independent variable that is in fact a subtle function of the outcome. Such variables can easily leak into your training data, especially when you have no knowledge or control of variable meaning preparation. The point is this: such variables won't actually be available in a real deployment and often are in training data packaged up by others.

---

[2] Data available from http://mng.bz/RDJF. We share the steps to prepare this data for modeling in R here: https://github.com/WinVector/zmPDSwR/tree/master/KDD2009.

[3] Checking if a column is actually going to be available during prediction (and not some later function of the unknown output) is a critical step in data science projects.

6.1.1 Getting started with KDD Cup 2009 data

For our example, we'll try to predict churn in the KDD dataset. The KDD contest was judged in terms of AUC (*area under the curve*, a measure of prediction quality discussed in section 5.2.3), so we'll also use AUC as our measure of performance.[4] The winning team achieved an AUC of 0.76 on churn, so we'll treat that as our upper bound on possible performance. Our lower bound on performance is an AUC of 0.5, as this is the performance of a useless model.

This problem has a large number of variables, many of which have a large number of possible levels. We're also using the AUC measure, which isn't particularly resistant to overfitting (not having built-in model complexity or chance corrections). Because of this concern, we'll split our data into three sets: training, calibration, and test. The intent of the three-way split is this: we'll use the training set for most of our work, and we'll never look at the test set (we'll reserve it for our final report of model performance). The calibration set is used to simulate the unseen test set during modeling—we'll look at performance on the calibration set to estimate if we're overfitting. This three-way split procedure is recommended by many researchers. In this book, we emphasize a two-way training and test split and suggest that, generally, steps like calibration and cross-validation estimates be performed by repeatedly splitting the training portion of the data (allowing for more efficient estimation than a single split, and keeping the test data completely out of the modeling effort). For simplicity in this example, we'll split the training portion of our data into training and calibration only a single time. Let's start work as shown in the following listing, where we prepare the data for analysis and modeling.

Listing 6.1 Preparing the KDD data for analysis

```
d <- read.table('orange_small_train.data.gz',
   header=T,
   sep='\t',
   na.strings=c('NA',''))
churn <- read.table('orange_small_train_churn.labels.txt',
   header=F,sep='\t')
d$churn <- churn$V1
appetency <- read.table('orange_small_train_appetency.labels.txt',
   header=F,sep='\t')
d$appetency <- appetency$V1
upselling <- read.table('orange_small_train_upselling.labels.txt',
   header=F,sep='\t')
```

- Read the file of independent variables. All data from https://github.com/WinVector/zmPDSwR/tree/master/KDD2009.
- Treat both NA and the empty string as missing data.
- Read churn dependent variable.
- Add churn as a new column.
- Add appetency as a new column.

[4] Also, as is common for example problems, we have no project sponsor to discuss metrics with, so our choice of evaluation is a bit arbitrary.

```
d$upselling <- upselling$V1
set.seed(729375)
d$rgroup <- runif(dim(d)[[1]])
dTrainAll <- subset(d,rgroup<=0.9)
dTest <- subset(d,rgroup>0.9)
outcomes=c('churn','appetency','upselling')
vars <- setdiff(colnames(dTrainAll),
   c(outcomes,'rgroup'))
catVars <- vars[sapply(dTrainAll[,vars],class) %in%
   c('factor','character')]
numericVars <- vars[sapply(dTrainAll[,vars],class) %in%
   c('numeric','integer')]
rm(list=c('d','churn','appetency','upselling'))
outcome <- 'churn'
pos <- '1'
useForCal <- rbinom(n=dim(dTrainAll)[[1]],size=1,prob=0.1)>0
dCal <- subset(dTrainAll,useForCal)
dTrain <- subset(dTrainAll,!useForCal)
```

Add upselling as a new column.

By setting the seed to the pseudo-random number generator, we make our work reproducible: someone redoing it will see the exact same results.

Split data into train and test subsets.

Identify which features are categorical variables.

Identify which features are numeric variables.

Remove unneeded objects from workspace.

Choose which outcome to model (churn).

Choose which outcome is considered positive.

Further split training data into training and calibration.

We have also saved an R workspace with most of the data, functions, and results of this chapter in the GitHub repository that you can load with the command `load('KDD2009.Rdata')`. We're now ready to build some single-variable models. Business analysts almost always build single-variable models using categorical features, so we'll start with these.

> **Subsample to prototype quickly**
>
> Often the data scientist will be so engrossed with the business problem, math, and data that they forget how much trial and error is needed. It's often an excellent idea to first work on a small subset of your training data, so that it takes seconds to debug your code instead of minutes. Don't work with expensive data sizes until you have to.

6.2 Building single-variable models

Single-variable models are simply models built using only one variable at a time. Single-variable models can be powerful tools, so it's worth learning how to work well with them before jumping into general modeling (which almost always means multiple variable models). We'll show how to build single-variable models from both categorical and numeric variables. By the end of this section, you should be able to build, evaluate, and cross-validate single-variable models with confidence.

6.2.1 Using categorical features

A single-variable model based on categorical features is easiest to describe as a table. For this task, business analysts use what's called a *pivot table* (which promotes values or levels of a feature to be families of new columns) and statisticians use what's called a *contingency table* (where each possibility is given a column name). In either case, the R command to produce a table is `table()`. To create a table comparing the levels of variable 218 against the labeled churn outcome, we run the table command shown in the following listing.

Listing 6.2 Plotting churn grouped by variable 218 levels

```
table218 <- table(
   Var218=dTrain[,'Var218'],
   churn=dTrain[,outcome],
   useNA='ifany')
print(table218)
      churn
Var218     -1      1
  cJvF 19101   1218
  UYBR 17599   1577
  <NA>   410    148
```

Tabulate levels of Var218.

Tabulate levels of churn outcome.

Include NA values in tabulation.

From this, we see variable 218 takes on two values plus NA, and we see the joint distribution of these values against the churn outcome. At this point it's easy to write down a single-variable model based on variable 218.

Listing 6.3 Churn rates grouped by variable 218 codes

```
> print(table218[,2]/(table218[,1]+table218[,2]))
      cJvF       UYBR       <NA>
0.05994389 0.08223821 0.26523297
```

This summary tells us that when variable 218 takes on a value of cJvF, around 6% of the customers churn; when it's UYBR, 8% of the customers churn; and when it's not recorded (NA), 27% of the customers churn. The utility of any variable level is a combination of how often the level occurs (rare levels aren't very useful) and how extreme the distribution of the outcome is for records matching a given level. Variable 218 seems like a feature that's easy to use and helpful with prediction. In real work, we'd want to research with our business partners why it has missing values and what's the best thing to do when values are missing (this will depend on how the data was prepared). We also need to design a strategy for what to do if a new level not seen during training were to occur during model use. Since this is a contest problem with no available project partners, we'll build a function that converts NA to a level (as it seems to be pretty informative) and also treats novel values as uninformative. Our function to convert a categorical variable into a single model prediction is shown in listing 6.4.

Listing 6.4 Function to build single-variable models for categorical variables

```
mkPredC <- function(outCol,varCol,appCol) {
   pPos <- sum(outCol==pos)/length(outCol)
   naTab <- table(as.factor(outCol[is.na(varCol)]))
   pPosWna <- (naTab/sum(naTab))[pos]
   vTab <- table(as.factor(outCol),varCol)
   pPosWv <- (vTab[pos,]+1.0e-3*pPos)/(colSums(vTab)+1.0e-3)
   pred <- pPosWv[appCol]
   pred[is.na(appCol)] <- pPosWna
   pred[is.na(pred)] <- pPos
   pred
}
```

- Given a vector of training outcomes (outCol), a categorical training variable (varCol), and a prediction variable (appCol), use outCol and varCol to build a single-variable model and then apply the model to appCol to get new predictions.
- Get stats on how often outcome is positive during training.
- Get stats on how often outcome is positive for NA values of variable during training.
- Get stats on how often outcome is positive, conditioned on levels of training variable.
- Make predictions by looking up levels of appCol.
- Add in predictions for NA levels of appCol.
- Add in predictions for levels of appCol that weren't known during training.
- Return vector of predictions.

Listing 6.4 may seem like a lot of work, but placing all of the steps in a function lets us apply the technique to many variables quickly. The dataset we're working with has 38 categorical variables, many of which are almost always NA, and many of which have over 10,000 distinct levels. So we definitely want to automate working with these variables as we have. Our first automated step is to adjoin a prediction or forecast (in this case, the predicted probability of churning) for each categorical variable, as shown in the next listing.

Listing 6.5 Applying single-categorical variable models to all of our datasets

```
for(v in catVars) {
  pi <- paste('pred',v,sep='')
  dTrain[,pi] <- mkPredC(dTrain[,outcome],dTrain[,v],dTrain[,v])
  dCal[,pi] <- mkPredC(dTrain[,outcome],dTrain[,v],dCal[,v])
  dTest[,pi] <- mkPredC(dTrain[,outcome],dTrain[,v],dTest[,v])
}
```

Note that in all cases we train with the training data frame and then apply to all three data frames dTrain, dCal, and dTest. We're using an extra calibration data frame (dCal) because we have so many categorical variables that have a very large number of levels and are subject to overfitting. We wish to have some chance of detecting this overfitting before moving on to the test data (which we're using as our final check, so it's data we mustn't use during model construction and evaluation, or we may have an exaggerated estimate of our model quality). Once we have the predictions, we can find the categorical variables that have a good AUC both on the training data and on the calibration data not used during training. These are likely the more useful variables and are identified by the loop in the next listing.

Listing 6.6 Scoring categorical variables by AUC

```
library('ROCR')

> calcAUC <- function(predcol,outcol) {
    perf <- performance(prediction(predcol,outcol==pos),'auc')
    as.numeric(perf@y.values)
  }

> for(v in catVars) {
   pi <- paste('pred',v,sep='')
   aucTrain <- calcAUC(dTrain[,pi],dTrain[,outcome])
   if(aucTrain>=0.8) {
      aucCal <- calcAUC(dCal[,pi],dCal[,outcome])
      print(sprintf("%s, trainAUC: %4.3f calibrationAUC: %4.3f",
        pi,aucTrain,aucCal))
   }
  }
[1] "predVar200, trainAUC: 0.828 calibrationAUC: 0.527"
[1] "predVar202, trainAUC: 0.829 calibrationAUC: 0.522"
[1] "predVar214, trainAUC: 0.828 calibrationAUC: 0.527"
[1] "predVar217, trainAUC: 0.898 calibrationAUC: 0.553"
```

Note how, as expected, each variable's training AUC is inflated compared to its calibration AUC. This is because many of these variables have thousands of levels. For example, `length(unique(dTrain$Var217))` is 12,434, indicating that variable 217 has 12,434 levels. A good trick to work around this is to sort the variables by their AUC score on the calibration set (not seen during training), which is a better estimate of the variable's true utility. In our case, the most promising variable is variable 206, which has both training and calibration AUCs of 0.59. The winning KDD entry, which was a model that combined evidence from multiple features, had a much larger AUC of 0.76.

6.2.2 Using numeric features

There are a number of ways to use a numeric feature to make predictions. A common method is to bin the numeric feature into a number of ranges and then use the range labels as a new categorical variable. R can do this quickly with its `quantile()` and `cut()` commands, as shown next.

Listing 6.7 Scoring numeric variables by AUC

```
> mkPredN <- function(outCol,varCol,appCol) {
   cuts <- unique(as.numeric(quantile(varCol,
      probs=seq(0, 1, 0.1),na.rm=T)))
   varC <- cut(varCol,cuts)
```

```
    appC <- cut(appCol,cuts)
    mkPredC(outCol,varC,appC)
}
> for(v in numericVars) {
    pi <- paste('pred',v,sep='')
    dTrain[,pi] <- mkPredN(dTrain[,outcome],dTrain[,v],dTrain[,v])
    dTest[,pi] <- mkPredN(dTrain[,outcome],dTrain[,v],dTest[,v])
    dCal[,pi] <- mkPredN(dTrain[,outcome],dTrain[,v],dCal[,v])
    aucTrain <- calcAUC(dTrain[,pi],dTrain[,outcome])
    if(aucTrain>=0.55) {
       aucCal <- calcAUC(dCal[,pi],dCal[,outcome])
       print(sprintf("%s, trainAUC: %4.3f calibrationAUC: %4.3f",
         pi,aucTrain,aucCal))
    }
  }
[1] "predVar6, trainAUC: 0.557 calibrationAUC: 0.554"
[1] "predVar7, trainAUC: 0.555 calibrationAUC: 0.565"
[1] "predVar13, trainAUC: 0.568 calibrationAUC: 0.553"
[1] "predVar73, trainAUC: 0.608 calibrationAUC: 0.616"
[1] "predVar74, trainAUC: 0.574 calibrationAUC: 0.566"
[1] "predVar81, trainAUC: 0.558 calibrationAUC: 0.542"
[1] "predVar113, trainAUC: 0.557 calibrationAUC: 0.567"
[1] "predVar126, trainAUC: 0.635 calibrationAUC: 0.629"
[1] "predVar140, trainAUC: 0.561 calibrationAUC: 0.560"
[1] "predVar189, trainAUC: 0.574 calibrationAUC: 0.599"
```

Notice in this case the numeric variables behave similarly on the training and calibration data. This is because our prediction method converts numeric variables into categorical variables with around 10 well-distributed levels, so our training estimate tends to be good and not overfit. We could improve our numeric estimate by interpolating between quantiles. Other methods we could've used are kernel-based density estimation and parametric fitting. Both of these methods are usually available in the variable treatment steps of Naive Bayes classifiers.

A good way to visualize the predictive power of a numeric variable is the double density plot, where we plot on the same graph the variable score distribution for positive examples and variable score distribution of negative examples as two groups. Figure 6.1 shows the performance of the single-variable model built from the numeric feature `Var126`.

The code to produce figure 6.1 is shown in the next listing.

Listing 6.8 Plotting variable performance

```
ggplot(data=dCal) +
   geom_density(aes(x=predVar126,color=as.factor(churn)))
```

What figure 6.1 is showing is the conditional distribution of `predVar126` for churning accounts (the dashed-line density plot) and the distribution of `predVar126` for non-churning accounts (the solid-line density plot). We can deduce that low values of `predVar126` are rare for churning accounts and not as rare for non-churning accounts (the graph is read by comparing areas under the curves). This (by Bayes

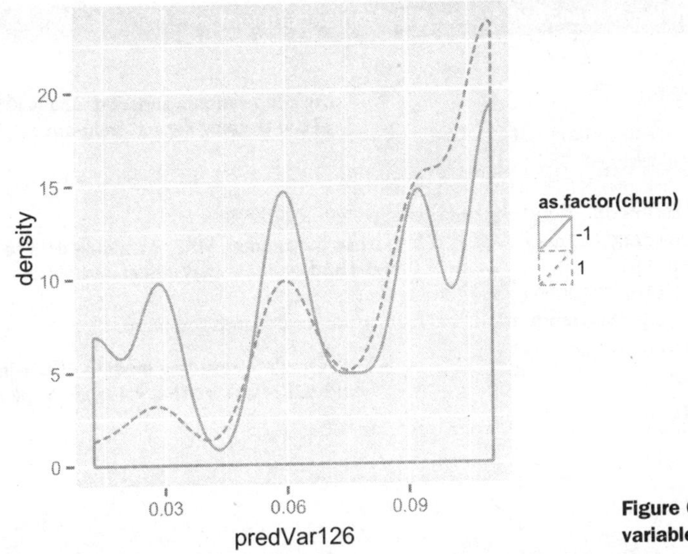

Figure 6.1 Performance of variable 126 on calibration data

law) lets us in turn say that a low value of `predVar126` is good evidence that an account will not churn.

> **Dealing with missing values in numeric variables**
> One of the best strategies we've seen for dealing with missing values in numeric variables is the following two-step process. First, for each numeric variable, introduce a new advisory variable that is 1 when the original variable had a missing value and 0 otherwise. Second, replace all missing values of the original variable with 0. You now have removed all of the missing values and have recorded enough details so that missing values aren't confused with actual zero values.

6.2.3 Using cross-validation to estimate effects of overfitting

We now have enough experience fitting the KDD dataset to try to estimate the degree of overfitting we're seeing in our models. We can use a procedure called *cross-validation* to estimate the degree of overfit we have hidden in our models. Cross-validation applies in *all* modeling situations. This is the first opportunity we have to demonstrate it, so we'll work through an example here.

In repeated cross-validation, a subset of the training data is used to build a model, and a complementary subset of the training data is used to score the model. We can implement a cross-validated estimate of the AUC of the single-variable model based on variable 217 with the code in the following listing.

Listing 6.9 Running a repeated cross-validation experiment

```
> var <- 'Var217'
> aucs <- rep(0,100)
> for(rep in 1:length(aucs)) {
   useForCalRep <- rbinom(n=dim(dTrainAll)[[1]],size=1,prob=0.1)>0
   predRep <- mkPredC(dTrainAll[!useForCalRep,outcome],
      dTrainAll[!useForCalRep,var],
      dTrainAll[useForCalRep,var])
   aucs[rep] <- calcAUC(predRep,dTrainAll[useForCalRep,outcome])
 }
> mean(aucs)
[1] 0.5556656
> sd(aucs)
[1] 0.01569345
```

For 100 iterations...

...select a random subset of about 10% of the training data as hold-out set,...

...use the random 90% of training data to train model and evaluate that model on hold-out set,...

...calculate resulting model's AUC using hold-out set; store that value and repeat.

This shows that the 100-fold replicated estimate of the AUC has a mean of 0.556 and a standard deviation of 0.016. So our original section 6.2 estimate of 0.553 as the AUC of this variable was very good. In some modeling circumstances, training set estimations are good enough (linear regression is often such an example). In many other circumstances, estimations from a single calibration set are good enough. And in extreme cases (such as fitting models with very many variables or level values), you're well advised to use replicated cross-validation estimates of variable utilities and model fits. Automatic cross-validation is *extremely* useful in all modeling situations, so it's critical you automate your modeling steps so you can perform cross-validation studies. We're demonstrating cross-validation here, as single-variable models are among the simplest to work with.

ASIDE: CROSS-VALIDATION IN FUNCTIONAL NOTATION
As a point of style, `for(){}` loops are considered an undesirable crutch in R. We used a for loop in our cross-validation example, as this is the style of programming that is likely to be most familiar to nonspecialists. The point is that for loops over-specify computation (they describe both what you want and the exact order of steps to achieve it). For loops tend to be less reusable and less composable than other computational methods. When you become proficient in R, you look to eliminate for loops from your code and use either vectorized or functional methods where appropriate. For example, the cross-validation we just demonstrated could be performed in a functional manner as shown in the following listing.

Listing 6.10 Empirically cross-validating performance

```
> fCross <- function() {
   useForCalRep <- rbinom(n=dim(dTrainAll)[[1]],size=1,prob=0.1)>0
   predRep <- mkPredC(dTrainAll[!useForCalRep,outcome],
      dTrainAll[!useForCalRep,var],
```

```
        dTrainAll[useForCalRep,var])
    calcAUC(predRep,dTrainAll[useForCalRep,outcome])
}
> aucs <- replicate(100,fCross())
```

What we've done is wrap our cross-reference work into a function instead of in a for-based code block. Advantages are that the function can be reused and run in parallel, and it's shorter (as it avoids needless details about result storage and result indices). The function is then called 100 times using the `replicate()` method (`replicate()` is a convenience method from the powerful `sapply()` family).

Note that we must write `replicate(100,fCross())`, *not* the more natural `replicate(100,fCross)`. This is because R is expecting an expression (a sequence that implies execution) as the second argument, and not the mere name of a function. The notation can be confusing and the reason it works is because function arguments in R are *not* evaluated prior to being passed in to a function, but instead are evaluated inside the function.[5] This is called *promise-based* argument evaluation and is powerful (it allows user-defined macros, lazy evaluation, placement of variable names on plots, user-defined control structures, and user-defined exceptions). This can also be complicated, so it's best to think of R as having mostly *call-by-value semantics* (see http://mng.bz/unf5), where arguments are passed to functions as values evaluated prior to entering the function and alterations of these values aren't seen outside of the function.

6.3 Building models using many variables

Models that combine the effects of many variables tend to be much more powerful than models that use only a single variable. In this section, you'll learn how to build some of the most fundamental multiple-variable models: decision trees, nearest neighbor, and Naive Bayes.

6.3.1 Variable selection

A key part of building many variable models is selecting what variables[6] to use and how the variables are to be transformed or treated. We've already discussed variable treatment in chapter 4, so we'll only discuss variable selection here (we're assuming you've discussed with your project sponsors what variables are available for or even legal to use in your model).

When variables are available has a huge impact on model utility. For instance, a variable that's coincident with (available near or even after) the time that the outcome occurs may make a very accurate model with little utility (as it can't be used for long-range prediction). The analyst has to watch out for variables that are functions of or "contaminated by" the value to be predicted. Which variables will actually be available

5 For just a taste of the complexity this introduces, try to read Thomas Lumley's "Standard nonstandard evaluation rules": http://developer.r-project.org/nonstandard-eval.pdf.

6 We'll call variables used to build the model variously *variables, independent variables, input variables, causal variables,* and so on to try and distinguish them from the item to be predicted (which we'll call *outcome* or *dependent*).

in production is something you'll want to discuss with your project sponsor. And sometimes you may want to improve model utility (at a possible cost of accuracy) by removing variables from the project design. An acceptable prediction one day before an event can be much more useful than a more accurate prediction one hour before the event.

Each variable we use represents a chance of explaining more of the outcome variation (a chance of building a better model) but also represents a possible source of noise and overfitting. To control this effect, we often preselect which subset of variables we'll use to fit. Variable selection can be an important defensive modeling step even for types of models that "don't need it" (as seen with decision trees in section 6.3.2). Listing 6.11 shows a hand-rolled variable selection loop where each variable is scored according to an AIC (Akaike information criterion) -inspired score, in which a variable is scored with a bonus proportional to the scaled log likelihood of the training data minus a penalty proportional to the complexity of the variable (which in this case is `2^entropy`). The score is a bit ad hoc, but tends to work well in selecting variables. Notice we're using performance on the calibration set (not the training set) to pick variables. Note that we don't use the test set for calibration; to do so lessens the reliability of the test set for model quality confirmation.

Listing 6.11 Basic variable selection

```
logLikelyhood <-
     function(outCol,predCol) {
  sum(ifelse(outCol==pos,log(predCol),log(1-predCol)))
}
selVars <- c()
minStep <- 5
baseRateCheck <- logLikelyhood(dCal[,outcome],
   sum(dCal[,outcome]==pos)/length(dCal[,outcome]))
for(v in catVars) {
  pi <- paste('pred',v,sep='')
  liCheck <- 2*((logLikelyhood(dCal[,outcome],dCal[,pi]) -
      baseRateCheck))
  if(liCheck>minStep) {
     print(sprintf("%s, calibrationScore: %g",
        pi,liCheck))
     selVars <- c(selVars,pi)
  }
}
for(v in numericVars) {
  pi <- paste('pred',v,sep='')
  liCheck <- 2*((logLikelyhood(dCal[,outcome],dCal[,pi]) -
      baseRateCheck) - 1)
  if(liCheck>=minStep) {
     print(sprintf("%s, calibrationScore: %g",
        pi,liCheck))
     selVars <- c(selVars,pi)
  }
}
```

Define a convenience function to compute log likelihood.

Run through categorical variables and pick based on a deviance improvement (related to difference in log likelihoods; see chapter 3).

Run through categorical variables and pick based on a deviance improvement.

In our case, this picks 27 of the 212 possible variables. The categorical and numeric variables selected are shown in the following listing.

Listing 6.12 Selected categorical and numeric variables

```
## [1] "predVar194, calibrationScore: 5.25759"
## [1] "predVar201, calibrationScore: 5.25521"
## [1] "predVar204, calibrationScore: 5.37414"
## [1] "predVar205, calibrationScore: 24.2323"
## [1] "predVar206, calibrationScore: 34.4434"
## [1] "predVar210, calibrationScore: 10.6681"
## [1] "predVar212, calibrationScore: 6.23409"
## [1] "predVar218, calibrationScore: 13.2455"
## [1] "predVar221, calibrationScore: 12.4098"
## [1] "predVar225, calibrationScore: 22.9074"
## [1] "predVar226, calibrationScore: 6.68931"
## [1] "predVar228, calibrationScore: 15.9644"
## [1] "predVar229, calibrationScore: 24.4946"

## [1] "predVar6, calibrationScore: 11.2431"
## [1] "predVar7, calibrationScore: 16.685"
## [1] "predVar13, calibrationScore: 8.06318"
## [1] "predVar28, calibrationScore: 9.38643"
## [1] "predVar65, calibrationScore: 7.96938"
## [1] "predVar72, calibrationScore: 10.5353"
## [1] "predVar73, calibrationScore: 46.2524"
## [1] "predVar74, calibrationScore: 17.6324"
## [1] "predVar81, calibrationScore: 6.8741"
## [1] "predVar113, calibrationScore: 21.136"
## [1] "predVar126, calibrationScore: 72.9556"
## [1] "predVar140, calibrationScore: 14.1816"
## [1] "predVar144, calibrationScore: 13.9858"
## [1] "predVar189, calibrationScore: 40.3059"
```

We'll show in section 6.3.2 the performance of a multiple-variable model with and without using variable selection.

6.3.2 *Using decision trees*

Decision trees are a simple model type: they make a prediction that is piecewise constant. This is interesting because the null hypothesis that we're trying to outperform is often a single constant for the whole dataset, so we can view a decision tree as a procedure to split the training data into pieces and use a simple memorized constant on each piece. Decision trees (especially a type called *classification and regression trees*, or *CART*) can be used to quickly predict either categorical or numeric outcomes. The best way to grasp the concept of decision trees is to think of them as machine-generated business rules.

FITTING A DECISION TREE MODEL

Building a decision tree involves proposing many possible *data cuts* and then choosing best cuts based on simultaneous competing criteria of predictive power, cross-validation strength, and interaction with other chosen cuts. One of the advantages of using a canned package for decision tree work is not having to worry about tree construction details. Let's start by building a decision tree model for churn. The simplest way to call `rpart()` is to just give it a list of variables and see what happens (`rpart()`, unlike many R modeling techniques, has built-in code for dealing with missing values).

Listing 6.13 Building a bad decision tree

```
> library('rpart')
> fV <- paste(outcome,'>0 ~ ',
   paste(c(catVars,numericVars),collapse=' + '),sep='')
> tmodel <- rpart(fV,data=dTrain)
> print(calcAUC(predict(tmodel,newdata=dTrain),dTrain[,outcome]))
[1] 0.9241265
> print(calcAUC(predict(tmodel,newdata=dTest),dTest[,outcome]))
[1] 0.5266172
> print(calcAUC(predict(tmodel,newdata=dCal),dCal[,outcome]))
[1] 0.5126917
```

What we get is pretty much a disaster. The model looks way too good to believe on the training data (which it has merely memorized, negating its usefulness) and not as good as our best single-variable models on withheld calibration and test data. A couple of possible sources of the failure are that we have categorical variables with very many levels, and we have a lot more NAs/missing data than `rpart()`'s surrogate value strategy was designed for. What we can do to work around this is fit on our reprocessed variables, which hide the categorical levels (replacing them with numeric predictions), and remove NAs (treating them as just another level).

Listing 6.14 Building another bad decision tree

```
> tVars <- paste('pred',c(catVars,numericVars),sep='')
> fV2 <- paste(outcome,'>0 ~ ',paste(tVars,collapse=' + '),sep='')
> tmodel <- rpart(fV2,data=dTrain)
> print(calcAUC(predict(tmodel,newdata=dTrain),dTrain[,outcome]))
[1] 0.928669
> print(calcAUC(predict(tmodel,newdata=dTest),dTest[,outcome]))
[1] 0.5390648
> print(calcAUC(predict(tmodel,newdata=dCal),dCal[,outcome]))
[1] 0.5384152
```

This result is about the same (also bad). So our next suspicion is that the overfitting is because our model is too complicated. To control `rpart()` model complexity, we need to monkey a bit with the controls. We pass in an extra argument, `rpart.control` (use `help('rpart')` for some details on this control), that changes the decision tree selection strategy.

Listing 6.15 Building yet another bad decision tree

```
> tmodel <- rpart(fV2,data=dTrain,
   control=rpart.control(cp=0.001,minsplit=1000,
      minbucket=1000,maxdepth=5)
 )
```

```
> print(calcAUC(predict(tmodel,newdata=dTrain),dTrain[,outcome]))
[1] 0.9421195
> print(calcAUC(predict(tmodel,newdata=dTest),dTest[,outcome]))
[1] 0.5794633
> print(calcAUC(predict(tmodel,newdata=dCal),dCal[,outcome]))
[1] 0.547967
```

This is a very small improvement. We can waste a lot of time trying variations of the `rpart()` controls. The best guess is that this dataset is unsuitable for decision trees and a method that deals better with overfitting issues is needed—such as random forests, which we'll demonstrate in chapter 9. The best result we could get for this dataset using decision trees was from using our selected variables (instead of all transformed variables).

Listing 6.16 Building a better decision tree

```
f <- paste(outcome,'>0 ~ ',paste(selVars,collapse=' + '),sep='')
> tmodel <- rpart(f,data=dTrain,
   control=rpart.control(cp=0.001,minsplit=1000,
      minbucket=1000,maxdepth=5)
 )
> print(calcAUC(predict(tmodel,newdata=dTrain),dTrain[,outcome]))
[1] 0.6906852
> print(calcAUC(predict(tmodel,newdata=dTest),dTest[,outcome]))
[1] 0.6843595
> print(calcAUC(predict(tmodel,newdata=dCal),dCal[,outcome]))
[1] 0.6669301
```

These AUCs aren't great (they're not near 1.0 or even particularly near the winning team's 0.76), but they are significantly better than any of the AUCs we saw from single-variable models when checked on non-training data. So we've finally built a legitimate multiple-variable model.

To tune `rpart` we suggest, in addition to trying variable selection (which is an odd thing to combine with decision tree methods), following the `rpart` documentation in trying different settings of the `method` argument. But we quickly get better results with KNN and logistic regression, so it doesn't make sense to spend too long trying to tune decision trees for this particular dataset.

HOW DECISION TREE MODELS WORK

At this point, we can look at the model and use it to explain how decision tree models work.

Listing 6.17 Printing the decision tree

```
> print(tmodel)
n= 40518

node), split, n, deviance, yval
      * denotes terminal node

 1) root 40518 2769.3550 0.07379436
   2) predVar126< 0.07366888 18188  726.4097 0.04167583
```

```
    4) predVar126< 0.04391312 8804   189.7251 0.02203544 *
    5) predVar126>=0.04391312 9384   530.1023 0.06010230
      10) predVar189< 0.08449448 8317   410.4571 0.05206204 *
      11) predVar189>=0.08449448 1067   114.9166 0.12277410 *
  3) predVar126>=0.07366888 22330 2008.9000 0.09995522
    6) predVar212< 0.07944508 8386   484.2499 0.06153112
      12) predVar73< 0.06813291 4084   167.5012 0.04285015 *
      13) predVar73>=0.06813291 4302   313.9705 0.07926546 *
    7) predVar212>=0.07944508 13944 1504.8230 0.12306370
      14) predVar218< 0.07134103 6728   580.7390 0.09542212
        28) predVar126< 0.1015407 3901   271.8426 0.07536529 *
        29) predVar126>=0.1015407 2827   305.1617 0.12309870
          58) predVar73< 0.07804522 1452   110.0826 0.08264463 *
          59) predVar73>=0.07804522 1375   190.1935 0.16581820 *
      15) predVar218>=0.07134103 7216   914.1502 0.14883590
        30) predVar74< 0.0797246 2579   239.3579 0.10352850 *
        31) predVar74>=0.0797246 4637   666.5538 0.17403490
          62) predVar189< 0.06775545 1031   102.9486 0.11251210 *
          63) predVar189>=0.06775545 3606   558.5871 0.19162510 *
```

Each row in listing 6.17 that starts with `#)` is called a *node* of the decision tree. This decision tree has 15 nodes. Node 1 is always called the *root*. Each node other than the root node has a parent, and the parent of node *k* is node `floor(k/2)`. The indentation also indicates how deep in the tree a node is. Each node other than the root is named by what condition must be true to move from the parent to the node. You move from node 1 to node 2 if `predVar126 < -0.002810871` (and otherwise you move to node 3, which has the complementary condition). So to score a row of data, we navigate from the root of the decision tree by the node conditions until we reach a node with no children, which is called a *leaf node*. Leaf nodes are marked with stars. The remaining three numbers reported for each node are the number of training items that navigated to the node, the deviance of the set of training items that navigated to the node (a measure of how much uncertainty remains at a given decision tree node), and the fraction of items that were in the positive class at the node (which is the prediction for leaf nodes).

We can get a graphical representation of much of this with the commands in the next listing that produce figure 6.2.

Listing 6.18 Plotting the decision tree

```
par(cex=0.7)
plot(tmodel)
text(tmodel)
```

6.3.3 Using nearest neighbor methods

A *k-nearest neighbor* (*KNN*) method scores an example by finding the *k* training examples nearest to the example and then taking the average of their outcomes as the score. The notion of nearness is basic Euclidean distance, so it can be useful to select nonduplicate variables, rescale variables, and orthogonalize variables.

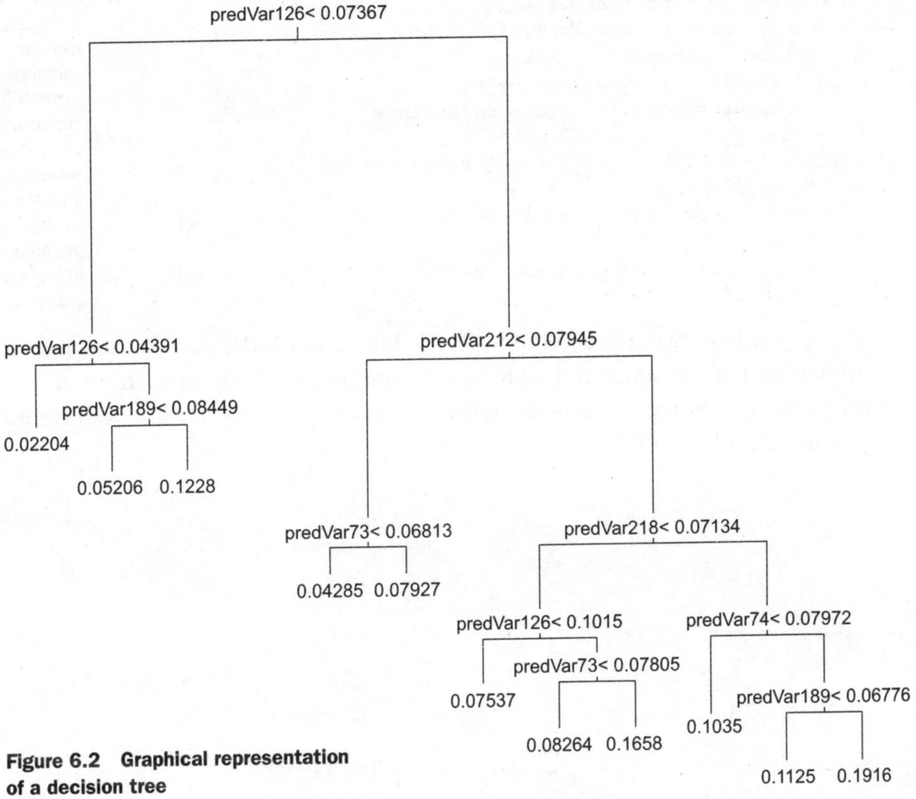

Figure 6.2 Graphical representation of a decision tree

One problem with KNN is the nature of its concept space. For example, if we were to run a 3-nearest neighbor analysis on our data, we have to understand that with three neighbors from the training data, we'll always see either zero, one, two, or three examples of churn. So the estimated probability of churn is always going to be one of 0%, 33%, 66%, or 100%. This is not going to work on an event as rare as churn, which has a rate of around 7% in our training data. For events with unbalanced outcomes (that is, probabilities not near 50%), we suggest using a large *k* so KNN can express a useful range of probabilities. For a good *k*, we suggest trying something such that you have a good chance of seeing 10 positive examples in each neighborhood (allowing your model to express rates smaller than your baseline rate to some precision). In our case, that's a *k* around `10/0.07 = 142`. You'll want to try a range of *k*, and we demonstrate a KNN run with `k=200` in the following listing.

Listing 6.19 Running k-nearest neighbors

```
> library('class')
> nK <- 200
> knnTrain <- dTrain[,selVars]
> knnCl <- dTrain[,outcome]==pos
```

Build a data frame with only the variables we wish to use for classification.

Build a vector with the known training outcomes.

Bind the knn() training function with our data in a new function.

```
> knnPred <- function(df) {
    knnDecision <- knn(knnTrain,df,knnCl,k=nK,prob=T)
    ifelse(knnDecision==TRUE,
       attributes(knnDecision)$prob,
       1-(attributes(knnDecision)$prob))
}
> print(calcAUC(knnPred(dTrain[,selVars]),dTrain[,outcome]))
[1] 0.7443927
> print(calcAUC(knnPred(dCal[,selVars]),dCal[,outcome]))
[1] 0.7119394
> print(calcAUC(knnPred(dTest[,selVars]),dTest[,outcome]))
[1] 0.718256
```

Convert knn's unfortunate convention of calculating probability as "proportion of the votes for the winning class" into the more useful "calculated probability of being a positive example."

This is our best result yet. What we're looking for are the two distributions to be unimodal[7] and, if not separated, at least not completely on top of each other. Notice how, under these criteria, the double density performance plot in figure 6.3 is much better looking than figure 6.1.

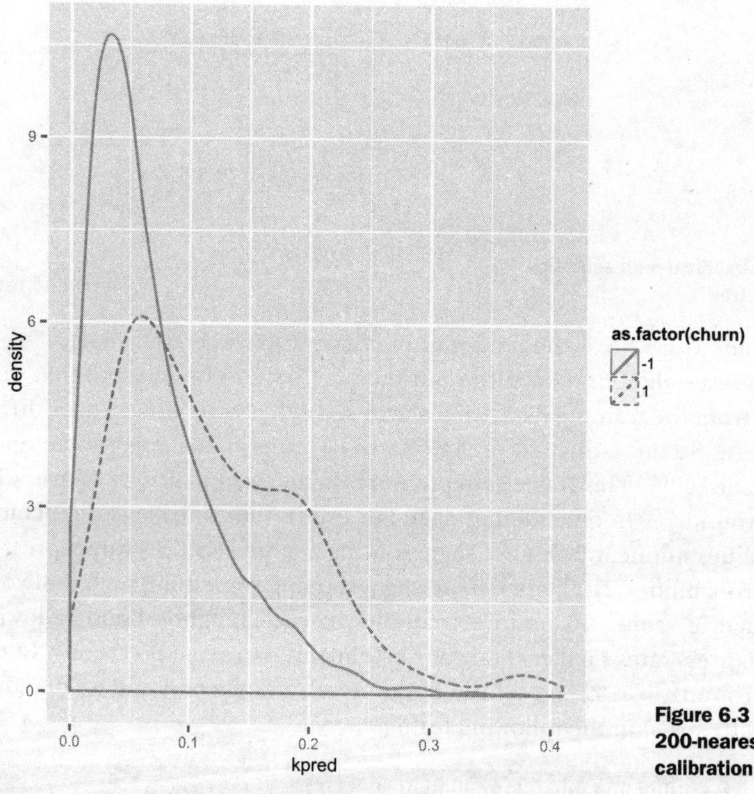

Figure 6.3 Performance of 200-nearest neighbors on calibration data

[7] Distributions that are multimodal are often evidence that there are significant effects we haven't yet explained. Distributions that are unimodal or even look normal are consistent with the unexplained effects being simple noise.

The code to produce figure 6.3 is shown in the next listing.

Listing 6.20 Platting 200-nearest neighbor performance

```
dCal$kpred <- knnPred(dCal[,selVars])
ggplot(data=dCal) +
   geom_density(aes(x=kpred,
      color=as.factor(churn),linetype=as.factor(churn)))
```

This finally gives us a result good enough to bother plotting the ROC curve for. The code in the next listing produces figure 6.4.

Listing 6.21 Plotting the receiver operating characteristic curve

```
plotROC <- function(predcol,outcol) {
   perf <- performance(prediction(predcol,outcol==pos),'tpr','fpr')
   pf <- data.frame(
      FalsePositiveRate=perf@x.values[[1]],
      TruePositiveRate=perf@y.values[[1]])
   ggplot() +
      geom_line(data=pf,aes(x=FalsePositiveRate,y=TruePositiveRate)) +
      geom_line(aes(x=c(0,1),y=c(0,1)))
}
print(plotROC(knnPred(dTest[,selVars]),dTest[,outcome]))
```

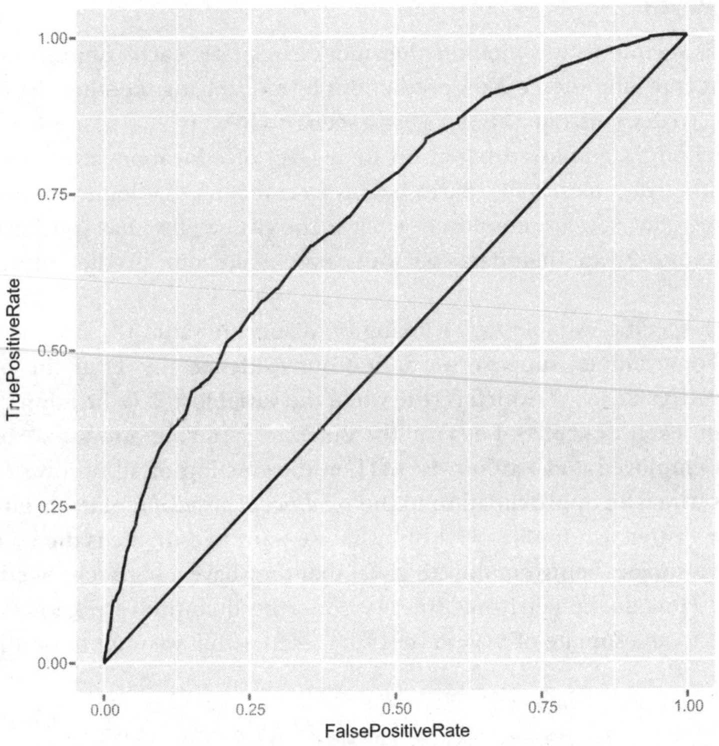

Figure 6.4 ROC of 200-nearest neighbors on calibration data

The ROC curve shows every possible classifier you can get by using different scoring thresholds on the same model. For example, you can achieve a high recall (high true positive rate, or TPR) at the expense of a high false positive rate (FPR) by selecting a threshold that moves you to the top right of the graph. Conversely, you can achieve high precision (high positive confirmation rate) at the expense of recall by selecting a threshold that moves you to the bottom left of the graph. Notice that score thresholds aren't plotted, just the resulting FPRs and TPRs.

KNN is expensive both in time and space. Sometimes we can get similar results with more efficient methods such as logistic regression (which we'll explain in detail in chapter 7). To demonstrate that a fast method can be competitive with KNN, we'll show the performance of logistic regression in the next listing.

Listing 6.22 Plotting the performance of a logistic regression model

```
> gmodel <- glm(as.formula(f),data=dTrain,family=binomial(link='logit'))
> print(calcAUC(predict(gmodel,newdata=dTrain),dTrain[,outcome]))
[1] 0.7309537
> print(calcAUC(predict(gmodel,newdata=dTest),dTest[,outcome]))
[1] 0.7234645
> print(calcAUC(predict(gmodel,newdata=dCal),dCal[,outcome]))
[1] 0.7170824
```

6.3.4 Using Naive Bayes

Naive Bayes is an interesting method that memorizes how each training variable is related to outcome, and then makes predictions by multiplying together the effects of each variable. To demonstrate this, let's use a scenario in which we're trying to predict whether somebody is employed based on their level of education, their geographic region, and other variables. Naive Bayes begins by reversing that logic and asking this question: Given that you are employed, what is the probability that you have a high school education? From that data, we can then make our prediction regarding employment.

Let's call a specific variable (`x_1`) taking on a specific value (`X_1`) a piece of *evidence:* `ev_1`. For example, suppose we define our evidence (`ev_1`) as the predicate `education=="High School"`, which is true when the variable `x_1` (education) takes on the value `X_1` (`"High School"`). Let's call the outcome `y` (taking on values `T` or `True` if the person is employed and `F` otherwise). Then the fraction of all positive examples where `ev_1` is true is an approximation to the *conditional probability* of `ev_1`, given `y==T`. This is usually written as `P(ev1|y==T)`. But what we want to estimate is the conditional probability of a subject being employed, given that they have a high school education: `P(y==T|ev1)`. How do we get from `P(ev1|y==T)` (the quantities we know from our training data) to an estimate of `P(y==T|ev1 ... evN)` (what we want to predict)?

Bayes' law tells us we can expand `P(y==T|ev1)` and `P(y==F|ev1)` like this:

$$P(y{=}{=}T \mid ev_1) = \frac{P(y{=}{=}T) \times P(ev_1 \mid y{=}{=}T)}{P(ev_1)}$$

$$P(y{=}{=}F \mid ev_1) = \frac{P(y{=}{=}F) \times (P(ev_1 \mid y{=}{=}F)}{P(ev_1)}$$

The left-hand side is what you want; the right-hand side is all quantities that can be estimated from the statistics of the training data. For a single feature `ev1`, this buys us little as we could derive `P(y==T|ev1)` as easily from our training data as from `P(ev1|y==T)`. For multiple features (`ev1 ... evN`) this sort of expansion is useful. The *Naive Bayes assumption* lets us assume that all the evidence is conditionally independent of each other for a given outcome:

$$P(ev_1\&\cdots ev_N \mid y{=}{=}T) \approx P(ev_1 \mid y{=}{=}T) \times P(ev_2 \mid y{=}{=}T) \times \cdots P(ev_N \mid y{=}{=}T)$$

$$P(ev_1\&\cdots ev_N \mid y{=}{=}F) \approx P(ev_1 \mid y{=}{=}F) \times P(ev_2 \mid y{=}{=}F) \times \cdots P(ev_N \mid y{=}{=}F)$$

This gives us the following:

$$P(y{=}{=}T \mid ev_1\&\cdots ev_N) \approx \frac{P(y{=}{=}T) \times (P(ev_1 \mid y{=}{=}T) \times \cdots P(ev_N \mid y{=}{=}T))}{P(ev_1\&\cdots ev_N)}$$

$$P(y{=}{=}F \mid ev_1\&\cdots ev_N) \approx \frac{P(y{=}{=}F) \times (P(ev_1 \mid y{=}{=}F) \times \cdots P(ev_N \mid y{=}{=}F))}{P(ev_1\&\cdots ev_N)}$$

The numerator terms of the right sides of the final expressions can be calculated efficiently from the training data, while the left sides can't. We don't have a direct scheme for estimating the denominators in the Naive Bayes expression (these are called the *joint probability of the evidence*). However, we can still estimate `P(y==T|evidence)` and `P(y==F|evidence)`, as we know by the law of total probability that we should have `P(y==T|evidence) + P(y==F|evidence) = 1`. So it's enough to pick a denominator such that our estimates add up to 1.

For numerical reasons, it's better to convert the products into sums, by taking the log of both sides. Since the denominator term is the same in both expressions, we can ignore it; we only want to determine which of the following expressions is greater:

$$\text{score}(T \mid ev_1\&\cdots ev_N) = log(P(y{=}{=}T)) + log(P(ev_1 \mid y{=}{=}T)) + \cdots log(P(ev_N \mid y{=}{=}T))$$

$$\text{score}(F \mid ev_1\&\cdots ev_N) = log(P(y{=}{=}F)) + log(P(ev_1 \mid y{=}{=}F)) + \cdots log(P(ev_N \mid y{=}{=}F))$$

It's also a good idea to add a smoothing term so that you're never taking the log of zero.

All of the single-variable models we've built up to now are estimates of the form `model(e_i) ~ P(y==T|e_i)`, so by another appeal to Bayes' law we can say that the proportions we need for the Naive Bayes calculation (the ratios of `P(e_i|y==T)` to `P(e_i|y==F)`) are identical to the ratios of `model(e_i)/P(y===T))` to `(1-model(e_i))/P(y===F)`. So our single-variable models can be directly used to build an overall Naive Bayes model (without any need for additional record keeping). We show such an implementation in the following listing.

Listing 6.23 Building, applying, and evaluating a Naive Bayes model

```
pPos <- sum(dTrain[,outcome]==pos)/length(dTrain[,outcome])
nBayes <- function(pPos,pf) {
   pNeg <- 1 - pPos
   smoothingEpsilon <- 1.0e-5
   scorePos <- log(pPos + smoothingEpsilon) +
      rowSums(log(pf/pPos + smoothingEpsilon))
   scoreNeg <- log(pNeg + smoothingEpsilon) +
      rowSums(log((1-pf)/(1-pPos) + smoothingEpsilon))
    m <- pmax(scorePos,scoreNeg)
   expScorePos <- exp(scorePos-m)
   expScoreNeg <- exp(scoreNeg-m)
   expScorePos/(expScorePos+expScoreNeg)
}
pVars <- paste('pred',c(numericVars,catVars),sep='')
dTrain$nbpredl <- nBayes(pPos,dTrain[,pVars])
dCal$nbpredl <- nBayes(pPos,dCal[,pVars])
dTest$nbpredl <- nBayes(pPos,dTest[,pVars])
 print(calcAUC(dTrain$nbpredl,dTrain[,outcome]))
## [1] 0.9757348
print(calcAUC(dCal$nbpredl,dCal[,outcome]))
## [1] 0.5995206
print(calcAUC(dTest$nbpredl,dTest[,outcome]))
## [1] 0.5956515
```

Define a function that performs the Naive Bayes prediction.

For each row, compute (with a smoothing term) the sum of log(P[positive & evidence_i]/P[positive]) across all columns. This is equivalent to the log of the product of P[evidence_i | positive] up to terms that don't depend on the positive/negative outcome.

Exponentiate to turn sums back into products, but make sure we don't cause a floating point overflow in doing so.

For each row, compute (with a smoothing term) the sum of log(P[negative & evidence_i]/P[negative]) across all columns. This is equivalent to the log of the product of P[evidence_i | negative] up to terms that don't depend on the positive/negative outcome.

Use the fact that the predicted positive probability plus the predicted negative probability should sum to 1.0 to find and eliminate Z. Return the correctly scaled predicted odds of being positive as our forecast.

Apply the function to make the predictions.

Calculate the AUCs. Notice the overfit—fantastic performance on the training set that isn't repeated on the calibration or test sets.

Intuitively, what we've done is built a new per-variable prediction column from each of our single-variable models. Each new column is the logarithm of the ratio of the single-variable model's predicted churn rate over the overall churn rate. When the model predicts a rate near the overall churn rate, this ratio is near 1.0 and therefore the logarithm is near 0. Similarly, for high predicted churn rates, the prediction column is a positive number, and for low predicted churn rates the column prediction is negative.

Summing these signed columns is akin to taking a net-consensus vote across all of the columns' variables. If all the evidence is conditionally independent given the outcome (this is the Naive Bayes assumption—and remember it's only an assumption), then this is exactly the right thing to do. The amazing thing about the Naive Bayes classifier is that it can perform well even when the conditional independence assumption isn't true.

Smoothing

The most important design parameter in Naive Bayes is how *smoothing* is handled. The idea of smoothing is an attempt to obey *Cromwell's rule* that no probability estimate of `0` should ever be used in probabilistic reasoning. This is because if you're combining probabilities by multiplication (the most common method of combining probability estimates), then once some term is 0, the entire estimate will be `0` *no matter what the values of the other terms are*. The most common form of smoothing is called *Laplace smoothing*, which counts `k` successes out of `n` trials as a success ratio of `(k+1)/(n+1)` and not as a ratio of `k/n` (defending against the `k=0` case). Frequentist statisticians think of smoothing as a form of regularization and Bayesian statisticians think of smoothing in terms of priors.

There are many discussions of Bayes Law and Naive Bayes methods that cover the math in much more detail. One thing to remember is that Naive Bayes doesn't perform any clever optimization, so it can be outperformed by methods like logistic regression and support vector machines (when you have enough training data). Also, variable selection is very important for Naive Bayes. Naive Bayes is particularly useful when you have a very large number of features that are rare and/or nearly independent.

Document classification and Naive Bayes

Naive Bayes is the workhorse method when classifying text documents (as done by email spam detectors). This is because the standard model for text documents (usually called *bag-of-words* or *bag-of-k-grams*) can have an extreme number of possible features. In the bag-of-k-grams model, we pick a small *k* (typically 2) and each possible consecutive sequence of *k* words is a possible feature. Each document is represented as a *bag*, which is a sparse vector indicating which k-grams are in the document. The number of possible features runs into the millions, but each document only has a non-zero value on a number of features proportional to *k* times the size of the document.

Of course we can also call a prepackaged Naive Bayes implementation (that includes its own variable treatments), as shown in the following listing.

Listing 6.24 Using a Naive Bayes package

```
library('e1071')
lVars <- c(catVars,numericVars)
ff <- paste('as.factor(',outcome,'>0) ~ ',
   paste(lVars,collapse=' + '),sep='')
nbmodel <- naiveBayes(as.formula(ff),data=dTrain)
dTrain$nbpred <- predict(nbmodel,newdata=dTrain,type='raw')[,'TRUE']
dCal$nbpred <- predict(nbmodel,newdata=dCal,type='raw')[,'TRUE']
dTest$nbpred <- predict(nbmodel,newdata=dTest,type='raw')[,'TRUE']
calcAUC(dTrain$nbpred,dTrain[,outcome])
## [1] 0.4643591
calcAUC(dCal$nbpred,dCal[,outcome])
## [1] 0.5544484
calcAUC(dTest$nbpred,dTest[,outcome])
## [1] 0.5679519
```

The `e1071` code is performing a bit below our expectations on raw data. We *do* see performance superior from `e1072` if we call it again with our processed and selected variables. This emphasizes the advantage of combining by hand variable processing with pre-made machine learning libraries.

6.4 Summary

The single-variable and multiple-variable memorization style models in this section are always worth trying first. This is especially true if most of your variables are categorical variables, as memorization is a good idea in this case. The techniques of this chapter are also a good repeat example of variable treatment and variable selection.

We have, at a bit of a stretch, called all of the modeling techniques of this chapter *memorization methods*. The reason for this is because, having worked an example using all of these models all in the same place, you now have enough experience to see the common memorization traits in these models: their predictions are all sums of summaries of the original training data.

The models of this chapter are conceptualized as follows:

- Single-variable models can be thought of as being simple memorizations or summaries of the training data. This is especially true for categorical variables where the model is essentially a contingency table or pivot table, where for every level of the variable we record the distribution of training outcomes (see section 6.2.1). Some sophisticated ideas (like smoothing, regularization, or shrinkage) may be required to avoid overfitting and to build good single-variable models. But in the end, single-variable models essentially organize the training data into a number of subsets indexed by the predictive variable and then store a summary of the distribution of outcome as their future prediction. These models are atoms or sub-assemblies that we sum in different ways to get the rest of the models of this chapter.

- Decision tree model decisions are also sums of summaries over subsets of the training data. For each scoring example, the model makes a prediction by choosing the summary of all training data that was placed in the same leaf node of the decision tree as the current example to be scored. There's some cleverness in the construction of the decision tree itself, but once we have the tree, it's enough to store a single data summary per tree leaf.
- K-nearest neighbor predictions are based on summaries of the *k* pieces of training data that are closest to the example to be scored. KNN models usually store all of their original training data instead of an efficient summary, so they truly do memorize the training data.
- Naive Bayes models partially memorize training data through intermediate features. Roughly speaking, Naive Bayes models form their decision by building a large collection of independent single-variable models.[8] The Naive Bayes prediction for a given example is just the product of all the applicable single-variable model adjustments (or, isomorphically, the sum of logarithms of the single-variable contributions). Note that Naive Bayes models are constructed without any truly clever functional forms or optimization steps. This is why we stretch terms a bit and call them memorization: their predictions are just sums of appropriate summaries of the original training data.

For all their fascinating features, at some point you'll have needs that push you away from memorization methods. For some problems, you'll want models that capture more of the functional or additive structure of relationships. In particular, you'll want to try regression for value prediction and logistic regression for category prediction, as we demonstrate in chapter 7.

Key takeaways

- Always try single-variable models before trying more complicated techniques.
- Single-variable modeling techniques give you a useful start on variable selection.
- Always compare your model performance to the performance of your best single-variable model.
- Consider decision trees, nearest neighbor, and naive Bayes models as basic data memorization techniques and, if appropriate, try them early in your projects.

[8] As you saw in section 6.3.4, these are slightly modified single-variable models, since they model feature-driven change in outcome distribution, or in Bayesian terms "have the priors pulled out."

7 Linear and logistic regression

This chapter covers

- Using linear regression to predict quantities
- Using logistic regression to predict probabilities or categories
- Extracting relations and advice from functional models
- Interpreting the diagnostics from R's `lm()` call
- Interpreting the diagnostics from R's `glm()` call

In the last chapter, we worked through using memorization methods for prediction. In this chapter, we'll talk about a different class of methods for both scoring and classification: functional methods. These are methods that learn a model that is a continuous function of its inputs (versus being a mere lookup table). This class of methods is especially useful when you don't just want to predict an outcome, but you also want to know the relationship between the input variables and the outcome. This knowledge can prove useful because this relationship can often be used as *advice* on how to get the outcome that you want.

In this chapter, we'll show how to use linear regression to predict customer income and logistic regression to predict the probability that a newborn baby will need extra medical attention. These are two of the most common functional methods (there are many others, including generalized additive models, neural nets, and support vector machines). We'll also walk through the diagnostics that R produces when you fit a linear or logistic model.

7.1 Using linear regression

Linear regression is the bread and butter prediction method for statisticians and data scientists. If you're trying to predict a numerical quantity like profit, cost, or sales volume, you should always try linear regression first. If it works well, you're done; if it fails, the detailed diagnostics produced give you a good clue as to what methods you should try next.

In this section, we'll use a real-world example (predicting personal income) to work through all of the steps of producing and using a linear regression model.

Before we get to the main example, let's take a quick overview of the method.

7.1.1 Understanding linear regression

Linear regression models the expected value of a numeric quantity (called the *dependent* or *response* variable) in terms of numeric and categorical inputs (called the *independent* or *explanatory* variables). For example, suppose we're trying to predict how many pounds a person on a diet and exercise plan will lose in a month. We'll base that prediction on other facts about that person, like their average daily caloric intake over that month and how many hours a day they exercised. In other words, for every person `i`, we want to predict `pounds.lost[i]` based on `daily.cals[i]` and `daily.exercise[i]`. Linear regression assumes that `pounds.lost[i]` is a linear combination of `daily.cals[i]` and `daily.exercise[i]`:

```
pounds.lost[i] = b.cals * daily.cals[i] + b.exercise * daily.exercise[i]
```

The goal is to find the values of `b.cals` and `b.exercise` so that the linear combination of `daily.cals[i]` and `daily.exercise[i]` comes very close to `pounds.lost[i]` for all persons `i` in the training data.

Let's put this in more general terms. Suppose that `y[i]` is the numeric quantity we want to predict, and `x[i,]` is a row of inputs that corresponds to output `y[i]`. Linear regression finds a fit function `f(x)` such that

```
y[i] ~ f(x[i,]) = b[1] x[i,1] + ... b[n] x[i,n]
```

We want numbers `b[1],...,b[n]` (called the *coefficients* or *betas*) such that `f(x[i,])` is as near as possible to `y[i]` for all `(x[i,],y[i])` pairs in our training data. R supplies a one-line command to find these coefficients: `lm()`.

In the idealized theoretic situation, linear regression is used to fit `y[i]`when the `y[i]` are themselves given by

```
y[i] = b[1] x[i,1] + b[2] x[i,2] + ... b[n] x[i,n] + e[i]
```

In particular, this means that `y` is linear in the values of `x`: a change in the value of `x[i,m]` by one unit (while holding all the other `x[i,k]`s constant) will change the value of `y[i]` by the amount `b[m]` always, no matter what the starting value of `x[i,m]` was. This is easier to see in one dimension. If `y = 3 + 2*x`, and if we increase `x` by 1, then `y` will always increase by 2, no matter what the starting value of `x` is. This wouldn't be true for, say, `y = 3 + 2*(x^2)`.

The last term, `e[i]`, represents what are called *unsystematic errors*, or noise. Unsystematic errors average to 0 (so they don't represent a net upward or net downward bias) and are uncorrelated with `x[i,]` and `y[i]`.

The technical meaning of *regression*

Regression means the unbiased prediction of the conditional expected value. A prediction is a function `f()` such that `f(x[i,])` is near the unknown ideal quantity `E[y[i]|x[i,]]` (where `E[|]` is the conditional expected value operator averaging over all possible `y[j]` where `x[j,]` is sufficiently similar to `x[i,]`). Unbiased predictors have `E[f(x[i,])-y[i]]=0` under an appropriate expectation operator `E[]` (note we're talking about properties of the model now, not properties of errors in the data). Regression isn't so much a prediction of an individual `y[i]` but a forecast of `E[y[i]|x[i,]]` (the conditional expectation). For a good regression model, we expect `f(x[i,])` to be a good estimate of `E[y[i]|x[i,]]` and to have low conditional variance (`y[i]` tending to be near `E[y[i]|x[i,]]`). When both of these conditions are met, then `f(x[i,])` is in general a good estimate for `y[i]`.

Under these assumptions, linear regression is absolutely relentless in finding the best coefficients. If there's some advantageous combination or cancellation of features, it'll find it. One thing that linear regression doesn't do is reshape variables to be linear. Oddly enough, linear regression often does an excellent job, even when the actual relation is not in fact linear.

THINKING ABOUT LINEAR REGRESSION When working with linear regression, you'll vacillate between "Adding is too simple to work," and "How is it even possible to estimate the coefficients?" This is natural and comes from the fact that the method is both simple and powerful. Our friend Philip Apps sums it up: "You have to get up pretty early in the morning to beat linear regression."

As a toy example, consider trying to fit the squares of the first 10 integers using only a linear function plus the constant 1. We're asking for coefficients `b[0]` and `b[1]` such that

```
x[i]^2 nearly equals b[0] + b[1] x[i]
```

This is clearly not a fair thing to ask, but linear regression still does a great job. It picks the following fit:

```
x[i]^2 nearly equals -22 + 11 x[i]
```

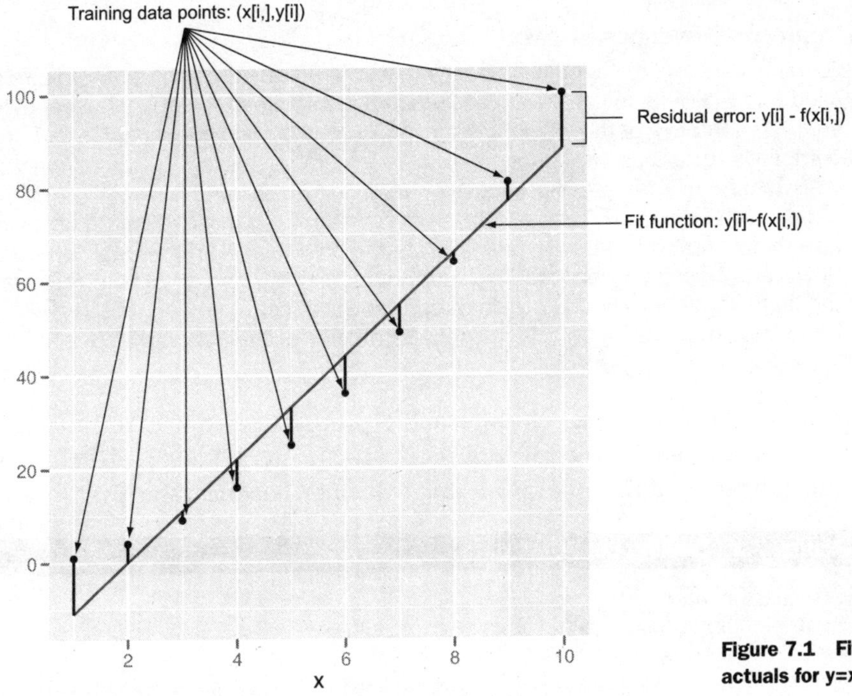

Figure 7.1 Fit versus actuals for $y=x^2$

As the figure 7.1 shows, this is a good fit in the region of values we trained on.

The example in figure 7.1 is typical of how linear regression is "used in the field"—we're using a linear model to predict something that is itself not linear. Be aware that this is a minor sin: in particular, note that the errors between the model's predictions and the true `y` are systematic. This is bad as the model underpredicts for specific ranges of x and overpredicts for others.

Next we'll work through an example of how to apply linear regression on more interesting real data. Our example task will be to predict personal income from other demographic variables such as age and education from 2011 US Census PUMS data. In addition to predicting income, we also have a secondary goal: to determine the effect of a bachelor's degree on income, relative to having no degree at all (the reference level "no high school diploma"). In section 2.2.3, we prepared a small sample of PUMS data which we'll use here. As a reminder, the data preparation steps included

- Restricting the data to full-time employees between 20 and 50 years of age, with an income between $1,000 and $250,000.
- Dividing the data into a training set, `dtrain`, and a test set, `dtest`.

> **Representativeness of data**
>
> For our examples, we're deliberately ignoring the 80 `PWGTP*` and `WGTP*` columns supplied with the Census data. The PUMS data is a sample of individual households that are representative of the US population *if* each person and household is counted proportionally to one of the `PWGTP*` and `WGTP*`columns. There are 80 columns so the researcher can evaluate the impact of sampling noise on their work (using `lm()`'s `weights` argument). To keep our examples simple, we'll model the data as-is and not worry about how this sample data is related to the larger (unreported) US population. However, it's critical when working with datasets like PUMS to become familiar with the steps taken to produce the data, and we would certainly want to use the `PWGTP*` weights before making any claims about statistics of the actual US population.

We can continue the example by loading `psub.RData` (which you can copy from https://github.com/WinVector/zmPDSwR/raw/master/PUMS/psub.RData) and performing the steps in the following listing (which we'll explain shortly).

Listing 7.1 Loading the PUMS data

```
load("psub.RData")
dtrain <- subset(psub,ORIGRANDGROUP >= 500)
dtest <- subset(psub,ORIGRANDGROUP < 500)
model <- lm(log(PINCP,base=10) ~ AGEP + SEX + COW + SCHL,data=dtrain)
dtest$predLogPINCP <- predict(model,newdata=dtest)
dtrain$predLogPINCP <- predict(model,newdata=dtrain)
```

Each row of PUMS data represents a single anonymized person or household. Personal data recorded includes occupation, level of education, personal income, and many other demographics variables.

For the analysis in this section, we'll consider the input variables age (`AGEP`), sex (`SEX`), class of worker (`COW`), and level of education (`SCHL`). The output variable is personal income (`PINCP`). We'll also set the *reference level*, or "default" sex to `M` (male); the reference level of class of worker to `Employee of a private for-profit`; and the reference level of education level to `no high school diploma`. We'll discuss reference levels later in this chapter.

Now on to the model building.

7.1.2 Building a linear regression model

The first step in either prediction or finding relations (advice) is to build the linear regression model. The command to build the linear regression model in R is `lm()`. The most important argument to `lm()` is a formula with ~ used in place of an equals sign. The formula specifies what column of the data frame is the quantity to be predicted, and what columns are to be used to make the predictions. Statisticians call the quantity to be predicted the *dependent variable* and the variables/columns used to make the prediction the *independent variables*. We find it is easier to call the quantity to be predicted the *y* and the variables used to make the predictions the *x*s. Our formula

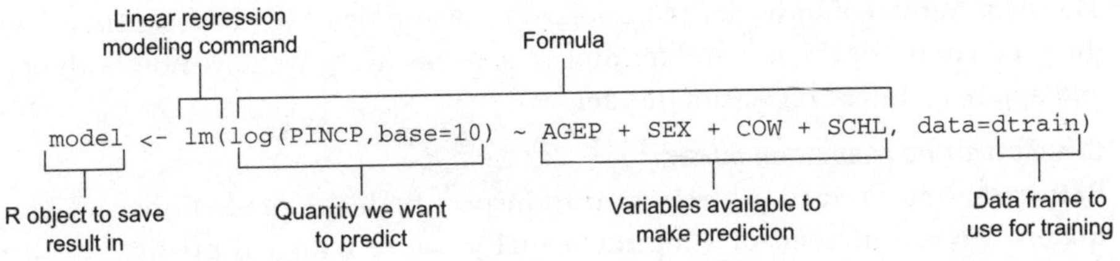

Figure 7.2 Building a linear model using the `lm()` command

is this: `log(PINCP,base=10) ~ AGEP + SEX + COW + SCHL`, which is read "Predict the log base 10 of income as a function of age, sex, employment class, and education."[1] The overall command is demonstrated in figure 7.2.

The command in figure 7.2 builds the linear regression model and stores the results in the new object called `model`. This model is able both to make predictions and to extract important advice from the data.

> **R STORES TRAINING DATA IN THE MODEL** R holds a copy of the training data in its model to supply the residual information seen in `summary(model)`. Holding a copy of the data this way is not strictly necessary and can needlessly run you out of memory. You can mitigate this problem somewhat by setting the parameters `model = F, x = F, y = F, qr = F` in the `lm()` call. If you're running low on memory (or swapping), you can dispose of R objects like `model` using the `rm()` command. In this case, you'd dispose of the model by running `rm("model")`.

7.1.3 *Making predictions*

Once you've called `lm()` to build the model, your first goal is to predict income. This is easy to do in R. To predict, you pass data into the `predict()` method. Figure 7.3 demonstrates this using both the test and training data frames `dtest` and `dtrain`.

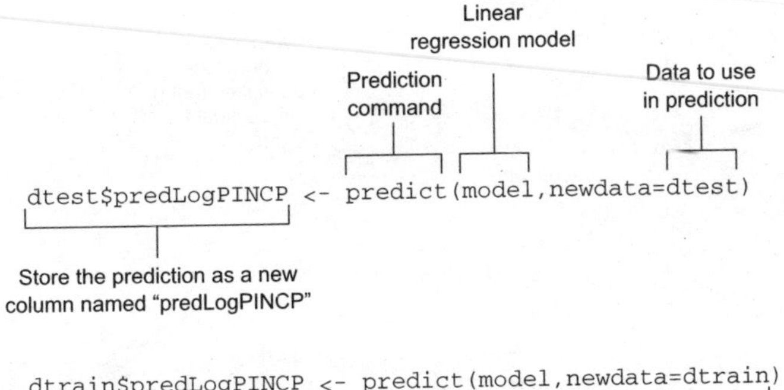

Figure 7.3 Making predictions with a linear regression model

1 Recall from the discussion of the lognormal distribution in section 4.1.2 that it's often useful to log transform monetary quantities.

The data frame columns dtest$predLogPINCP and dtrain$predLogPINCP now store the predictions for the test and training sets, respectively. We have now both produced and applied a linear regression model.

CHARACTERIZING PREDICTION QUALITY

Before sharing predictions, you want to inspect both the predictions and model for quality. We recommend plotting the actual y you're trying to predict as if it were a function of your prediction. In this case, plot log(PINCP,base=10) as if it were a function of predLogPINCP. If the predictions are very good, then the plot will be dots arranged near the line y=x, which we call *the line of perfect prediction* (the phrase is not standard terminology; we use it to make talking about the graph easier). The commands to produce this for figure 7.4 are shown in the next listing.

Listing 7.2 Plotting log income as a function of predicted log income

```
ggplot(data=dtest,aes(x=predLogPINCP,y=log(PINCP,base=10))) +
   geom_point(alpha=0.2,color="black") +
   geom_smooth(aes(x=predLogPINCP,
      y=log(PINCP,base=10)),color="black") +
   geom_line(aes(x=log(PINCP,base=10),
      y=log(PINCP,base=10)),color="blue",linetype=2) +
   scale_x_continuous(limits=c(4,5)) +
   scale_y_continuous(limits=c(3.5,5.5))
```

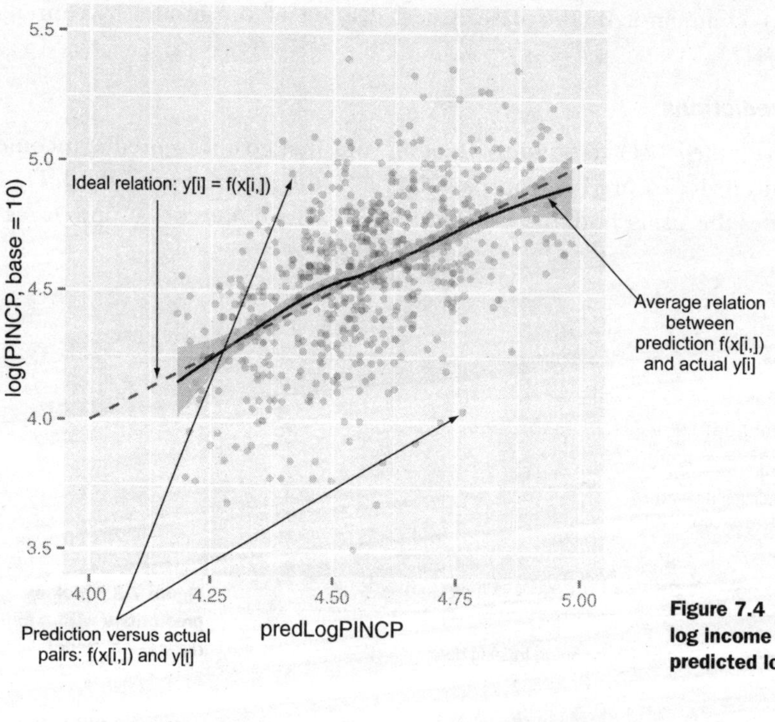

Figure 7.4 Plot of actual log income as a function of predicted log income

Statisticians prefer the residual plot shown in figure 7.5, where the predictions errors `predLogPINCP-log(PINCP,base=10)` are plotted as a function of `predLogPINCP`. In this case, the line of perfect prediction is the line `y=0`. Notice the points are scattered widely from this line (a possible sign of low-quality fit). The residual plot in figure 7.5 is prepared with the R commands in the next listing.

Listing 7.3 Plotting residuals income as a function of predicted log income

```
ggplot(data=dtest,aes(x=predLogPINCP,
                     y=predLogPINCP-log(PINCP,base=10))) +
  geom_point(alpha=0.2,color="black") +
  geom_smooth(aes(x=predLogPINCP,
                  y=predLogPINCP-log(PINCP,base=10)),
                  color="black")
```

When you look at the true-versus-fitted or residual graphs, you're looking for some specific things that we'll discuss next.

On average, are the predictions correct?

In other words, does the smoothing curve lie more or less along the line of perfect prediction? Ideally, the points will all lie very close to that line, but you may instead get a wider cloud of points (as we do in figures 7.4 and 7.5) if your input variables don't explain the output too closely. But if the smoothing curve lies along the line of perfect

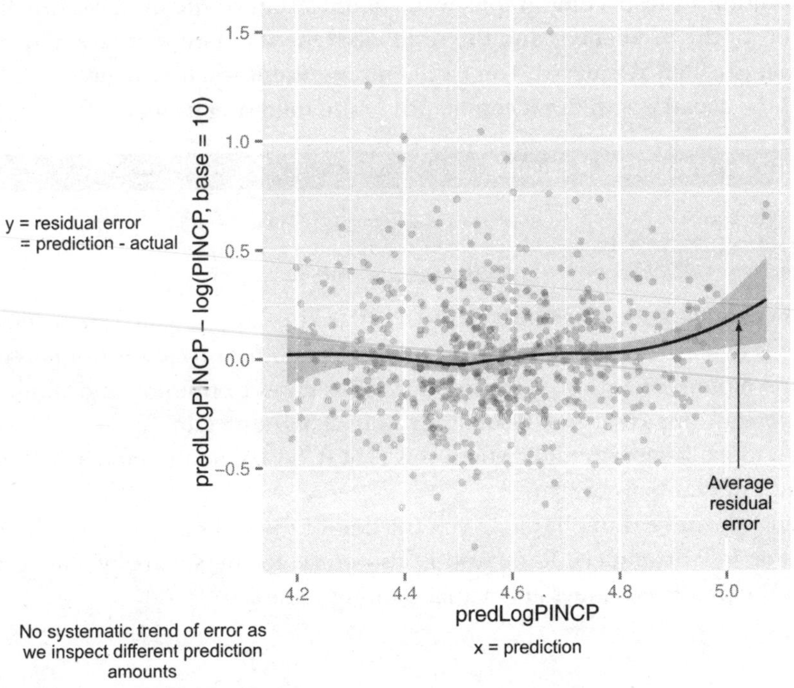

Figure 7.5 Plot of residual error as a function of prediction

> **Why are the predictions, not the true values, on the x-axis?**
> The two graphs (plotting residuals as a function of true values or as a function of predicted values) answer different questions. Statisticians tend to prefer the graph as shown in figure 7.5, with predictions on the x-axis.
>
> A residual graph with *predictions* on the x-axis gives you a sense of when the model may be under- or overpredicting, based on the model's output. A residual graph with the *true outcome* on the x-axis instead gives you a sense of where the model under- or overpredicts based on the actual outcome.

prediction, then the model predicts correctly on average: it underpredicts about as much as it overpredicts.

Are there systematic errors?
If the smoothing curve veers off the line of perfect prediction too much, this is a sign of systematic under- or overprediction in certain ranges: the error is correlated with `y[i]`. Many of the theoretical claims about linear regression depend on the observation error being uncorrelated with `y[i]`. Unstructured observation errors (the good case) are called *homoscedastic,* and structured observation errors are called *heteroscedastic* and introduce prediction bias. For example, the toy fit in section 7.1 is heteroscedastic and is unsafe to use for values outside of its training range.

In addition to inspecting graphs, you should produce quantitative summaries of the quality of the predictions and the residuals. One standard measure of quality of a prediction is called R-squared. You can compute the R-squared between the prediction and the actual `y` with the R commands in the following listing.

Listing 7.4 Computing R-squared

```
rsq <- function(y,f) { 1 - sum((y-f)^2)/sum((y-mean(y))^2) }
rsq(log(dtrain$PINCP,base=10),predict(model,newdata=dtrain))
rsq(log(dtest$PINCP,base=10),predict(model,newdata=dtest))
```

You want R-squared to be fairly large (1.0 is the largest you can achieve) and R-squareds that are similar on test and training. A significantly lower R-squared on test data is a symptom of an overfit model that looks good in training and won't work in production. In our case, our R-squareds were 0.338 on training and 0.261 on test. We'd like to see R-squares higher than this (say, 0.7–1.0). So the model is of low quality, but not substantially overfit.

R-squared can be thought of as what fraction of the `y` variation is explained by the model. For well-fit models, R-squared is also equal to the square of the correlation between the predicted values and actual training values.

R-squared can be overoptimistic

In general, R-squared on training data will be higher for models with more input parameters, independently of whether the additional variables actually improve the model or not. That's why many people prefer the adjusted R-squared (which we'll discuss later in this chapter).

Also, R-squared is related to correlation, and the correlation can be artificially inflated if the model correctly predicts a few outliers (because the increased data range makes the overall data cloud appear "tighter" against the line of perfect prediction). Here's a toy example. Let `y <- c(1,2,3,4,5,9,10)` and `pred <- c(0.5,0.5,0.5,0.5,0.5,9,10)`. This corresponds to a model that's completely uncorrelated to the true outcome for the first five points, and perfectly predicts the last two points, which are somewhat far away from the first five. You can check for yourself that this obviously poor model has a correlation `cor(y,pred)` of about 0.926, with a corresponding R-squared of 0.858. So it's an excellent idea to look at the true-versus-fitted graph in addition to checking R-squared.

Another good measure to consider is root mean square error (RMSE).

Listing 7.5 Calculating root mean square error

```
rmse <- function(y, f) { sqrt(mean( (y-f)^2 )) }
rmse(log(dtrain$PINCP,base=10),predict(model,newdata=dtrain))
rmse(log(dtest$PINCP,base=10),predict(model,newdata=dtest))
```

You can think of the RMSE as a measure of the width of the data cloud around the line of perfect prediction. We'd like RMSE to be small, and one way to achieve this is to introduce more useful explanatory variables.

7.1.4 *Finding relations and extracting advice*

Recall that our other goal, beyond predicting income, is to find the value of having a bachelor's degree. We'll show how this value, and other relations in the data, can be read directly off a linear regression model.

All of the information in a linear regression model is stored in a block of numbers called the *coefficients*. The coefficients are available through the `coefficients(model)` command. The coefficients of our income model are shown in figure 7.6.

REPORTED COEFFICIENTS

Our original modeling variables were only `AGEP`, `SEX`, `COW`, and `SCHL`; yet the model reports many more coefficients than these four. We'll explain what all the reported coefficients are.

In figure 7.6, there are eight coefficients that start with `SCHL`. The original variable `SCHL` took on these eight string values plus one more not shown: `no high school diploma`. Each of these possible strings is called a *level*, and `SCHL` itself is called a *categorical variable* or a *factor variable*. The level that isn't shown is called the *reference level*; the coefficients of the other levels are measured with respect to the reference level.

```
> coefficients(model)
                          (Intercept)                                  AGEP
                           3.97328317                            0.01171695
                                 SEXF       COWFederal government employee
                          -0.09313262                            0.05972743
        COWLocal government employee COWPrivate not-for-profit employee
                          -0.03441690                           -0.13352439
      COWSelf-employed incorporated  COWSelf-employed not incorporated
                          -0.07242727                           -0.06060878
        COWState government employee                SCHLAssociate's degree
                          -0.08128385                            0.22143196
                 SCHLBachelor's degree                SCHLDoctorate degree
                           0.39383406                            0.30655376
     SCHLGED or alternative credential                  SCHLMaster's degree
                           0.13776759                            0.47728422
              SCHLProfessional degree       SCHLRegular high school diploma
                           0.67877416                            0.10174598
   SCHLsome college credit, no degree
                           0.16315219
```

The modeled values of a bachelor's degree versus a high school diploma

Figure 7.6 The model coefficients

For example, in `SCHLBachelor's degree` we find the coefficient 0.39, which is read as "The model gives a 0.39 bonus to log income for having a bachelor's degree, relative to not having a high school degree." This means that the income ratio between someone with a bachelor's degree and the equivalent person (same sex, age, and class of work) without a high school degree is about `10^0.39`, or 2.45 times higher.

And under `SCHLRegular high school diploma` we find the coefficient 0.10. This is read as "The model believes that having a bachelor's degree tends to add 0.39–0.10 units to the predicted log income (relative to a high school degree)." The modeled relation between the bachelor's degree holder's expected income and high school graduate's (all other variables being equal) is `10^(0.39-0.10)`, or about 1.8 times greater. The advice: college is worth it if you can find a job (remember that we limited our analysis to the fully employed, so this is assuming you can find a job).

`SEX` and `COW` are also discrete variables, and the coefficients that correspond to the different levels of `SEX` and `COW` can be interpreted in a similar manner. `AGEP` is a continuous variable with coefficient 0.0117. You can interpret this as a one-year increase in age, adding a 0.0117 bonus to log income; in other words, an increase in age of one year corresponds to an increase of income of `10^0.0117`, or a factor of 1.027—about a 2.7% increase in income (all other variables being equal).

The coefficient `(Intercept)` corresponds to a variable that always has a value of 1, which is implicitly added to linear regression models unless you use the special `0+` notation in the formula during the call to `lm()`. This coefficient is a rough center for the model predictions.

The preceding interpretations of the coefficients assume that the model has provided good estimates of the coefficients. We'll see how to check that in the next section.

> **Indicator variables**
>
> Most modeling methods handle a string-valued (categorical) variable with *n* possible levels by converting it to *n* (or *n-1*) binary variables, or *indicator variables*. R has commands to explicitly control the conversion of string-valued variables into well-behaved indicators: `as.factor()` creates categorical variables from string variables; `relevel()` allows the user to specify the reference level.
>
> But beware of variables with a very large number of levels, like ZIP codes. The runtime of linear (and logistic) regression increases as roughly the cube of the number of coefficients. Too many levels (or too many variables in general) will bog the algorithm down and require much more data for reliable inference.[2]

7.1.5 Reading the model summary and characterizing coefficient quality

In section 7.1.3, we checked whether our income predictions were to be trusted. We'll now show how to check whether model coefficients are reliable. This is especially urgent, as we've been discussing showing coefficients' relations to others as advice.

Most of what we need to know is already in the model summary, which is produced using the `summary()` command: `summary(model)`. This produces the output shown in figure 7.7, which looks intimidating, but contains a lot of useful information and diagnostics. You're likely to be asked about elements of figure 7.7 when presenting results, so we'll demonstrate how all of these fields are derived and what the fields mean.

We'll first break down the `summary()` into pieces.

THE ORIGINAL MODEL CALL

The first part of the `summary()` is how the `lm()` model was constructed:

```
Call:
lm(formula = log(PINCP, base = 10) ~ AGEP + SEX + COW + SCHL,
    data = dtrain)
```

This is a good place to double-check whether we used the correct data frame, performed our intended transformations, and used the right variables. For example, we can double-check whether we used the data frame `dtrain` and not the data frame `dtest`.

THE RESIDUALS SUMMARY

The next part of the `summary()` is the residuals summary:

```
Residuals:
     Min       1Q   Median       3Q      Max
-1.29220 -0.14153  0.02458  0.17632  0.62532
```

2 To see a trick for dealing with factors with very many levels, see http://mng.bz/ytFY.

Model call summary

```
Call:
lm(formula = log(PINCP, base = 10) ~ AGEP + SEX + COW + SCHL,
    data = dtrain)
```

Residuals summary

```
Residuals:
     Min       1Q   Median       3Q      Max
-1.29220 -0.14153  0.02458  0.17632  0.62532
```

Coefficients

```
Coefficients:
                                    Estimate Std. Error t value Pr(>|t|)
(Intercept)                         3.973283   0.059343  66.954  < 2e-16 ***
AGEP                                0.011717   0.001352   8.666  < 2e-16 ***
SEXF                               -0.093133   0.023405  -3.979 7.80e-05 ***
COWFederal government employee      0.059727   0.060927   0.980 0.327343
COWLocal government employee       -0.034417   0.048030  -0.717 0.473928
COWPrivate not-for-profit employee -0.133524   0.039223  -3.404 0.000709 ***
COWSelf-employed incorporated      -0.072427   0.068093  -1.064 0.287928
COWSelf-employed not incorporated  -0.060609   0.069244  -0.875 0.381779
COWState government employee       -0.081284   0.057796  -1.406 0.160146
SCHLAssociate's degree              0.221432   0.052094   4.251 2.49e-05 ***
SCHLBachelor's degree               0.393834   0.043249   9.106  < 2e-16 ***
SCHLDoctorate degree                0.306554   0.160127   1.914 0.056058 .
SCHLGED or alternative credential   0.137768   0.078192   1.762 0.078612 .
SCHLMaster's degree                 0.477284   0.050895   9.378  < 2e-16 ***
SCHLProfessional degree             0.678774   0.087321   7.773 3.52e-14 ***
SCHLRegular high school diploma     0.101746   0.042628   2.387 0.017316 *
SCHLsome college credit, no degree  0.163152   0.042729   3.818 0.000149 ***
---
Signif. codes:  0 '***' 0.001 '**' 0.01 '*' 0.05 '.' 0.1 ' ' 1
```

Model quality summary

```
Residual standard error: 0.2691 on 578 degrees of freedom
Multiple R-squared: 0.3383, Adjusted R-squared: 0.3199
F-statistic: 18.47 on 16 and 578 DF,  p-value: < 2.2e-16
```

Figure 7.7 Model summary

In linear regression, the residuals are everything. Most of what we want to know about the quality of our model fit is in the residuals. The residuals are our errors in prediction: `log(dtrain$PINCP,base=10) - predict(model,newdata=dtrain)`. We can find useful summaries of the residuals for both the training and test sets, as shown in the following listing.

Listing 7.6 Summarizing residuals

```
> summary(log(dtrain$PINCP,base=10) - predict(model,newdata=dtrain))
    Min.  1st Qu.   Median     Mean  3rd Qu.     Max.
-1.29200 -0.14150  0.02458  0.00000  0.17630  0.62530
> summary(log(dtest$PINCP,base=10) - predict(model,newdata=dtest))
     Min.   1st Qu.    Median      Mean   3rd Qu.      Max.
-1.494000 -0.165300  0.018920 -0.004637  0.175500  0.868100
```

In linear regression, the coefficients are chosen to minimize the sum of squares of the residuals. This is the why the method is also often called the *least squares method*. So for good models, we expect the residuals to be small.

In the residual summary, you're given the `Min.` and `Max.`, which are the smallest and largest residuals seen. You're also given three quantiles of the residuals: `1st. Qu.`,

`Median`, and `3rd Qu.` An r-quantile is a number *r* such that an r-fraction of the residuals is less than x and a (1-r)-fraction of residuals is greater than x. The `1st. Qu.`, `Median`, and `3rd Qu.` quantiles' values are the values of the 0.25, 0.5, and 0.75 quantiles.

What you hope to see in the residual summary is the median near 0 and symmetry in that `1st. Qu.` is near `-3rd Qu.` (with neither too large). The `1st. Qu.` and `3rd Qu.` quantiles are interesting because exactly half of the training data has a residual in this range. If you drew a random training example, its residual would be in this range exactly half the time. So you really expect to commonly see prediction errors of these magnitudes. If these errors are too big for your application, you don't have a usable model.

THE COEFFICIENTS TABLE

The next part of the `summary(model)` is the coefficients table, as shown in figure 7.8. A matrix form of this table can be retrieved as `summary(model)$coefficients`.

Each model coefficient forms a row of the summary coefficients table. The columns report the estimated coefficient, the uncertainty of the estimate, how large the coefficient is relative to the uncertainty, and how likely such a ratio would be due to mere chance. Figure 7.8 gives the names and interpretations of the columns.

We set out to study income and the impact on income of getting a bachelor's degree. But we must look at all of the coefficients to check for interfering effects.

For example, the coefficient of -0.093 for `SEXF` means that our model learned a penalty of -0.093 to `log(PINCP,base=10)` for being female. Females are modeled as earning `1-10^-0.093` relative to males, or 19% less, all other model parameters being equal. Note we said "all other model parameters being equal" not "all other things

```
Coefficients:
                                    Estimate Std. Error t value Pr(>|t|)
(Intercept)                         3.973283   0.059343  66.954  < 2e-16 ***
AGEP                                0.011717   0.001352   8.666  < 2e-16 ***
SEXF                               -0.093133   0.023405  -3.979 7.80e-05 ***
COWFederal government employee      0.059727   0.060927   0.980 0.327343
COWLocal government employee       -0.034417   0.048030  -0.717 0.473928
COWPrivate not-for-profit employee -0.133524   0.039223  -3.404 0.000709 ***
COWSelf-employed incorporated      -0.072427   0.068093  -1.064 0.287928
COWSelf-employed not incorporated  -0.060609   0.069244  -0.875 0.381779
COWState government employee       -0.081284   0.057796  -1.406 0.160146
SCHLAssociate's degree              0.221432   0.052094   4.251 2.49e-05 ***
SCHLBachelor's degree               0.393834   0.043249   9.106  < 2e-16 ***
SCHLDoctorate degree                0.306554   0.160127   1.914 0.056058 .
SCHLGED or alternative credential   0.137768   0.078192   1.762 0.078612 .
SCHLMaster's degree                 0.477284   0.050895   9.378  < 2e-16 ***
SCHLProfessional degree             0.678774   0.087321   7.773 3.52e-14 ***
SCHLRegular high school diploma     0.101746   0.042628   2.387 0.017316 *
SCHLsome college credit, no degree  0.163152   0.042729   3.818 0.000149 ***
```

Name of coefficient

Coefficient estimate

Standard error in estimate

t-value: Number of standard errors estimate is away from zero

p-value: Probability of such a large t-value forming by mere chance

Figure 7.8 Model summary coefficient columns

being equal." That's because we're not modeling the number of years in the workforce (which age may not be a reliable proxy for) or occupation/industry type (which has a big impact on income). This model is not, with the features it was given, capable of testing if, on average, a female in the same job with the same number of years of experience is paid less.

Statistics as an attempt to correct bad experimental design

The absolute best experiment to test if there's a sex-driven difference in income distribution would be to compare incomes of individuals who were identical in all possible variables (age, education, years in industry, performance reviews, race, region, and so on) but differ only in sex. We're unlikely to have access to such data, so we'd settle for a good experimental design: a population where there's no correlation between any other feature and sex. Random selection can help in experimental design, but it's not a complete panacea. Barring a good experimental design, the usual pragmatic strategy is this: introduce extra variables to represent effects that may have been interfering with the effect we were trying to study. Thus a study of the effect of sex on income may include other variables like education and age to try to disentangle the competing effects.

The *p-value* (also called the *significance*) is one of the most important diagnostic columns in the coefficient summary. The p-value estimates the probability of seeing a coefficient with a magnitude as large as we observe if the true coefficient is really 0 (if the variable has no effect on the outcome). Don't trust the estimate of any coefficient with a large p-value. The general rule of thumb, `p>=0.05`, is not to be trusted. The estimate of the coefficient may be good, but you want to use more data to build a model that reliably shows that the estimate is good. However, lower p-values aren't always "better" once they're good enough. There's no reason to prefer a coefficient with a p-value of 1e-23 to one with a p-value of 1e-08; at this point you know both coefficients are likely good estimates and you should prefer the ones that explain the most variance.

Collinearity also lowers significance

Sometimes, a predictive variable won't appear significant because it's collinear (or correlated) with another predictive variable. For example, if we did try to use both age and number of years in the workforce to predict income, neither variable may appear significant. This is because age tends to be correlated with number of years in the workforce. If you remove one of the variables and the other one gains significance, this is a good indicator of correlation.

Another possible indication of collinearity in the inputs is seeing coefficients with an unexpected sign: for example, seeing that income is *negatively* correlated with years in the workforce.

The overall model can still predict income quite well, even when the inputs are correlated; it just can't determine which variable deserves the credit for the prediction. Using regularization (especially ridge regression as found in `lm.ridge()` in the package `MASS`) is helpful in collinear situations (we prefer it to "*x*-alone" variable preprocessing, such as principal components analysis). If you want to use the coefficient values as advice as well as to make good predictions, try to avoid collinearity in the inputs as much as possible.

OVERALL MODEL QUALITY SUMMARIES

The last part of the `summary(model)` report is the overall model quality statistics. It's a good idea to check the overall model quality before sharing any predictions or coefficients. The summaries are as follows:

```
Residual standard error: 0.2691 on 578 degrees of freedom
Multiple R-squared: 0.3383,     Adjusted R-squared: 0.3199
F-statistic: 18.47 on 16 and 578 DF,  p-value: < 2.2e-16
```

The *degrees of freedom* is the number of data rows minus the number of coefficients fit; in our case, this:

```
df <- dim(dtrain)[1] - dim(summary(model)$coefficients)[1]
```

The degrees of freedom is thought of as the number of training data rows you have after correcting for the number of coefficients you tried to solve for. You want the degrees of freedom to be large compared to the number of coefficients fit to avoid overfitting. Overfitting is when you find chance relations in your training data that aren't present in the general population. Overfitting is bad: you think you have a good model when you don't.

The *residual standard error* is the sum of the square of the residuals (or the sum of squared error) divided by the degrees of freedom. So it's similar to the RMSE (root mean squared error) that we discussed earlier, except with the number of data rows adjusted to be the degrees of freedom; in R, this:

```
modelResidualError <- sqrt(sum(residuals(model)^2)/df)
```

Multiple R-squared is just the R-squared (discussed in section 7.1.3).

The *adjusted R-squared* is the multiple R-squared penalized by the ratio of the degrees of freedom to the number of training examples. This attempts to correct the fact that more complex models tend to look better on training data due to overfitting. Usually it's better to rely on the adjusted R-squared. Better still is to compute the R-squared between predictions and actuals on hold-out test data. In section 7.1.3, we showed the R-squared on test data was 0.26, which is significantly lower than the reported adjusted R-squared of 0.32. So the adjusted R-squared discounts for overfitting, but not always enough. This is one of the reasons we advise preparing both training and test datasets;

the test dataset estimates can be more representative of production model performance than statistical formulas.

The F-statistic is similar to the p-values we saw with the model coefficients. It's used to measure whether the linear regression model predicts outcome better than the constant mode (the mean value of *y*). The F-statistic gets its name from the F-test, which is the technique used to check if two variances—in this case, the variance of the residuals from the constant model and the variance of the residuals from the linear model—are significantly different. The corresponding p-value is the estimate of the probability that we would've observed an F-statistic this large or larger if the two variances in question are in reality the same. So you want the p-value to be small (rule of thumb: less than 0.05).

In our example, the model is doing better than just the constant model, and the improvement is incredibly unlikely to have arisen from sampling error.

INTERPRETING MODEL SIGNIFICANCES Most of the tests of linear regression, including the tests for coefficient and model significance, are based on the error terms, or residuals are normally distributed. It's important to examine graphically or using quantile analysis to determine if the regression model is appropriate.

7.1.6 Linear regression takeaways

Here's what you should remember about linear regression:

- Linear regression is the go-to statistical modeling method for quantities.
- You should always try linear regression first, and only use more complicated methods if they actually outperform a linear regression model.
- Linear regression will have trouble with problems that have a very large number of variables, or categorical variables with a very large number of levels.
- You can enhance linear regression by adding new variables or transforming variables (like we did with the `log()` transform of `y`, but always be wary when transforming `y` as it changes the error model).
- With linear regression, you think in terms of residuals. You look for variables that correlate with your errors and add them to try and eliminate systematic modeling errors.
- Linear regression can predict well even in the presence of correlated variables, but correlated variables lower the quality of the advice.
- Overly large coefficient magnitudes, overly large standard errors on the coefficient estimates, and the wrong sign on a coefficient could be indications of correlated inputs.
- Linear regression packages have some of the best built-in diagnostics available, but rechecking your model on test data is still your most effective safety check.

7.2 Using logistic regression

Logistic regression is the most important (and probably most used) member of a class of models called *generalized linear models.* Unlike linear regression, logistic regression can directly predict values that are restricted to the (0,1) interval, such as probabilities. It's the go-to method for predicting probabilities or rates, and like linear regression, the coefficients of a logistic regression model can be treated as *advice.* It's also a good first choice for binary classification problems.

In this section, we'll use a medical classification example (predicting whether a newborn will need extra medical attention) to work through all of the steps of producing and using a logistic regression model.[3]

7.2.1 Understanding logistic regression

Logistic regression predicts the probability `y` that an instance belongs to a specific category—for instance, the probability that a flight will be delayed. When `x[i,]` is a row of inputs (for example, a flight's origin and destination, the time of year, the weather, the air carrier), logistic regression finds a fit function `f(x)` such that

```
P[y[i] in class] ~ f(x[i,]) = s(a+b[1] x[i,1] + ... b[n] x[i,n])
```

Here, `s(z)` is the so-called *sigmoid function,* defined as `s(z) = 1/(1+exp(z))`. If the `y[i]` are the probabilities that the `x[i,]` belong to the class of interest (in our example, that a flight with certain characteristics will be delayed), then the task of fitting is to find the `b[1], ..., b[n]` such that `f(x[i,])` is the best possible estimate of `y[i]`. R supplies a one-line command to find these coefficients: `glm()`.[4] Note that we don't need to supply `y[i]` that are probability estimates to run `glm()`; the training method only requires `y[i]` that say whether a given training example is in the target class.

The sigmoid function maps real numbers to the interval (0,1)—that is, to probabilities. The inverse of the sigmoid is the *logit,* which is defined as `log(p/(1-p))`, where `p` is a probability. The ratio `p/(1-p)` is known as the *odds,* so in the flight example, the logit is the log of the odds (or *log-odds*) that a flight will be delayed. In other words, you can think of logistic regression as a linear regression that finds the log-odds of the probability that you're interested in.

In particular, logistic regression assumes that `logit(y)` is linear in the values of `x`. Like linear regression, logistic regression will find the best coefficients to predict `y`, including finding advantageous combinations and cancellations when the inputs are correlated.

For the example task, imagine that you're working at a hospital. The goal is to design a plan that provisions neonatal emergency equipment to delivery rooms. Newborn

---

[3] Logistic regression is usually used to perform classification, but logistic regression and its close cousin *beta regression* are also useful in estimating *rates.* In fact, R's standard `glm()` call will work with prediction numeric values between 0 and 1.0 in addition to predicting classifications.

[4] Logistic regression can be used for classifying into any number of categories (as long as the categories are disjoint and cover all possibilities: every `x` has to belong to one of the given categories). But `glm()` only handles the two-category case, so our discussion will focus on this case.

babies are assessed at one and five minutes after birth using what's called the *Apgar test*, which is designed to determine if a baby needs immediate emergency care or extra medical attention. A baby who scores below 7 (on a scale from 0 to 10) on the Apgar scale needs extra attention.

Such at-risk babies are rare, so the hospital doesn't want to provision extra emergency equipment for every delivery. On the other hand, at-risk babies may need attention quickly, so provisioning resources proactively to appropriate deliveries can save lives. The goal of this project is to identify ahead of time situations with a higher probability of risk, so that resources can be allocated appropriately.

We'll use a sample dataset from the CDC 2010 natality public-use data file (http://mng.bz/pnGy). This dataset records statistics for all births registered in the 50 US States and the District of Columbia, including facts about the mother and father, and about the delivery. We'll use a sample of just over 26,000 births in a data frame called `sdata`.[5] The data is split into training and test sets, using the random grouping column that we added, as recommended in section 2.2.2.

Listing 7.7 Loading the CDC data

```
load("NatalRiskData.rData")
train <- sdata[sdata$ORIGRANDGROUP<=5,]
test <- sdata[sdata$ORIGRANDGROUP>5,]
```

Table 7.1 lists the columns of the dataset that we'll use. Because the goal is to anticipate at-risk infants ahead of time, we'll restrict variables to those whose values are known before delivery or can be determined during labor. For example, facts about the mother's weight or health history are valid inputs, but postbirth facts like infant birth weight are not. We can consider in-labor complications like breech birth by reasoning that the model can be updated in the delivery room (via a protocol or checklist) in time for emergency resources to be allocated before delivery.

Table 7.1 Some variables in natality dataset

Variable	Type	Description
`atRisk`	Logical	`TRUE` if 5-minute Apgar score < 7; `FALSE` otherwise
`PWGT`	Numeric	Mother's prepregnancy weight
`UPREVIS`	Numeric (integer)	Number of prenatal medical visits
`CIG_REC`	Logical	`TRUE` if smoker; `FALSE` otherwise
`GESTREC3`	Categorical	Two categories: `<37 weeks` (premature) and `>=37 weeks`

5 Our pre-prepared file is at https://github.com/WinVector/zmPDSwR/tree/master/CDC/NatalRiskData.rData; we also provide a script file (https://github.com/WinVector/zmPDSwR/blob/master/CDC/PrepNatalRiskData.R), which prepares the data frame from an extract of the full natality data set. Details found at https://github.com/WinVector/zmPDSwR/blob/master/CDC/README.md.

Table 7.1 Some variables in natality dataset *(continued)*

Variable	Type	Description
DPLURAL	Categorical	Birth plurality, three categories: single/twin/triplet+
ULD_MECO	Logical	TRUE if moderate/heavy fecal staining of amniotic fluid
ULD_PRECIP	Logical	TRUE for unusually short labor (< three hours)
ULD_BREECH	Logical	TRUE for breech (pelvis first) birth position
URF_DIAB	Logical	TRUE if mother is diabetic
URF_CHYPER	Logical	TRUE if mother has chronic hypertension
URF_PHYPER	Logical	TRUE if mother has pregnancy-related hypertension
URF_ECLAM	Logical	TRUE if mother experienced eclampsia: pregnancy-related seizures

Now we're ready to build the model.

7.2.2 Building a logistic regression model

The command to build a logistic regression model in R is `glm()`. In our case, the dependent variable `y` is the logical (or Boolean) `atRisk`; all the other variables in table 7.1 are the independent variables `x`. The formula for building a model to predict `atRisk` using these variables is rather long to type in by hand; you can generate the formula with the commands shown in the next listing.

Listing 7.8 Building the model formula

```
complications <- c("ULD_MECO","ULD_PRECIP","ULD_BREECH")
 riskfactors <- c("URF_DIAB", "URF_CHYPER", "URF_PHYPER",
                  "URF_ECLAM")
y <- "atRisk"
x <- c("PWGT",
       "UPREVIS",
       "CIG_REC",
       "GESTREC3",
       "DPLURAL",
       complications,
       riskfactors)
fmla <- paste(y, paste(x, collapse="+"), sep="~")
```

Now we build the logistic regression model, using the training dataset.

Listing 7.9 Fitting the logistic regression model

```
print(fmla)
[1] "atRisk ~ PWGT+UPREVIS+CIG_REC+GESTREC3+DPLURAL+ULD_MECO+ULD_PRECIP+
          ULD_BREECH+URF_DIAB+URF_CHYPER+URF_PHYPER+URF_ECLAM"

model <- glm(fmla, data=train, family=binomial(link="logit"))
```

This is similar to the linear regression call to `lm()`, with one additional argument: `family=binomial(link="logit")`. The `family` function specifies the assumed distribution of the dependent variable `y`. In our case, we're modeling `y` as a binomial distribution, or as a coin whose probability of heads depends on `x`. The `link` function "links" the output to a linear model—pass `y` through the `link` function, and then model the resulting value as a linear function of the `x` values. Different combinations of `family` functions and `link` functions lead to different kinds of generalized linear models (for example, Poisson, or probit). In this book, we'll only discuss logistic models, so we'll only need to use the binomial family with the logit link.

> **DON'T FORGET THE FAMILY ARGUMENT!** Without an explicit `family` argument, `glm` defaults to standard linear regression (like `lm`).

As before, we've stored the results in the object `model`.

7.2.3 Making predictions

Making predictions with a logistic model is similar to making predictions with a linear model—use the `predict()` function.

Listing 7.10 Applying the logistic regression model

```
train$pred <- predict(model, newdata=train, type="response")
test$pred <- predict(model, newdata=test, type="response")
```

We've again stored the predictions for the training and test sets as the column `pred` in the respective data frames. Note the additional parameter `type="response"`. This tells the `predict()` function to return the predicted probabilities `y`. If you don't specify `type="response"`, then by default `predict()` will return the output of the `link` function, `logit(y)`.

One strength of logistic regression is that it preserves the marginal probabilities of the training data. That means that if you sum up the predicted probability scores for the entire training set, that quantity will be equal to the number of positive outcomes (`atRisk == T`) in the training set. This is also true for subsets of the data determined by variables included in the model. For example, in the subset of the training data that has `train$GESTREC=="<37 weeks"` (the baby was premature), the sum of the predicted probabilities equals the number of positive training examples (see, for example http://mng.bz/j338).

CHARACTERIZING PREDICTION QUALITY

If our goal is to use the model to classify new instances into one of two categories (in this case, at-risk or not-at-risk), then we want the model to give high scores to positive instances and low scores otherwise. We can check if this is so by plotting the distribution of scores for both the positive and negative instances. Let's do this on the training set (we should also plot the test set, to make sure that the performance is of similar quality).

Listing 7.11 Plotting distribution of prediction score grouped by known outcome

```
library(ggplot2)
ggplot(train, aes(x=pred, color=atRisk, linetype=atRisk)) +
    geom_density()
```

The result is shown in figure 7.9. Ideally, we'd like the distribution of scores to be separated, with the scores of the negative instances (`FALSE`) to be concentrated on the left, and the distribution for the positive instances to be concentrated on the right. Earlier we showed an example of a classifier that separates the positives and the negatives quite well in figure 5.8. In the current case, both distributions are concentrated on the left, meaning that both positive and negative instances score low. This isn't surprising, since the positive instances (the ones with the baby at risk) are rare (about 1.8% of all births in the dataset). The distribution of scores for the negative instances dies off sooner than the distribution for positive instances. This means that the model did identify subpopulations in the data where the rate of at-risk newborns is higher than the average.

In order to use the model as a classifier, you must pick a threshold; scores above the threshold will be classified as positive, those below as negative. When you pick a threshold, you're trying to balance the *precision* of the classifier (what fraction of the predicted positives are true positives) and its *recall* (how many of the true positives the classifier finds).

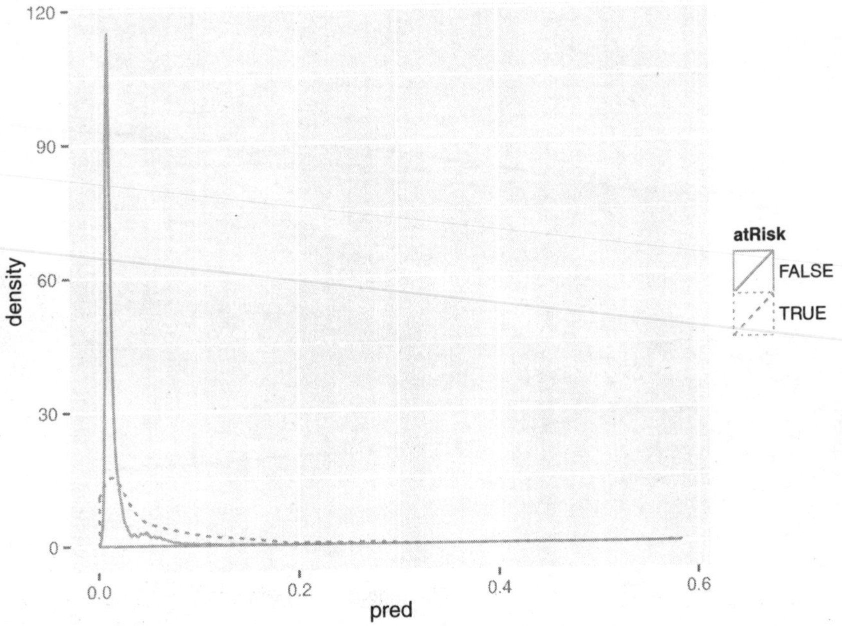

Figure 7.9 Distribution of score broken up by positive examples (`TRUE`) and negative examples (`FALSE`)

If the score distributions of the positive and negative instances are well separated, as in figure 5.8, we can pick an appropriate threshold in the "valley" between the two peaks. In the current case, the two distributions aren't well separated, which indicates that the model can't build a classifier that simultaneously achieves good recall and good precision. But we can build a classifier that identifies a subset of situations with a higher-than-average rate of at-risk births, so preprovisioning resources to those situations may be advised. We'll call the ratio of the classifier precision to the average rate of positives the *enrichment rate.*

The higher we set the threshold, the more precise the classifier will be (we'll identify a set of situations with a much higher-than-average rate of at-risk births); but we'll also miss a higher percentage of at-risk situations, as well. When picking the threshold, we'll use the training set, since picking the threshold is part of classifier-building. We can then use the test set to evaluate classifier performance.

To help pick the threshold, we can use a plot like figure 7.10, which shows both enrichment and recall as a functions of the threshold.

Looking at figure 7.10, you see that higher thresholds result in more precise classifications, at the cost of missing more cases; a lower threshold will identify more cases, at the cost of many more false positives. The best trade-off between precision and recall is a function of how many resources the hospital has available to allocate, and

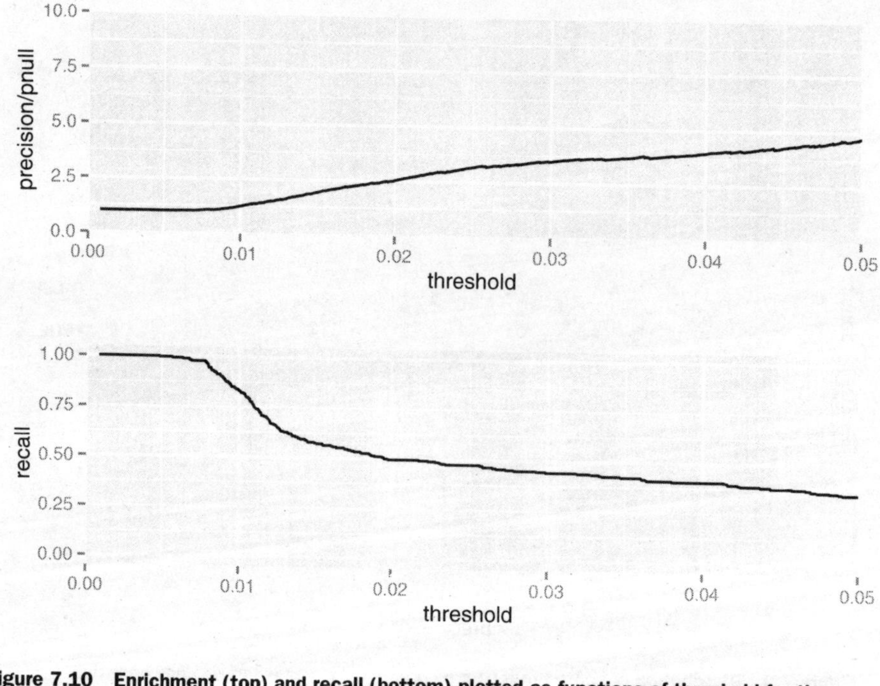

Figure 7.10 Enrichment (top) and recall (bottom) plotted as functions of threshold for the training set

how many they can keep in reserve (or redeploy) for situations that the classifier missed. A threshold of 0.02 (which incidentally is about the overall rate of at-risk births in the training data) might be a good trade-off. The resulting classifier will identify a set of potential at-risk situations that finds about half of all the true at-risk situations, with a true positive rate 2.5 times higher than the overall population.

We can produce figure 7.10 with the ROCR package, which we discussed in more detail in chapter 5.

Listing 7.12 Exploring modeling trade-offs

```
library(ROCR)
library(grid)

predObj <- prediction(train$pred, train$atRisk)
precObj <- performance(predObj, measure="prec")
recObj <- performance(predObj, measure="rec")

precision <- (precObj@y.values)[[1]]
prec.x <- (precObj@x.values)[[1]]
recall <- (recObj@y.values)[[1]]

rocFrame <- data.frame(threshold=prec.x, precision=precision,
                       recall=recall)

nplot <- function(plist) {
  n <- length(plist)
  grid.newpage()
  pushViewport(viewport(layout=grid.layout(n,1)))
  vplayout=function(x,y) {viewport(layout.pos.row=x, layout.pos.col=y)}
  for(i in 1:n) {
    print(plist[[i]], vp=vplayout(i,1))
  }
}

pnull <-
   mean(as.numeric(train$atRisk))

p1 <- ggplot(rocFrame, aes(x=threshold)) +
  geom_line(aes(y=precision/pnull)) +
  coord_cartesian(xlim = c(0,0.05), ylim=c(0,10) )
```

Load ROCR library.

Load grid library (you'll need this for the nplot function below).

Create ROCR prediction object.

Create ROCR object to calculate precision as a function of threshold.

Create ROCR object to calculate recall as a function of threshold.

ROCR objects are what R calls S4 objects; the slots (or fields) of an S4 object are stored as lists within the object. You extract the slots from an S4 object using @ notation.

The x values (thresholds) are the same in both predObj and recObj, so you only need to extract them once.

Build data frame with thresholds, precision, and recall.

Function to plot multiple plots on one page (stacked).

Calculate rate of at-risk births in the training set.

Plot enrichment rate as a function of threshold.

```
p2 <- ggplot(rocFrame, aes(x=threshold)) +     <-- Plot recall as a function of threshold.
  geom_line(aes(y=recall)) +
  coord_cartesian(xlim = c(0,0.05) )

nplot(list(p1, p2))                             <-- Show both plots simultaneously.
```

Once we've picked an appropriate threshold, we can evaluate the resulting classifier by looking at the confusion matrix, as we discussed in section 5.2.1. Let's use the test set to evaluate the classifier, with a threshold of 0.02.

Listing 7.13 Evaluating our chosen model

```
Build confusion matrix.
-> > ctab.test <- table(pred=test$pred>0.02, atRisk=test$atRisk)
 > ctab.test
       atRisk                              <-- Rows contain predicted negatives
pred    FALSE TRUE                             and positives; columns contain
  FALSE  9487   93                             actual negatives and positives.
  TRUE   2405  116
> precision <- ctab.test[2,2]/sum(ctab.test[2,])
> precision
[1] 0.04601349
> recall <- ctab.test[2,2]/sum(ctab.test[,2])
> recall
[1] 0.5550239
> enrich <- precision/mean(as.numeric(test$atRisk))
> enrich
[1] 2.664159
```

The resulting classifier is low-precision, but identifies a set of potential at-risk cases that contains 55.5% of the true positive cases in the test set, at a rate 2.66 times higher than the overall average. This is consistent with the results on the training set.

In addition to making predictions, a logistic regression model also helps you extract useful information and advice. We'll show this in the next section.

7.2.4 Finding relations and extracting advice from logistic models

The coefficients of a logistic regression model encode the relationships between the input variables and the output in a way similar to how the coefficients of a linear regression model do. You can get the model's coefficients with the call `coefficients(model)`.

Listing 7.14 The model coefficients

```
> coefficients(model)
              (Intercept)                          PWGT
              -4.41218940                    0.00376166
                  UPREVIS                   CIG_RECTRUE
              -0.06328943                    0.31316930
       GESTREC3< 37 weeks DPLURALtriplet or higher
               1.54518311                    1.39419294
              DPLURALtwin                  ULD_MECOTRUE
               0.31231871                    0.81842627
```

```
ULD_PRECIPTRUE          ULD_BREECHTRUE
    0.19172008              0.74923672
  URF_DIABTRUE          URF_CHYPERTRUE
   -0.34646672              0.56002503
URF_PHYPERTRUE           URF_ECLAMTRUE
    0.16159872              0.49806435
```

Negative coefficients that are statistically significant[6] correspond to variables that are negatively correlated to the odds (and hence to the probability) of a positive outcome (the baby being at risk). Positive coefficients that are statistically significant are positively correlated to the odds of a positive outcome.

As with linear regression, every categorical variable is expanded to a set of indicator variables. If the original variable has *n* levels, there will be *n*-1 indicator variables; the remaining level is the reference level.

For example, the variable `DPLURAL` has three levels corresponding to single births, twins, and triplets or higher. The logistic regression model has two corresponding coefficients: `DPLURALtwin` and `DPLURALtriplet or higher`. The reference level is single births. Both of the `DPLURAL` coefficients are positive, indicating that multiple births have higher odds of being at risk than single births do, all other variables being equal.

> **LOGISTIC REGRESSION ALSO DISLIKES A VERY LARGE VARIABLE COUNT** And as with linear regression, you should avoid categorical variables with too many levels.

INTERPRETING THE COEFFICIENTS

Interpreting coefficient values is a little more complicated with logistic than with linear regression. If the coefficient for the variable `x[,k]` is `b[k]`, then the odds of a positive outcome are multiplied by a factor of `exp(b[k])` for every unit change in `x[,k]`.

The coefficient for `GESTREC3< 37 weeks` (for a premature baby) is 1.545183. So for a premature baby, the odds of being at risk are `exp(1.545183)=4.68883` times higher compared to a baby that's born full-term, with all other input variables unchanged. As an example, suppose a full-term baby with certain characteristics has a 1% probability of being at risk (odds are `p/(1-p)`, or `0.01/0.99 = 0.0101`); then the odds for a premature baby with the same characteristics are `0.0101*4.68883 = 0.047`. This corresponds to a probability of being at risk of `odds/(1+odds)`, or `0.047/1.047`—about 4.5%.

Similarly, the coefficient for `UPREVIS` (number of prenatal medical visits) is about -0.06. This means every prenatal visit lowers the odds of an at-risk baby by a factor of `exp(-0.06)`, or about 0.94. Suppose the mother of our premature baby had made no prenatal visits; a baby in the same situation whose mother had made three prenatal visits would have odds of being at risk of about `0.047 * 0.94 * 0.94 * 0.94 = 0.039`. This corresponds to a probability of being at risk of 3.75%.

---

6 We'll show how to check for statistical significance in the next section.

So the general advice in this case might be to keep a special eye on premature births (and multiple births), and encourage expectant mothers to make regular prenatal visits

7.2.5 Reading the model summary and characterizing coefficients

As we mentioned earlier, conclusions about the coefficient values are only to be trusted if the coefficient values are statistically significant. We also want to make sure that the model is actually explaining something. The diagnostics in the model summary will help us determine some facts about model quality. The call, as before, is `summary(model)`.

Listing 7.15 The model summary

```
> summary(model)

Call:
glm(formula = fmla, family = binomial(link = "logit"), data = train)

Deviance Residuals:
    Min       1Q   Median       3Q      Max
-0.9732  -0.1818  -0.1511  -0.1358   3.2641

Coefficients:
                          Estimate Std. Error z value Pr(>|z|)
(Intercept)              -4.412189   0.289352 -15.249  < 2e-16 ***
PWGT                      0.003762   0.001487   2.530 0.011417 *
UPREVIS                  -0.063289   0.015252  -4.150 3.33e-05 ***
CIG_RECTRUE               0.313169   0.187230   1.673 0.094398 .
GESTREC3< 37 weeks        1.545183   0.140795  10.975  < 2e-16 ***
DPLURALtriplet or higher  1.394193   0.498866   2.795 0.005194 **
DPLURALtwin               0.312319   0.241088   1.295 0.195163
ULD_MECOTRUE              0.818426   0.235798   3.471 0.000519 ***
ULD_PRECIPTRUE            0.191720   0.357680   0.536 0.591951
ULD_BREECHTRUE            0.749237   0.178129   4.206 2.60e-05 ***
URF_DIABTRUE             -0.346467   0.287514  -1.205 0.228187
URF_CHYPERTRUE            0.560025   0.389678   1.437 0.150676
URF_PHYPERTRUE            0.161599   0.250003   0.646 0.518029
URF_ECLAMTRUE             0.498064   0.776948   0.641 0.521489
---
Signif. codes:  0 '***' 0.001 '**' 0.01 '*' 0.05 '.' 0.1 ' ' 1

(Dispersion parameter for binomial family taken to be 1)

    Null deviance: 2698.7  on 14211  degrees of freedom
Residual deviance: 2463.0  on 14198  degrees of freedom
AIC: 2491

Number of Fisher Scoring iterations: 7
```

THE ORIGINAL MODEL CALL

The first line of the summary is the call to `glm()`:

```
Call:
glm(formula = fmla, family = binomial(link = "logit"), data = train)
```

Here is where we check that we've used the correct training set and the correct formula (although in our case, the formula itself is in another variable). We can also verify that we used the correct family and link function to produce a logistic model.

THE DEVIANCE RESIDUALS SUMMARY

The deviance residuals are the analog to the residuals of a linear regression model:

```
Deviance Residuals:
    Min        1Q    Median        3Q       Max
-0.9732   -0.1818   -0.1511   -0.1358    3.2641
```

In linear regression, the residuals are the vector of differences between the true outcome values and the predicted output values (the errors). In logistic regression, the deviance residuals are related to the *log likelihoods* of having observed the true outcome, given the predicted probability of that outcome. The idea behind log likelihood is that positive instances `y` should have high probability `py` of occurring under the model; negative instances should have low probability of occurring (or putting it another way, `(1-py)` should be large). The log likelihood function rewards "matches" between the outcome `y` and the predicted probability `py`, and penalizes mismatches (high `py` for negative instances, and vice versa).

Listing 7.16 Calculating deviance residuals

```
pred <- predict(model, newdata=train, type="response")
 llcomponents <- function(y, py) {
   y*log(py) + (1-y)*log(1-py)
}

edev <- sign(as.numeric(train$atRisk) - pred) *
   sqrt(-2*llcomponents(as.numeric(train$atRisk), pred))

> summary(edev)
   Min. 1st Qu.  Median    Mean 3rd Qu.    Max.
-0.9732 -0.1818 -0.1511 -0.1244 -0.1358  3.2640
```

Create vector of predictions for training data.

Function to return the log likelihoods for each data point. Argument y is the true outcome (as a numeric variable, 0/1); argument py is the predicted probability.

Calculate deviance residuals.

Linear regression models are found by minimizing the sum of the squared residuals; logistic regression models are found by minimizing the sum of the squared residual deviances, which is equivalent to maximizing the log likelihood of the data, given the model.

Logistic models can also be used to explicitly compute rates: given several groups of identical data points (identical except the outcome), predict the rate of positive outcomes in each group. This kind of data is called *grouped data*. In the case of grouped data, the deviance residuals can be used as a diagnostic for model fit. This is why the deviance residuals are included in the summary. We're using *ungrouped data*—every data point in the training set is potentially unique. In the case of ungrouped data, the model fit diagnostics that use the deviance residuals are no longer valid.[7]

---

[7] See Daniel Powers and Yu Xie, *Statistical Methods for Categorical Data Analysis, 2nd Ed.*, Emerald Group Publishing Ltd., 2008.

THE SUMMARY COEFFICIENTS TABLE

The summary coefficients table for logistic regression has the same format as the coefficients table for linear regression:

```
Coefficients:
                            Estimate Std. Error z value Pr(>|z|)
(Intercept)                -4.412189   0.289352 -15.249  < 2e-16 ***
PWGT                        0.003762   0.001487   2.530 0.011417 *
UPREVIS                    -0.063289   0.015252  -4.150 3.33e-05 ***
CIG_RECTRUE                 0.313169   0.187230   1.673 0.094398 .
GESTREC3< 37 weeks          1.545183   0.140795  10.975  < 2e-16 ***
DPLURALtriplet or higher    1.394193   0.498866   2.795 0.005194 **
DPLURALtwin                 0.312319   0.241088   1.295 0.195163
ULD_MECOTRUE                0.818426   0.235798   3.471 0.000519 ***
ULD_PRECIPTRUE              0.191720   0.357680   0.536 0.591951
ULD_BREECHTRUE              0.749237   0.178129   4.206 2.60e-05 ***
URF_DIABTRUE               -0.346467   0.287514  -1.205 0.228187
URF_CHYPERTRUE              0.560025   0.389678   1.437 0.150676
URF_PHYPERTRUE              0.161599   0.250003   0.646 0.518029
URF_ECLAMTRUE               0.498064   0.776948   0.641 0.521489
---
Signif. codes:  0 '***' 0.001 '**' 0.01 '*' 0.05 '.' 0.1 ' ' 1
```

The columns of the table represent

- A coefficient
- Its estimated value
- The error around that estimate
- The signed distance of the estimated coefficient value from 0 (using the standard error as the unit of distance)
- The probability of seeing a coefficient value at least as large as we observed, under the null hypothesis that the coefficient value is really 0

This last value, called the *p-value* or *significance*, tells us whether we should trust the estimated coefficient value. The standard rule of thumb is that coefficients with p-values less than 0.05 are reliable, although some researchers prefer stricter thresholds.

For the birth data, we can see from the coefficient summary that premature birth and triplet birth are strong predictors of the newborn needing extra medical attention: the coefficient magnitudes are non-negligible and the p-values indicate significance. Other variables that affect the outcome are the mother's prepregnancy weight (heavier mothers indicate higher risk—slightly surprising); the number of prenatal medical visits (the more visits, the lower the risk); meconium staining in the amniotic fluid; and breech position at birth. There might be a positive correlation between mother's smoking and an at-risk birth, but the data doesn't indicate it definitively. None of the other variables show a strong relationship to an at-risk birth.

Lack of significance could mean collinear inputs

As with linear regression, logistic regression can predict well with collinear (or correlated) inputs, but the correlations can mask good advice.

To see this for yourself, we left data about the babies' birth weight in grams in the dataset `sdata`. It's present in both the test and training data as the column `DBWT`. Try adding `DBWT` to the logistic regression model in addition to all the other variables; you'll see that the coefficient for baby's birth weight will be non-negligible (has a substantial impact on prediction) and significant, and negatively correlated with risk. The coefficient for `DPLURALtriplet or higher` will appear insignificant, and the coefficient for `GESTREC3< 37 weeks` has a much smaller magnitude. This is because low birth weight is correlated to both prematurity and multiple birth. Of the three related variables, birth weight is the best single predictor of the outcome: knowing that the baby is a triplet adds no additional useful information, and knowing the baby is premature adds only a little information.

In the context of the modeling goal—to proactively allocate emergency resources where they're more likely to be needed—birth weight isn't as useful a variable, because we don't know the baby's weight until it's born. We do know ahead of time if it's being born prematurely, or if it's one of multiple babies. So it's better to use `GESTREC3` and `DPLURAL` as input variables, instead of `DBWT`.

Other signs of possibly collinear inputs are coefficients with the wrong sign and unusually large coefficient magnitudes.

OVERALL MODEL QUALITY SUMMARIES

The next section of the summary contains the model quality statistics:

```
Null deviance: 2698.7  on 14211  degrees of freedom
Residual deviance: 2463.0  on 14198  degrees of freedom
AIC: 2491
```

Null and residual deviances

Deviance is again a measure of how well the model fits the data. It is 2 times the negative log likelihood of the dataset, given the model. If you think of deviance as analogous to variance, then the *null deviance* is similar to the variance of the data around the average rate of positive examples. The *residual deviance* is similar to the variance of the data around the model. We can calculate the deviances for both the training and test sets.

Listing 7.17 Computing deviance

```
loglikelihood <- function(y, py) {
   sum(y * log(py) + (1-y)*log(1 - py))
}

pnull <- mean(as.numeric(train$atRisk))
```

Function to calculate the log likelihood of a dataset. Variable y is the outcome in numeric form (1 for positive examples, 0 for negative). Variable py is the predicted probability that y==1.

Calculate rate of positive examples in dataset.

```
null.dev <- -2*loglikelihood(as.numeric(train$atRisk), pnull)    # Calculate null deviance.

> pnull
[1] 0.01920912
> null.dev
[1] 2698.716
> model$null.deviance        # For training data, the null deviance is stored in the slot model$null.deviance.
 [1] 2698.716

pred <- predict(model, newdata=train, type="response")    # Predict probabilities for training data.
 resid.dev <- -
     2*loglikelihood(as.numeric(train$atRisk), pred)    # Calculate deviance of model for training data.

> resid.dev
[1] 2462.992
> model$deviance        # For training data, model deviance is stored in the slot model$deviance.
 [1] 2462.992

testy <- as.numeric(test$atRisk)    # Calculate null deviance and residual deviance for test data.
 testpred <- predict(model, newdata=test,
                        type="response")
pnull.test <- mean(testy)
null.dev.test <- -2*loglikelihood(testy, pnull.test)
resid.dev.test <- -2*loglikelihood(testy, testpred)

> pnull.test
[1] 0.0172713
> null.dev.test
[1] 2110.91
> resid.dev.test
[1] 1947.094
```

The first thing we can do with the null and residual deviances is check whether the model's probability predictions are better than just guessing the average rate of positives, statistically speaking. In other words, is the reduction in deviance from the model meaningful, or just something that was observed by chance? This is similar to calculating the F-test statistics that are reported for linear regression. In the case of logistic regression, the test you'll run is the *chi-squared test*. To do that, you need to know the degrees of freedom for the null model and the actual model (which are reported in the summary). The degrees of freedom of the null model is the number of data points minus 1: `df.null = dim(train)[[1]] - 1`. The degrees of freedom of the model that you fit is the number of data points minus the number of coefficients in the model: `df.model = dim(train)[[1]] - length(model$coefficients)`.

If the number of data points in the training set is large, and `df.null - df.model` is small, then the probability of the difference in deviances `null.dev - resid.dev` being as large as we observed is approximately distributed as a chi-squared distribution with `df.null - df.model` degrees of freedom.

Listing 7.18 Calculating the significance of the observed fit

```
df.null <- dim(train)[[1]] - 1
df.model <- dim(train)[[1]] -
     length(model$coefficients)

> df.null
[1] 14211
> df.model
[1] 14198

delDev <- null.dev - resid.dev
deldf <- df.null - df.model
p <- pchisq(delDev, deldf, lower.tail=F)

> delDev
[1] 235.724
> deldf
[1] 13
> p
[1] 5.84896e-43
```

Null model has (number of data points - l) degrees of freedom.

Fitted model has (number of data points - number of coefficients) degrees of freedom.

Compute difference in deviances and difference in degrees of freedom.

Estimate probability of seeing the observed difference in deviances under null model (the p-value) using chi-squared distribution.

The p-value is very small; it's extremely unlikely that we could've seen this much reduction in deviance by chance.

The pseudo R-squared

A useful goodness of fit measure based on the deviances is the pseudo R-squared: `1 - (dev.model/dev.null)`. The pseudo R-squared is the analog to the R-squared measure for linear regression. It's a measure of how much of the deviance is "explained" by the model. Ideally, you want the pseudo R-squared to be close to 1. Let's calculate the pseudo-R-squared for both the test and training data.

Listing 7.19 Calculating the pseudo R-squared

```
pr2 <- 1-(resid.dev/null.dev)

> print(pr2)
[1] 0.08734674
> pr2.test <- 1-(resid.dev.test/null.dev.test)
> print(pr2.test)
[1] 0.07760427
```

The model only explains about 7.7–8.7% of the deviance; it's not a highly predictive model (you should have suspected that already, from figure 7.9). This tells us that we haven't yet identified all the factors that actually predict at-risk births.

Goodness of fit versus significance

It's worth noting that the model we found is a legitimate model, just not a complete one. The good p-value tells us that the model is legitimate: it gives us more information than the average rate of at-risk births does alone. The poor pseudo R-squared means that the model isn't giving us enough information to predict at-risk births with high reliability.

It's also possible to have good pseudo R-squared (on the training data) with a bad p-value. This is an indication of overfit. That's why it's a good idea to check both, or better yet, check the pseudo R-squared of the model on both training and test data.

The AIC

The last metric given in the section of the summary is the AIC, or the *Akaike information criterion.* The AIC is the log likelihood adjusted for the number of coefficients. Just as the R-squared of a linear regression is generally higher when the number of variables is higher, the log likelihood also increases with the number of variables.

Listing 7.20 Calculating the Akaike information criterion

```
aic <- 2*(length(model$coefficients) -
          loglikelihood(as.numeric(train$atRisk), pred))
> aic
[1] 2490.992
```

The AIC is usually used to decide which and how many input variables to use in the model. If you train many different models with different sets of variables on the same training set, you can consider the model with the lowest AIC to be the best fit.

FISHER SCORING ITERATIONS

The last line of the model summary is the number of Fisher scoring iterations:

```
Number of Fisher Scoring iterations: 7
```

The Fisher scoring method is an iterative optimization method similar to Newton's method that `glm()` uses to find the best coefficients for the logistic regression model. You should expect it to converge in about six to eight iterations. If there are more iterations than that, then the algorithm may not have converged, and the model may not be valid.

Separation and quasi-separation

The probable reason for nonconvergence is separation or quasi-separation: one of the model variables or some combination of the model variables predicts the outcome perfectly for at least a subset of the training data. You'd think this would be a good thing, but ironically logistic regression fails when the variables are too powerful. Ideally, `glm()` will issue a warning when it detects separation or quasi-separation:

```
Warning message:
glm.fit: fitted probabilities numerically 0 or 1 occurred
```

Unfortunately, there are situations when it seems that no warning is issued, but there are other warning signs:

- An unusually high number of Fisher iterations
- Very large coefficients, usually with extremely large standard errors
- Residual deviances larger than the null deviances

If you see any of these signs, the model is suspect. To try to fix the problem, remove any variables with unusually large coefficients; they're probably causing the separation. You can try using a decision tree on the variables that you remove to detect regions of perfect prediction. The data that the decision tree doesn't predict perfectly on can still be used for building a logistic regression model. The overall model would then be a hybrid: the decision tree to predict the too-good data, and a logistic regression model for the rest.

The right way to deal with separation

We admit, it doesn't feel right to remove variables or data that are "too good" from the modeling process. The correct way to handle separation is to regularize. Unfortunately, the default, `glm()` doesn't regularize. The package `glmnet` can. But its calling interface isn't the standard interface that `lm()`, `glm()`, and other modeling functions in this book use. It also doesn't have the nice diagnostic output of the other packages. For these reasons, we consider a discussion of `glmnet` beyond the scope of this book.

To regularize `glm()` in an ad hoc way, you can use the `weights` argument. The `weights` argument lets you pass a vector of weights (one per datum) to the `glm()` call. Add another copy of the data, but with *opposite* outcomes, and use this faux data in `glm()` with a small weight. An example of this trick can be found in the blog article "A Pathological GLM Problem that Doesn't Issue a Warning" (http://mng.bz/G8RS).

Another way to deal with separation is to build a two-stage model starting with a decision tree (section 6.3.2) and use a different `glm()` for a different set of variables on each induced partition of your data.

7.2.6 *Logistic regression takeaways*

What you should remember about logistic regression:

- Logistic regression is the go-to statistical modeling method for binary classification. Try logistic regression first, and then more complicated methods if logistic regression doesn't perform well.
- Logistic regression will have trouble with problems with a very large number of variables, or categorical variables with a very large number of levels.
- Logistic regression is well calibrated: it reproduces the marginal probabilities of the data.
- Logistic regression can predict well even in the presence of correlated variables, but correlated variables lower the quality of the advice.

- Overly large coefficient magnitudes, overly large standard errors on the coefficient estimates, and the wrong sign on a coefficient could be indications of correlated inputs.
- Too many Fisher iterations, or overly large coefficients with very large standard errors, could be signs that an input or combination of inputs is perfectly correlated with a subset of your responses. You may have to segment the data to deal with this issue.
- `glm()` provides good diagnostics, but rechecking your model on test data is still your most effective diagnostic.
- Pseudo R-squared is a useful goodness-of-fit heuristic.

7.3 Summary

In this chapter, you've started building models that go beyond training data memorization and infer a functional form of model. You've learned how to predict numerical quantities with linear regression models and to predict probabilities or classify using logistic regression models. You've also learned how to interpret the models that you've produced.

Both linear and logistic regression assume that the outcome is a function of a linear combination of the inputs. This seems restrictive, but in practice linear and logistic regression models can perform well even when the theoretical assumptions aren't exactly met. We'll show how to further work around these limits in chapter 9.

Linear and logistic regression can also provide *advice* by quantifying the relationships between the outcomes and the model's inputs. Since the models are expressed completely by their coefficients, they're small, portable, and efficient—all valuable qualities when putting a model into production. If the model's errors are homoscedastic (uncorrelated with y), the model might be trusted to extrapolate predictions outside the training range. Extrapolation is never completely safe, but it's sometimes necessary.

The methods that we discussed in this chapter and in the previous chapter use data about known outcomes to build models that predict future outcomes. But what if you don't yet know what to predict? The next chapter looks at *unsupervised methods*: algorithms that discover previously unknown relationships in data.

Key takeaways

- Functional models allow you to better explore how changes in inputs affect predictions.
- Linear regression is a good first technique for modeling quantities.
- Logistic regression is good first technique for modeling probabilities.
- Models with simple forms come with very powerful summaries and diagnostics.

8 *Unsupervised methods*

This chapter covers

- Using R's clustering functions to explore data and look for similarities
- Choosing the right number of clusters
- Evaluating a clustering
- Using R's association rules functions to find patterns of co-occurrence in data
- Evaluating a set of association rules

The methods that we've discussed in previous chapters build models to predict outcomes. In this chapter, we'll look at methods to discover unknown relationships in data. These methods are called *unsupervised methods*. With unsupervised methods, there's no outcome that you're trying to predict; instead, you want to discover patterns in the data that perhaps you hadn't previously suspected. For example, you may want to find groups of customers with similar purchase patterns, or correlations between population movement and socioeconomic factors. Unsupervised analyses are often not ends in themselves; rather, they're ways of finding relationships and patterns that can be used to build predictive models. In fact, we encourage you to think of unsupervised methods as exploratory—procedures that help you get your hands in the data—rather than as black-box approaches that mysteriously and automatically give you "the right answer."

In this chapter, we'll look at two classes of unsupervised methods. *Cluster analysis* finds groups in your data with similar characteristics. *Association rule mining* finds elements or properties in the data that tend to occur together.

8.1 Cluster analysis

In cluster analysis, the goal is to group the observations in your data into *clusters* such that every datum in a cluster is more similar to other datums in the same cluster than it is to datums in other clusters. For example, a company that offers guided tours might want to cluster its clients by behavior and tastes: which countries they like to visit; whether they prefer adventure tours, luxury tours, or educational tours; what kinds of activities they participate in; and what sorts of sites they like to visit. Such information can help the company design attractive travel packages and target the appropriate segments of their client base with them.

Cluster analysis is a topic worthy of a book in itself; in this chapter, we'll discuss two approaches. *Hierarchical clustering* finds nested groups of clusters. An example of hierarchical clustering might be the standard plant taxonomy, which classifies plants by family, then genus, then species, and so on. The second approach we'll cover is *k-means*, which is a quick and popular way of finding clusters in quantitative data.

> **Clustering and density estimation**
> Historically, cluster analysis is related to the problem of *density estimation*: if you think of your data as living in a large dimensional space, then you want to find the regions of the space where the data is densest. If those regions are distinct, or nearly so, then you have clusters.

8.1.1 Distances

In order to cluster, you need the notions of *similarity* and *dissimilarity*. Dissimilarity can be thought of as distance, so that the points in a cluster are closer to each other than they are to the points in other clusters. This is shown in figure 8.1.

Different application areas will have different notions of distance and dissimilarity. In this section, we'll cover a few of the most common ones:

- Euclidean distance
- Hamming distance
- Manhattan (city block) distance
- Cosine similarity

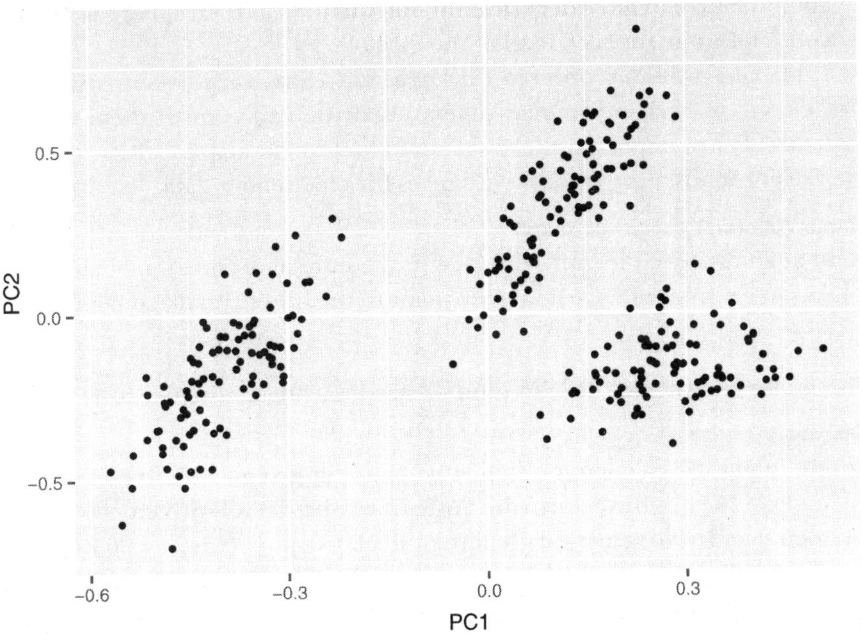

Figure 8.1 An example of data in three clusters

EUCLIDEAN DISTANCE

The most common distance is *Euclidean distance.* The Euclidean distance between two vectors x and y is defined as

```
edist(x, y) <- sqrt((x[1]-y[1])^2 + (x[2]-y[2])^2 + ...)
```

This is the measure people tend to think of when they think of "distance." Optimizing squared Euclidean distance is the basis of k-means. Of course, Euclidean distance only makes sense when all the data is real-valued (quantitative). If the data is categorical (in particular, binary), then other distances can be used.

HAMMING DISTANCE

For categorical variables (`male/female`, or `small/medium/large`), you can define the distance as `0` if two points are in the same category, and `1` otherwise. If all the variables are categorical, then you can use *Hamming distance,* which counts the number of mismatches:

```
hdist(x, y) <- sum((x[1] != y[1]) + (x[2] != y[2]) + ...)
```

Here, `a != b` is defined to have a value of `1` if the expression is true, and a value of `0` if the expression is false.

You can also expand categorical variables to indicator variables (as we discussed in section 7.1.4), one for each level of the variable.

If the categories are ordered (like `small/medium/large`) so that some categories are "closer" to each other than others, then you can convert them to a numerical sequence. For example, (`small/medium/large`) might map to (`1/2/3`). Then you can use Euclidean distance, or other distances for quantitative data.

MANHATTAN (CITY BLOCK) DISTANCE

Manhattan distance measures distance in the number of horizontal and vertical units it takes to get from one (real-valued) point to the other (no diagonal moves):

```
mdist(x, y) <- sum(abs(x[1]-y[1]) + abs(x[2]-y[2]) + ...)
```

This is also known as *L1 distance* (and squared Euclidean distance is *L2 distance*).

COSINE SIMILARITY

Cosine similarity is a common similarity metric in text analysis. It measures the smallest angle between two vectors (the angle `theta` between two vectors is assumed to be between 0 and 90 degrees). Two perpendicular vectors (`theta` = 90 degrees) are the most dissimilar; the cosine of 90 degrees is 0. Two parallel vectors are the most similar (identical, if you assume they're both based at the origin); the cosine of 0 degrees is 1. From elementary geometry, you can derive that the cosine of the angle between two vectors is given by the normalized dot product between the two vectors:

```
dot(x, y) <- sum( x[1]*y[1] + x[2]*y[2] + ... )
cossim(x, y) <- dot(x, y)/(sqrt(dot(x,x)*dot(y,y)))
```

You can turn the cosine similarity into a pseudo distance by subtracting it from 1.0 (though to get an actual metric, you should use `1 - 2*acos(cossim(x,y))/pi`).

Different distance metrics will give you different clusters, as will different clustering algorithms. The application domain may give you a hint as to the most appropriate distance, or you can try several distance metrics. In this chapter, we'll use (squared) Euclidean distance, as it's the most natural distance for quantitative data.

8.1.2 Preparing the data

To demonstrate clustering, we'll use a small dataset from 1973 on protein consumption from nine different food groups in 25 countries in Europe.[1] The goal is to group the countries based on patterns in their protein consumption. The dataset is loaded into R as a data frame called `protein`, as shown in the next listing.

---

1 The original dataset can be found at http://mng.bz/y2Vw. A tab-separated text file with the data can be found at https://github.com/WinVector/zmPDSwR/tree/master/Protein/. The data file is called protein.txt; additional information can be found in the file protein_README.txt.

Listing 8.1 Reading the protein data

```
protein <- read.table("protein.txt", sep="\t", header=TRUE)
summary(protein)
          Country       RedMeat          WhiteMeat           Eggs
 Albania       : 1   Min.   : 4.400   Min.   : 1.400   Min.   :0.500
 Austria       : 1   1st Qu.: 7.800   1st Qu.: 4.900   1st Qu.:2.700
 Belgium       : 1   Median : 9.500   Median : 7.800   Median :2.900
 Bulgaria      : 1   Mean   : 9.828   Mean   : 7.896   Mean   :2.936
 Czechoslovakia: 1   3rd Qu.:10.600   3rd Qu.:10.800   3rd Qu.:3.700
 Denmark       : 1   Max.   :18.000   Max.   :14.000   Max.   :4.700
 (Other)       :19
      Milk            Fish           Cereals          Starch
 Min.   : 4.90   Min.   : 0.200   Min.   :18.60   Min.   :0.600
 1st Qu.:11.10   1st Qu.: 2.100   1st Qu.:24.30   1st Qu.:3.100
 Median :17.60   Median : 3.400   Median :28.00   Median :4.700
 Mean   :17.11   Mean   : 4.284   Mean   :32.25   Mean   :4.276
 3rd Qu.:23.30   3rd Qu.: 5.800   3rd Qu.:40.10   3rd Qu.:5.700
 Max.   :33.70   Max.   :14.200   Max.   :56.70   Max.   :6.500

      Nuts           Fr.Veg
 Min.   :0.700   Min.   :1.400
 1st Qu.:1.500   1st Qu.:2.900
 Median :2.400   Median :3.800
 Mean   :3.072   Mean   :4.136
 3rd Qu.:4.700   3rd Qu.:4.900
 Max.   :7.800   Max.   :7.900
```

UNITS AND SCALING

The documentation for this dataset doesn't mention what the units of measurement are, though we can assume all the columns are measured in the same units. This is important: units (or more precisely, disparity in units) affect what clusterings an algorithm will discover. If you measure vital statistics of your subjects as age in years, height in feet, and weight in pounds, you'll get different distances—and possibly different clusters—than if you measure age in years, height in meters, and weight in kilograms.

Ideally, you want a unit of change in each coordinate to represent the same degree of difference. In the `protein` dataset, we assume that the measurements are all in the same units, so it might seem that we're okay. This may well be a correct assumption, but different food groups provide different amounts of protein. Animal-based food sources in general have more grams of protein per serving than plant-based food sources, so one could argue that a change in consumption of 5 grams is a bigger difference in terms of vegetable consumption than it is in terms of red meat consumption.

One way to try to make the clustering more coordinate-free is to transform all the columns to have a mean value of 0 and a standard deviation of 1. This makes the standard deviation the unit of measurement in each coordinate. Assuming that your training data has a distribution that accurately represents the population at large, then a standard deviation represents approximately the same degree of difference in every coordinate. You can scale the data in R using the function `scale()`.

Listing 8.2 Rescaling the dataset

```
vars.to.use <- colnames(protein)[-1]
pmatrix <- scale(protein[,vars.to.use])
pcenter <- attr(pmatrix, "scaled:center")
pscale <- attr(pmatrix, "scaled:scale")
```

Use all the columns except the first (Country).

The output of scale() is a matrix. For the purposes of this chapter, you can think of a matrix as a data frame with all numeric columns (this isn't strictly true, but it's close enough).

The scale() function annotates its output with two attributes—scaled:center returns the mean values of all the columns, and scaled:scale returns the standard deviations. You'll store these away so you can "unscale" the data later.

Now on to clustering. We'll start with hierarchical.

8.1.3 Hierarchical clustering with hclust()

The `hclust()` function takes as input a distance matrix (as an object of class `dist`), which records the distances between all pairs of points in the data (using any one of a variety of metrics). It returns a *dendrogram*: a tree that represents the nested clusters. `hclust()` uses one of a variety of clustering methods to produce a tree that records the nested cluster structure. You can compute the distance matrix using the function `dist()`.

`dist()` will calculate distance functions using the (squared) Euclidean distance (`method="euclidean"`), the Manhattan distance (`method="manhattan"`), and something like the Hamming distance, when categorical variables are expanded to indicators (`method="binary"`). If you want to use another distance metric, you'll have to compute the appropriate distance matrix and convert it to a `dist` object using the `as.dist()` call (see `help(dist)` for further details).

Let's cluster the protein data. We'll use Ward's method, which starts out with each data point as an individual cluster and merges clusters iteratively so as to minimize the *total within sum of squares (WSS)* of the clustering (we'll explain more about WSS later in the chapter).

Listing 8.3 Hierarchical clustering

```
d <- dist(pmatrix, method="euclidean")      <-- Create the distance matrix.
pfit <- hclust(d, method="ward")            <-- Do the clustering.
plot(pfit, labels=protein$Country)          <-- Plot the dendrogram.
```

The dendrogram suggests five clusters (as shown in figure 8.2). You can draw the rectangles on the dendrogram using the function `rect.hclust()`:

```
rect.hclust(pfit, k=5)
```

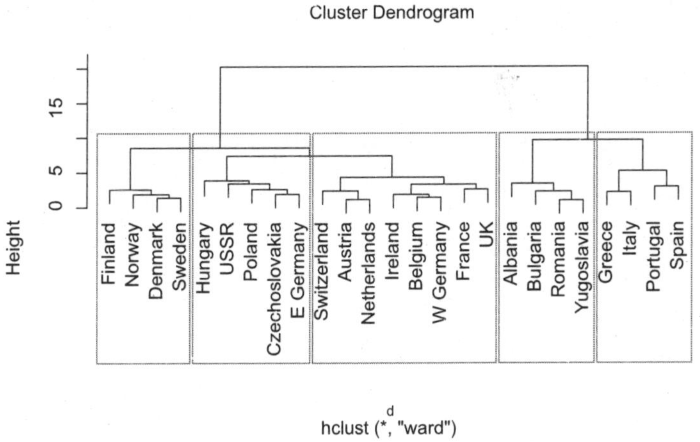

Figure 8.2 Dendrogram of countries clustered by protein consumption

To extract the members of each cluster from the `hclust` object, use `cutree()`.

Listing 8.4 Extracting the clusters found by `hclust()`

```
groups <- cutree(pfit, k=5)

print_clusters <- function(labels, k) {
  for(i in 1:k) {
    print(paste("cluster", i))
    print(protein[labels==i,c("Country","RedMeat","Fish","Fr.Veg")])
  }
}

> print_clusters(groups, 5)
[1] "cluster 1"
      Country RedMeat Fish Fr.Veg
1     Albania    10.1  0.2    1.7
4    Bulgaria     7.8  1.2    4.2
18    Romania     6.2  1.0    2.8
25 Yugoslavia     4.4  0.6    3.2
[1] "cluster 2"
       Country RedMeat Fish Fr.Veg
2      Austria     8.9  2.1    4.3
3      Belgium    13.5  4.5    4.0
9       France    18.0  5.7    6.5
12     Ireland    13.9  2.2    2.9
14 Netherlands     9.5  2.5    3.7
21 Switzerland    13.1  2.3    4.9
22          UK    17.4  4.3    3.3
24   W Germany    11.4  3.4    3.8
[1] "cluster 3"
          Country RedMeat Fish Fr.Veg
5  Czechoslovakia     9.7  2.0    4.0
7       E Germany     8.4  5.4    3.6
11        Hungary     5.3  0.3    4.2
```

A convenience function for printing out the countries in each cluster, along with the values for red meat, fish, and fruit/vegetable consumption. We'll use this function throughout this section. Note that the function is hardcoded for the protein dataset.

```
16         Poland     6.9  3.0    6.6
23           USSR     9.3  3.0    2.9
[1] "cluster 4"
   Country RedMeat Fish Fr.Veg
6  Denmark    10.6  9.9    2.4
8  Finland     9.5  5.8    1.4
15  Norway     9.4  9.7    2.7
20  Sweden     9.9  7.5    2.0
[1] "cluster 5"
    Country RedMeat Fish Fr.Veg
10   Greece    10.2  5.9    6.5
13    Italy     9.0  3.4    6.7
17 Portugal     6.2 14.2    7.9
19    Spain     7.1  7.0    7.2
```

There's a certain logic to these clusters: the countries in each cluster tend to be in the same geographical region. It makes sense that countries in the same region would have similar dietary habits. You can also see that

- Cluster 2 is made of countries with higher-than-average red meat consumption.
- Cluster 4 contains countries with higher-than-average fish consumption but low produce consumption.
- Cluster 5 contains countries with high fish and produce consumption.

This dataset has only 25 points; it's harder to "eyeball" the clusters and the cluster members when there are very many data points. In the next few sections, we'll look at some ways to examine clusters more holistically.

VISUALIZING CLUSTERS

As we mentioned in chapter 3, visualization is an effective way to get an overall view of the data, or in this case, the clusters. We can try to visualize the clustering by projecting the data onto the first two *principal components* of the data.[2] If N is the number of variables that describe the data, then the principal components describe the hyperellipsoid in N-space that bounds the data. If you order the principal components by the length of the hyperellipsoid's corresponding axes (longest first), then the first two principal components describe a plane in N-space that captures as much of the variation of the data as can be captured in two dimensions. We'll use the `prcomp()` call to do the principal components decomposition.

Listing 8.5 Projecting the clusters on the first two principal components

```
library(ggplot2)
princ <- prcomp(pmatrix)
nComp <- 2
project <- predict(princ, newdata=pmatrix)[,1:nComp]
```

Calculate the principal components of the data. (annotates `princ <- prcomp(pmatrix)`)

The predict() function will rotate the data into the space described by the principal components. We only want the projection on the first two axes. (annotates `project <- predict(...)`)

---

2 We can project the data onto any two of the principal components, but the first two are the most likely to show useful information.

```
project.plus <- cbind(as.data.frame(project),
                      cluster=as.factor(groups),
                      country=protein$Country)
ggplot(project.plus, aes(x=PC1, y=PC2)) +
  geom_point(aes(shape=cluster)) +
  geom_text(aes(label=country),
            hjust=0, vjust=1)
```

Create a data frame with the transformed data, along with the cluster label and country label of each point.

Plot it.

You can see in figure 8.3 that the Romania/Yugoslavia/Bulgaria/Albania cluster and the Mediterranean cluster (Spain and so on) are separated from the others. The other three clusters co-mingle in this projection, though they're probably more separated in other projections.

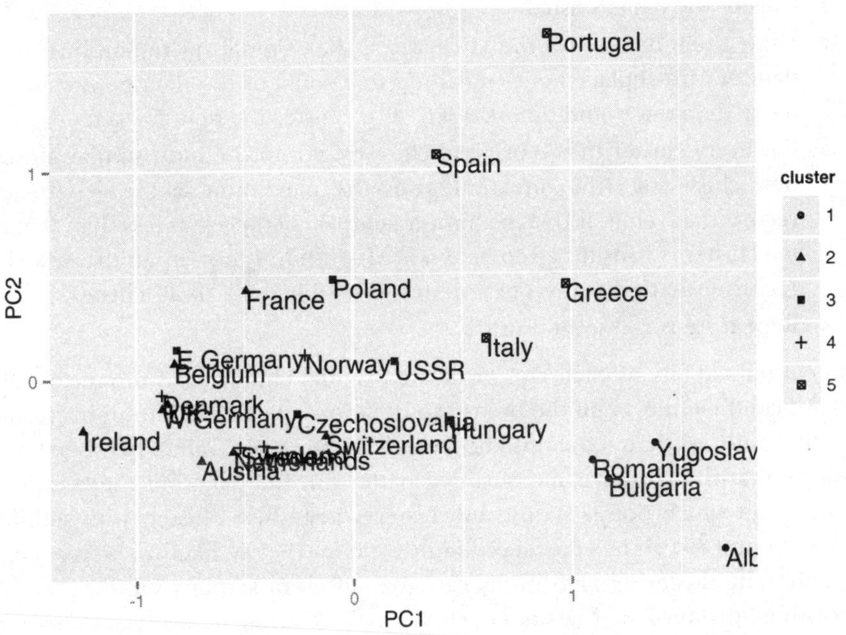

Figure 8.3 Plot of countries clustered by protein consumption, projected onto first two principal components

BOOTSTRAP EVALUATION OF CLUSTERS

An important question when evaluating clusters is whether a given cluster is "real"—does the cluster represent actual structure in the data, or is it an artifact of the clustering algorithm? As you'll see, this is especially important with clustering algorithms like k-means, where the user has to specify the number of clusters *a priori*. It's been our experience that clustering algorithms will often produce several clusters that represent actual structure or relationships in the data, and then one or two clusters that are buckets that represent "other" or "miscellaneous." Clusters of "other" tend to be made up of data points that have no real relationship to each other; they just don't fit anywhere else.

One way to assess whether a cluster represents true structure is to see if the cluster holds up under plausible variations in the dataset. The `fpc` package has a function called `clusterboot()` that uses bootstrap resampling to evaluate how stable a given cluster is.[3] `clusterboot()` is an integrated function that both performs the clustering and evaluates the final produced clusters. It has interfaces to a number of R clustering algorithms, including both `hclust` and `kmeans`.

`clusterboot`'s algorithm uses the *Jaccard coefficient*, a similarity measure between sets. The Jaccard similarity between two sets A and B is the ratio of the number of elements in the intersection of A and B over the number of elements in the union of A and B. The basic general strategy is as follows:

1. Cluster the data as usual.
2. Draw a new dataset (of the same size as the original) by resampling the original dataset with replacement (meaning that some of the data points may show up more than once, and others not at all). Cluster the new dataset.
3. For every cluster in the original clustering, find the most similar cluster in the new clustering (the one that gives the maximum Jaccard coefficient) and record that value. If this maximum Jaccard coefficient is less than 0.5, the original cluster is considered to be *dissolved*—it didn't show up in the new clustering. A cluster that's dissolved too often is probably not a "real" cluster.
4. Repeat steps 2–3 several times.

The cluster stability of each cluster in the original clustering is the mean value of its Jaccard coefficient over all the bootstrap iterations. As a rule of thumb, clusters with a stability value less than 0.6 should be considered unstable. Values between 0.6 and 0.75 indicate that the cluster is measuring a pattern in the data, but there isn't high certainty about which points should be clustered together. Clusters with stability values above about 0.85 can be considered highly stable (they're likely to be real clusters).

Different clustering algorithms can give different stability values, even when the algorithms produce highly similar clusterings, so `clusterboot()` is also measuring how stable the clustering algorithm is.

Let's run `clusterboot()` on the protein data, using hierarchical clustering with five clusters.

Listing 8.6 Running `clusterboot()` on the protein data

```
library(fpc)

kbest.p<-5
```

Load the fpc package. You may have to install it first. We'll discuss installing R packages in appendix A.

Set the desired number of clusters.

[3] For a full description of the algorithm, see Christian Henning, "Cluster-wise assessment of cluster stability," Research Report 271, Dept. of Statistical Science, University College London, December 2006. The report can be found online at http://mng.bz/3XzA.

```
cboot.hclust <- clusterboot(pmatrix,clustermethod=hclustCBI,
                            method="ward", k=kbest.p)
```

Run clusterboot() with hclust ('clustermethod=hclustCBI') using Ward's method ('method="ward"') and kbest.p clusters ('k=kbest.p'). Return the results in an object called cboot.hclust.

```
> summary(cboot.hclust$result)
              Length Class  Mode
result         7     hclust list
noise          1     -none- logical
nc             1     -none- numeric
clusterlist    5     -none- list
partition     25     -none- numeric
clustermethod  1     -none- character
nccl           1     -none- numeric
```

The results of the clustering are in cboot.hclust$result. The output of the hclust() function is in cboot.hclust$result$result.

```
> groups<-cboot.hclust$result$partition
> print_clusters(groups, kbest.p)
[1] "cluster 1"
      Country RedMeat Fish Fr.Veg
1     Albania    10.1  0.2    1.7
4    Bulgaria     7.8  1.2    4.2
18    Romania     6.2  1.0    2.8
25 Yugoslavia     4.4  0.6    3.2
[1] "cluster 2"
       Country RedMeat Fish Fr.Veg
2      Austria     8.9  2.1    4.3
3      Belgium    13.5  4.5    4.0
9       France    18.0  5.7    6.5
12     Ireland    13.9  2.2    2.9
14 Netherlands     9.5  2.5    3.7
21 Switzerland    13.1  2.3    4.9
22          UK    17.4  4.3    3.3
24   W Germany    11.4  3.4    3.8
[1] "cluster 3"
          Country RedMeat Fish Fr.Veg
5  Czechoslovakia     9.7  2.0    4.0
7       E Germany     8.4  5.4    3.6
11        Hungary     5.3  0.3    4.2
16         Poland     6.9  3.0    6.6
23           USSR     9.3  3.0    2.9
[1] "cluster 4"
   Country RedMeat Fish Fr.Veg
6  Denmark    10.6  9.9    2.4
8  Finland     9.5  5.8    1.4
15  Norway     9.4  9.7    2.7
20  Sweden     9.9  7.5    2.0
[1] "cluster 5"
    Country RedMeat Fish Fr.Veg
10   Greece    10.2  5.9    6.5
13    Italy     9.0  3.4    6.7
17 Portugal     6.2 14.2    7.9
19    Spain     7.1  7.0    7.2
> cboot.hclust$bootmean
```

cboot.hclust$result$partition returns a vector of cluster labels.

The clusters are the same as those produced by a direct call to hclust().

The vector of cluster stabilities.

```
[1] 0.7905000 0.7990913 0.6173056 0.9312857 0.7560000
> cboot.hclust$bootbrd
[1] 25 11 47  8 35
```

The count of how many times each cluster was dissolved. By default clusterboot() runs 100 bootstrap iterations.

The `clusterboot()` results show that the cluster of countries with high fish consumption (cluster 4) is highly stable. Clusters 1 and 2 are also quite stable; cluster 5 less so (you can see in figure 8.4 that the members of cluster 5 are separated from the other countries, but also fairly separated from each other). Cluster 3 has the characteristics of what we've been calling the "other" cluster.

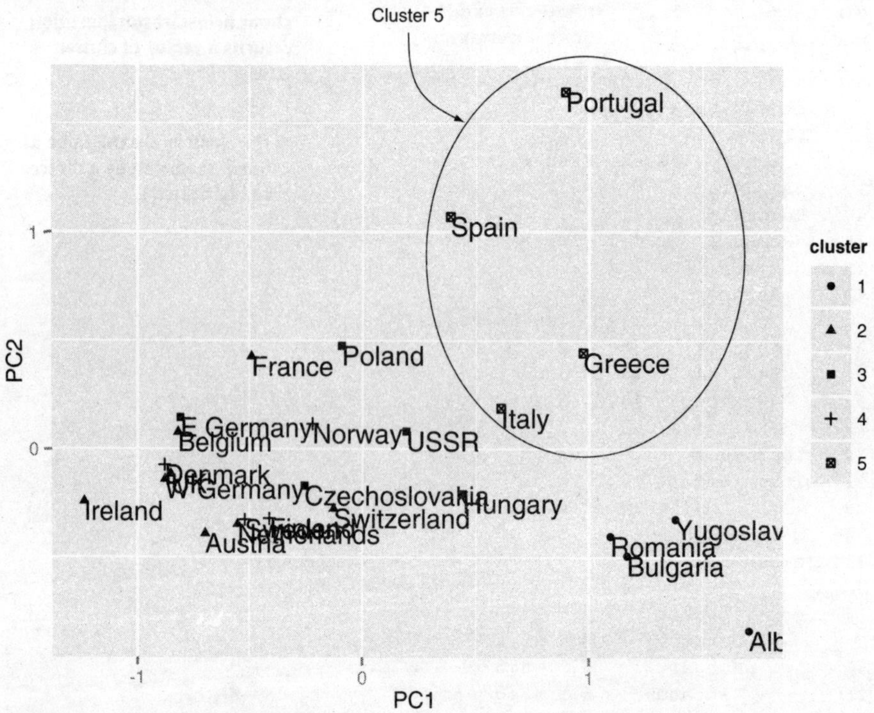

Figure 8.4 Cluster 5: The Mediterranean cluster. Its members are separated from the other clusters, but also from each other.

`clusterboot()` assumes that you know the number of clusters, *k*. We eyeballed the appropriate *k* from the dendrogram, but this isn't always feasible with a large dataset. Can we pick a plausible *k* in a more automated fashion? We'll look at this question in the next section.

PICKING THE NUMBER OF CLUSTERS

There are a number of heuristics and rules-of-thumb for picking clusters; a given heuristic will work better on some datasets than others. It's best to take advantage of domain knowledge to help set the number of clusters, if that's possible. Otherwise, try a variety of heuristics, and perhaps a few different values of *k*.

Total within sum of squares

One simple heuristic is to compute the *total within sum of squares (WSS)* for different values of *k* and look for an "elbow" in the curve. Define the cluster's *centroid* as the point that is the mean value of all the points in the cluster. The within sum of squares for a single cluster is the average squared distance of each point in the cluster from the cluster's centroid. The total within sum of squares is the sum of the within sum of squares of all the clusters. We show the calculation in the following listing.

Listing 8.7 Calculating total within sum of squares

```
sqr_edist <- function(x, y) {
  sum((x-y)^2)
}

wss.cluster <- function(clustermat) {
  c0 <- apply(clustermat, 2, FUN=mean)
  sum(apply(clustermat, 1, FUN=function(row){sqr_edist(row,c0)}))
}
```

Function to calculate squared distance between two vectors.

Function to calculate the WSS for a single cluster, which is represented as a matrix (one row for every point).

Calculate the centroid of the cluster (the mean of all the points).

Calculate the squared difference of every point in the cluster from the centroid, and sum all the distances.

```
wss.total <- function(dmatrix, labels) {
  wsstot <- 0
  k <- length(unique(labels))
  for(i in 1:k)
    wsstot <- wsstot + wss.cluster(subset(dmatrix, labels==i))
  wsstot
}
```

Function to compute the total WSS from a set of data points and cluster labels.

Extract each cluster, calculate the cluster's WSS, and sum all the values.

The total WSS will decrease as the number of clusters increases, because each cluster will be smaller and tighter. The hope is that the rate at which the WSS decreases will slow down for *k* beyond the optimal number of clusters. In other words, the graph of WSS versus *k* should flatten out beyond the optimal *k*, so the optimal *k* will be at the "elbow" of the graph. Unfortunately, this elbow can be difficult to see.

Calinski-Harabasz index

The *Calinski-Harabasz index* of a clustering is the ratio of the between-cluster variance (which is essentially the variance of all the cluster centroids from the dataset's grand centroid) to the total within-cluster variance (basically, the average WSS of the clusters in the clustering). For a given dataset, the *total sum of squares (TSS)* is the squared distance of all the data points from the dataset's centroid. The TSS is independent of the clustering. If WSS(k) is the total WSS of a clustering with k clusters, then the *between sum of squares* BSS(k) of the clustering is given by `BSS(k) = TSS - WSS(k)`. WSS(k) measures how close the points in a cluster are to each other. BSS(k) measures how far apart the clusters are from each other. A good clustering has a small WSS(k) and a large BSS(k).

The within-cluster variance W is given by `WSS(k)/(n-k)`, where n is the number of points in the dataset. The between-cluster variance B is given by `BSS(k)/(k-1)`. The within-cluster variance will decrease as k increases; the rate of decrease should slow down past the optimal k. The between-cluster variance will increase as k, but the rate of increase should slow down past the optimal k. So in theory, the ratio of B to W should be maximized at the optimal k.

Let's write a function to calculate the Calinski-Harabasz (CH) index. The function will accommodate both a `kmeans` clustering and an `hclust` clustering.

Listing 8.8 The Calinski-Harabasz index

```
totss <- function(dmatrix) {
  grandmean <- apply(dmatrix, 2, FUN=mean)
  sum(apply(dmatrix, 1, FUN=function(row){sqr_edist(row, grandmean)}))
}

ch_criterion <- function(dmatrix, kmax, method="kmeans") {
  if(!(method %in% c("kmeans", "hclust"))) {
    stop("method must be one of c('kmeans', 'hclust')")
  }
  npts <- dim(dmatrix)[1]  # number of rows.

  totss <- totss(dmatrix)

  wss <- numeric(kmax)
  crit <- numeric(kmax)
  wss[1] <- (npts-1)*sum(apply(dmatrix, 2, var))
  for(k in 2:kmax) {
    if(method=="kmeans") {
      clustering<-kmeans(dmatrix, k, nstart=10, iter.max=100)
      wss[k] <- clustering$tot.withinss
    }else {  # hclust
      d <- dist(dmatrix, method="euclidean")
      pfit <- hclust(d, method="ward")
      labels <- cutree(pfit, k=k)
      wss[k] <- wss.total(dmatrix, labels)
    }
  }
```

Annotations:

- Convenience function to calculate the total sum of squares.
- A function to calculate the CH index for a number of clusters from 1 to kmax.
- The total sum of squares is independent of the clustering.
- Calculate WSS for k=1 (which is really just total sum of squares).
- Calculate WSS for k from 2 to kmax. kmeans() returns the total WSS as one of its outputs.
- For hclust(), calculate total WSS by hand.

```
  bss <- totss - wss                     <— Calculate BSS for k from 1 to kmax.
  crit.num <- bss/(0:(kmax-1))           <— Normalize BSS by k-1.
  crit.denom <- wss/(npts - 1:kmax)      <— Normalize WSS by npts - k.
  list(crit = crit.num/crit.denom, wss = wss, totss = totss)   <—
}
```

Return a vector of CH indices and of WSS for k from 1 to kmax. Also return total sum of squares.

We can calculate both indices for the protein dataset and plot them.

Listing 8.9 Evaluating clusterings with different numbers of clusters

```
library(reshape2)
clustcrit <- ch_criterion(pmatrix, 10, method="hclust")
critframe <- data.frame(k=1:10, ch=scale(clustcrit$crit),
                        wss=scale(clustcrit$wss))
critframe <- melt(critframe, id.vars=c("k"),
                  variable.name="measure",
                  value.name="score")
ggplot(critframe, aes(x=k, y=score, color=measure)) +
  geom_point(aes(shape=measure)) + geom_line(aes(linetype=measure)) +
  scale_x_continuous(breaks=1:10, labels=1:10)
```

- **Load the reshape2 package (for the melt() function).** (annotates `library(reshape2)`)
- **Calculate both criteria for 1–10 clusters.** (annotates `clustcrit <- ...`)
- **Create a data frame with the number of clusters, the CH criterion, and the WSS criterion. We'll scale both the CH and WSS criteria to similar ranges so that we can plot them both on the same graph.** (annotates `critframe <- data.frame(...)`)
- **Use the melt() function to put the data frame in a shape suitable for ggplot.** (annotates `critframe <- melt(...)`)
- **Plot it.** (annotates `ggplot(...)`)

Looking at figure 8.5, you see that the CH criterion is maximized at k=2, with another local maximum at k=5. If you squint your eyes, you can convince yourself that the WSS plot has an elbow at k=2. The k=2 clustering corresponds to the first split of the dendrogram in figure 8.2; if you use `clusterboot()` to do the clustering, you'll see that the clusters are highly stable, though perhaps not very informative.

There are several other indices that you can try when picking *k*. The *gap statistic*[4] is an attempt to automate the "elbow finding" on the WSS curve. It works best when the data comes from a mix of populations that all have approximately Gaussian distributions (a *mixture of Gaussian*). We'll see one more measure, the *average silhouette width*, when we discuss `kmeans()`.

[4] See Robert Tibshirani, Guenther Walther, and Trevor Hastie, "Estimating the number of clusters in a data set via the gap statistic," *Journal of the Royal Statistical Society B*, 2001, 63(2), pp. 411-423; www.stanford.edu/~hastie/Papers/gap.pdf.

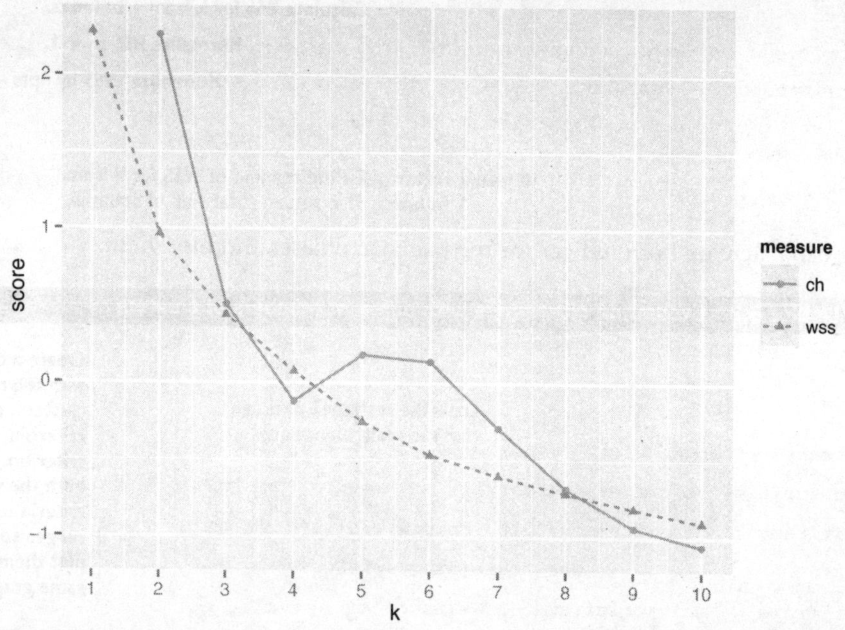

Figure 8.5 Plot of the Calinski-Harabasz and WSS indices for 1–10 clusters, on protein data

8.1.4 The k-means algorithm

K-means is a popular clustering algorithm when the data is all numeric and the distance metric is squared Euclidean (though you could in theory run it with other distance metrics). It's fairly ad hoc and has the major disadvantage that you must pick *k* in advance. On the plus side, it's easy to implement (one reason it's so popular) and can be faster than hierarchical clustering on large datasets. It works best on data that looks like a mixture of Gaussians (which the `protein` data unfortunately doesn't appear to be).

THE KMEANS() FUNCTION

The function to run k-means in R is `kmeans()`. The output of `kmeans()` includes the cluster labels, the centers (centroids) of the clusters, the total sum of squares, total WSS, total BSS, and the WSS of each cluster. The k-means algorithm is illustrated in figure 8.6, with $k = 2$.

This algorithm isn't guaranteed to have a unique stopping point. K-means can be fairly unstable, in that the final clusters depend on the initial cluster centers. It's good practice to run k-means several times with different random starts, and then select the clustering with the lowest total WSS. The `kmeans()` function can do this automatically, though it defaults to only using one random start.

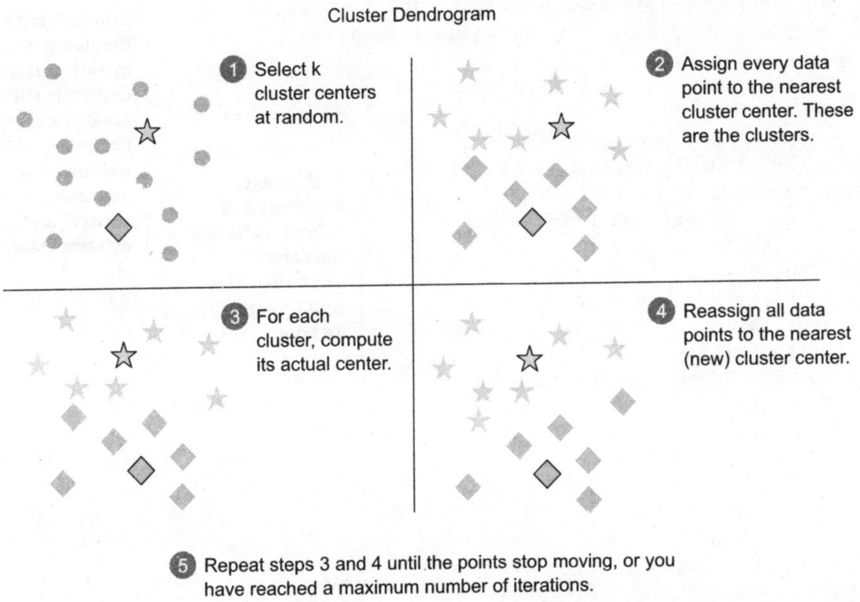

Figure 8.6 The k-means procedure. The two cluster centers are represented by the outlined star and diamond.

Let's run `kmeans()` on the `protein` data (scaled to 0 mean and unit standard deviation, as before). We'll use `k=5`, as shown in the next listing.

Listing 8.10 Running k-means with k=5

```
> pclusters <- kmeans(pmatrix, kbest.p. nstart=100, iter.max=100)
 > summary(pclusters)
             Length Class  Mode
cluster      25     -none- numeric
centers      45     -none- numeric
totss         1     -none- numeric
withinss      5     -none- numeric
tot.withinss  1     -none- numeric
betweenss     1     -none- numeric
size          5     -none- numeric

> pclusters$centers
       RedMeat  WhiteMeat        Eggs       Milk       Fish
1 -0.807569986 -0.8719354 -1.55330561 -1.0783324 -1.0386379
2  0.006572897 -0.2290150  0.19147892  1.3458748  1.1582546
3 -0.570049402  0.5803879 -0.08589708 -0.4604938 -0.4537795
4  1.011180399  0.7421332  0.94084150  0.5700581 -0.2671539
5 -0.508801956 -1.1088009 -0.41248496 -0.8320414  0.9819154
     Cereals     Starch       Nuts      Fr.Veg
1  1.7200335 -1.4234267  0.9961313 -0.64360439
2 -0.8722721  0.1676780 -0.9553392 -1.11480485
3  0.3181839  0.7857609 -0.2679180  0.06873983
```

Run kmeans() with five clusters (kbest.p=5), 100 random starts, and 100 maximum iterations per run.

kmeans() returns all the sum of squares measures.

pclusters$centers is a matrix whose rows are the centroids of the clusters. Note that pclusters$centers is in the scaled coordinates, not the original protein coordinates.

```
4 -0.6877583  0.2288743 -0.5083895  0.02161979
5  0.1300253 -0.1842010  1.3108846  1.62924487
> pclusters$size
[1] 4 4 5 8 4
> groups <- pclusters$cluster
> print_clusters(groups, kbest.p)
[1] "cluster 1"
      Country RedMeat Fish Fr.Veg
1     Albania    10.1  0.2    1.7
4    Bulgaria     7.8  1.2    4.2
18    Romania     6.2  1.0    2.8
25 Yugoslavia     4.4  0.6    3.2
[1] "cluster 2"
   Country RedMeat Fish Fr.Veg
6  Denmark    10.6  9.9    2.4
8  Finland     9.5  5.8    1.4
15  Norway     9.4  9.7    2.7
20  Sweden     9.9  7.5    2.0
[1] "cluster 3"
          Country RedMeat Fish Fr.Veg
5  Czechoslovakia     9.7  2.0    4.0
7       E Germany     8.4  5.4    3.6
11        Hungary     5.3  0.3    4.2
16         Poland     6.9  3.0    6.6
23           USSR     9.3  3.0    2.9
[1] "cluster 4"
       Country RedMeat Fish Fr.Veg
2      Austria     8.9  2.1    4.3
3      Belgium    13.5  4.5    4.0
9       France    18.0  5.7    6.5
12     Ireland    13.9  2.2    2.9
14 Netherlands     9.5  2.5    3.7
21 Switzerland    13.1  2.3    4.9
22          UK    17.4  4.3    3.3
24   W Germany    11.4  3.4    3.8
[1] "cluster 5"
    Country RedMeat Fish Fr.Veg
10   Greece    10.2  5.9    6.5
13    Italy     9.0  3.4    6.7
17 Portugal     6.2 14.2    7.9
19    Spain     7.1  7.0    7.2
```

pclusters$size returns the number of points in each cluster. Generally (though not always) a good clustering will be fairly well balanced: no extremely small clusters and no extremely large ones.

pclusters$cluster is a vector of cluster labels.

In this case, kmeans() and hclust() returned the same clustering. This won't always be true.

THE KMEANSRUNS() FUNCTION FOR PICKING K

To run `kmeans()`, you must know *k*. The `fpc` package (the same package that has `clusterboot()`) has a function called `kmeansruns()` that calls `kmeans()` over a range of *k* and estimates the best *k*. It then returns its pick for the best value of *k*, the output of `kmeans()` for that value, and a vector of criterion values as a function of *k*. Currently, `kmeansruns()` has two criteria: the *Calinski-Harabasz Index* (`"ch"`), and the *average silhouette width* (`"asw"`; for more about silhouette clustering, see http://mng.bz/Qe15). It's a good idea to plot the criterion values over the entire range of *k*, since you may see evidence for a *k* that the algorithm didn't automatically pick (as we did in figure 8.5), as we demonstrate in the following listing.

Listing 8.11 Plotting cluster criteria

Run kmeansruns() from 1–10 clusters, and the CH criterion. By default, kmeansruns() uses 100 random starts and 100 maximum iterations per run.

The CH criterion picks two clusters.

Run kmeansruns() from 1–10 clusters, and the average silhouette width criterion. Average silhouette width picks 3 clusters.

The vector of criterion values is called crit.

Compare the CH values for kmeans() and hclust(). They're not quite the same, because the two algorithms didn't pick the same clusters.

Plot the values for the two criteria.

kmeansruns() also returns the output of kmeans for k=bestk.

```
> clustering.ch <- kmeansruns(pmatrix, krange=1:10, criterion="ch")
> clustering.ch$bestk
[1] 2
> clustering.asw <- kmeansruns(pmatrix, krange=1:10, criterion="asw")
> clustering.asw$bestk
[1] 3

> clustering.ch$crit
 [1]  0.000000 14.094814 11.417985 10.418801 10.011797  9.964967
 [7]  9.861682  9.412089  9.166676  9.075569
> clustcrit$crit
 [1]       NaN 12.215107 10.359587  9.690891 10.011797  9.964967
 [7]  9.506978  9.092065  8.822406  8.695065

> critframe <- data.frame(k=1:10, ch=scale(clustering.ch$crit),
            asw=scale(clustering.asw$crit))
> critframe <- melt(critframe, id.vars=c("k"),
                  variable.name="measure",
                   value.name="score")
> ggplot(critframe, aes(x=k, y=score, color=measure)) +
   geom_point(aes(shape=measure)) + geom_line(aes(linetype=measure)) +
   scale_x_continuous(breaks=1:10, labels=1:10)
> summary(clustering.ch)
             Length Class  Mode
cluster      25     -none- numeric
centers      18     -none- numeric
totss         1     -none- numeric
withinss      2     -none- numeric
tot.withinss  1     -none- numeric
betweenss     1     -none- numeric
size          2     -none- numeric
crit         10     -none- numeric
bestk         1     -none- numeric
```

Figure 8.7 shows the results of the two clustering criteria provided by kmeansruns. They suggest two to three clusters as the best choice. However, if you compare the values of `clustering.ch$crit` and `clustcrit$crit` in the listing, you'll see that the CH

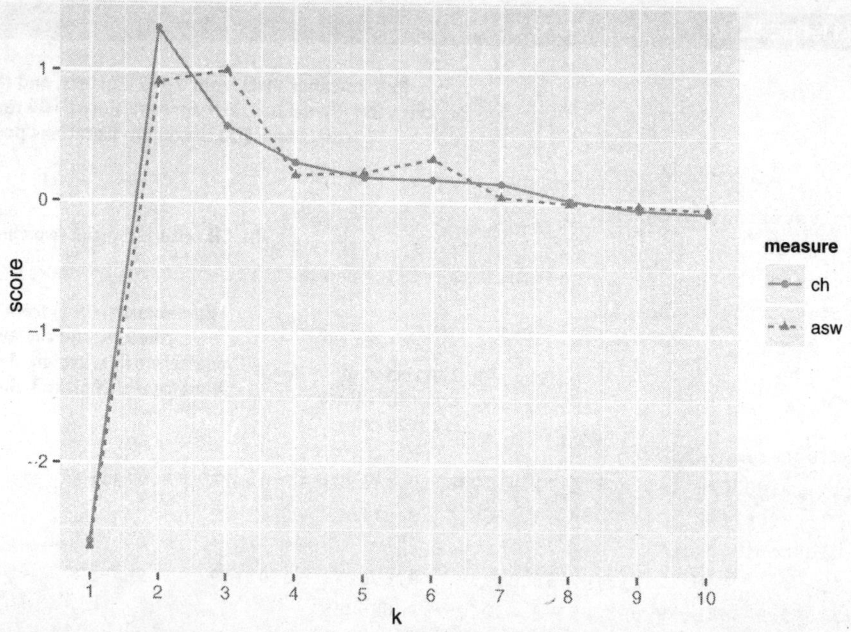

Figure 8.7 Plot of the Calinski-Harabasz and average silhouette width indices for 1–10 clusters, on protein data

criterion produces different curves for `kmeans()` and `hclust()` clusterings, but it did pick the same value (which probably means it picked the same clusters) for `k=5`, and `k=6`, which might be taken as evidence that either five or six is the optimal choice for *k*.

CLUSTERBOOT() REVISITED

We can run `clusterboot()` using the k-means algorithm, as well.

Listing 8.12 Running `clusterboot()` with k-means

```
kbest.p<-5
cboot<-clusterboot(pmatrix, clustermethod=kmeansCBI,
            runs=100,iter.max=100,
            krange=kbest.p, seed=15555)

> groups <- cboot$result$partition
> print_clusters(cboot$result$partition, kbest.p)
[1] "cluster 1"
      Country RedMeat Fish Fr.Veg
1     Albania    10.1  0.2    1.7
4    Bulgaria     7.8  1.2    4.2
18    Romania     6.2  1.0    2.8
25 Yugoslavia     4.4  0.6    3.2
[1] "cluster 2"
   Country RedMeat Fish Fr.Veg
6  Denmark    10.6  9.9    2.4
8  Finland     9.5  5.8    1.4
```

We've set the seed for the random generator so the results are reproducible.

```
15  Norway       9.4  9.7     2.7
20  Sweden       9.9  7.5     2.0
[1] "cluster 3"
           Country RedMeat Fish Fr.Veg
5  Czechoslovakia      9.7  2.0    4.0
7       E Germany      8.4  5.4    3.6
11        Hungary      5.3  0.3    4.2
16         Poland      6.9  3.0    6.6
23           USSR      9.3  3.0    2.9
[1] "cluster 4"
       Country RedMeat Fish Fr.Veg
2      Austria     8.9  2.1    4.3
3      Belgium    13.5  4.5    4.0
9       France    18.0  5.7    6.5
12     Ireland    13.9  2.2    2.9
14 Netherlands     9.5  2.5    3.7
21 Switzerland    13.1  2.3    4.9
22          UK    17.4  4.3    3.3
24   W Germany    11.4  3.4    3.8
[1] "cluster 5"
     Country RedMeat Fish Fr.Veg
10    Greece    10.2  5.9    6.5
13     Italy     9.0  3.4    6.7
17  Portugal     6.2 14.2    7.9
19     Spain     7.1  7.0    7.2
> cboot$bootmean
[1] 0.8670000 0.8420714 0.6147024 0.7647341 0.7508333
> cboot$bootbrd
[1] 15 20 49 17 32
```

Note that the stability numbers as given by `cboot$bootmean` (and the number of times that the clusters were "dissolved" as given by `cboot$bootbrd`) are different for the hierarchical clustering and k-means, even though the discovered clusters are the same. This shows that the stability of a clustering is partly a function of the clustering algorithm, not just the data. Again, the fact that both clustering algorithms discovered the same clusters might be taken as an indication that five is the optimal number of clusters.

8.1.5 Assigning new points to clusters

Clustering is often used as part of data exploration, or as a precursor to other supervised learning methods. But you may want to use the clusters that you discovered to categorize new data, as well. One common way to do so is to treat the centroid of each cluster as the representative of the cluster as a whole, and then assign new points to the cluster with the nearest centroid. Note that if you scaled the original data before clustering, then you should also scale the new data point the same way before assigning it to a cluster.

Listing 8.13 A function to assign points to a cluster

```
assign_cluster <- function(newpt, centers, xcenter=0, xscale=1) {
  xpt <- (newpt - xcenter)/xscale
  dists <- apply(centers, 1, FUN=function(c0){sqr_edist(c0, xpt)})
  which.min(dists)
}
```

- A function to assign a new data point newpt to a clustering described by centers, a matrix where each row is a cluster centroid. If the data was scaled (using scale()) before clustering, then xcenter and xscale are the scaled:center and scaled:scale attributes, respectively.
- Center and scale the new data point.
- Calculate how far the new data point is from each of the cluster centers.
- Return the cluster number of the closest centroid.

Note that the function sqr_edist (the squared Euclidean distance) was defined previously, in section 8.1.1.

Let's look at an example of assigning points to clusters, using synthetic data.

Listing 8.14 An example of assigning points to clusters

```
rnorm.multidim <- function(n, mean, sd, colstr="x") {
   ndim <- length(mean)
   data <- NULL
   for(i in 1:ndim) {
     col <- rnorm(n, mean=mean[[i]], sd=sd[[i]])
     data<-cbind(data, col)
   }
   cnames <- paste(colstr, 1:ndim, sep='')
   colnames(data) <- cnames
   data
}

mean1 <- c(1, 1, 1)
sd1 <- c(1, 2, 1)

mean2 <- c(10, -3, 5)
sd2 <- c(2, 1, 2)

mean3 <- c(-5, -5, -5)
sd3 <- c(1.5, 2, 1)

clust1 <- rnorm.multidim(100, mean1, sd1)
clust2 <- rnorm.multidim(100, mean2, sd2)
clust3 <- rnorm.multidim(100, mean3, sd3)
toydata <- rbind(clust3, rbind(clust1, clust2))
```

- A function to generate n points drawn from a multidimensional Gaussian distribution with centroid mean and standard deviation sd. The dimension of the distribution is given by the length of the vector mean.
- The parameters for three Gaussian distributions.
- Create a dataset with 100 points each drawn from the above distributions.

```
tmatrix <- scale(toydata)
tcenter <- attr(tmatrix, "scaled:center")
tscale<-attr(tmatrix, "scaled:scale")
kbest.t <- 3
tclusters <- kmeans(tmatrix, kbest.t, nstart=100, iter.max=100)

tclusters$size
[1] 100 101  99

unscale <- function(scaledpt, centervec, scalevec) {
  scaledpt*scalevec + centervec
}

> unscale(tclusters$centers[1,], tcenter, tscale)
       x1        x2        x3
 9.978961 -3.097584  4.864689
> mean2
[1] 10 -3  5

> unscale(tclusters$centers[2,], tcenter, tscale)
       x1        x2        x3
-4.979523 -4.927404 -4.908949
> mean3
[1] -5 -5 -5

> unscale(tclusters$centers[3,], tcenter, tscale)
       x1        x2        x3
1.0003356 1.3037825 0.9571058
> mean1
[1] 1 1 1

> assign_cluster(rnorm.multidim(1, mean1, sd1),
               tclusters$centers,
               tcenter, tscale)
3
3

> assign_cluster(rnorm.multidim(1, mean2, sd1),
               tclusters$centers,
               tcenter, tscale)
1
1
```

Scale the dataset.

Store the centering and scaling parameters for future use.

Cluster the dataset, using k-means with three clusters.

The resulting clusters are about the right size.

A function to "unscale" data points (put them back in the coordinates of the original dataset).

Unscale the first centroid. It corresponds to our original distribution 2.

The second centroid corresponds to the original distribution 3.

The third centroid corresponds to the original distribution 1.

Generate a random point from the original distribution 1 and assign it to one of the discovered clusters.

It's assigned to cluster 3, as we would expect.

Generate a random point from the original distribution 2 and assign it.

It's assigned to cluster 1.

```
> assign_cluster(rnorm.multidim(1, mean3, sd1),
                 tclusters$centers,
                 tcenter, tscale)
2
2
```

Generate a random point from the original distribution 3 and assign it.

It's assigned to cluster 2.

8.1.6 *Clustering takeaways*

Here's what you should remember about clustering:

- The goal of clustering is to discover or draw out similarities among subsets of your data.
- In a good clustering, points in the same cluster should be more similar (nearer) to each other than they are to points in other clusters.
- When clustering, the units that each variable is measured in matter. Different units cause different distances and potentially different clusterings.
- Ideally, you want a unit change in each coordinate to represent the same degree of change. One way to approximate this is to transform all the columns to have a mean value of 0 and a standard deviation of 1.0, for example by using the function `scale()`.
- Clustering is often used for data exploration or as a precursor to supervised learning methods.
- Like visualization, it's more iterative and interactive, and less automated than supervised methods.
- Different clustering algorithms will give different results. You should consider different approaches, with different numbers of clusters.
- There are many heuristics for estimating the best number of clusters. Again, you should consider the results from different heuristics and explore various numbers of clusters.

Sometimes, rather than looking for subsets of data points that are highly similar to each other, you'd like to know what kind of data (or which data attributes) tend to occur together. In the next section, we'll look at one approach to this problem.

8.2 *Association rules*

Association rule mining is used to find objects or attributes that frequently occur together—for example, products that are often bought together during a shopping session, or queries that tend to occur together during a session on a website's search engine. Such information can be used to recommend products to shoppers, to place frequently bundled items together on store shelves, or to redesign websites for easier navigation.

8.2.1 Overview of association rules

The unit of "togetherness" when mining association rules is called a *transaction*. Depending on the problem, a transaction could be a single shopping basket, a single user session on a website, or even a single customer. The objects that comprise a transaction are referred to as *items* in an *itemset*: the products in the shopping basket, the pages visited during a website session, the actions of a customer. Sometimes transactions are referred to as *baskets*, from the shopping basket analogy.

Mining for association rules occurs in two steps:

1. Look for all the itemsets (subsets of transactions) that occur more often than in a minimum fraction of the transactions.
2. Turn those itemsets into rules.

Let's consider the example of books that are checked out from a library. When a library patron checks out a set of books, that's a transaction; the books that the patron checked out are the itemset that comprise the transaction. Table 8.1 represents a database of transactions.

Table 8.1 A database of library transactions

Transaction ID	Books checked out
1	*The Hobbit, The Princess Bride*
2	*The Princess Bride, The Last Unicorn*
3	*The Hobbit*
4	*The Neverending Story*
5	*The Last Unicorn*
6	*The Hobbit, The Princess Bride, The Fellowship of the Ring*
7	*The Hobbit, The Fellowship of the Ring, The Two Towers, The Return of the King*
8	*The Fellowship of the Ring, The Two Towers, The Return of the King*
9	*The Hobbit, The Princess Bride, The Last Unicorn*
10	*The Last Unicorn, The Neverending Story*

Looking over all the transactions in table 8.1, you find that *The Hobbit* is in 50% of all transactions, and *The Princess Bride* is in 40% of them (you run a library where fantasy is quite popular). Both books are checked out together in 30% of all transaction. We'd say the *support* of the itemset {*The Hobbit, The Princess Bride*} is 30%. Of the five transactions that include *The Hobbit*, three (60%) also include *The Princess Bride*. So you can make a rule "People who check out *The Hobbit* also check out *The Princess Bride*." This rule should be correct (according to your data) 60% of the time. We'd say that the *confidence* of the rule is 60%. Conversely, of the four times *The Princess Bride* was checked out, *The Hobbit* appeared three times, or 75% of the time. So the rule "People who check out *The Princess Bride* also check out *The Hobbit*" has 75% confidence.

Let's define support and confidence formally. The rule "if X, then Y" means that every time you see the itemset X in a transaction, you expect to also see Y (with a given confidence). For the apriori algorithm (which we'll look at in this section), Y is always an itemset with one item. Suppose that your database of transactions is called T. Then `support(X)` is the number of transactions that contain X divided by the total number of transactions in T. The confidence of the rule "if X, then Y" is given by `conf(X=>Y) = support(union(X,Y))/support(X)`, where `union(X, Y)` means that you're referring to itemsets that contain both the items in X and the items in Y.

The goal in association rule mining is to find all the interesting rules in the database with at least a given minimum support (say, 10%) and a minimum given confidence (say, 60%).

8.2.2 The example problem

For our example problem, let's imagine that we're working for a bookstore, and we want to identify books that our customers are interested in, based on (all of) their previous purchases and book interests. We can get information about their book interests two ways: either they've purchased a book from us, or they've rated the book on our website (even if they bought the book somewhere else). In this case, a transaction is a customer, and an itemset is all the books that they've expressed an interest in, either by purchase or by rating.

The data that we'll use is based on data collected in 2004 from the book community Book-Crossing[5] for research conducted at the Institut für Informatik, University of Freiburg.[6] We've condensed the information into a single tab-separated text file called bookdata.tsv. Each row of the file consists of a user ID, a book title (which we've designed as a unique ID for each book), and the rating (which we won't actually use in this example):

```
"token" "userid"          "rating"         "title"
" a light in the storm" 55927    0         " A Light in the Storm"
```

The `token` column contains lower-cased column strings; we used the tokens to identify books with different ISBNs (the original book IDs) that had the same title except for

[5] The original data repository can be found at http://mng.bz/2052. Since some artifacts in the original files caused errors when reading into R, we're providing copies of the data as a prepared RData object:https://github.com/WinVector/zmPDSwR/blob/master/Bookdata/bxBooks.RData. The prepared version of the data that we'll use in this section is at https://github.com/WinVector/zmPDSwR/blob/master/Bookdata/bookdata.tsv.gz. Further information and scripts for preparing the data can be found at https://github.com/WinVector/zmPDSwR/tree/master/Bookdata.

[6] The researchers' original paper is "Improving Recommendation Lists Through Topic Diversification," Cai-Nicolas Ziegler, Sean M. McNee, Joseph A. Konstan, Georg Lausen; Proceedings of the 14th International World Wide Web Conference (WWW '05), May 10-14, 2005, Chiba, Japan. It can be found online at http://mng.bz/7trR.

casing. The `title` column holds properly capitalized title strings; these are unique per book, so we'll use them as book IDs.

In this format, the transaction (customer) information is diffused through the data, rather than being all in one row; this reflects the way the data would naturally be stored in a database, since the customer's activity would be diffused throughout time. Books generally come in different editions or from different publishers. We've condensed all different versions into a single item; hence different copies or printings of *Little Women* will all map to the same item ID in our data (namely, the title `Little Women`).

The original data includes approximately a million ratings of 271,379 books from 278,858 readers. Our data will have fewer books due to the mapping that we discussed earlier.

Now we're ready to mine.

8.2.3 Mining association rules with the arules package

We'll use the package `arules` for association rule mining. `arules` includes an implementation of the popular association rule algorithm *apriori,* as well as implementations to read in and examine transaction data.[7] The package uses special data types to hold and manipulate the data; we'll explore these data types as we work the example.

READING IN THE DATA

We can read the data directly from the bookdata.tsv.gz file into the object `bookbaskets` using the function `read.transaction()`.

Listing 8.15 Reading in the book data

```
library(arules)                      <- Load the arules package.

bookbaskets <- read.transactions("bookdata.tsv.gz", format="single",   <- Specify the file and the file format.
                       sep="\t",                 <- Specify the column separator (a tab).
                       cols=c("userid", "title"),    <- Specify the column of transaction IDs and of item IDs, respectively.
                       rm.duplicates=T)          <- Tell the function to look for and remove duplicate entries (for example, multiple entries for The Hobbit by the same user).
```

The `read.transactions()` function reads data in two formats: the format where every row corresponds to a single item (like `bookdata.tsv.gz`), and a format where each row corresponds to a single transaction, possibly with a transaction ID, like table 8.1. To read data in the first format, use the argument `format="single"`; to read data in the second format, use the argument `format="basket"`.

---

7 For a more comprehensive introduction to `arules` than we can give in this chapter, please see Hahsler, Grin, Hornik, and Buchta, "Introduction to arules—A computational environment for mining association rules and frequent item sets," online at cran.r-project.org/web/packages/arules/vignettes/arules.pdf.

It sometimes happens that a reader will buy one edition of a book and then later add a rating for that book under a different edition. Because of the way we're representing books for this example, these two actions will result in duplicate entries. The `rm.duplicates=T` argument will eliminate them. It will also output some (not too useful) diagnostics about the duplicates.

Once you've read in the data, you can inspect the resulting object.

EXAMINING THE DATA

Transactions are represented as a special object called `transactions`. You can think of a `transactions` object as a 0/1 matrix, with one row for every transaction and one column for every possible item. The matrix entry *(i,j)* is 1 if the *i* transaction contains item *j*. There are a number of calls you can use to examine the transaction data, as the next listing shows.

Listing 8.16 Examining the transaction data

```
> class(bookbaskets)                    <-- The object is of class transactions.
[1] "transactions"
attr(,"package")
[1] "arules"
> bookbaskets                           <-- Printing the object tells you its dimensions.
transactions in sparse format with
 92108 transactions (rows) and
 220447 items (columns)
> dim(bookbaskets)                      <-- You can also use dim() to see the dimensions of the matrix.
[1]  92108 220447
> colnames(bookbaskets)[1:5]            <-- The columns are labeled by book title.
[1] " A Light in the Storm:[...]"
[2] " Always Have Popsicles"
[3] " Apple Magic"
[4] " Ask Lily"
[5] " Beyond IBM: Leadership Marketing and Finance for the 1990s"
> rownames(bookbaskets)[1:5]
[1] "10"      "1000"    "100001" "100002" "100004"    <-- The rows are labeled by customer.
```

You can examine the distribution of transaction sizes (or basket sizes) with the function `size()`:

```
> basketSizes <- size(bookbaskets)
> summary(basketSizes)
   Min. 1st Qu.  Median    Mean 3rd Qu.    Max.
    1.0     1.0     1.0    11.1     4.0 10250.0
```

Most customers (at least half of them, in fact) only expressed interest in one book. But someone has expressed interest in more than 10,000! You probably want to look more closely at the size distribution to see what's going on.

Listing 8.17 Examining the size distribution

```
> quantile(basketSizes, probs=seq(0,1,0.1))
   0%    10%    20%    30%    40%    50%    60%    70%    80%    90%  100%
    1      1      1      1      1      1      2      3      5     13 10253
> library(ggplot2)
> ggplot(data.frame(count=basketSizes)) +
  geom_density(aes(x=count), binwidth=1) +
  scale_x_log10()
```

Look at the basket size distribution, in 10% increments.

Plot the distribution to get a better look.

Figure 8.8 shows the distribution of basket sizes. 90% of customers expressed interest in fewer than 15 books; most of the remaining customers expressed interest in up to about 100 books or so (the call `quantile(basketSizes, probs=c(0.99, 1))` will show you that 99% of customers expressed interest in 179 books or fewer). Still, there are a few people who have expressed interest in several hundred, or even several thousand books.

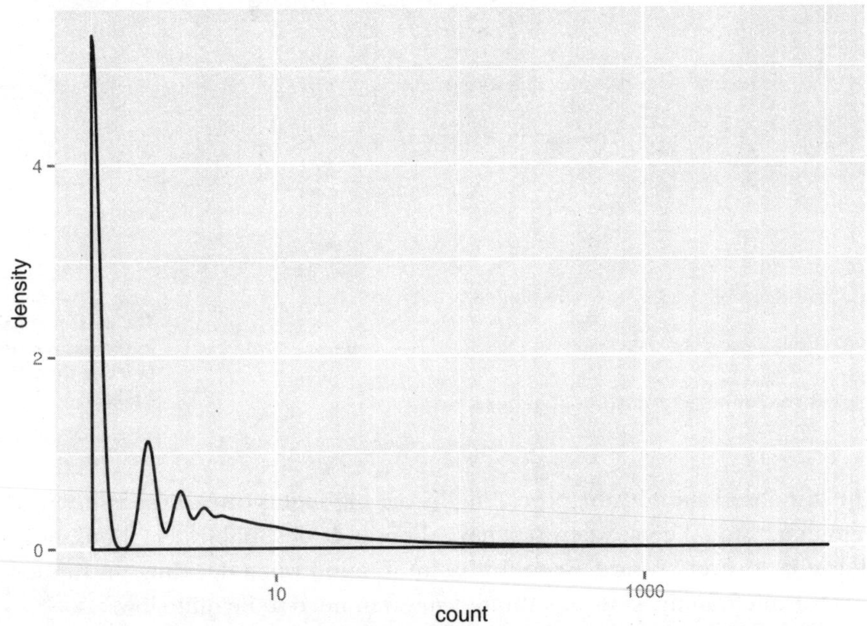

Figure 8.8 A density plot of basket sizes

Which books are they reading? The function `itemFrequency()` will give you the relative frequency of each book in the transaction data:

```
> bookFreq <- itemFrequency(bookbaskets)
summary(bookFreq)
     Min.   1st Qu.    Median      Mean   3rd Qu.      Max.
1.086e-05 1.086e-05 1.086e-05 5.035e-05 3.257e-05 2.716e-02

> sum(bookFreq)
[1] 11.09909
```

Note that the frequencies don't sum to 1. You can recover the number of times that each book occurred in the data by normalizing the item frequencies and multiplying by the total number of items.

Listing 8.18 Finding the ten most frequent books

```
> bookCount <- (bookFreq/sum(bookFreq))*sum(basketSizes)
> summary(bookCount)
   Min.  1st Qu.   Median     Mean  3rd Qu.      Max.
  1.000    1.000    1.000    4.637    3.000 2502.000
> orderedBooks <- sort(bookCount, decreasing=T)
> orderedBooks[1:10]
                                   Wild Animus
                                          2502
                     The Lovely Bones: A Novel
                                          1295
                             She's Come Undone
                                           934
                             The Da Vinci Code
                                           905
         Harry Potter and the Sorcerer's Stone
                                           832
                    The Nanny Diaries: A Novel
                                           821
                               A Painted House
                                           819
                         Bridget Jones's Diary
                                           772
                       The Secret Life of Bees
                                           762
Divine Secrets of the Ya-Ya Sisterhood: A Novel
                                           737
> orderedBooks[1]/dim(bookbaskets)[1]
Wild Animus
 0.02716376
```

Get the absolute count of book occurrences.

Sort the count and list the 10 most popular books.

The most popular book in the dataset occurred in fewer than 3% of the baskets.

The last observation in the preceding listing highlights one of the issues with mining high-dimensional data: when you have thousands of variables, or thousands of items, almost every event is rare. Keep this point in mind when deciding on support thresholds for rule mining; your thresholds will often need to be quite low.

Before we get to the rule mining, let's refine the data a bit more. As we observed earlier, half of the customers in the data only expressed interest in a single book. Since you want to find books that occur together in people's interest lists, you can't make any direct use of people who haven't yet shown interest in multiple books. You can restrict the dataset to customers who have expressed interest in at least two books:

```
> bookbaskets_use <- bookbaskets[basketSizes > 1]
> dim(bookbaskets_use)
[1]  40822 220447
```

Now you're ready to look for association rules.

THE APRIORI() FUNCTION

In order to mine rules, you need to decide on a minimum support level and a minimum threshold level. For this example, let's try restricting the itemsets that we'll consider to those that are supported by at least 100 people. This leads to a minimum support of `100/dim(bookbaskets_use)[1] = 100/40822`. This is about 0.002, or 0.2%. We'll use a confidence threshold of 75%.

Listing 8.19 Finding the association rules

```
> rules <- apriori(bookbaskets_use,
            parameter =list(support = 0.002, confidence=0.75))
```

Call apriori() with a minimum support of 0.002 and a minimum confidence of 0.75.

```
> summary(rules)
set of 191 rules
```

The summary of the apriori() output reports the number of rules found;...

```
rule length distribution (lhs + rhs):sizes
  2   3   4   5
 11 100  66  14

   Min. 1st Qu.  Median    Mean 3rd Qu.    Max.
  2.000   3.000   3.000   3.435   4.000   5.000
```

...the distribution of rule lengths (in this example, most rules contain 3 items—2 on the left side, X (lhs), and one on the right side, Y (rhs));...

```
summary of quality measures:
    support           confidence          lift
 Min.   :0.002009   Min.   :0.7500   Min.   : 40.89
 1st Qu.:0.002131   1st Qu.:0.8113   1st Qu.: 86.44
 Median :0.002278   Median :0.8468   Median :131.36
 Mean   :0.002593   Mean   :0.8569   Mean   :129.68
 3rd Qu.:0.002695   3rd Qu.:0.9065   3rd Qu.:158.77
 Max.   :0.005830   Max.   :0.9882   Max.   :321.89
```

...a summary of rule quality measures, including support and confidence;...

```
mining info:
            data ntransactions support confidence
 bookbaskets_use         40822   0.002       0.75
```

...and some information on how apriori() was called.

The quality measures on the rules include not only the rules' support and confidence, but also a quantity called *lift*. Lift compares the frequency of an observed pattern with how often you'd expect to see that pattern just by chance. The lift of a rule "if X, then Y" is given by `support(union(X, Y))/(support(X)*support(Y))`. If the lift is near 1, then there's a good chance that the pattern you observed is occurring just by chance. The larger the lift, the more likely that the pattern is "real." In this case, all the discovered rules have a lift of at least 40, so they're likely to be real patterns in customer behavior.

INSPECTING AND EVALUATING RULES

There are also other metrics and interest measures you can use to evaluate the rules by using the function `interestMeasure()`. We'll look at two of these measures: `coverage` and `fishersExactTest`. *Coverage* is the support of the left side of the rule (X); it tells you how often the rule would be applied in the dataset. *Fisher's exact test* is a significance test for whether an observed pattern is real, or chance (the same thing lift measures; Fisher's test is more formal). Fisher's exact test returns the p-value, or the probability that you would see the observed pattern by chance; you want the p-value to be small.

Listing 8.20 Scoring rules

```
> measures <- interestMeasure(rules,
+                    method=c("coverage", "fishersExactTest"),
+                    transactions=bookbaskets_use)
> summary(measures)
    coverage              fishersExactTest
 Min.    :0.002082    Min.     : 0.000e+00
 1st Qu.:0.002511    1st Qu.: 0.000e+00
 Median :0.002719    Median : 0.000e+00
 Mean    :0.003039    Mean    :5.080e-138
 3rd Qu.:0.003160    3rd Qu.: 0.000e+00
 Max.    :0.006982    Max.    :9.702e-136
```

The call to interestMeasure() takes as arguments the discovered rules,...

...a list of interest measures to apply,...

...and a dataset to evaluate the interest measures over. This is usually the same set used to mine the rules, but it needn't be. For instance, you can evaluate the rules over the full dataset, bookbaskets, to get coverage estimates that reflect all the customers, not just the ones who showed interest in more than one book.

The coverage of the discovered rules ranges from 0.002–0.007, equivalent to a range of about 100–250 people. All the p-values from Fisher's test are small, so it's likely that the rules reflect actual customer behavior patterns.

You can also call `interestMeasure()` with methods `support`, `confidence`, and `lift`, among others. This would be useful in our example if you wanted to get support, confidence, and lift estimates for the full dataset `bookbaskets`, rather than the filtered dataset `bookbaskets_use`—or for a subset of the data, for instance, only customers from the United States.

The function `inspect()` pretty-prints the rules. The function `sort()` allows you to sort the rules by a quality or interest measure, like confidence. To print the five most confident rules in the dataset, you could use the following command:

```
inspect(head((sort(rules, by="confidence")), n=5))
```

For legibility, we show the output of this command in table 8.2.

Table 8.2 The five most confident rules discovered in the data

Left side	Right side	Support	Confidence	Lift
Four to Score *High Five* *Seven Up* *Two for the Dough*	*Three to Get Deadly*	0.002	0.988	165

Table 8.2 The five most confident rules discovered in the data *(continued)*

Left side	Right side	Support	Confidence	Lift
Harry Potter and the Order of the Phoenix *Harry Potter and the Prisoner of Azkaban* *Harry Potter and the Sorcerer's Stone*	*Harry Potter and the Chamber of Secrets*	0.003	0.966	73
Four to Score *High Five* *One for the Money* *Two for the Dough*	*Three to Get Deadly*	0.002	0.966	162
Four to Score *Seven Up* *Three to Get Deadly* *Two for the Dough*	*High Five*	0.002	0.966	181
High Five *Seven Up* *Three to Get Deadly* *Two for the Dough*	*Four to Score*	0.002	0.966	168

There are two things to notice in table 8.2. First, the rules concern books that come in series: the numbered series of novels about bounty hunter Stephanie Plum, and the Harry Potter series. So these rules essentially say that if a reader has read four Stephanie Plum or Harry Potter books, they're almost sure to buy another one.

The second thing to notice is that rules 1, 4, and 5 are permutations of the same itemset. This is likely to happen when the rules get long.

RESTRICTING WHICH ITEMS TO MINE

You can restrict which items appear in the left side or right side of a rule. Suppose you're interested specifically in books that tend to co-occur with the novel *The Lovely Bones*. You can do this by restricting which books appear on the right side of the rule, using the `appearance` parameter.

Listing 8.21 Finding rules with restrictions

```
brules <- apriori(bookbaskets_use,
                  parameter =list(support = 0.001,
                                  confidence=0.6),
                  appearance=list(rhs=c("The Lovely Bones: A Novel"),
                                  default="lhs"))

> summary(brules)
set of 46 rules
```

Relax the minimum support to 0.001 and the minimum confidence to 0.6.

Only The Lovely Bones is allowed to appear on the right side of the rules.

By default, all the books can go into the left side of the rules.

```
rule length distribution (lhs + rhs):sizes
 3  4
44  2

   Min. 1st Qu.  Median    Mean 3rd Qu.    Max.
  3.000   3.000   3.000   3.043   3.000   4.000

summary of quality measures:
    support           confidence          lift
 Min.   :0.001004   Min.   :0.6000   Min.   :21.81
 1st Qu.:0.001029   1st Qu.:0.6118   1st Qu.:22.24
 Median :0.001102   Median :0.6258   Median :22.75
 Mean   :0.001132   Mean   :0.6365   Mean   :23.14
 3rd Qu.:0.001219   3rd Qu.:0.6457   3rd Qu.:23.47
 Max.   :0.001396   Max.   :0.7455   Max.   :27.10

mining info:
            data ntransactions support confidence
 bookbaskets_use         40822   0.001        0.6
```

The supports, confidences, and lifts are lower than they were in our previous example, but the lifts are still much greater than 1, so it's likely that the rules reflect real customer behavior patterns.

Let's inspect the rules, sorted by confidence. Since they'll all have the same right side, you can use the `lhs()` function to only look at the left sides.

Listing 8.22 Inspecting rules

```
brulesConf <- sort(brules, by="confidence")

> inspect(head(lhs(brulesConf), n=5))
  items
1 {Divine Secrets of the Ya-Ya Sisterhood: A Novel,
   Lucky : A Memoir}
2 {Lucky : A Memoir,
   The Notebook}
3 {Lucky : A Memoir,
   Wild Animus}
4 {Midwives: A Novel,
   Wicked: The Life and Times of the Wicked Witch of the West}
5 {Lucky : A Memoir,
   Summer Sisters}
```

Sort the rules by confidence.

Use the lhs() function to get the left itemsets of each rule; then inspect the top five.

Note that four of the five most confident rules include *Lucky: A Memoir* in the left side, which perhaps isn't surprising, since *Lucky* was written by the author of *The Lovely Bones*. Suppose you want to find out about works by other authors that are interesting to people who showed interest in *The Lovely Bones*; you can use `subset()` to filter down to only rules that don't include *Lucky*.

Listing 8.23 Inspecting rules with restrictions

```
brulesSub <- subset(brules, subset=!(lhs %in% "Lucky : A Memoir"))
brulesConf <- sort(brulesSub, by="confidence")

> inspect(head(lhs(brulesConf), n=5))
  items
1 {Midwives: A Novel,
   Wicked: The Life and Times of the Wicked Witch of the West}
2 {She's Come Undone,
   The Secret Life of Bees,
   Wild Animus}
3 {A Walk to Remember,
   The Nanny Diaries: A Novel}
4 {Beloved,
   The Red Tent}
5 {The Da Vinci Code,
   The Reader}
```

Restrict to the subset of rules where Lucky is not in the left side.

These examples show that association rule mining is often highly interactive. To get interesting rules, you must often set the support and confidence levels fairly low; as a result you can get many, many rules. Some rules will be more interesting or surprising to you than others; to find them requires sorting the rules by different interest measures, or perhaps restricting yourself to specific subsets of rules.

8.2.4 *Association rule takeaways*

Here's what you should remember about association rules:

- The goal of association rule mining is to find relationships in the data: items or attributes that tend to occur together.
- A good rule "if X, then Y" should occur more often than you'd expect to observe by chance. You can use lift or Fisher's exact test to check if this is true.
- When a large number of different possible items can be in a basket (in our example, thousands of different books), most events will be rare (have low support).
- Association rule mining is often interactive, as there can be many rules to sort and sift through.

8.3 *Summary*

In this chapter, you've learned how to find similarities in data using two different clustering methods in R, and how to find items that tend to occur together in data using association rules. You've also learned how to evaluate your discovered clusters and your discovered rules.

Unsupervised methods like the ones we've covered in this chapter are really more exploratory in nature. Unlike with supervised methods, there's no "ground truth" to evaluate your findings against. But the findings from unsupervised methods can be the starting point for more focused experiments and modeling.

In the last few chapters, we've covered the most basic modeling and data analysis techniques; they're all good first approaches to consider when you're starting a new project. In the next chapter, we'll touch on a few more advanced methods.

Key takeaways

- Unsupervised methods find structure in the data, often as a prelude to predictive modeling.
- The goal of clustering is to discover or draw out similarities among subsets of your data.
- When clustering, you'll find that scaling is important.
- The goal of association rule mining is to find relationships in the data: items or attributes that tend to occur together.
- In association rule mining, most events will be rare, so support and confidence levels must often be set low.

9 Exploring advanced methods

This chapter covers

- Reducing training variance with bagging and random forests
- Learning non-monotone relationships with generalized additive models
- Increasing data separation with kernel methods
- Modeling complex decision boundaries with support vector machines

In the last few chapters, we've covered basic predictive modeling algorithms that you should have in your toolkit. These machine learning methods are usually a good place to start. In this chapter, we'll look at more advanced methods that resolve specific weaknesses of the basic approaches. The main weaknesses we'll address are training variance, non-monotone effects, and linearly inseparable data.

To illustrate the issues, let's consider a silly health prediction model. Suppose we have for a number of patients (of widely varying but unrecorded ages) recorded height (as *h* in feet) and weight (as *w* in pounds), and an appraisal of "healthy" or "unhealthy." The modeling question is this: can height and weight accurately predict health appraisal? Models built off such limited features provide quick examples of the following common weaknesses:

- *Training variance*—Training variance is when small changes in the makeup of the training set result in models that make substantially different predictions. Decision trees can exhibit this effect. Both *bagging* and *random forests* can reduce training variance and sensitivity to overfitting.
- *Non-monotone effects*—Linear regression and logistic regression (see chapter 7) both treat numeric variables in a monotone matter: if more of a quantity is good, then much more of the quantity is better. This is often not the case in the real world. For example, ideal healthy weight is in a bounded range, not arbitrarily heavy or arbitrarily light. *Generalized additive models* add the ability to model interesting variable effects and ranges to linear models and generalized linear models (such as logistic regression).
- *Linearly inseparable data*—Often the concept we're trying to learn is not a linear combination of the original variables. Take BMI, or body mass index, for example: BMI purports to relate height (h) and weight (w) through the expression w/h^2 to health (rightly or wrongly). The term w/h^2 is not a linear combination of w and h, so neither linear regression or logistic regression would directly discover such a relation. It's reasonable to expect that a model that has a term of w/h^2 could produce better predictions of health appraisal than a model that only has linear combinations of h and w. This is because the data is more "separable" with respect to a w/h^2-shaped decision surface than to an h-shaped decision surface. *Kernel methods* allow the data scientist to introduce new nonlinear combination terms to models (like w/h^2), and *support vector machines (SVMs)* use both kernels and training data to build useful decision surfaces.

These issues don't always cause modeling efforts to *visibly* fail. Instead they often leave you with a model that's not as powerful as it could be. In this chapter, we'll use a few advanced methods to fix such modeling weaknesses lurking in earlier examples. We'll start with a demonstration of bagging and random forests.

9.1 Using bagging and random forests to reduce training variance

In section 6.3.2, we looked at using decision trees for classification and regression. As we mentioned there, decision trees are an attractive method for a number of reasons:

- They take any type of data, numerical or categorical, without any distributional assumptions and without preprocessing.
- Most implementations (in particular, R's) handle missing data; the method is also robust to redundant and nonlinear data.
- The algorithm is easy to use, and the output (the tree) is relatively easy to understand.
- Once the model is fit, scoring is fast.

On the other hand, decision trees do have some drawbacks:

- They have a tendency to overfit, especially without pruning.
- They have high training variance: samples drawn from the same population can produce trees with different structures and different prediction accuracy.
- Prediction accuracy can be low, compared to other methods.[1]

For these reasons a technique called *bagging* is often used to improve decision tree models, and a more specialized approach called *random forests* directly combines decision trees with bagging. We'll work examples of both techniques.

9.1.1 Using bagging to improve prediction

One way to mitigate the shortcomings of decision tree models is by bootstrap aggregation, or bagging. In bagging, you draw bootstrap samples (random samples with replacement) from your data. From each sample, you build a decision tree model. The final model is the average of all the individual decision trees.[2] To make this concrete, suppose that `x` is an input datum, `y_i(x)` is the output of the *i*th tree, `c(y_1(x), y_2(x), ... y_n(x))` is the vector of individual outputs, and `y` is the output of the final model:

- For regression, or for estimating class probabilities, `y(x)` is the average of the scores returned by the individual trees: `y(x) = mean(c(y_1(x), ... y_n(x)))`.
- For classification, the final model assigns the class that got the most votes from the individual trees.

Bagging decision trees stabilizes the final model by lowering the variance; this improves the accuracy. A bagged ensemble of trees is also less likely to overfit the data.

> **Bagging classifiers**
>
> The proofs that bagging reduces variance are only valid for regression and for estimating class probabilities, not for classifiers (a model that only returns class membership, not class probabilities). Bagging a bad classifier can make it worse. So you definitely want to work over estimated class probabilities, if they're at all available. But it can be shown that for CART trees (which is the decision tree implementation in R) under mild assumptions, bagging tends to increase classifier accuracy. See Clifton D. Sutton, "Classification and Regression Trees, Bagging, and Boosting," *Handbook of Statistics, Vol. 24* (Elsevier, 2005) for more details.

---

1 See Lim, Loh, and Shih, "A Comparison of Prediction Accuracy, Complexity, and Training Time of Thirty-three Old and New Classification Algorithms," *Machine Learning*, 2000. 40, 203–229; online at http://mng.bz/rwKM.

2 Bagging and random forests (which we'll describe in the next section) are two variations of a general technique called *ensemble learning*. An ensemble model is composed of the combination of several smaller simple models (often small decision trees). Giovanni Seni and John Elder's *Ensemble Methods in Data Mining* (Morgan & Claypool, 2010) is an excellent introduction to the general theory of ensemble learning.

The Spambase dataset (also used in chapter 5) provides a good example of the bagging technique. The dataset consists of about 4,600 documents and 57 features that describe the frequency of certain key words and characters. First we'll train a decision tree to estimate the probability that a given document is spam, and then we'll evaluate the tree's deviance (which you'll recall from discussions in chapters 5 and 7 is similar to variance) and its prediction accuracy.

First, let's load the data. As we did in section 5.2, let's download a copy of *spamD.tsv* (https://github.com/WinVector/zmPDSwR/raw/master/Spambase/spamD.tsv). Then we'll write a few convenience functions and train a decision tree, as in the following listing.

Listing 9.1 Preparing Spambase data and evaluating the performance of decision trees

```
spamD <- read.table('spamD.tsv',header=T,sep='\t')
spamTrain <- subset(spamD,spamD$rgroup>=10)
spamTest <- subset(spamD,spamD$rgroup<10)
```

Load the data and split into training (90% of data) and test (10% of data) sets.

```
spamVars <- setdiff(colnames(spamD),list('rgroup','spam'))
spamFormula <- as.formula(paste('spam=="spam"',
                          paste(spamVars,collapse=' + '),sep=' ~ '))
```

Use all the features and do binary classification, where TRUE corresponds to spam documents.

```
loglikelihood <- function(y, py) {
  pysmooth <- ifelse(py==0, 1e-12,
                ifelse(py==1, 1-1e-12, py))

  sum(y * log(pysmooth) + (1-y)*log(1 - pysmooth))
}
```

A function to calculate log likelihood (for calculating deviance).

A function to calculate and return various measures on the model: normalized deviance, prediction accuracy, and fl, which is the product of precision and recall.

```
accuracyMeasures <- function(pred, truth, name="model") {
  dev.norm <- -2*loglikelihood(as.numeric(truth), pred)/length(pred)
  ctable <- table(truth=truth,
               pred=(pred>0.5))
  accuracy <- sum(diag(ctable))/sum(ctable)
  precision <- ctable[2,2]/sum(ctable[,2])
  recall <- ctable[2,2]/sum(ctable[2,])
  f1 <- precision*recall
  data.frame(model=name, accuracy=accuracy, f1=f1, dev.norm)
}
```

Normalize the deviance by the number of data points so that we can compare the deviance across training and test sets.

Convert the class probability estimator into a classifier by labeling documents that score greater than 0.5 as spam.

```
library(rpart)
treemodel <- rpart(spamFormula, spamTrain)
```

Load the rpart library and fit a decision tree model.

```
accuracyMeasures(predict(treemodel, newdata=spamTrain),
```

Evaluate the decision tree model against the training and test sets.

```
                  spamTrain$spam=="spam",
                  name="tree, training")

accuracyMeasures(predict(treemodel, newdata=spamTest),
                  spamTest$spam=="spam",
                  name="tree, test")
```

The output of the last two calls to accuracyMeasures() produces the following output. As expected, the accuracy and F1 scores both degrade on the test set, and the deviance increases (we want the deviance to be small):

```
          model  accuracy        f1  dev.norm
tree, training 0.9104514 0.7809002 0.5618654

          model  accuracy        f1  dev.norm
    tree, test 0.8799127 0.7091151 0.6702857
```

Now let's try bagging the decision trees.

Listing 9.2 Bagging decision trees

```
ntrain <- dim(spamTrain)[1]
n <- ntrain
ntree <- 100

samples <- sapply(1:ntree,
                  FUN = function(iter)
                    {sample(1:ntrain, size=n, replace=T)})

treelist <-lapply(1:ntree,
                   FUN=function(iter)
                   {samp <- samples[,iter];
                    rpart(spamFormula, spamTrain[samp,])})

predict.bag <- function(treelist, newdata) {
  preds <- sapply(1:length(treelist),
                  FUN=function(iter) {
                    predict(treelist[[iter]], newdata=newdata)})
  predsums <- rowSums(preds)
  predsums/length(treelist)
}

accuracyMeasures(predict.bag(treelist, newdata=spamTrain),
                  spamTrain$spam=="spam",
                  name="bagging, training")

accuracyMeasures(predict.bag(treelist, newdata=spamTest),
```

Use bootstrap samples the same size as the training set, with 100 trees.

Build the bootstrap samples by sampling the row indices of spamTrain with replacement. Each column of the matrix samples represents the row indices into spamTrain that comprise the bootstrap sample.

Train the individual decision trees and return them in a list. Note: this step can take a few minutes.

predict.bag assumes the underlying classifier returns decision probabilities, not decisions.

Evaluate the bagged decision trees against the training and test sets.

```
                    spamTest$spam=="spam",
                    name="bagging, test")
```

This results in the following:

```
            model  accuracy        f1  dev.norm
bagging, training 0.9220372 0.8072953 0.4702707

            model  accuracy        f1 dev.norm
    bagging, test 0.9061135 0.7646497 0.528229
```

As you see, bagging improves accuracy and F1, and reduces deviance over both the training and test sets when compared to the single decision tree (we'll see a direct comparison of the scores a little later on). The improvement is more dramatic on the test set: the bagged model has less generalization error[3] than the single decision tree. We can further improve model performance by going from bagging to *random forests.*

9.1.2 Using random forests to further improve prediction

In bagging, the trees are built using randomized datasets, but each tree is built by considering the exact same set of features. This means that all the individual trees are likely to use very similar sets of features (perhaps in a different order or with different split values). Hence, the individual trees will tend to be overly correlated with each other. If there are regions in feature space where one tree tends to make mistakes, then all the trees are likely to make mistakes there, too, diminishing our opportunity for correction. The random forest approach tries to de-correlate the trees by randomizing the set of variables that each tree is allowed to use. For each individual tree in the ensemble, the random forest method does the following:

1. Draws a bootstrapped sample from the training data
2. For each sample, grows a decision tree, and at each node of the tree
   1. Randomly draws a subset of `mtry` variables from the `p` total features that are available
   2. Picks the best variable and the best split from that set of `mtry` variables
   3. Continues until the tree is fully grown

The final ensemble of trees is then bagged to make the random forest predictions. This is quite involved, but fortunately all done by a single-line random forest call.

By default, the `randomForest()` function in R draws `mtry = p/3` variables at each node for regression trees and `m = sqrt(p)` variables for classification trees. In theory, random forests aren't terribly sensitive to the value of `mtry`. Smaller values will grow the trees faster; but if you have a very large number of variables to choose from, of which only a small fraction are actually useful, then using a larger `mtry` is better, since

[3] Generalization error is the difference in accuracy of the model on data it's never seen before, as compared to its error on the training set.

with a larger `mtry` you're more likely to draw some useful variables at every step of the tree-growing procedure.

Continuing from the data in section 9.1, let's build a spam model using random forests.

Listing 9.3 Using random forests

```
library(randomForest)

set.seed(5123512)

fmodel <- randomForest(x=spamTrain[,spamVars],
        y=spamTrain$spam,
        ntree=100,
        nodesize=7,
        importance=T)

accuracyMeasures(predict(fmodel,
   newdata=spamTrain[,spamVars],type='prob')[,'spam'],
   spamTrain$spam=="spam",name="random forest, train")
##                    model  accuracy        f1  dev.norm
## 1 random forest, train 0.9884142 0.9706611 0.1428786
accuracyMeasures(predict(fmodel,
   newdata=spamTest[,spamVars],type='prob')[,'spam'],
   spamTest$spam=="spam",name="random forest, test")
##                   model  accuracy        f1  dev.norm
## 1 random forest, test 0.9541485 0.8845029 0.3972416
```

Load the randomForest package. (library(randomForest))

Set the pseudo-random seed to a known value to try and make the random forest run repeatable. (set.seed)

Call the randomForest() function to build the model with explanatory variables as x and the category to be predicted as y.

Use 100 trees to be compatible with our bagging example. The default is 500 trees. (ntree=100)

Specify that each node of a tree must have a minimum of 7 elements, to be compatible with the default minimum node size that rpart() uses on this training set. (nodesize=7)

Tell the algorithm to save information to be used for calculating variable importance (we'll see this later). (importance=T)

Report the model quality.

Let's summarize the results for all three of the models we've looked at:

```
# Performance on the training set
        model  accuracy        f1  dev.norm
         Tree 0.9104514 0.7809002 0.5618654
      Bagging 0.9220372 0.8072953 0.4702707
Random Forest 0.9884142 0.9706611 0.1428786

# Performance on the test set
        model  accuracy        f1  dev.norm
         Tree 0.8799127 0.7091151 0.6702857
      Bagging 0.9061135 0.7646497 0.5282290
Random Forest 0.9541485 0.8845029 0.3972416

# Performance change between training and test:
# The decrease in accuracy and f1 in the test set
# from training, and the increase in dev.norm
```

```
# in the test set from training.
# (So in every case, smaller is better)
        model   accuracy         f1    dev.norm
         Tree 0.03053870 0.07178505 -0.10842030
      Bagging 0.01592363 0.04264557 -0.05795832
Random Forest 0.03426572 0.08615813 -0.254363
```

The random forest model performed dramatically better than the other two models in both training and test. But the random forest's generalization error was comparable to that of a single decision tree (and almost twice that of the bagged model).[4]

Random forests can overfit!

It's lore among random forest proponents that "random forests don't overfit." In fact, they can. Hastie et al. back up this observation in their chapter on random forests in *The Elements of Statistical Learning, Second Edition* (Springer, 2009). Look for unreasonably good fits on the training data as evidence of useless overfit and memorization. Also, it's important to evaluate your model's performance on a holdout set.

You can also mitigate the overfitting problem by limiting how deep the trees can be grown (using the `maxnodes` parameter to `randomForest()`). When you do this, you're deliberately degrading model performance on training data so that you can more usefully distinguish between models and falsify bad training decisions.

EXAMINING VARIABLE IMPORTANCE

A useful feature of the `randomForest()` function is its variable importance calculation. Since the algorithm uses a large number of bootstrap samples, each data point `x` has a corresponding set of *out-of-bag samples*: those samples that don't contain the point `x`. The out-of-bag samples can be used is a way similar to *N*-fold cross validation, to estimate the accuracy of each tree in the ensemble.

To estimate the "importance" of a variable `v`, the variable's values are randomly permuted in the out-of-bag samples, and the corresponding decrease in each tree's accuracy is estimated. If the average decrease over all the trees is large, then the variable is considered important—its value makes a big difference in predicting the outcome. If the average decrease is small, then the variable doesn't make much difference to the outcome. The algorithm also measures the decrease in node purity that occurs from splitting on a permuted variable (how this variable affects the quality of the tree).

We can calculate the variable importance by setting `importance=T` in the `randomForest()` call, and then calling the functions `importance()` and `varImpPlot()`.

[4] When a machine learning algorithm shows an implausibly good fit (like 0.99+ accuracy), it can be a symptom that you don't have enough training data to falsify bad modeling alternatives. Limiting the complexity of the model can cut down on generalization error and overfitting and can be worthwhile, even if it decreases training performance.

Listing 9.4 `randomForest` variable `importance()`

```
> varImp <- importance(fmodel)                    <— Call importance() on the spam model.

> varImp[1:10, ]
                     non-spam       spam MeanDecreaseAccuracy
word.freq.make       2.096811  3.7304353             4.334207
word.freq.address    3.603167  3.9967031             4.977452
word.freq.all        2.799456  4.9527834             4.924958
word.freq.3d         3.000273  0.4125932             2.917972
word.freq.our        9.037946  7.9421391            10.731509
word.freq.over       5.879377  4.2402613             5.751371
word.freq.remove    16.637390 13.9331691            17.753122
word.freq.internet   7.301055  4.4458342             7.947515
word.freq.order      3.937897  4.3587883             4.866540
word.freq.mail       5.022432  3.4701224             6.103929

varImpPlot(fmodel, type=1)
```

The importance() function returns a matrix of importance measures (larger values = more important).

Plot the variable importance as measured by accuracy change.

The result of the `varImpPlot()` call is shown in figure 9.1.

Knowing which variables are most important (or at least, which variables contribute the most to the structure of the underlying decision trees) can help you with variable reduction. This is useful not only for building smaller, faster trees, but for choosing variables to be used by another modeling algorithm, if that's desired. We can

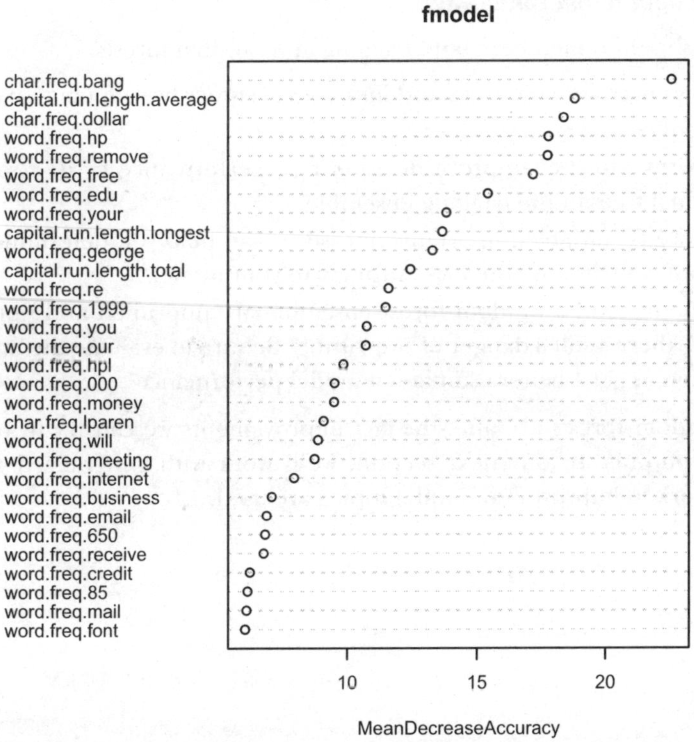

Figure 9.1 Plot of the most important variables in the spam model, as measured by accuracy

reduce the number of variables in this spam example from 57 to 25 without affecting the quality of the final model.

Listing 9.5 Fitting with fewer variables

```
selVars <- names(sort(varImp[,1], decreasing=T))[1:25]

fsel <- randomForest(x=spamTrain[,selVars],y=spamTrain$spam,
                     ntree=100,
                     nodesize=7,
                     importance=T)

accuracyMeasures(predict(fsel,
   newdata=spamTrain[,selVars],type='prob')[,'spam'],
   spamTrain$spam=="spam",name="RF small, train")
##          model  accuracy        f1  dev.norm
## 1 RF small, train 0.9876901 0.9688546 0.1506817

accuracyMeasures(predict(fsel,
   newdata=spamTest[,selVars],type='prob')[,'spam'],
   spamTest$spam=="spam",name="RF small, test")
##         model  accuracy        f1  dev.norm
## 1 RF small, test 0.9497817 0.8738142 0.400825
```

Sort the variables by their importance, as measured by accuracy change.

Build a random forest model using only the 25 most important variables.

The smaller model performs just as well as the random forest model built using all 57 variables.

9.1.3 Bagging and random forest takeaways

Here's what you should remember about bagging and random forests:

- Bagging stabilizes decision trees and improves accuracy by reducing variance.
- Bagging reduces generalization error.
- Random forests further improve decision tree performance by de-correlating the individual trees in the bagging ensemble.
- Random forests' variable importance measures can help you determine which variables are contributing the most strongly to your model.
- Because the trees in a random forest ensemble are unpruned and potentially quite deep, there's still a danger of overfitting. Be sure to evaluate the model on holdout data to get a better estimate of model performance.

Bagging and random forests are after-the-fact improvements we can try in order to improve model outputs. In our next section, we'll work with generalized additive models, which work to improve how model inputs are used.

9.2 Using generalized additive models (GAMs) to learn non-monotone relationships

In chapter 7, we looked at how to use linear regression to model and predict quantitative output, and how to use logistic regression to predict class probabilities. Linear and logistic regression models are powerful tools, especially when you want to understand the relationship between the input variables and the output. They're robust to correlated variables (when regularized), and logistic regression preserves the marginal probabilities of the data. The primary shortcoming of both these models is that they assume that the relationship between the inputs and the output is monotone. That is, if more is good, than much more is always better.

But what if the actual relationship is non-monotone? For example, for underweight patients, increasing weight can increase health. But there's a limit: at some point more weight is bad. Linear and logistic regression miss this distinction (but still often perform surprisingly well, hiding the issue). *Generalized additive models (GAMs)* are a way to model non-monotone responses within the framework of a linear or logistic model (or any other generalized linear model).

9.2.1 Understanding GAMs

Recall that, if `y[i]` is the numeric quantity you want to predict, and `x[i,]` is a row of inputs that corresponds to output `y[i]`, then linear regression finds a function `f(x)` such that

```
f(x[i,]) = b0 + b[1] x[i,1] + b[2] x[i,2] + ... b[n] x[i,n]
```

And `f(x[i,])` is as close to `y[i]` as possible.

In its simplest form, a GAM model relaxes the linearity constraint and finds a set of functions `s_i()` (and a constant term `a0`) such that

```
f(x[i,]) = a0 + s_1(x[i,1]) + s_2(x[i,2]) + ... s_n(x[i,n])
```

And `f(x[i,])` is as close to `y[i]` as possible. The functions `s_i()` are smooth curve fits that are built up from polynomials. The curves are called *splines* and are designed to pass as closely as possible through the data without being too "wiggly" (without overfitting). An example of a spline fit is shown in figure 9.2.

Let's work on a concrete example.

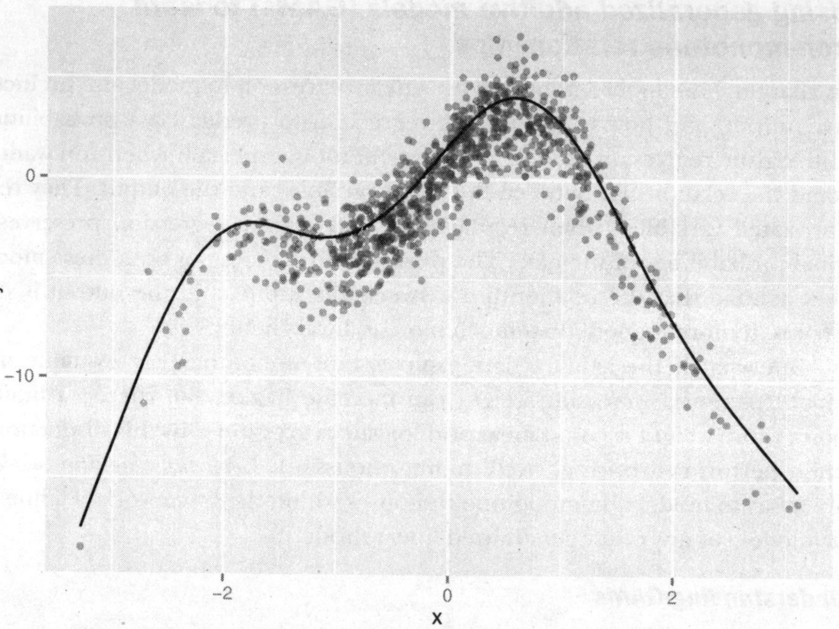

Figure 9.2 A spline that has been fit through a series of points

9.2.2 A one-dimensional regression example

Let's consider a toy example where the response y is a noisy nonlinear function of the input variable x (in fact, it's the function shown in figure 9.2). As usual, we'll split the data into training and test sets.

Listing 9.6 Preparing an artificial problem

```
set.seed(602957)

x <- rnorm(1000)
noise <- rnorm(1000, sd=1.5)

y <- 3*sin(2*x) + cos(0.75*x) - 1.5*(x^2 ) + noise

select <- runif(1000)
frame <- data.frame(y=y, x = x)

train <- frame[select > 0.1,]
test <-frame[select <= 0.1,]
```

Given the data is from the nonlinear functions sin() and cos(), there shouldn't be a good linear fit from x to y. We'll start by building a (poor) linear regression.

Listing 9.7 Linear regression applied to our artificial example

```
> lin.model <- lm(y ~ x, data=train)
> summary(lin.model)
```

```
Call:
lm(formula = y ~ x, data = train)

Residuals:
    Min      1Q  Median      3Q     Max
-17.698  -1.774   0.193   2.499   7.529

Coefficients:
            Estimate Std. Error t value Pr(>|t|)
(Intercept)  -0.8330     0.1161  -7.175 1.51e-12 ***
x             0.7395     0.1197   6.180 9.74e-10 ***
---
Signif. codes:  0 '***' 0.001 '**' 0.01 '*' 0.05 '.' 0.1 ' ' 1

Residual standard error: 3.485 on 899 degrees of freedom
Multiple R-squared:  0.04075,   Adjusted R-squared:  0.03968
F-statistic: 38.19 on 1 and 899 DF,  p-value: 9.737e-10

#
# calculate the root mean squared error (rmse)
#
> resid.lin <- train$y-predict(lin.model)
> sqrt(mean(resid.lin^2))
[1] 3.481091
```

The resulting model's predictions are plotted versus true response in figure 9.3. As expected, it's a very poor fit, with an R-squared of about 0.04. In particular, the errors

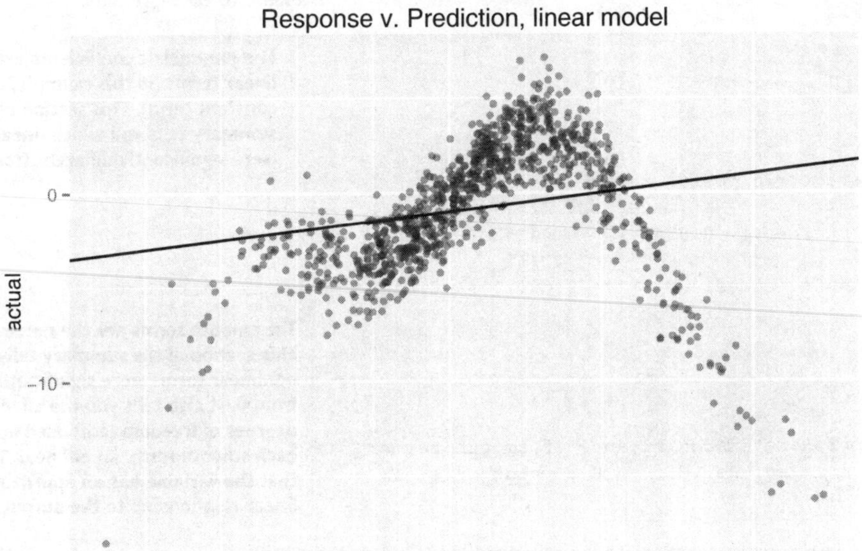

Figure 9.3 Linear model's predictions versus actual response. The solid line is the line of perfect prediction (prediction=actual).

are *heteroscedastic*:[5] there are regions where the model systematically underpredicts and regions where it systematically overpredicts. If the relationship between x and y were truly linear (with noise), then the errors would be *homoscedastic*: the errors would be evenly distributed (mean 0) around the predicted value everywhere.

Let's try finding a nonlinear model that maps x to y. We'll use the function gam() in the package mgcv.[6] When using gam(), you can model variables as either linear or nonlinear. You model a variable x as nonlinear by wrapping it in the s() notation. In this example, rather than using the formula y ~ x to describe the model, you'd use the formula y ~s(x). Then gam() will search for the spline s() that best describes the relationship between x and y, as shown in listing 9.8. Only terms surrounded by s() get the GAM/spline treatment.

Listing 9.8 GAM applied to our artificial example

```
> library(mgcv)
> glin.model <- gam(y~s(x), data=train)
> glin.model$converged
[1] TRUE

> summary(glin.model)


Family: gaussian
Link function: identity


Formula:
y ~ s(x)


Parametric coefficients:
            Estimate Std. Error t value Pr(>|t|)
(Intercept) -0.83467    0.04852   -17.2   <2e-16 ***
---
Signif. codes:  0 '***' 0.001 '**' 0.01 '*' 0.05 '.' 0.1 ' ' 1


Approximate significance of smooth terms:
       edf Ref.df      F p-value
```

Load the mgcv package.

Build the model, specifying that x should be treated as a nonlinear variable.

The converged parameter tells you if the algorithm converged. You should only trust the output if this is TRUE.

Setting family=gaussian and link=identity tells you that the model was treated with the same distributions assumptions as a standard linear regression.

The parametric coefficients are the linear terms (in this example, only the constant term). This section of the summary tells you which linear terms were significantly different from 0.

The smooth terms are the nonlinear terms. This section of the summary tells you which nonlinear terms were significantly different from 0. It also tells you the effective degrees of freedom (edf) used up to build each smooth term. An edf near 1 indicates that the variable has an approximately linear relationship to the output.

---

5 Heteroscedastic errors are errors whose magnitude is correlated with the quantity to be predicted. Heteroscedastic errors are bad because they're systematic and violate the assumption that errors are uncorrelated with outcomes, which is used in many proofs of the good properties of regression methods.

6 There's an older package called gam, written by Hastie and Tibshirani, the inventors of GAMs. The gam package works fine. But it's incompatible with the mgcv package, which ggplot already loads. Since we're using ggplot for plotting, we'll use mgcv for our examples.

```
s(x) 8.685  8.972 497.8  <2e-16 ***
---
Signif. codes:  0 '***' 0.001 '**' 0.01 '*' 0.05 '.' 0.1 ' ' 1

R-sq.(adj) =  0.832   Deviance explained = 83.4%
GCV score =  2.144  Scale est. = 2.121      n = 901

#
# calculate the root mean squared error (rmse)
#
> resid.glin <- train$y-predict(glin.model)
> sqrt(mean(resid.glin^2))
[1] 1.448514
```

"R-sq (adj)" is the adjusted R-squared. "Deviance explained" is the raw R-squared (0.834).

The resulting model's predictions are plotted versus true response in figure 9.4. This fit is much better: the model explains over 80% of the variance (R-squared of 0.83), and the root mean squared error (RMSE) over the training data is less than half the RMSE of the linear model. Note that the points in figure 9.4 are distributed more or less evenly around the line of perfect prediction. The GAM has been fit to be homoscedastic, and any given prediction is as likely to be an overprediction as an underprediction.

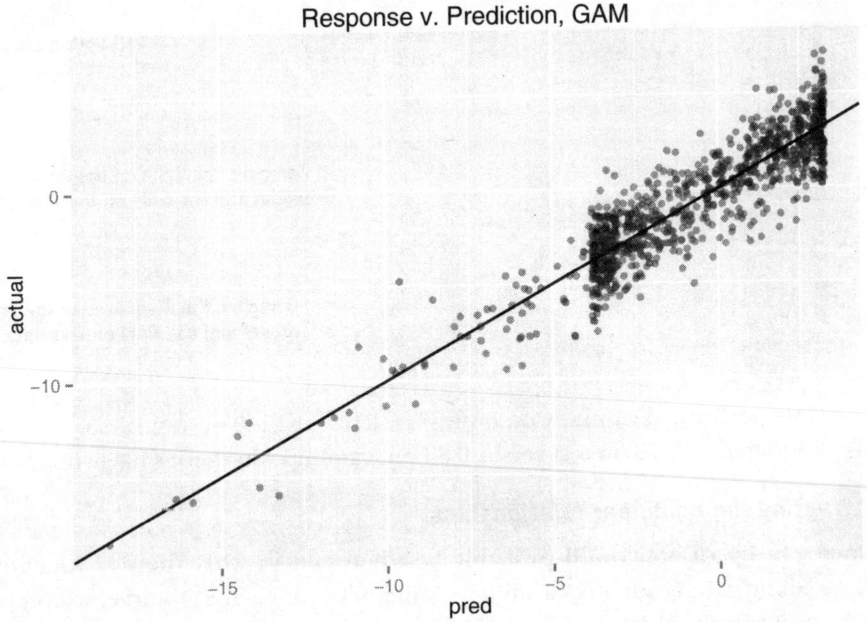

Figure 9.4 GAM's predictions versus actual response. The solid line is the theoretical line of perfect prediction (prediction=actual).

Modeling linear relationships using gam()

By default, `gam()` will perform standard linear regression. If you were to call `gam()` with the formula `y ~ x`, you'd get the same model that you got using `lm()`. More generally, the call `gam(y ~ x1 + s(x2), data=...)` would model the variable `x1` as having a linear relationship with `y`, and try to fit the best possible smooth curve to model the relationship between `x2` and `y`. Of course, the best smooth curve could be a straight line, so if you're not sure whether the relationship between `x` and `y` is linear, you can use `s(x)`. If you see that the coefficient has an `edf` (effective degrees of freedom—see the model summary in listing 9.8) of about 1, then you can try refitting the variable as a linear term.

The use of splines gives GAMs a richer model space to choose from; this increased flexibility brings a higher risk of overfitting. Let's check the models' performances on the test data.

Listing 9.9 Comparing linear regression and GAM performance

```
> actual <- test$y
> pred.lin <- predict(lin.model, newdata=test)
> pred.glin <- predict(glin.model, newdata=test)
> resid.lin <- actual-pred.lin
> resid.glin <- actual-pred.glin

> sqrt(mean(resid.lin^2))
[1] 2.792653
> sqrt(mean(resid.glin^2))
[1] 1.401399

> cor(actual, pred.lin)^2
[1] 0.1543172
> cor(actual, pred.glin)^2
[1] 0.7828869
```

- Call both models on the test data.
- Compare the RMSE of the linear model and the GAM on the test data.
- Compare the R-squared of the linear model and the GAM on test data.

The GAM performed similarly on both sets (RMSE of 1.40 on test versus 1.45 on training; R-squared of 0.78 on test versus 0.83 on training). So there's likely no overfit.

9.2.3 Extracting the nonlinear relationships

Once you fit a GAM, you'll probably be interested in what the `s()` functions look like. Calling `plot()` on a GAM will give you a plot for each `s()` curve, so you can visualize nonlinearities. In our example, `plot(glin.model)` produces the top curve in figure 9.5.

The shape of the curve is quite similar to the scatter plot we saw in figure 9.2 (which is reproduced as the lower half of figure 9.5). In fact, the spline that's superimposed on the scatter plot in figure 9.2 is the same curve.

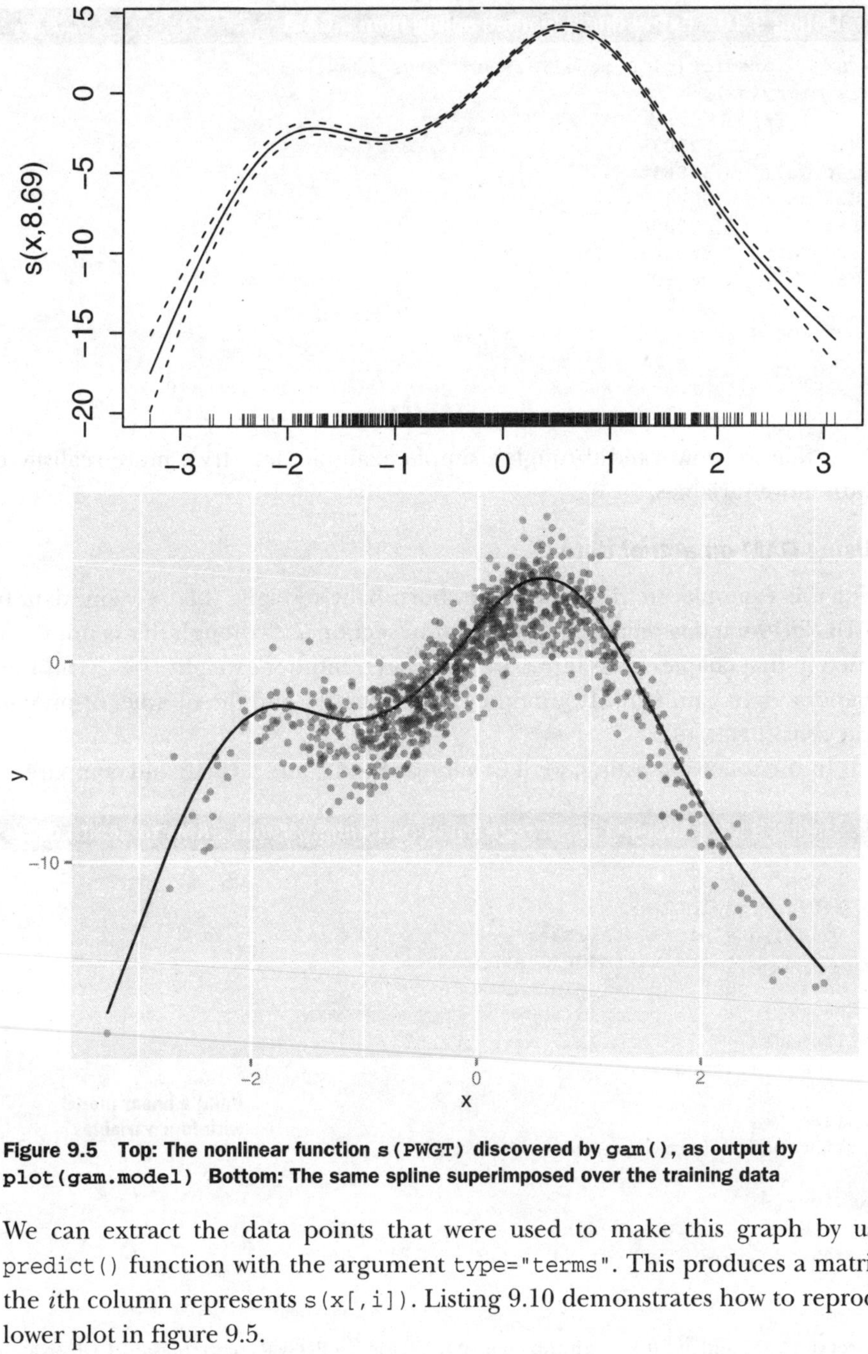

Figure 9.5 Top: The nonlinear function `s(PWGT)` discovered by `gam()`, as output by `plot(gam.model)` Bottom: The same spline superimposed over the training data

We can extract the data points that were used to make this graph by using the `predict()` function with the argument `type="terms"`. This produces a matrix where the *i*th column represents `s(x[,i])`. Listing 9.10 demonstrates how to reproduce the lower plot in figure 9.5.

Listing 9.10 Extracting a learned spline from a GAM

```
> sx <- predict(glin.model, type="terms")
> summary(sx)
      s(x)
 Min.    :-17.527035
 1st Qu.: -2.378636
 Median :  0.009427
 Mean   :  0.000000
 3rd Qu.:  2.869166
 Max.   :  4.084999

> xframe <- cbind(train, sx=sx[,1])

> ggplot(xframe, aes(x=x)) + geom_point(aes(y=y), alpha=0.4) +
                             geom_line(aes(y=sx))
```

Now that we've worked through a simple example, let's try a more realistic example with more variables.

9.2.4 Using GAM on actual data

For this example, we'll predict a newborn baby's weight (`DBWT`) using data from the CDC 2010 natality dataset that we used in section 7.2 (though this is not the risk data used in that chapter).[7] As input, we'll consider mother's weight (`PWGT`), mother's pregnancy weight gain (`WTGAIN`), mother's age (`MAGER`), and the number of prenatal medical visits (`UPREVIS`).[8]

In the following listing, we'll fit a linear model and a GAM, and compare.

Listing 9.11 Applying linear regression (with and without GAM) to health data

```
> library(mgcv)
> library(ggplot2)
> load("NatalBirthData.rData")
> train <- sdata[sdata$ORIGRANDGROUP<=5,]
> test <- sdata[sdata$ORIGRANDGROUP>5,]
> form.lin <- as.formula("DBWT ~ PWGT + WTGAIN + MAGER + UPREVIS")
> linmodel <- lm(form.lin, data=train)          <- Build a linear model
> summary(linmodel)                                with four variables.

Call:
lm(formula = form.lin, data = train)

Residuals:
     Min       1Q   Median       3Q      Max
-3155.43  -272.09    45.04   349.81  2870.55
```

[7] The dataset can be found at https://github.com/WinVector/zmPDSwR/blob/master/CDC/NatalBirthData.rData. A script for preparing the dataset from the original CDC extract can be found at https://github.com/WinVector/zmPDSwR/blob/master/CDC/prepBirthWeightData.R.

[8] We've chosen this example to highlight the mechanisms of `gam()`, not to find the best model for birth weight. Adding other variables beyond the four we've chosen will improve the fit, but obscure the exposition.

```
Coefficients:
             Estimate Std. Error t value Pr(>|t|)
(Intercept) 2419.7090    31.9291  75.784  < 2e-16 ***
PWGT           2.1713     0.1241  17.494  < 2e-16 ***
WTGAIN         7.5773     0.3178  23.840  < 2e-16 ***
MAGER          5.3213     0.7787   6.834  8.6e-12 ***
UPREVIS       12.8753     1.1786  10.924  < 2e-16 ***
---
Signif. codes:  0 '***' 0.001 '**' 0.01 '*' 0.05 '.' 0.1 ' ' 1

Residual standard error: 562.7 on 14381 degrees of freedom
Multiple R-squared:  0.06596, Adjusted R-squared:  0.0657
F-statistic: 253.9 on 4 and 14381 DF,  p-value: < 2.2e-16

> form.glin <- as.formula("DBWT ~ s(PWGT) + s(WTGAIN) +
                s(MAGER) + s(UPREVIS)")
> glinmodel <- gam(form.glin, data=train)
> glinmodel$converged
[1] TRUE
> summary(glinmodel)

Family: gaussian
Link function: identity

Formula:
DBWT ~ s(PWGT) + s(WTGAIN) + s(MAGER) + s(UPREVIS)

Parametric coefficients:
            Estimate Std. Error t value Pr(>|t|)
(Intercept) 3276.948      4.623   708.8   <2e-16 ***
---
Signif. codes:  0 '***' 0.001 '**' 0.01 '*' 0.05 '.' 0.1 ' ' 1

Approximate significance of smooth terms:
             edf Ref.df       F  p-value
s(PWGT)    5.374  6.443  68.981  < 2e-16 ***
s(WTGAIN)  4.719  5.743 102.313  < 2e-16 ***
s(MAGER)   7.742  8.428   6.959 1.82e-09 ***
s(UPREVIS) 5.491  6.425  48.423  < 2e-16 ***
---
Signif. codes:  0 '***' 0.001 '**' 0.01 '*' 0.05 '.' 0.1 ' ' 1

R-sq.(adj) =  0.0927   Deviance explained = 9.42%
GCV score = 3.0804e+05  Scale est. = 3.0752e+05  n = 14386
```

The model explains about 7% of the variance; all coefficients are significantly different from 0.

Build a GAM with the same variables.

Verify that the model has converged.

The model explains just under 10% of the variance; all variables have a nonlinear effect significantly different from 0.

The GAM has improved the fit, and all four variables seem to have a nonlinear relationship with birth weight, as evidenced by `edf`s all greater than 1. We could use `plot(glinmodel)` to examine the shape of the `s()` functions; instead, we'll compare them with a direct smoothing curve of each variable against mother's weight.

Listing 9.12 Plotting GAM results

```
> terms <- predict(glinmodel, type="terms")        <-- Get the matrix of s() functions.

> tframe <-

     cbind(DBWT = train$DBWT, as.data.frame(terms))        <-- Bind in birth weight; convert to data frame.

> colnames(tframe) <- gsub('[()]', '', colnames(tframe))

> pframe <- cbind(tframe, train[,c("PWGT", "WTGAIN",

                                   "MAGER", "UPREVIS")])        <-- Bind in the input variables.

> p1 <- ggplot(pframe, aes(x=PWGT)) +

   geom_point(aes(y=scale(sPWGT, scale=F))) +        <-- Plot s(PWGT) shifted to be zero mean versus PWGT (mother's weight) as points.

   geom_smooth(aes(y=scale(DBWT, scale=F))) +        <-- Plot the smoothing curve of DWBT (birth weight) shifted to be zero mean versus PWGT (mother's weight).

[...]        <-- Repeat for remaining variables (omitted for brevity).
```

Make the column names reference-friendly ("s(PWGT)" is converted to "sPWGT", etc.).

The plots of the s() splines compared with the smooth curves directly relating the input variables to birth weight are shown in figure 9.6. The smooth curves in each case are similar to the corresponding s() in shape, and nonlinear for all of the variables. As usual, we should check for overfit with hold-out data.

Listing 9.13 Checking GAM model performance on hold-out data

```
pred.lin <- predict(linmodel, newdata=test)        <-- Run both the linear model and the GAM on the test data.
pred.glin <- predict(glinmodel, newdata=test)

cor(pred.lin, test$DBWT)^2        <-- Calculate R-squared for both models.
# [1] 0.0616812
cor(pred.glin, test$DBWT)^2
# [1] 0.08857426
```

The performance of the linear model and the GAM were similar on the test set, as they were on the training set, so in this example there's no substantial overfit.

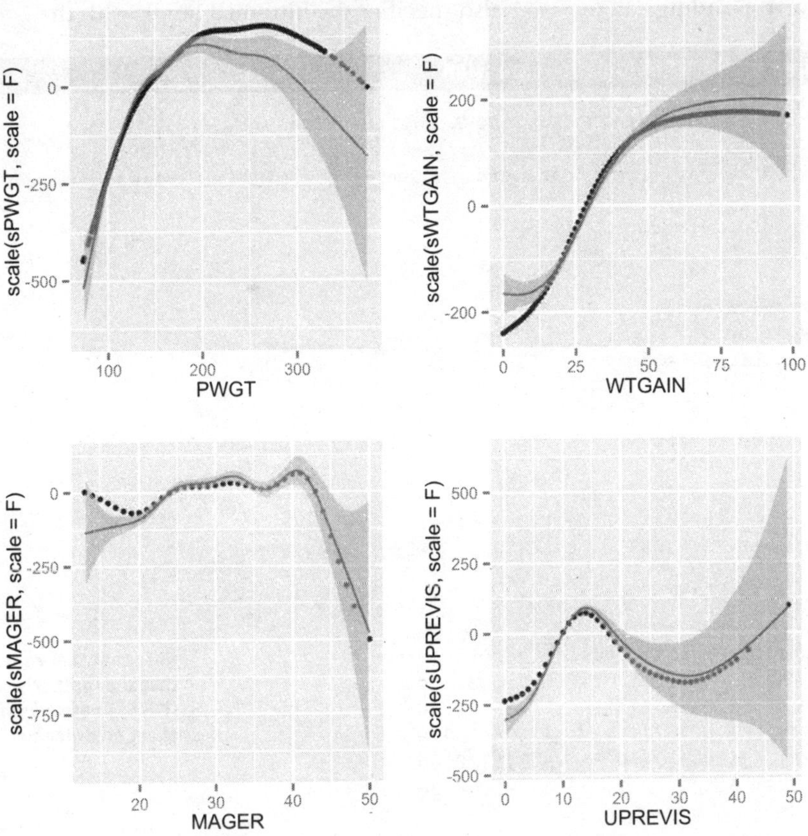

Figure 9.6 Smoothing curves of each of the four input variables plotted against birth weight, compared with the splines discovered by `gam()`. All curves have been shifted to be zero mean for comparison of shape.

9.2.5 *Using GAM for logistic regression*

The `gam()` function can be used for logistic regression as well. Suppose that we wanted to predict the birth of underweight babies (defined as `DBWT < 2000`) from the same variables we've been using. The logistic regression call to do that would be as shown in the following listing.

Listing 9.14 GLM logistic regression

```
form <- as.formula("DBWT < 2000 ~ PWGT + WTGAIN + MAGER + UPREVIS")
logmod <- glm(form, data=train, family=binomial(link="logit"))
```

The corresponding call to gam() also specifies the binomial family with the logit link.

Listing 9.15 GAM logistic regression

```
> form2 <- as.formula("DBWT<2000~s(PWGT)+s(WTGAIN)+
                                          s(MAGER)+s(UPREVIS)")
> glogmod <- gam(form2, data=train, family=binomial(link="logit"))

> glogmod$converged
[1] TRUE

> summary(glogmod)
Family: binomial
Link function: logit

Formula:
DBWT < 2000 ~ s(PWGT) + s(WTGAIN) + s(MAGER) + s(UPREVIS)

Parametric coefficients:
            Estimate Std. Error z value Pr(>|z|)
(Intercept) -3.94085    0.06794     -58   <2e-16 ***
---
Signif. codes:  0 '***' 0.001 '**' 0.01 '*' 0.05 '.' 0.1 ' ' 1

Approximate significance of smooth terms:
             edf Ref.df  Chi.sq  p-value
s(PWGT)    1.905  2.420   2.463  0.36412
s(WTGAIN)  3.674  4.543  64.426 1.72e-12 ***
s(MAGER)   1.003  1.005   8.335  0.00394 **
s(UPREVIS) 6.802  7.216 217.631  < 2e-16 ***
---
Signif. codes:  0 '***' 0.001 '**' 0.01 '*' 0.05 '.' 0.1 ' ' 1

R-sq.(adj) =  0.0331   Deviance explained = 9.14%
UBRE score = -0.76987  Scale est. = 1         n = 14386
```

Note that there's no proof that the mother's weight (PWGT) has a significant effect on outcome.

"Deviance explained" is the pseudo R-squared: 1 - (deviance/null.deviance)

As with the standard logistic regression call, we recover the class probabilities with the call predict(glogmodel, newdata=train, type="response"). Again these models are coming out with low quality, and in practice we would look for more explanatory variables to build better screening models.

The gam() package requires explicit formulas as input

You may have noticed that when calling lm(), glm(), or rpart(), we can input the formula specification as a string. These three functions quietly convert the string into a formula object. Unfortunately, neither gam() nor randomForest(), which you saw in section 9.1.2, will do this automatic conversion. You must explicitly call as.formula() to convert the string into a formula object.

9.2.6 GAM takeaways

Here's what you should remember about GAMs:

- GAMs let you represent nonlinear and non-monotonic relationships between variables and outcome in a linear or logistic regression framework.
- In the `mgcv` package, you can extract the discovered relationship from the GAM model using the `predict()` function with the `type="terms"` parameter.
- You can evaluate the GAM with the same measures you'd use for standard linear or logistic regression: residuals, deviance, R-squared, and pseudo R-squared. The `gam()` summary also gives you an indication of which variables have a significant effect on the model.
- Because GAMs have increased complexity compared to standard linear or logistic regression models, there's more risk of overfit.

GAMs allow you to extend linear methods (and generalized linear methods) to allow variables to have nonlinear (or even non-monotone) effects on outcome. But we've only considered each variable's impact individually. Another approach is to form new variables from nonlinear combinations of existing variables. The hope is that with access to enough of these new variables, your modeling problem becomes easier.

In the next two sections, we'll work with two of the most popular ways to add and manage new variables: *kernel methods* and *support vector machines.*

9.3 Using kernel methods to increase data separation

Often your available variables aren't quite good enough to meet your modeling goals. The most powerful way to get new variables is to get new, better measurements from the domain expert. Acquiring new measurements may not be practical, so you'd also use methods to create new variables from combinations of the measurements you already have at hand. We call these new variables *synthetic* to emphasize that they're synthesized from combinations of existing variables and don't represent actual new measurements. Kernel methods are one way to produce new variables from old and to increase the power of machine learning methods.[9] With enough synthetic variables, data where points from different classes are mixed together can often be lifted to a space where the points from each class are grouped together, and separated from out-of-class points.

One misconception about kernel methods is that they're automatic or self-adjusting. They're not; beyond a few "automatic bandwidth adjustments," it's up to the data scientist to specify a useful kernel instead of the kernel being automatically found from

[9] The standard method to create synthetic variables is to add *interaction* terms. An interaction between variables occurs when a change in outcome due to two (or more) variables is more than the changes due to each variable alone. For example, too high a sodium intake will increase the risk of hypertension, but this increase is disproportionately higher for people with a genetic susceptibility to hypertension. The probability of becoming hypertensive is a function of the interaction of the two factors (diet and genetics). For details on using interaction terms in R, see `help('formula')`. In models such as `lm()`, you can introduce an interaction term by adding a colon (`:`) to a pair of terms in your formula specification.

the data. But many of the standard kernels (inner-product, Gaussian, and cosine) are so useful that it's often profitable to try a few kernels to see what improvements they offer.

THE WORD KERNEL IS USED IN MANY DIFFERENT SENSES The word *kernel* has many different incompatible definitions in mathematics and statistics. The machine learning sense of the word used here is taken from operator theory and the sense used in Mercer's theorem. The kernels we want are two argument functions that behave a lot like an inner product. The other common (incompatible) statistical use of kernel is in density estimation, where kernels are single argument functions that represent probability density functions or distributions.

In the next few sections, we'll work through the definition of a kernel function. We'll give a few examples of transformations that can be implemented by kernels and a few examples of transformations that can't be implemented as kernels. We'll then work through a few examples.

9.3.1 Understanding kernel functions

To understand kernel functions, we'll work through the definition, why they're useful, and some examples of important kernel functions.

FORMAL DEFINITION OF A KERNEL FUNCTION

In our application, a kernel is a function with a very specific definition. Let `u` and `v` be any pair of variables. `u` and `v` are typically vectors of input or independent variables (possibly taken from two rows of a dataset). A function `k(,)` that maps pairs `(u,v)` to numbers is called a *kernel function* if and only if there is some function `phi()` mapping `(u,v)`s to a vector space such that `k(u,v) = phi(u) %*% phi(v)` for all `u,v`.[10] We'll informally call the expression `k(u,v) = phi(u) %*% phi(v)` the *Mercer expansion of the kernel* (in reference to Mercer's theorem; see http://mng.bz/xFD2) and consider `phi()` the certificate that tells us `k(,)` is a good kernel. This is much easier to understand from a concrete example. In listing 9.16, we'll develop an example function `k(,)` and the matching `phi()` that demonstrates that `k(,)` is in fact a kernel over two dimensional vectors.

Listing 9.16 An artificial kernel example

```
> u <- c(1,2)
> v <- c(3,4)
> k <- function(u,v) {
      u[1]*v[1] + u[2]*v[2] +
        u[1]*u[1]*v[1]*v[1] + u[2]*u[2]*v[2]*v[2] +
        u[1]*u[2]*v[1]*v[2]
   }
```

Define a function of two vector variables (both two dimensional) as the sum of various products of terms.

[10] `%*%` is R's notation for dot product or inner product; see `help('%*%')` for details. Note that `phi()` is allowed to map to very large (and even infinite) vector spaces.

```
> phi <- function(x) {
    x <- as.numeric(x)
    c(x,x*x,combn(x,2,FUN=prod))
  }
> print(k(u,v))
[1] 108
> print(phi(u))
[1] 1 2 1 4 2
> print(phi(v))
[1]  3  4  9 16 12
> print(as.numeric(phi(u) %*% phi(v)))
[1] 108
```

Define a function of a single vector variable that returns a vector containing the original entries plus all products of entries.

Example evaluation of k(,).

Confirm phi() agrees with k(,). phi() is the certificate that shows k(,) is in fact a kernel.

Figure 9.7 illustrates[11] what we hope for from a good kernel: our data being pushed around so it's easier to sort or classify. By using a kernel transformation, we move to a situation where the distinction we're trying to learn is representable by a linear operator in our transformed data.

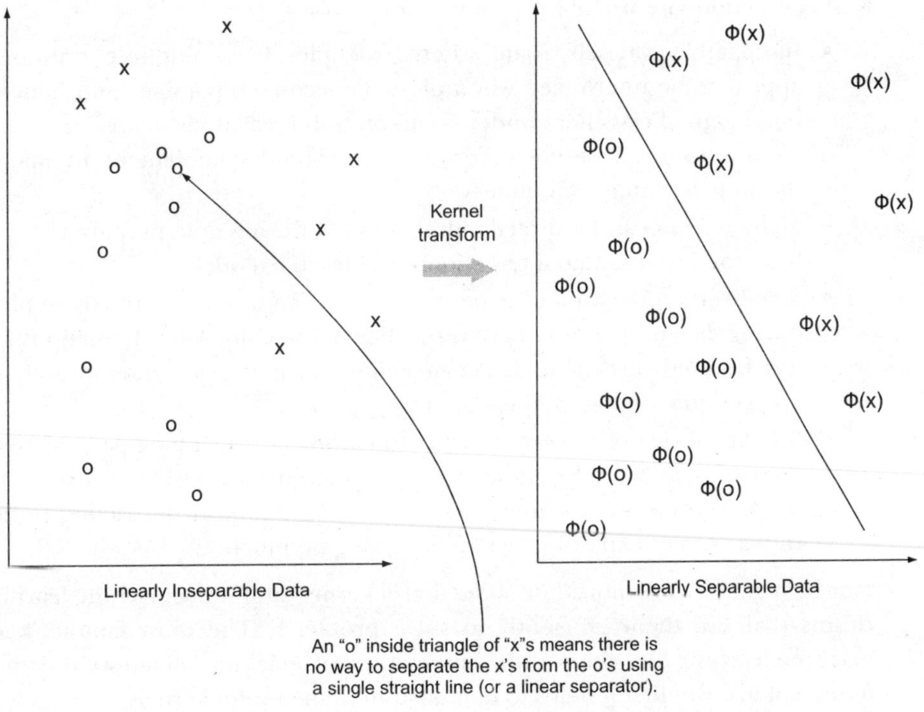

Figure 9.7 Notional illustration of a kernel transform (based on Cristianini and Shawe-Taylor, 2000)

[11] See Nello Cristianini and John Shawe-Taylor, *An Introduction to Support Vector Machines and Other Kernel-based Learning Methods*, Cambridge University Press, 2000.

Most kernel methods use the function `k(,)` directly and only use properties of `k(,)` guaranteed by the matching `phi()` to ensure method correctness. The `k(,)` function is usually quicker to compute than the notional function `phi()`. A simple example of this is what we'll call the *dot-product similarity* of documents. The dot-product document similarity is defined as the dot product of two vectors where each vector is derived from a document by building a huge vector of indicators, one for each possible feature. For instance, if the features you're considering are word pairs, then for every pair of words in a given dictionary, the document gets a feature of 1 if the pair occurs as a consecutive utterance in the document and 0 if not. This method is the `phi()`, but in practice we never use the `phi()` procedure. Instead, for one document each consecutive pair of words is generated and a bit of score is added if this pair is both in the dictionary and found consecutively in the other document. For moderate-sized documents and large dictionaries, this direct `k(,)` implementation is vastly more efficient than the `phi()` implementation.

WHY ARE KERNEL FUNCTIONS USEFUL?

Kernel functions are useful for a number of reasons:

- Inseparable datasets (data where examples from multiple training classes appear to be intermixed when plotted) become separable (and hence we can build a good classifier) under common nonlinear transforms. This is known as *Cover's theorem.* Nonlinear kernels are a good complement to many linear machine learning techniques.
- Many `phi()`s can be directly implemented during data preparation. Never be too proud to try some interaction variables in a model.
- Some very powerful and expensive `phi()`s that can't be directly implemented during data preparation have very efficient matching kernel functions `k(,)` that can be used directly in select machine learning algorithms without needing access to the highly complex `phi()`.
- All symmetric positive semidefinite functions `k(,)` mapping pairs of variables to the reals can be represented as `k(u,v) = phi(u) %*% phi(v)` for some function `phi()`. This is a consequence of *Mercer's theorem.* So by restricting to functions with a Mercer expansion, we're not giving up much.

Our next goal is to demonstrate some useful kernels and some machine learning algorithms that use them efficiently to solve problems. The most famous kernelized machine learning algorithm is the support vector machine, which we'll demonstrate in section 9.4. But first it helps to demonstrate some useful kernels.

SOME IMPORTANT KERNEL FUNCTIONS

Let's look at some practical uses for some important kernels in table 9.1.

Table 9.1 Some important kernels and their uses

Kernel name	Informal description and use
Definitional (or explicit) kernels	Any method that explicitly adds additional variables (such as interactions) can be expressed as a kernel over the original data. These are kernels where you explicitly implement and use `phi()`.
Linear transformation kernels	Any positive semidefinite linear operation (like projecting to principal components) can also be expressed as a kernel.
Gaussian or radial kernel	Many decreasing non-negative functions of distance can be expressed as kernels. This is also an example of a kernel where `phi()` maps into an infinite dimensional vector space (essentially the Taylor series of `exp()`) and therefore `phi(u)` doesn't have an easy-to-implement representation (you must instead use `k(,)`).
Cosine similarity kernel	Many similarity measures (measures that are large for identical items and small for dissimilar items) can be expressed as kernels.
Polynomial kernel	Much is made of the fact that positive integer powers of kernels are also kernels. The derived kernel does have many more terms derived from powers and products of terms from the original kernel, but the modeling technique isn't able to independently pick coefficients for all of these terms simultaneously. Polynomial kernels do introduce some extra options, but they're not magic.

At this point, it's important to mention that not everything is a kernel. For example, the common squared distance function (`k = function(u,v) {(u-v) %*% (u-v)}`) isn't a kernel. So kernels can express similarities, but can't directly express distances.[12]

Only now that we've touched on *why* some common kernels are useful is it appropriate to look at the formal mathematical definitions. Remember, we pick kernels for their utility, not because the mathematical form is exciting. Now let's take a look at six important kernel definitions.

Mathematical definitions of common kernels

A definitional kernel is any kernel that is an explicit inner product of two applications of a vector function:

$$k(u, v) = \phi(u) \cdot \phi(v)$$

The dot product or identity kernel is just the inner product applied to actual vectors of data:

$$k(u, v) = u \cdot v$$

[12] Some more examples of kernels (and how to build new kernels from old) can be found at http://mng.bz/1F78.

A linear transformation kernel is a matrix form like the following:

$$k(u, v) = u^T L^T Lv$$

The Gaussian or radial kernel has the following form:

$$k(u, v) = e^{-c||u-v||^2}$$

The cosine similarity kernel is a rescaled dot product kernel:

$$k(u, v) = \frac{u \cdot v}{\sqrt{u \cdot u \cdot v \cdot v}}$$

A polynomial kernel is a dot product with a transform (shift and power) applied as shown here:

$$k(u, v) = (su \cdot v + c)^d$$

9.3.2 Using an explicit kernel on a problem

Let's demonstrate explicitly choosing a kernel function on a problem we've already worked with.

REVISITING THE PUMS LINEAR REGRESSION MODEL

To demonstrate using a kernel on an actual problem, we'll reprepare the data used in section 7.1.3 to again build a model predicting the logarithm of income from a few other factors. We'll resume this analysis by using `load()` to reload the data from a copy of the file https://github.com/WinVector/zmPDSwR/raw/master/PUMS/psub.RData. Recall that the basic model (for purposes of demonstration) used only a few variables; we'll redo producing a stepwise improved linear regression model for `log(PINCP)`.

Listing 9.17 Applying stepwise linear regression to PUMS data

```
dtrain <- subset(psub,ORIGRANDGROUP >= 500)
dtest <- subset(psub,ORIGRANDGROUP < 500)
m1 <- step(
   lm(log(PINCP,base=10) ~ AGEP + SEX + COW + SCHL,
      data=dtrain),
   direction='both')
rmse <- function(y, f) { sqrt(mean( (y-f)^2 )) }
print(rmse(log(dtest$PINCP,base=10),
```

Split data into test and training.

Build the basic linear regression model.

Ask that the linear regression model we're building be stepwise improved, which is a powerful automated procedure for removing variables that don't seem to have significant impacts (can improve generalization performance).

Define the RMSE function.

```
  predict(m1,newdata=dtest)))
# [1] 0.2752171
```

Calculate the RMSE between the prediction and the actuals.

The quality of prediction was middling (the RMSE isn't that small), but the model exposed some of the important relationships. In a real project, you'd do your utmost to find new explanatory variables. But you'd also be interested to see if any combination of variables you were already using would help with prediction. We'll work through finding some of these combinations using an explicit `phi()`.

INTRODUCING AN EXPLICIT TRANSFORM

Explicit kernel transforms are a formal way to unify ideas like reshaping variables and adding interaction terms.[13]

In listing 9.18, we'll set up a `phi()` function and use it to build a new larger data frame with new modeling variables.

Listing 9.18 Applying an example explicit kernel transform

```
phi <- function(x) {
    x <- as.numeric(x)
    c(x,x*x,combn(x,2,FUN=prod))
  }
phiNames <- function(n) {
     c(n,paste(n,n,sep=':'),
        combn(n,2,FUN=function(x) {paste(x,collapse=':')}))
  }
modelMatrix <- model.matrix(~ 0 + AGEP + SEX + COW + SCHL,psub)
colnames(modelMatrix) <- gsub('[^a-zA-Z0-9]+','_',
   colnames(modelMatrix))
pM <- t(apply(modelMatrix,1,phi))
vars <- phiNames(colnames(modelMatrix))
vars <- gsub('[^a-zA-Z0-9]+','_',vars)
colnames(pM) <- vars
pM <- as.data.frame(pM)
```

Define our primal kernel function: map a vector to a copy of itself plus all square terms and cross-multiplied terms.

Define a function similar to our primal kernel, but working on variable names instead of values.

Convert data to a matrix where all categorical variables are encoded as multiple numeric indicators.

Remove problematic characters from matrix column names.

Apply the primal kernel function to every row of the matrix and transpose results so they're written as rows (not as a list as returned by apply()).

Extend names from original matrix to names for compound variables in new matrix.

[13] See `help('formula')` for how to add interactions using the `:` and `*` operators.

```
pM$PINCP <- psub$PINCP

pM$ORIGRANDGROUP <- psub$ORIGRANDGROUP

pMtrain <- subset(pM,ORIGRANDGROUP >= 500)

pMtest <- subset(pM,ORIGRANDGROUP < 500)
```

Add in outcomes, test/train split columns, and prepare new data for modeling.

The steps to use this new expanded data frame to build a model are shown in the following listing.

Listing 9.19 Modeling using the explicit kernel transform

```
formulaStr2 <- paste('log(PINCP,base=10)',
   paste(vars,collapse=' + '),
   sep=' ~ ')
m2 <- lm(as.formula(formulaStr2),data=pMtrain)
coef2 <- summary(m2)$coefficients
interestingVars <- setdiff(rownames(coef2)[coef2[,'Pr(>|t|)']<0.01],
                          '(Intercept)')
interestingVars <- union(colnames(modelMatrix),interestingVars)
```

Select a set of interesting variables by building an initial model using all of the new variables and retaining an interesting subset. This is an ad hoc move to speed up the stepwise regression by trying to quickly dispose of many useless derived variables. By introducing many new variables, the primal kernel method also introduces many new degrees of freedom, which can invite overfitting.

```
formulaStr3 <- paste('log(PINCP,base=10)',
                     paste(interestingVars,collapse=' + '),
                     sep=' ~ ')
m3 <- step(lm(as.formula(formulaStr3),data=pMtrain),direction='both')
print(rmse(log(pMtest$PINCP,base=10),predict(m3,newdata=pMtest)))
# [1] 0.2735955
```

Stepwise regress on subset of variables to get new model.

Calculate the RMSE between the prediction and the actuals.

We see RMSE is improved by a small amount on the test data. With such a small improvement, we have extra reason to confirm its statistical significance using a cross-validation procedure as demonstrated in section 6.2.3. Leaving these issues aside, let's look at the summary of the new model to see what new variables the phi() procedure introduced. The next listing shows the structure of the new model.

Listing 9.20 Inspecting the results of the explicit kernel model

```
> print(summary(m3))

Call:
lm(formula = log(PINCP, base = 10) ~ AGEP + SEXM +
    COWPrivate_not_for_profit_employee +
    SCHLAssociate_s_degree + SCHLBachelor_s_degree +
    SCHLDoctorate_degree +
    SCHLGED_or_alternative_credential + SCHLMaster_s_degree +
```

```
    SCHLProfessional_degree + SCHLRegular_high_school_diploma +
    SCHLsome_college_credit_no_degree + AGEP_AGEP, data = pMtrain)

Residuals:
     Min       1Q   Median       3Q      Max
-1.29264 -0.14925  0.01343  0.17021  0.61968

Coefficients:
                                Estimate Std. Error t value Pr(>|t|)
(Intercept)                    2.9400460  0.2219310  13.248  < 2e-16 ***
AGEP                           0.0663537  0.0124905   5.312 1.54e-07 ***
SEXM                           0.0934876  0.0224236   4.169 3.52e-05 ***
COWPrivate_not_for_profit_em -0.1187914  0.0379944  -3.127  0.00186 **
SCHLAssociate_s_degree         0.2317211  0.0509509   4.548 6.60e-06 ***
SCHLBachelor_s_degree          0.3844459  0.0417445   9.210  < 2e-16 ***
SCHLDoctorate_degree           0.3190572  0.1569356   2.033  0.04250 *
SCHLGED_or_alternative_creden 0.1405157  0.0766743   1.833  0.06737 .
SCHLMaster_s_degree            0.4553550  0.0485609   9.377  < 2e-16 ***
SCHLProfessional_degree        0.6525921  0.0845052   7.723 5.01e-14 ***
SCHLRegular_high_school_diplo 0.1016590  0.0415834   2.445  0.01479 *
SCHLsome_college_credit_no_de 0.1655906  0.0416345   3.977 7.85e-05 ***
AGEP_AGEP                     -0.0007547  0.0001704  -4.428 1.14e-05 ***
---
Signif. codes:  0 '***' 0.001 '**' 0.01 '*' 0.05 '.' 0.1 ' ' 1

Residual standard error: 0.2649 on 582 degrees of freedom
Multiple R-squared:  0.3541,    Adjusted R-squared:  0.3408
F-statistic: 26.59 on 12 and 582 DF,  p-value: < 2.2e-16
```

In this case, the only new variable is `AGEP_AGEP`. The model is using `AGEP*AGEP` to build a non-monotone relation between age and log income.[14]

The `phi()` method is automatic and can therefore be applied in many modeling situations. In our example, we can think of the crude function that multiplies all pairs of variables as our `phi()` or think of the implied function that took the original set of variables to the new set called `interestingVars` as the actual training data-dependent `phi()`. Explicit `phi()` kernel notation adds some capabilities, but algorithms that are designed to work directly with implicit kernel definitions in `k(,)` notation can be much more powerful. The most famous such method is the support vector machine, which we'll use in the next section.

9.3.3 Kernel takeaways

Here's what you should remember about kernel methods:

- Kernels provide a systematic way of creating interactions and other synthetic variables that are combinations of individual variables.
- The goal of kernelizing is to lift the data into a space where the data is separable, or where linear methods can be used directly.

[14] Of course, this sort of relation could be handled quickly by introducing an `AGEP*AGEP` term directly in the model or by using a generalized additive model to discover the optimal (possibly nonlinear) shape of the relation between `AGEP` and log income (see section 9.2).

Now we're ready to work with the most well-known use of kernel methods: support vector machines.

9.4 Using SVMs to model complicated decision boundaries

The idea behind SVMs is to use entire training examples as classification landmarks (called *support vectors*). We'll describe the bits of the theory that affect use and move on to applications.

9.4.1 Understanding support vector machines

A support vector machine with a given function `phi()` builds a model where for a given example `x` the machine decides `x` is in the class if

```
w %*% phi(x) + b >= 0
```

for some `w` and `b`, and not in the class otherwise. The model is completely determined by the vector `w` and the scalar offset `b`. The general idea is sketched out in figure 9.8. In "real space" (left), the data is separated by a nonlinear boundary. When the data is lifted into the higher-dimensional kernel space (right), the lifted points are separated by a hyperplane whose normal is `w` and that is offset from the origin by `b` (not shown). Essentially, all the data that makes a positive dot product with `w` is on one side of the hyperplane (and all belong to one class); data that makes a negative dot product with the `w` belongs to the other class.

Finding `w` and `b` is performed by the support vector training operation. There are variations on the support vector machine that make decisions between more than two classes, perform scoring/regression, and detect novelty. But we'll discuss only the support vector machines for simple classification.

As a user of support vector machines, you don't immediately need to know how the training procedure works; that's what the software does for you. But you do need to have some notion of what it's trying to do. The model `w,b` is ideally picked so that

```
w %*% phi(x) + b >= u
```

for all training xs that were in the class, and

```
w %*% phi(x) + b <= v
```

for all training examples not in the class. The data is called *separable* if `u>v` and the size of the separation `(u-v)/sqrt(w %*% w)` is called the *margin*. The goal of the SVM optimizer is to maximize the margin. A large margin can actually ensure good behavior on future data (good generalization performance). In practice, real data isn't always separable even in the presence of a kernel. To work around this, most SVM implementations implement the so-called *soft margin* optimization goal.

A soft margin optimizer adds additional error terms that are used to allow a limited fraction of the training examples to be on the wrong side of the decision surface.[15] The

[15] A common type of dataset that is inseparable under any kernel is any dataset where there are at least two examples belonging to different outcome classes with the exact same values for all input or `x` variables. The original "hard margin" SVM couldn't deal with this sort of data and was for that reason not considered to be practical.

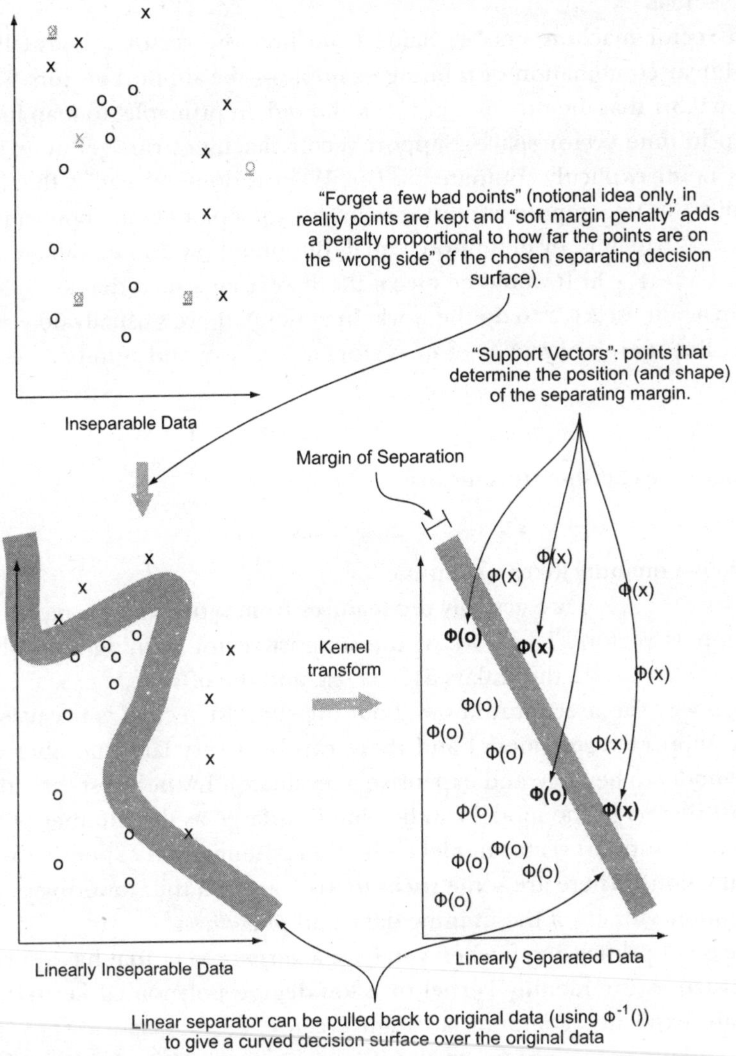

Figure 9.8 Notional illustration of SVM

model doesn't actually perform well on the altered training examples, but trades the error on these examples against increased margin on the remaining training examples. For most implementations, there's a control that determines the trade-off between margin width for the remaining data and how much data is pushed around to achieve the margin. Typically the control is named `C` and setting it to values higher than `1` increases the penalty for moving data.[16]

[16] For more details on support vector machines, we recommend Cristianini and Shawe-Taylor's *An Introduction to Support Vector Machines and Other Kernel-based Learning Methods.*

THE SUPPORT VECTORS

The support vector machine gets its name from how the vector `w` is usually represented: as a linear combination of training examples—the support vectors. Recall we said in section 9.3.1 that the function `phi()` is allowed, in principle, to map into a very large or even infinite vector space. Support vector machines can get away with this because they never explicitly compute `phi(x)`. What is done instead is that any time the algorithm wants to compute `phi(u) %*% phi(v)` for a pair of data points, it instead computes `k(u,v)` which is, by definition, equal. But then how do we evaluate the final model `w %*% phi(x) + b`? It would be nice if there were an `s` such that `w = phi(s)`, as we could then again use `k(,)` to do the work. In general, there's usually no `s` such that `w = phi(s)`. But there's always a set of vectors `s1,...,sm` and numbers `a1,...,am` such that

```
w = sum(a1*phi(s1),...,am*phi(sm))
```

With some math, we can show this means

```
w %*% phi(x) + b = sum(a1*k(s1,x),...,am*k(sm,x)) + b
```

The right side is a quantity we can compute.

The vectors `s1,...,sm` are actually the features from `m` training examples and are called the support vectors. The work of the support vector training algorithm is to find the vectors `s1,...,sm`, the scalars `a1,...,am`, and the offset `b`.[17]

The reason why the user must know about the support vectors is because they're stored in the support vector model and there can be a very large number of them (causing the model to be large and expensive to evaluate). In the worst case, the number of support vectors in the model can be almost as large as the number of training examples (making support vector model evaluation potentially as expensive as nearest neighbor evaluation). There are some tricks to work around this: lowering `C`, training models on random subsets of the training data, and *primalizing*.

The easy case of primalizing is when you have a kernel `phi()` that has a simple representation (such as the identity kernel or a low-degree polynomial kernel). In this case, you can explicitly compute a single vector `w = sum(a1*phi(s1),... am*phi(sm))` and use `w %*% phi(x)` to classify a new `x` (notice you don't need to keep the support vectors `s1,...sm` when you have `w`).

For kernels that don't map into a finite vector space (such as the popular radial or Gaussian kernel), you can also hope to find a vector function `p()` such that `p(u) %*% p(v)` is very near `k(u,v)` for all of your training data and then use

```
w ~ sum(a1*p(s1),...,am*p(sm))
```

[17] Because SVMs work in terms of support vectors, not directly in terms of original variables or features, a feature that's predictive can be lost if it doesn't show up strongly in kernel-specified similarities between support vectors.

along with b as an approximation of your support vector model. But many support vector packages are unable to convert to a primal form model (it's mostly seen in Hadoop implementations), and often converting to primal form takes as long as the original model training.

9.4.2 Trying an SVM on artificial example data

Support vector machines excel at learning concepts of the form "examples that are near each other should be given the same classification." This is because they can use support vectors and margin to erect a moat that groups training examples into classes. In this section, we'll quickly work some examples. One thing to notice is how little knowledge of the internal working details of the support vector machine are needed. The user mostly has to choose the kernel to control what is similar/dissimilar, adjust C to try and control model complexity, and pick `class.weights` to try and value different types of errors.

SPIRAL EXAMPLE

Let's start with an example adapted from R's kernlab library documentation. Listing 9.21 shows the recovery of the famous spiral machine learning counter-example[18] using kernlab's spectral clustering method.

Listing 9.21 Setting up the spirals data as an example classification problem

```
library('kernlab')
data('spirals')
sc <- specc(spirals, centers = 2)
s <- data.frame(x=spirals[,1],y=spirals[,2],
   class=as.factor(sc))
library('ggplot2')
ggplot(data=s) +
   geom_text(aes(x=x,y=y,
      label=class,color=class)) +
   coord_fixed() +
   theme_bw() + theme(legend.position='none')
```

- Load the kernlab kernel and support vector machine package and then ask that the included example "spirals" be made available.
- Use kernlab's spectral clustering routine to identify the two different spirals in the example dataset.
- Combine the spiral coordinates and the spiral label into a data frame.
- Plot the spirals with class labels.

Figure 9.9 shows the labeled spiral dataset. Two classes (represented digits) of data are arranged in two interwoven spirals. This dataset is difficult for learners that don't have a rich enough concept space (perceptrons, shallow neural nets) and easy for more sophisticated learners that can introduce the right new features. Support vector machines, with the right kernel, are a technique that finds the spiral easily.

18 See K. J. Lang and M. J. Witbrock, "Learning to tell two spirals apart," in Proceedings of the 1988 Connectionist Models Summer School, D. Touretzky, G. Hinton, and T. Sejnowski (eds), Morgan Kaufmann, 1988 (pp. 52-59).

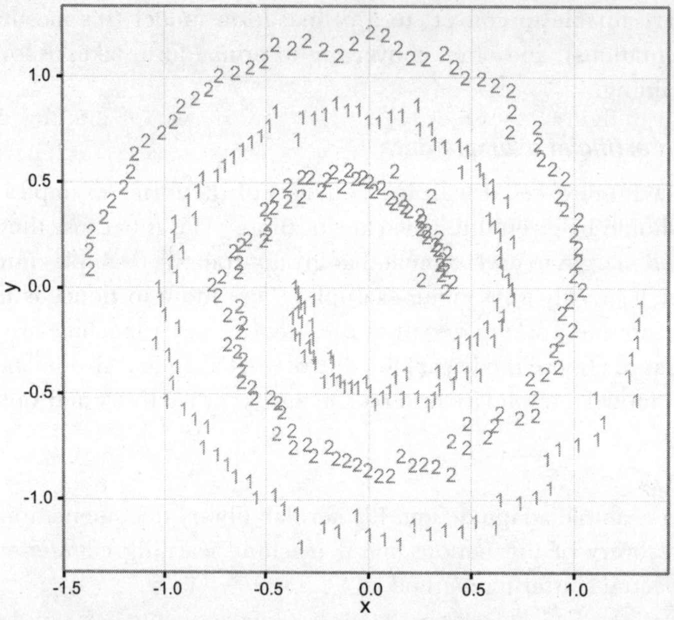

Figure 9.9 The spiral counter-example

SUPPORT VECTOR MACHINES WITH THE WRONG KERNEL

Support vector machines are powerful, but without the correct kernel they have difficulty with some concepts (such as the spiral example). Listing 9.22 shows a failed attempt to learn the spiral concept with a support vector machine using the identity or dot-product kernel.

Listing 9.22 SVM with a poor choice of kernel

```
set.seed(2335246L)
s$group <- sample.int(100,size=dim(s)[[1]],replace=T)
sTrain <- subset(s,group>10)
sTest <- subset(s,group<=10)
mSVMV <- ksvm(class~x+y,data=sTrain,kernel='vanilladot')
sTest$predSVMV <- predict(mSVMV,newdata=sTest,type='response')
ggplot() +
   geom_text(data=sTest,aes(x=x,y=y,
      label=predSVMV),size=12) +
   geom_text(data=s,aes(x=x,y=y,
      label=class,color=class),alpha=0.7) +
```

Prepare to try to learn spiral class label from coordinates using a support vector machine.

Build the support vector model using a vanilladot kernel (not a very good kernel).

Use the model to predict class on held-out data.

```
  coord_fixed() +
  theme_bw() + theme(legend.position='none')
```

Plot the predictions on top of a grey copy of all the data so we can see if predictions agree with the original markings.

This attempt results in figure 9.10. In the figure, we plot the total dataset in light grey and the SVM classifications of the test dataset in solid black. Note that the plotted predictions look a lot more like the concept `y < 0` than the spirals. The SVM didn't produce a good model with the identity kernel. In the next section, we'll repeat the process with the Gaussian radial kernel and get a much better result.

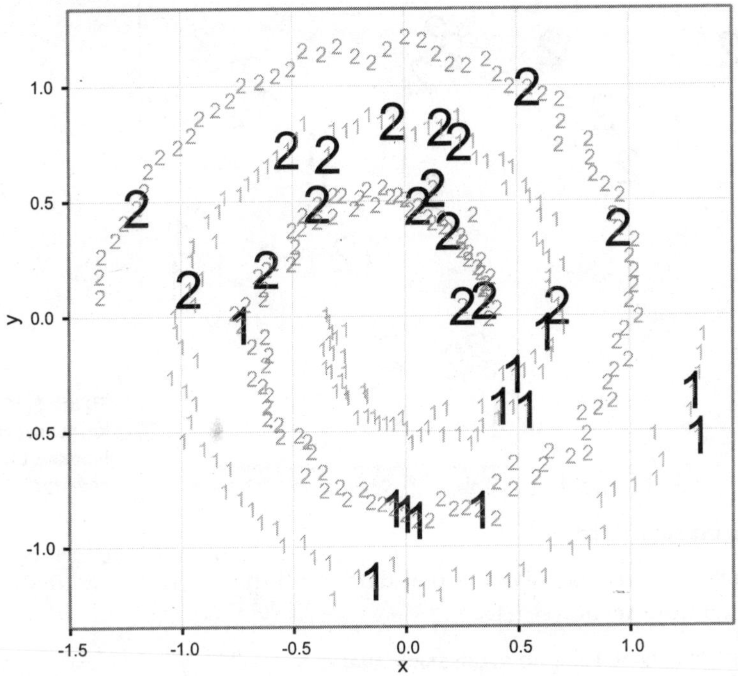

Figure 9.10 Identity kernel failing to learn the spiral concept

SUPPORT VECTOR MACHINES WITH A GOOD KERNEL

In listing 9.23, we'll repeat the SVM fitting process, but this time specifying the Gaussian or radial kernel. We'll again plot the SVM test classifications in black (with the entire dataset in light grey) in figure 9.11. Note that this time the actual spiral has been learned and predicted.

Listing 9.23 SVM with a good choice of kernel

This time use the "radial" or Gaussian kernel, which is a nice geometric similarity measure.

```
mSVMG <- ksvm(class~x+y,data=sTrain,kernel='rbfdot')
sTest$predSVMG <- predict(mSVMG,newdata=sTest,type='response')
ggplot() +
  geom_text(data=sTest,aes(x=x,y=y,
```

```
        label=predSVMG),size=12) +
    geom_text(data=s,aes(x=x,y=y,
        label=class,color=class),alpha=0.7) +
    coord_fixed() +
    theme_bw() + theme(legend.position='none')
```

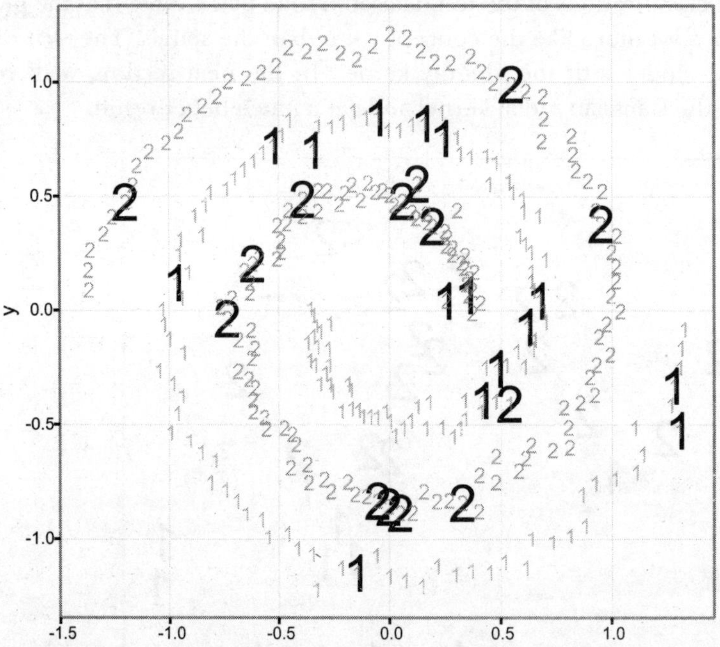

Figure 9.11 Radial kernel successfully learning the spiral concept

9.4.3 Using SVMs on real data

To demonstrate the use of SVMs on real data, we'll quickly redo the analysis of the Spambase data from section 5.2.1.

REPEATING THE SPAMBASE LOGISTIC REGRESSION ANALYSIS

In section 5.2.1, we originally built a logistic regression model and confusion matrix. We'll continue working on this example in listing 9.24 (after downloading the dataset from https://github.com/WinVector/zmPDSwR/raw/master/Spambase/spamD.tsv).

Listing 9.24 Revisiting the Spambase example with GLM

```
spamD <- read.table('spamD.tsv',header=T,sep='\t')
spamTrain <- subset(spamD,spamD$rgroup>=10)
spamTest <- subset(spamD,spamD$rgroup<10)
spamVars <- setdiff(colnames(spamD),list('rgroup','spam'))
spamFormula <- as.formula(paste('spam=="spam"',
   paste(spamVars,collapse=' + '),sep=' ~ '))
spamModel <- glm(spamFormula,family=binomial(link='logit'),
   data=spamTrain)
spamTest$pred <- predict(spamModel,newdata=spamTest,
   type='response')
```

```
print(with(spamTest,table(y=spam,glPred=pred>=0.5)))
##           glPred
## y          FALSE TRUE
##   non-spam   264   14
##   spam        22  158
```

APPLYING A SUPPORT VECTOR MACHINE TO THE SPAMBASE EXAMPLE

The SVM modeling steps are about as simple as the previous regression analysis, and are shown in the following listing.

Listing 9.25 Applying an SVM to the Spambase example

```
library('kernlab')
spamFormulaV <- as.formula(paste('spam',
   paste(spamVars,collapse=' + '),sep=' ~ '))
svmM <- ksvm(spamFormulaV,data=spamTrain,
     kernel='rbfdot',
     C=10,
     prob.model=T,cross=5,
     class.weights=c('spam'=1,'non-spam'=10)
     )
spamTest$svmPred <- predict(svmM,newdata=spamTest,type='response')
print(with(spamTest,table(y=spam,svmPred=svmPred)))
##           svmPred
## y          non-spam spam
##   non-spam      269    9
##   spam           27  153
```

Build a support vector model for the Spambase problem.

Ask for the radial dot or Gaussian kernel (in fact the default kernel).

Set the "soft margin penalty" high; prefer not moving training examples over getting a wider margin. Prefer a complex model that applies weakly to all the data over a simpler model that applies strongly on a subset of the data.

Ask that, in addition to a predictive model, an estimate of a model estimating class probabilities also be built. Not all SVM libraries support this operation, and the probabilities are essentially built after the model (through a cross-validation procedure) and may not be as high-quality as the model itself.

Explicitly control the trade-off between false positive and false negative errors. In this case, we say non-spam classified as spam (a false positive) should be considered an expensive mistake.

Listing 9.26 shows the standard summary and print display for the support vector model. Very few model diagnostics are included (other than training error, which is a simple accuracy measure), so we definitely recommend using the model critique techniques from chapter 5 to validate model quality and utility. A few things to look for are which kernel was used, the *SV type* (`classification` is the type we want),[19] and the number of support vectors retained (this is the degree of memorization going on). In this case, 1,118 training examples were retained as support vectors, which seems like

[19] The `ksvm` call only performs classification on factors; if a Boolean or numeric quantity is used as the quantity to be predicted, the `ksvm` call may return a regression model (instead of the desired classification model).

way too complicated a model, as this number is much larger than the original number of variables (57) and with an order of magnitude of the number of training examples (4143). In this case, we're seeing more memorization than useful generalization.

Listing 9.26 Printing the SVM results summary

```
print(svmM)
Support Vector Machine object of class "ksvm"

SV type: C-svc  (classification)
 parameter : cost C = 10

Gaussian Radial Basis kernel function.
 Hyperparameter : sigma =  0.0299836801848002

Number of Support Vectors : 1118

Objective Function Value : -4642.236
Training error : 0.028482
Cross validation error : 0.076998
Probability model included.
```

COMPARING RESULTS

Note that the two confusion matrices are very similar. But the SVM model has a lower false positive count of 9 than the GLM's 14. Some of this is due to setting `C=10` (which tells the SVM to prefer training accuracy and margin over model simplicity) and setting `class.weights` (telling the SVM to prefer precision over recall). For a more apples-to-apples comparison, we can look at the GLM model's top 162 spam candidates (the same number the SVM model proposed: 153 + 9).

Listing 9.27 Shifting decision point to perform an apples-to-apples comparison

```
sameCut <- sort(spamTest$pred)[length(spamTest$pred)-162]
print(with(spamTest,table(y=spam,glPred=pred>sameCut)))
##            glPred

## y          FALSE TRUE
##   non-spam   267   11
##   spam        29  151
```

Find out what GLM score threshold has 162 examples above it. (annotates the `sameCut` line)

Ask the GLM model for its predictions that are above the threshold. We're essentially asking the model for its 162 best candidate spam prediction results. (annotates the `print` line)

Note that the new shifted GLM confusion matrix in listing 9.27 is pretty much indistinguishable from the SVM confusion matrix. Where SVMs excel is in cases where unknown combinations of variables are important effects, and also when similarity of examples is strong evidence of examples being in the same class (not a property of the email spam example we have here). Problems of this nature tend to benefit from use of either SVM or nearest neighbor techniques.[20]

9.4.4 Support vector machine takeaways

Here's what you should remember about SVMs:

- SVMs are a kernel-based classification approach where the kernels are represented in terms of a (possibly very large) subset of the training examples.
- SVMs try to lift the problem into a space where the data is linearly separable (or as near to separable as possible).
- SVMs are useful in cases where the useful interactions or other combinations of input variables aren't known in advance. They're also useful when similarity is strong evidence of belonging to the same class.

9.5 Summary

In this chapter, we demonstrated some advanced methods to fix specific issues with basic modeling approaches. We used

- *Bagging and random forests*—To reduce the sensitivity of models to early modeling choices and reduce modeling variance
- *Generalized additive models*—To remove the (false) assumption that each model feature contributes to the model in a monotone fashion
- *Kernel methods*—To introduce new features that are nonlinear combinations of existing features, increasing the power of our model
- *Support vector machines*—To use training examples as landmarks (support vectors), again increasing the power of our model

You should understand that you bring in advanced methods and techniques to fix specific modeling problems, not because they have exotic names or exciting histories. We also feel you should at least try to find an existing technique to fix a problem you suspect is hiding in your data *before* building your own custom technique (often the existing technique incorporates a lot of tuning and wisdom). Finally, the goal of learning the theory of advanced techniques is not to be able to recite the steps of the common implementations, but to know when the techniques apply and what trade-offs they represent. The data scientist needs to supply thought and judgment and realize that the platform can supply implementations.

[20] For some examples of the connections between support vector machines and kernelized nearest neighbor methods please see http://mng.bz/1F78.

The actual point of a modeling project is to deliver results for deployment and to present useful documentation and evaluations to your partners. The next part of this book will address best practices for delivering your results.

Key takeaways

- Use advanced methods to fix specific problems, not for the excitement.
- Advanced methods can help fix overfit, variable interactions, non-additive relations, and unbalanced distributions, but not lack of features or data.
- Which method is best depends on the data, and there are many advanced methods to try.
- Only deliver advanced models if you can show they are outperforming simpler methods.

Part 3

Delivering results

In part 2, we covered how to build a model that addresses the problem that you want to solve. The next steps are to implement your solution and communicate your results to other interested parties. In part 3, we conclude with the important steps of deploying work into production, documenting work, and building effective presentations.

Chapter 10 covers the documentation necessary for sharing or transferring your work to others, in particular those who will be deploying your model in an operational environment. This includes effective code commenting practices, as well as proper version management and collaboration with the version control software, `git`. We also discuss the practice of *reproducible research* using `knitr`. Chapter 10 also covers how to export models you've built from R, or deploy them as HTTP services.

Chapter 11 discusses how to present the results of your projects to different audiences. Project sponsors, project consumers (people in the organization who'll be using or interpreting the results of your model), and fellow data scientists will all have different perspectives and interests. In chapter 11, we give examples of how to tailor your presentations to the needs and interests of a specific audience.

On completing part 3, you'll understand how to document and transfer the results of your project and how to effectively communicate your findings to other interested parties.

10 Documentation and deployment

This chapter covers

- Producing effective milestone documentation
- Managing project history using source control
- Deploying results and making demonstrations

In this chapter, we'll work through producing effective milestone documentation, code comments, version control records, and demonstration deployments. The idea is that these can all be thought of as important documentation of the work you've done. Table 10.1 expands a bit on our goals for this chapter.

This chapter explains how to share your work. We'll discuss how to use knitr to create substantial project milestone documentation and automate reproduction of graphs and other results. You'll learn about using effective comments in code, and using Git for version management and for collaboration. We'll also discuss deploying models as HTTP services and exporting model results.

Table 10.1 Chapter goals

Goal	Description
Produce effective milestone documentation	A readable summary of project goals, data provenance, steps taken, and technical results (numbers and graphs). Milestone documentation is usually read by collaborators and peers, so it can be concise and can often include actual code. We'll demonstrate a great tool for producing excellent milestone documentation: the R *knitr* package. knitr is a product of the "reproducible research" movement (see Christopher Gandrud's *Reproducible Research with R and RStudio*, Chapman and Hall, 2013) and is an excellent way to produce a reliable snapshot that not only shows the state of a project, but allows others to confirm the project works.
Manage a complete project history	It makes little sense to have exquisite milestone or checkpoint documentation of how your project worked last February if you can't get a copy of February's code and data. This is why you need a good version control discipline.
Deploy demonstrations	True production deployments are best done by experienced engineers. These engineers know the tools and environment they will be deploying to. A good way to jump-start production deployment is to have a reference deployment. This allows engineers to experiment with your work, test corner cases, and build acceptance tests.

10.1 The buzz dataset

Our example dataset for this and the following chapter is the buzz dataset from http://ama.liglab.fr/datasets/buzz/. We'll work with the data found in TomsHardware-Relative-Sigma-500.data.txt.[1] The original supplied documentation (TomsHardware-Relative-Sigma-500.names.txt and BuzzDataSetDoc.pdf) tells us the buzz data is structured as shown in table 10.2.

Table 10.2 Buzz data description

Attribute	Description
Rows	Each row represents many different measurements of the popularity of a technical personal computer discussion topic.
Topics	Topics include technical issues about personal computers such as brand names, memory, overclocking, and so on.
Measurement types	For each topic, measurement types are quantities such as the number of discussions started, number of posts, number of authors, number of readers, and so on. Each measurement is taken at eight different times.
Times	The eight relative times are named 0 through 7 and are likely days (the original variable documentation is not completely clear and the matching paper has not yet been released). For each measurement type all eight relative times are stored in different columns in the same data row.

[1] All files mentioned in this chapter are available from https://github.com/WinVector/zmPDSwR/tree/master/Buzz.

Table 10.2 Buzz data description *(continued)*

Attribute	Description
Buzz	The quantity to be predicted is called *buzz* and is defined as being `true` or `1` if the ongoing rate of additional discussion activity is at least 500 events per day averaged over a number of days after the observed days. Likely buzz is a future average of the seven variables labeled *NAC* (the original documentation is unclear on this).

In *our* initial buzz documentation, we list what we know (and, importantly, admit what we're not sure about). We don't intend any disrespect in calling out issues in the supplied buzz documentation. That documentation is about as good as you see at the beginning of a project. In an actual project, you'd clarify and improve unclear points through discussions and work cycles. This is one reason having access to active project sponsors and partners is critical in real-world projects.

The buzz problem demonstrates some features that are common in actual data science projects:

- This is a project where we're trying to predict the future from past features. These sorts of projects are particularly desirable, as we can expect to produce a lot of training data by saving past measurements.
- The quantity to be predicted is a function of future values of variables we're measuring. So part of the problem is relearning the business rules that make the determination. In such cases, it may be better to steer the project to predict estimates of the future values in question and leave the decision rules to the business.
- A domain-specific reshaping of the supplied variables would be appropriate. We're given daily popularities of articles over eight days; we'd prefer variables that represent popularity summed over the measured days, variables that measure topic age, variables that measure shape (indicating topics that are falling off fast or slow), and other time series–specific features.

In this chapter, we'll use the buzz dataset as-is and concentrate on demonstrating the tools and techniques used in producing documentation, deployments, and presentations. In actual projects, we advise you to start by producing notes like those in table 10.2. You'd also incorporate meeting notes to document your actual project goals. As this is only a demonstration, we'll emphasize technical documentation: data provenance and an initial trivial analysis to demonstrate we have control of the data. Our example initial buzz analysis is found here: https://github.com/WinVector/zmPDSwR/blob/master/Buzz/buzzm.md.[2] We suggest you skim it before we work through the tools and steps used to produce these documents in our next section.

[2] Also available in PDF form: https://github.com/WinVector/zmPDSwR/raw/master/Buzz/buzz.pdf.

10.2 Using knitr to produce milestone documentation

The first audience you'll have to prepare documentation for is yourself and your peers. You may need to return to previous work months later, and it may be in an urgent situation like an important bug fix, presentation, or feature improvement. For self/peer documentation, you want to concentrate on facts: what the stated goals were, where the data came from, and what techniques were tried. You assume as long as you use standard terminology or references that the reader can figure out anything else they need to know. You want to emphasize any surprises or exceptional issues, as they're exactly what's expensive to relearn. You can't expect to share this sort of documentation with clients, but you can later use it as a basis for building wider documentation and presentations.

The first sort of documentation we recommend is project milestone or checkpoint documentation. At major steps of the project you should take some time out to repeat your work in a clean environment (proving you know what's in intermediate files and you can in fact recreate them). An important, and often neglected, milestone is the start of a project. In this section, we'll use the knitr R package to document starting work with the buzz data.

10.2.1 What is knitr?

knitr is an R package that allows the inclusion of R code and results inside documents. knitr's operation is similar in concept to Knuth's literate programming and to the R Sweave package. In practice you maintain a master file that contains both user-readable documentation and chunks of program source code. The document types supported by knitr include LaTeX, Markdown, and HTML. LaTeX format is a good choice for detailed typeset technical documents. Markdown format is a good choice for online documentation and wikis. Direct HTML format may be appropriate for some web applications.

knitr's main operation is called a *knit*: knitr extracts and executes all of the R code and then builds a new result document that assembles the contents of the original document plus pretty-printed code and results (see figure 10.1).

The process is best demonstrated with a few examples.

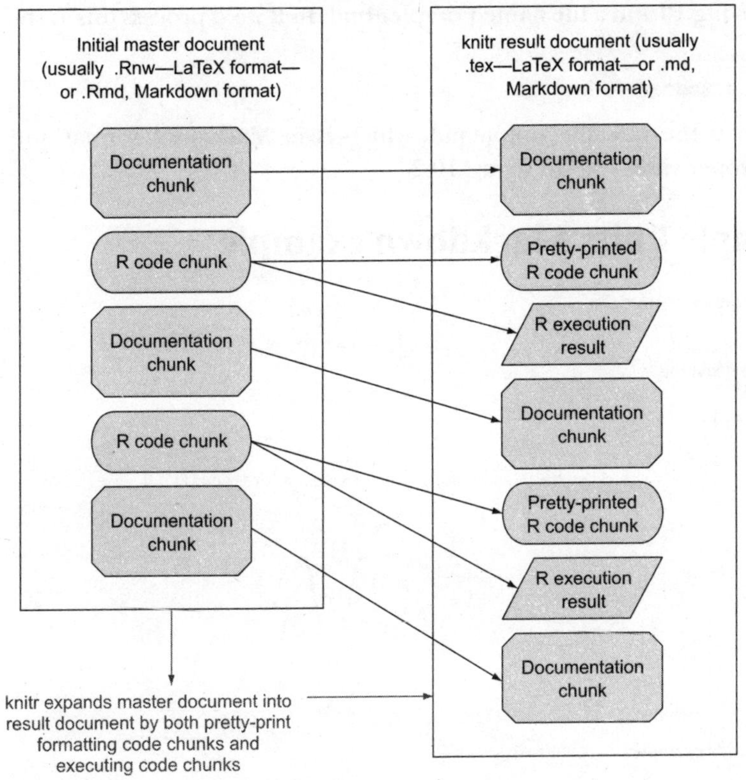

Figure 10.1 knitr process schematic

A SIMPLE KNITR MARKDOWN EXAMPLE

Markdown (http://daringfireball.net/projects/markdown/) is a simple web-ready format that's used in many wikis. The following listing shows a simple Markdown document with knitr annotation blocks denoted with ```.

Listing 10.1 knitr-annotated Markdown

```
# Simple knitr Markdown example                     <- Markdown text and formatting

Two examples:

* plotting
* calculating
                                                     knitr chunk open with option assignments
Plot example:
```{r plotexample, fig.width=2, fig.height=2, fig.align='center'}
library(ggplot2)                                     <- R code
ggplot(data=data.frame(x=c(1:100),y=sin(0.1*c(1:100)))) +
   geom_line(aes(x=x,y=y))
```                                   <- knitr chunk close

Calculation example: <- More Markdown text
```{r calcexample}                   <- Another R code chunk
pi*pi
```
```

We'll save listing 10.1 in a file named simple.Rmd. In R we'd process this as shown next:

```
library(knitr)
knit('simple.Rmd')
```

This produces the new file simple.md, which is in Markdown format and appears (with the proper viewer) as in figure 10.2.[3]

Documentation —

Simple knitr Markdown example

Two examples:

- plotting
- calculating

Plot example:

R code —

```
library(ggplot2)
ggplot(data = data.frame(x = c(1:100), y = sin(0.1 * c(1:100)))) + geom_line(aes(x = x,
    y = y))
```

R results —

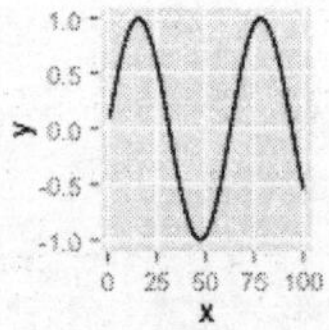

Documentation — Calculation example:

R code —

```
pi * pi
```

R results —

```
## [1] 9.87
```

Figure 10.2 Simple knitr Markdown result

A SIMPLE KNITR LATEX EXAMPLE

LaTeX is a powerful document preparation system suitable for publication-quality typesetting both for articles and entire books. To show how to use knitr with LaTeX, we'll work through a simple example. The main new feature is that in LaTeX, code blocks are marked with << and @ instead of ```. A simple LaTeX document with knitr chunks looks like the following listing.

Listing 10.2 knitr LaTeX example

```
\documentclass{article}
\begin{document}
<<nameofblock>>=
1+2
@
\end{document}
```

- `\documentclass{article}` / `\begin{document}`: **LaTeX declarations (not knitr)**
- `<<nameofblock>>=`: **knit start chunk marker**
- `1+2`: **R code**
- `@`: **knit end chunk marker**
- `\end{document}`: **LaTeX declarations (not knitr)**

3 We used `pandoc -o simple.html simple.md` to convert the file to easily viewable HTML.

We'll save this content into a file named add.Rnw and then (using the Bash shell) run R in batch to produce the file add.tex. At a shell prompt, we then run LaTeX to create the final add.pdf file:

```
echo "library(knitr); knit('add.Rnw')" | R --vanilla
pdflatex add.tex
```

Use R in batch mode to create add.tex from add.Rnw.

Use LaTeX to create add.pdf from add.tex.

This produces the PDF as shown in figure 10.3.

R code
```
1 + 2
```
R results
```
## [1] 3
```

Figure 10.3 Simple knitr LaTeX result

PURPOSE OF KNITR

The purpose of knitr is to produce reproducible work.[4] When you distribute your work in knitr format (as we do in section 10.2.3), anyone can download your work and, without great effort, rerun it to confirm they get the same results you did. This is the ideal standard of scientific research, but is rarely met, as scientists usually are deficient in sharing all of their code, data, and actual procedures. knitr collects and automates all the steps, so it becomes obvious if something is missing or doesn't actually work as claimed. knitr automation may seem like a mere convenience, but it makes the essential work listed in table 10.3 much easier (and therefore more likely to actually be done).

Table 10.3 Maintenance tasks made easier by knitr

Task	Discussion
Keeping code in sync with documentation	With only one copy of the code (already in the document), it's not so easy to get out of sync.
Keeping results in sync with data	Eliminating all by-hand steps (such as cutting and pasting results, picking filenames, and including figures) makes it much more likely you'll correctly rerun and recheck your work.
Handing off correct work to others	If the steps are sequenced so a machine can run them, then it's much easier to rerun and confirm them. Also, having a container (the master document) to hold all your work makes managing dependencies much easier.

10.2.2 knitr technical details

To use knitr on a substantial project, you need to know more about how knitr code chunks work. In particular you need to be clear how chunks are marked and what common chunk options you'll need to manipulate.

[4] The knitr community calls this *reproducible research*, but that's because scientific work is often called *research*.

KNITR BLOCK DECLARATION FORMAT

In general, a knitr code block starts with the block declaration (``` in Markdown and << in LaTeX). The first string is the name of the block (must be unique across the entire project). After that, a number of comma-separated `option=value` chunk option assignments are allowed.

KNITR CHUNK OPTIONS

A sampling of useful option assignments is given in table 10.4.

Table 10.4 Some useful knitr options

Option name	Purpose
`cache`	Controls whether results are cached. With `cache=F` (the default), the code chunk is always executed. With `cache=T`, the code chunk isn't executed if valid cached results are available from previous runs. Cached chunks are essential when you're revising knitr documents, but you should always delete the cache directory (found as a subdirectory of where you're using knitr) and do a clean rerun to make sure your calculations are using current versions of the data and settings you've specified in your document.
`echo`	Controls whether source code is copied into the document. With `echo=T` (the default), pretty formatted code is added to the document. With `echo=F`, code isn't echoed (useful when you only want to display results).
`eval`	Controls whether code is evaluated. With `eval=T` (the default), code is executed. With `eval=F`, it's not (useful for displaying instructions).
`message`	Set `message=F` to direct R `message()` commands to the console running R instead of to the document. This is useful for issuing progress messages to the user that you don't want in the final document.
`results`	Controls what's to be done with R output. Usually you don't set this option and output is intermingled (with `##` comments) with the code. A useful option is `results='hide'`, which suppresses output.
`tidy`	Controls whether source code is reformatted before being printed. You almost always want to set `tidy=F`, as the current version of knitr often breaks code due to mishandling of R comments when reformatting.

Most of these options are demonstrated in our buzz example, which we'll work through in the next section.

10.2.3 Using knitr to document the buzz data

For a more substantial example, we'll use knitr to document the initial data treatment and initial trivial model for the buzz data (recall from section 10.1 that buzz is records of computer discussion topic popularity). We'll produce a document that outlines the initial steps of working with the buzz data (the sorts of steps we had, up until now, been including in this book whenever we introduce a new dataset). This example works through advanced knitr topics such as caching (to speed up reruns), messages (to alert the user), and advanced formatting. We supply two examples of knitr for the buzz data at https://github.com/WinVector/zmPDSwR/tree/master/Buzz. The first example is in Markdown format and found in the knitr file buzzm.Rmd, which knits to the Markdown file buzzm.md. The second example is in LaTeX format and found in the knitr file buzz.Rnw, which knits to the LaTeX file buzz.tex (which in turn is used to produce the viewable file buzz.pdf). All steps we'll mention in this section are completely demonstrated in both of these files. We'll show excerpts from buzz.Rmd (using the ``` delimiter) and excerpts from buzz.Rnw (using the << delimiter).

BUZZ DATA NOTES For the buzz data, the preparation notes can be found in the files buzz.md, buzz.html, or buzz.pdf. We suggest viewing one of these files and table 10.2. The original description files from the buzz project (TomsHardware-Relative-Sigma-500.names.txt and BuzzDataSetDoc.pdf) are also available at https://github.com/WinVector/zmPDSwR/tree/master/Buzz.

SETTING UP CHUNK CACHE DEPENDENCIES

For a substantial knitr project, you'll want to enable caching. Otherwise, rerunning knitr to correct typos becomes prohibitively expensive. The standard way to enable knitr caching is to add the cache=T option to all knitr chunks. You'll also probably want to set up the chunk cache dependency calculator by inserting the following invisible chunk toward the top of your file.

Listing 10.3 Setting knitr dependency options

```
% set up caching and knitr chunk dependency calculation
% note: you will want to do clean re-runs once in a while to make sure
% you are not seeing stale cache results.
<<setup,tidy=F,cache=F,eval=T,echo=F,results='hide'>>=
opts_chunk$set(autodep=T)
dep_auto()
@
```

CONFIRMING DATA PROVENANCE

Because knitr is automating steps, you can afford to take a couple of extra steps to confirm the data you're analyzing is in fact the data you thought you had. For example, we'll start our buzz data analysis by confirming that the SHA cryptographic hash of the data we're starting from matches what we thought we had downloaded. This is done (assuming your system has the sha cryptographic hash installed) as shown in the following listing (note: always look to the first line of chunks for chunk options such as cache=T).

Listing 10.4 Using the `system()` command to compute a file hash

```
<<dataprep,tidy=F,cache=T>>=
infile <- "TomsHardware-Relative-Sigma-500.data.txt"
paste('checked at',date())
system(paste('shasum',infile),intern=T)
 buzzdata <- read.table(infile, header=F, sep=",")
...
```

Run a system-installed cryptographic hash program (this program is outside of R's install image).

This code sequence depends on a program named "shasum" being on your execution path. You have to have a cryptographic hash installed, and you can supply a direct path to the program if necessary. Common locations for a cryptographic hash include /usr/bin/shasum, /sbin/md5, and fciv.exe, depending on your actual system configuration.

This code produces the output shown in figure 10.4. In particular, we've documented that the data we loaded has the same cryptographic hash we recorded when we first downloaded the data. Having confidence you're still working with the exact same data you started with can speed up debugging when things go wrong. Note that we're using the cryptographic hash to defend only against accident (using the wrong version of a file or seeing a corrupted file) and not to defend against true adversaries, so it's okay to use a cryptographic hash that's convenient even if it's becoming out of date.

```
infile <- "TomsHardware-Relative-Sigma-500.data.txt"
paste('checked at',date())

## [1] "checked at Fri Nov  8 15:01:39 2013"

system(paste('shasum',infile),intern=T)  # write down file hash

## [1] "c239182c786baf678b55f559b3d0223da91e869c  TomsHardware-Relative-Sigma-500.data.txt"
```

Figure 10.4 knitr documentation of buzz data load

RECORDING THE PERFORMANCE OF THE NAIVE ANALYSIS

The initial milestone is a good place to try to record the results of a naive "just apply a standard model to whatever variables are present" analysis. For the buzz data analysis, we'll use a random forest modeling technique (not shown here, but in our knitr documentation) and apply the model to test data.

Listing 10.5 Calculating model performance

```
rtest <- data.frame(truth=buzztest$buzz,
  pred=predict(fmodel, newdata=buzztest))
print(accuracyMeasures(rtest$pred, rtest$truth))
## [1] "precision= 0.809782608695652 ; recall= 0.84180790960452"
##      pred
## truth   0   1
##     0 579  35
##     1  28 149
##   model accuracy     f1 dev.norm
## 1 model   0.9204 0.6817    4.401
```

USING MILESTONES TO SAVE TIME

Now that we've gone to all the trouble to implement, write up, and run the buzz data preparation steps, we'll end our knitr analysis by saving the R workspace. We can then start additional analyses (such as introducing better shape features for the time-varying data) from the saved workspace. In the following listing, we'll show a conditional saving of the data (to prevent needless file churn) and again produce a cryptographic hash of the file (so we can confirm work that starts from a file with the same name is in fact starting from the same data).

Listing 10.6 Conditionally saving a file

```
Save prepared R environment.
% Another way to conditionally save, check for file.
% message=F is letting message() calls get routed to console instead
% of the document.
<<save,tidy=F,cache=F,message=F,eval=T>>=
fname <- 'thRS500.Rdata'
if(!file.exists(fname)) {
   save(list=ls(),file=fname)
   message(paste('saved',fname))  # message to running R console
   print(paste('saved',fname))    # print to document
} else {
   message(paste('skipped saving',fname)) # message to running R console
   print(paste('skipped saving',fname))   # print to document
}
paste('checked at',date())
system(paste('shasum',fname),intern=T)  # write down file hash
@
```

Figure 10.5 shows the result. The data scientists can safely start their analysis on the saved workspace and have documentation that allows them to confirm that a workspace file they're using is in fact one produced by this version of the preparation steps.

Save prepared R environment.

```
fname <- 'thRS500.Rdata'
if(!file.exists(fname)) {
   save(list=ls(),file=fname)
   message(paste('saved',fname))  # message to running R console
   print(paste('saved',fname))    # print to document
} else {
   message(paste('skipped saving',fname)) # message to running R console
   print(paste('skipped saving',fname))   # print to document
}

## [1] "skipped saving thRS500.Rdata"

paste('checked at',date())

## [1] "checked at Fri Nov  8 15:32:54 2013"

system(paste('shasum',fname),intern=T)  # write down file hash

## [1] "304895b8b5860ac5c995e10bd3b8c995820d60a0  thRS500.Rdata"
```

Figure 10.5 knitr documentation of prepared buzz workspace

KNITR TAKEAWAY

In our knitr example, we worked through the steps we've done for every dataset in this book: load data, manage columns/variables, perform an initial analysis, present results, and save a workspace. The key point is that because we took the extra effort to do this work in knitr, we have the following:

- Nicely formatted documentation (buzz.md and buzz.pdf)
- Shared executable code (buzz.Rmd and buzz.Rnw)

This makes debugging (which usually involves repeating and investigating earlier work), sharing, and documentation much easier and more reliable.

10.3 Using comments and version control for running documentation

Another essential record of your work is what we call *running documentation*. Running documentation is more informal than milestone/checkpoint documentation and is easiest maintained in the form of code comments and version control records. Undocumented, untracked code runs up a great deal of *technical debt* (see http://mng.bz/IaTd) that can cause problems down the road.

In this section, we'll work through producing effective code comments and using Git for version control record keeping.

10.3.1 Writing effective comments

R's comment style is simple: everything following a # (that isn't itself quoted) until the end of a line is a comment and ignored by the R interpreter. The following listing is an example of a well-commented block of R code.

Listing 10.7 Example code comment

```
#    Return the pseudo logarithm of x, which is close to
# sign(x)*log10(abs(x)) for x such that abs(x) is large
# and doesn't "blow up" near zero.  Useful
# for transforming wide-range variables that may be negative
# (like profit/loss).
# See: http://www.win-vector.com/blog
#  /2012/03/modeling-trick-the-signed-pseudo-logarithm/
#    NB: This transform has the undesirable property of making most
# signed distributions appear bimodal around the origin, no matter
# what the underlying distribution really looks like.
# The argument x is assumed be numeric and can be a vector.
pseudoLog10 <- function(x) { asinh(x/2)/log(10) }
```

Good comments include what the function does, what types arguments are expected to be, limits of domain, why you should care about the function, and where it's from. Of critical importance are any `NB` (*nota bene* or *note well*) or `TODO` notes. It's vastly more important to document any unexpected features or limitations in your code than to try to explain the obvious. Because R variables don't have types (only objects they're pointing to have types), you may want to document what types of arguments you're expecting. It's critical to know if a function works correctly on lists, data frame rows, vectors, and so on.

Note that in our comments we didn't bother with anything listed in table 10.5.

Table 10.5 Things not to worry about in comments

Item	Why not to bother
Pretty ASCII-art formatting	It's enough that the comment be there and be readable. Formatting into a beautiful block just makes the comment harder to maintain and decreases the chance of the comment being up to date.
Anything we see in the code itself	There's no point repeating the name of the function, saying it takes only one argument, and so on.
Anything we can get from version control	We don't bother recording the author or date the function was written. These facts, though important, are easily recovered from your version control system with commands like `git blame`.
Any sort of Javadoc/ Doxygen-style annotations	The standard way to formally document R functions is in separate .Rd (R documentation) files in a package structure (see http://cran.r-project.org/doc/manuals/R-exts.html). In our opinion, the R package system is too specialized and toilsome to use in regular practice (though it's good for final delivery). For formal code documentation, we recommend knitr.

Also, avoid comments that add no actual content, such as in the following listing.

Listing 10.8 Useless comment

```
########################################
# Function: addone
# Author: John Mount
# Version: 1.3.11
# Location: RSource/helperFns/addone.R
# Date: 10/31/13
# Arguments: x
# Purpose: Adds one
########################################
addone <- function(x) { x + 1 }
```

The only thing worse than no documentation is documentation that's wrong. At all costs avoid comments that are incorrect, as in listing 10.9 (the comment says "adds one" when the code clearly adds two)—and *do* delete such comments if you find them.

Listing 10.9 Worse than useless comment

```
# adds one
addtwo <- function(x) { x + 2 }
```

10.3.2 Using version control to record history

Version control can both maintain critical snapshots of your work in earlier states and produce running documentation of what was done by whom and when in your project. Figure 10.6 shows a cartoon "version control saves the day" scenario that is in fact common.

In this section, we'll explain the basics of using Git (http://git-scm.com/) as a version control system. To really get familiar with Git, we recommend a good book such

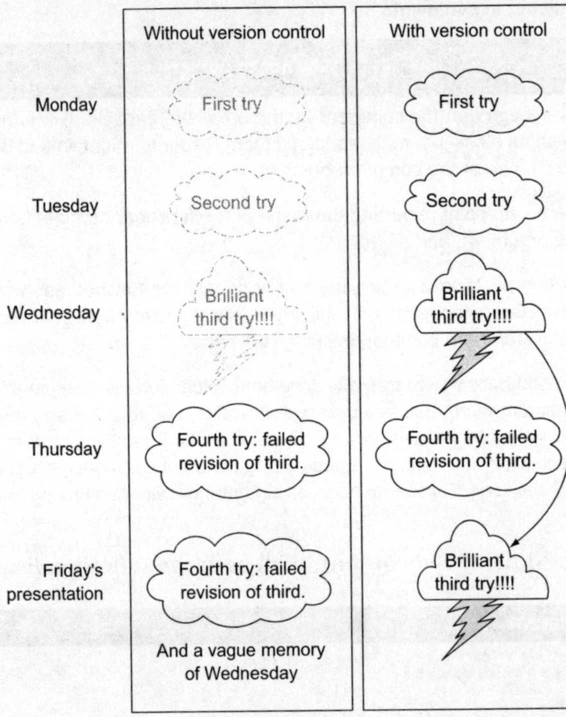

Figure 10.6 Version control saving the day

as Jon Loeliger and Matthew McCullough's *Version Control with Git*, 2nd Edition (O'Reilly, 2012). Or, better yet, work with people who know Git. In this chapter, we assume you know how to run an interactive shell on your computer (on Linux and OS X you tend to use `bash` as your shell; on Windows you can install Cygwin—http://www.cygwin.com).

WORKING IN BRIGHT LIGHT Sharing your Git repository means you're sharing a lot of information about your work habits and also sharing your mistakes. You're much more exposed than when you just share final work or status reports. Make this a virtue: know you're working in bright light. One of the most critical features in a good data scientist (perhaps even before analytic skill) is scientific honesty.

As a single user, to get most of the benefit from Git, you need to become familiar with a few commands:

- `git init .`
- `git add -A .`
- `git commit`
- `git status`
- `git log`
- `git diff`
- `git checkout`

Unfortunately, we don't have space to explain all of these commands. We'll demonstrate how to think about Git and the main path of commands you need to maintain your work history.

CHOOSING A PROJECT DIRECTORY STRUCTURE

Before starting with source control, it's important to settle on and document a good project directory structure. Christopher Gandrud's *Reproducible Research with R and RStudio* (Chapman & Hall, 2013) has good advice and instructions on how to do this. A pattern that's worked well for us is to start a new project with the directory structure described in table 10.6.

Table 10.6 A possible project directory structure

Directory	Description
Data	Where we save original downloaded data. This directory must usually be excluded from version control (using the .gitignore feature) due to file sizes, so you must ensure it's backed up. We tend to save each data refresh in a separate subdirectory named by date.
Scripts	Where we store all code related to analysis of the data.
Derived	Where we store intermediate results that are derived from data and scripts. This directory must be excluded from source control. You also should have a master script that can rebuild the contents of this directory in a single command (and test the script from time to time). Typical contents of this directory are compressed files and file-based databases (H2, SQLite).
Results	Similar to derived, but this directory holds smaller later results (often based on derived) and hand-written content. These include important saved models, graphs, and reports. This directory is under version control, so collaborators can see what was said when. Any report shared with partners should come from this directory.

STARTING A GIT PROJECT USING THE COMMAND LINE

When you've decided on your directory structure and want to start a version-controlled project, do the following:

1. Start the project in a new directory. Place any work either in this directory or in subdirectories.
2. Move your interactive shell into this directory and type `git init .`. It's okay if you've already started working and there are already files present.
3. Exclude any subdirectories you don't want under source control with .gitignore control files.

You can check if you've already performed the init step by typing `git status`. If the init hasn't been done, you'll get a message similar to `fatal: Not a git repository (or any of the parent directories): .git.`. If the init has been done, you'll get a status message telling you something like `on branch master` and listing facts about many files.

The init step sets up in your directory a single hidden file tree called .git and prepares you to keep extra copies of every file in your directory (including subdirectories). Keeping all of these extra copies is called *versioning* and what is meant by *version control*. You can now start working on your project: save everything related to your work in this directory or some subdirectory of this directory.

Again, you only need to init a project once. Don't worry about accidentally running `git init .` a second time; that's harmless.

USING ADD/COMMIT PAIRS TO CHECKPOINT WORK

As often as practical, enter the following two commands into an interactive shell in your project directory:

```
git add -A .
git commit
```

Stage results to commit (specify what files should be committed). (`git add -A .`)

Actually perform the commit. (`git commit`)

GET NERVOUS ABOUT UNCOMMITTED STATE A good rule of thumb for Git: you should be as nervous about having uncommitted changes as you should be about not having clicked Save. You don't need to push/pull often, but you do need to make local commits often (even if you later squash them with a Git technique called *rebasing*).

Checking in a file is split into two stages: add and commit. This has some advantages (such as allowing you to inspect before committing), but for now just consider the two commands as always going together. The `commit` command should bring up an editor where you enter a comment as to what you're up to. Until you're a Git expert, allow yourself easy comments like "update," "going to lunch," "just added a paragraph," or "corrected spelling." Run the add/commit pair of commands after every minor accomplishment on your project. Run these commands every time you leave your project (to go to lunch, to go home, or to work on another project). Don't fret if you forget to do this; just run the commands next time you remember.

> **A "wimpy commit" is better than no commit**
>
> We've been a little loose in our instructions to commit often and don't worry too much about having a long commit message. Two things to keep in mind are that usually you want commits to be meaningful with the code working (so you tend not to commit in the middle of an edit with syntax errors), and good commit notes are to be preferred (just don't forgo a commit because you don't feel like writing a good commit note).

USING GIT LOG AND GIT STATUS TO VIEW PROGRESS

Any time you want to know about your work progress, type either `git status` to see if there are any edits you can put through the add/commit cycle, or `git log` to see the history of your work (from the viewpoint of the add/commit cycles).

The following listing shows the `git status` from our copy of this book's examples repository (https://github.com/WinVector/zmPDSwR).

Listing 10.10 Checking your project status

```
$ git status
# On branch master
nothing to commit (working directory clean)
```

And the next listing shows a `git log` from the same project.

Listing 10.11 Checking your project history

```
commit c02839e0b34172f54fd68201f64895295b9d7609
Author: John Mount <jmount@win-vector.com>
Date:   Sat Nov 9 13:28:30 2013 -0800

    add export of random forest model

commit 974a8d5b95bdf25b95d23ef75d08d8aa6c0d74fe
Author: John Mount <jmount@win-vector.com>
Date:   Sat Nov 9 12:01:14 2013 -0800

    Add rook examples
```

The indented lines are the text we entered at the `git commit` step; the dates are tracked automatically.

USING GIT THROUGH RSTUDIO

The RStudio IDE supplies a graphical user interface to Git that you should try. The add/commit cycle can be performed as follows in RStudio:

- Start a new project. From the RStudio command menu, select Project > Create Project, and choose New Project. Then select the name of the project, what directory to create the new project directory in, leave the type as (Default), and make sure Create a Git Repository for this Project is checked. When the new project pane looks something like figure 10.7, click Create Project, and you have a new project.
- Do some work in your project. Create new files by selecting File > New > R Script. Type some R code (like `1/5`) into the editor pane and then click the Save icon to save the file. When saving the file, be sure to choose your project directory or a subdirectory of your project.
- Commit your changes to version control. Figure 10.7 shows how to do this. Select the Git control pane in the top right of RStudio. This pane shows all changed files as line items. Check the Staged check box for any files you want to stage for this commit. Then click Commit, and you're done.

You may not yet deeply understand or like Git, but you're able to safely check in all of your changes every time you remember to stage and commit. This means all of your work history is there; you can't clobber your committed work just by deleting your

Figure 10.7 RStudio new project pane

working file. Consider all of your working directory as "scratch work"—only checked-in work is safe from loss.

Your Git history can be seen by pulling down on the Other Commands gear (shown in the Git pane in figure 10.8) and selecting History (don't confuse this with the nearby History pane, which is command history, not Git history). In an emergency, you can find Git help and find your earlier files. If you've been checking in, then your older versions are there; it's just a matter of getting some help in accessing them. Also, if you're working with others, you can use the push/pull menu items to publish and receive updates. Here's all we want to say about version control at this point: *commit often, and if you're committing often, all problems can be solved with some further research.* Also, be aware that since your primary version control is on your own machine, you need to make sure you have an independent backup of your machine. If your machine fails and your work hasn't been backed up or shared, then you lose both your work and your version repository.

10.3.3 Using version control to explore your project

Up until now, our model of version control has been this: Git keeps a complete copy of all of our files each time we successfully enter the pair of add/commit lines. We'll now use these commits. If you add/commit often enough, Git is ready to help you with any of the following tasks:

- Tracking your work over time
- Recovering a deleted file
- Comparing two past versions of a file

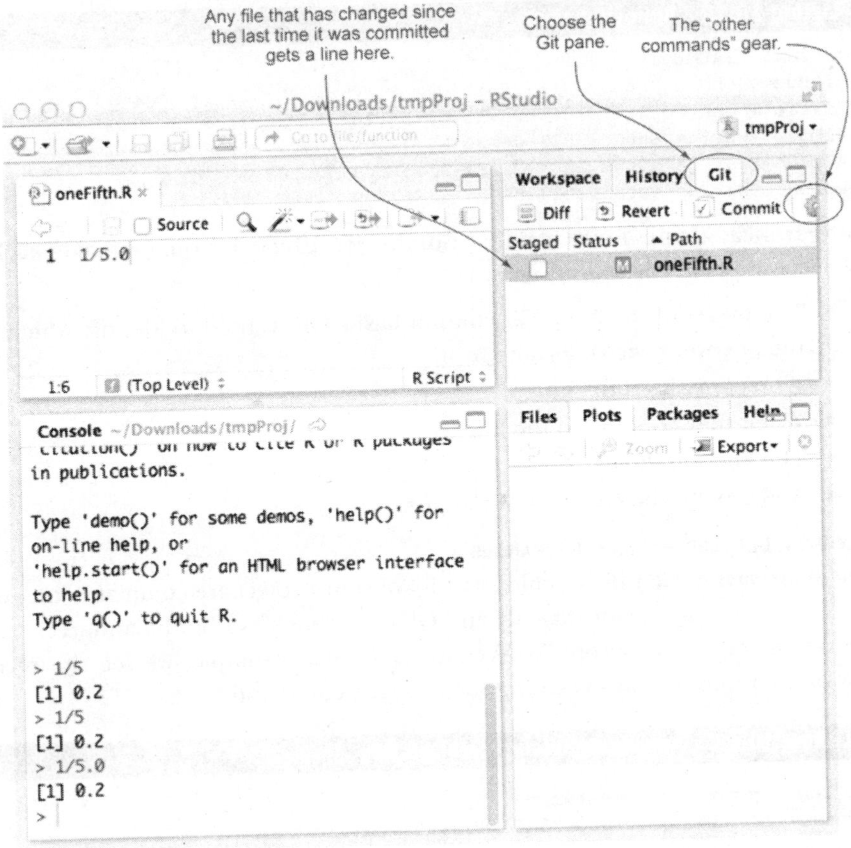

Figure 10.8 RStudio Git controls

- Finding when you added a specific bit of text
- Recovering a whole file or a bit of text from the past (undo an edit)
- Sharing files with collaborators
- Publicly sharing your project (à la GitHub at https://github.com/, or Bitbucket at https://bitbucket.org)
- Maintaining different versions (branches) of your work

And that's why you want to add and commit often.

GETTING HELP ON GIT For any Git command, you can type `git help [command]` to get usage information. For example, to learn about `git log`, type `git help log`.

FINDING OUT WHO WROTE WHAT AND WHEN

In section 10.3.1, we implied that a good version control system can produce a lot of documentation on its own. One powerful example is the command `git blame`. Look what happens if we download the Git repository https://github.com/WinVector/zmPDSwR (with the command `git clone git@github.com:WinVector/zmPDSwR.git`) and run the command `git blame README.md`.

Listing 10.12 Annoying work

```
git blame README.md
376f9bce (John Mount   2013-05-15 07:58:14 -0700  1) ## Support ...
376f9bce (John Mount   2013-05-15 07:58:14 -0700  2) # by Nina   ...
2541bb0b (Marius Butuc 2013-04-24 23:52:09 -0400  3)
2541bb0b (Marius Butuc 2013-04-24 23:52:09 -0400  4) Works deri ...
2541bb0b (Marius Butuc 2013-04-24 23:52:09 -0400  5)
```

We've truncated lines for readability. But the `git blame` information takes each line of the file and prints the following:

- The prefix of the line's Git commit hash. This is used to identify which commit the line we're viewing came from.
- Who committed the line.
- When they committed the line.
- The line number.
- And, finally, the contents of the line.

VIEWING A DETAILED HISTORY OF CHANGES

The main ways to view the detailed history of your project are command-line tools like `git log --graph --name-status` and GUI tools such as RStudio and `gitk`. Continuing our https://github.com/WinVector/zmPDSwR example, we see the recent history of the repository by executing the `git log` command.

Listing 10.13 Viewing detailed project history

```
git log --graph --name-status
* commit c49c853cbcbb1e5a923d6e1127aa54ec7335d1b3
| Author: John Mount <jmount@win-vector.com>
| Date:   Sat Oct 26 09:22:02 2013 -0700
|
|     Add knitr and rendered result
|
| A     Buzz/.gitignore
| A     Buzz/buzz.Rnw
| A     Buzz/buzz.pdf
|
* commit 6ce20dd33c5705b6de7e7f9390f2150d8d212b42
| Author: John Mount <jmount@win-vector.com>
| Date:   Sat Oct 26 07:40:59 2013 -0700
|
|     update
|
| M     CodeExamples.zip
```

This variation of the `git log` command draws a graph of the history (mostly a straight line, which is the simplest possible history) and what files were added (the `A` lines), modified (the `M` lines), and so on. Commit comments are shown. Note that commit comments can be short. We can say things like "update" instead of "update CodeExamples.zip" because Git records what files were altered in each commit. The `gitk`

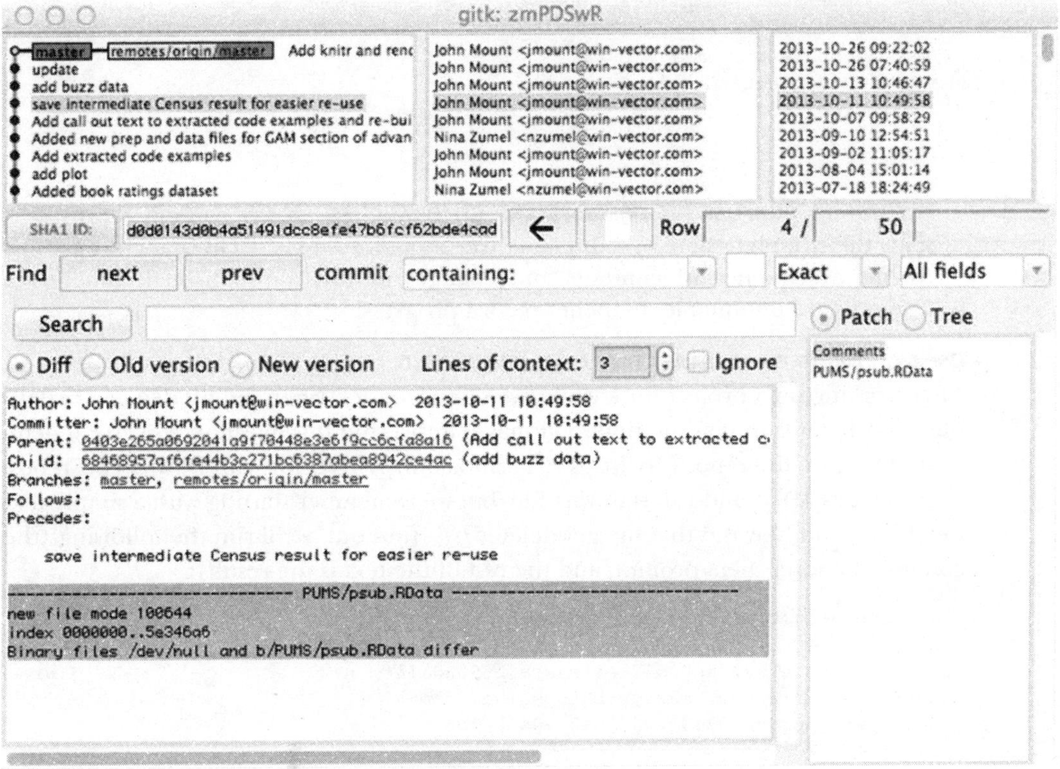

Figure 10.9 `gitk` browsing https://github.com/WinVector/zmPDSwR

GUI allows similar views and browsing through the detailed project history, as shown in figure 10.9.

USING GIT DIFF TO COMPARE FILES FROM DIFFERENT COMMITS

The `git diff` command allows you to compare any two committed versions of your project, or even to compare your current uncommitted work to any earlier version. In Git, commits are named using large hash keys, but you're allowed to use prefixes of the hashes as names of commits.[5] For example, listing 10.14 demonstrates finding the differences in two versions of https://github.com/WinVector/zmPDSwR in a diff or patch format.

Listing 10.14 Finding line-based differences between two committed versions

```
diff --git a/CDC/NatalBirthData.rData b/CDC/NatalBirthData.rData
...
+++ b/CDC/prepBirthWeightData.R
@@ -0,0 +1,83 @@
+data <- read.table("natal2010Sample.tsv.gz",
```

---

[5] You can also create meaningful names for commits with the `git tag` command.

```
+                    sep="\t", header=T, stringsAsFactors=F)
+
+# make a boolean from Y/N data
+makevarYN = function(col) {
+  ifelse(col %in% c("", "U"), NA, ifelse(col=="Y", T, F))
+}
...
```

TRY NOT TO CONFUSE GIT COMMITS AND GIT BRANCHES A Git commit represents the complete state of a directory tree at a given time. A Git branch represents a sequence of commits and changes as you move through time. Commits are immutable; branches record progress.

USING GIT LOG TO FIND THE LAST TIME A FILE WAS AROUND

After working on a project for a while, we often wonder, when did we delete a certain file and what was in it at the time? Git makes answering this question easy. We'll demonstrate this in the repository https://github.com/WinVector/zmPDSwR. This repository has a README.md (Markdown) file, but we remember starting with a simple text file. When and how did that file get deleted? To find out, we'll run the following (the command is after the `$` prompt, and the rest of the text is the result):

```
$ git log --name-status -- README.txt

commit 2541bb0b9a2173eb1d471e11d4aca3b690a011ef
Author: Marius Butuc <marius.butuc@gmail.com>
Date:   Wed Apr 24 23:52:09 2013 -0400

    Translate readme to Markdown

D       README.txt

commit 9534cff7579607316397cbb40f120d286b7e4b58
Author: John Mount <jmount@win-vector.com>
Date:   Thu Mar 21 17:58:48 2013 -0700

    update licenses

M       README.txt
```

Ah—the file was deleted by Marius Butuc, an early book reader who generously composed a pull request to change our text file to Markdown (we reviewed and accepted the request at the time). We can view the contents of this older file with `git show 9534cf -- README.txt` (the `9534cff` is the prefix of the commit number before the deletion; manipulating these commit numbers isn't hard if you use copy and paste). And we can recover that copy of the file with `git checkout 9534cf -- README.txt`.

10.3.4 Using version control to share work

In addition to producing work, you must often share it with peers. The common (and bad) way to do this is emailing zip files. Most of the bad sharing practices take excessive effort, are error-prone, and rapidly cause confusion. We advise using version control to share work with peers. To do that effectively with Git, you need to start using additional commands such as `git pull`, `git rebase`, and `git push`. Things seem more confusing at this point (though you still don't need to worry about branching in its full generality), but are in fact far less confusing and less error-prone than ad hoc solutions. We almost always advise sharing work in *star workflow*, where each worker has their own repository, and a single common "naked" repository (a repository with only Git data structures and no ready-to-use files) is used to coordinate (thought of as a server or gold standard, often named *origin*).

The usual shared workflow is like this:

- Continuously: work, work, work.
- Frequently: commit results to the local repository using a `git add`/`git commit` pair.
- Every once in a while: pull a copy of the remote repository into our view with some variation of `git pull` and then use `git push` to push work upstream.

The main rule of Git is this: don't try anything clever (push/pull, and so on) unless you're in a "clean" state (everything committed, confirmed with `git status`).

SETTING UP REMOTE REPOSITORY RELATIONS

For two or more Git repositories to share work, the repositories need to know about each other through a relation called *remote*. A Git repository is able to share its work to a remote repository by the `push` command and pick up work from a remote repository by the `pull` command. Listing 10.15 shows the declared remotes for the authors' local copy of the https://github.com/WinVector/zmPDSwR repository.

Listing 10.15 `git remote`

```
$ git remote --verbose
origin  git@github.com:WinVector/zmPDSwR.git (fetch)
origin  git@github.com:WinVector/zmPDSwR.git (push)
```

The remote relation is set when you create a copy of a repository using the `git clone` command or can be set using the `git remote add` command. In listing 10.15, the remote repository is called `origin`—this is the traditional name for a remote repository that you're using as your master or gold standard. (Git tends not to use the name *master* for repositories because master is the name of the branch you're usually working on.)

USING PUSH AND PULL TO SYNCHRONIZE WORK WITH REMOTE REPOSITORIES

Once your local repository has declared some other repository as remote, you can push and pull between the repositories. When pushing or pulling, always make sure you're clean (have no uncommitted changes), and you usually want to pull before you push (as that's the quickest way to spot and fix any potential conflicts). For a description of what version control conflicts are and how to deal with them, see http://mng.bz/5pTv.

Usually for simple tasks we don't use branches (a technical version control term), and we use the `rebase` option on pull so that it appears that every piece of work is recorded into a simple linear order, even though collaborators are actually working in parallel. This is what we call an *essential* difficulty of working with others: time and order become separate ideas and become hard to track (and this is *not* a needless complexity added by using Git—there *are* such needless complexities, but this is not one of them).

The new Git commands you need to learn are these:

- `git push` (usually used in the `git push -u origin master` variation)
- `git pull` (usually used in the `git fetch; git merge -m pull master origin/master` or `git pull --rebase origin master` variations)

Typically two authors may be working on different files in the same project at the same time. As you can see in figure 10.10, the second author to push their results to the

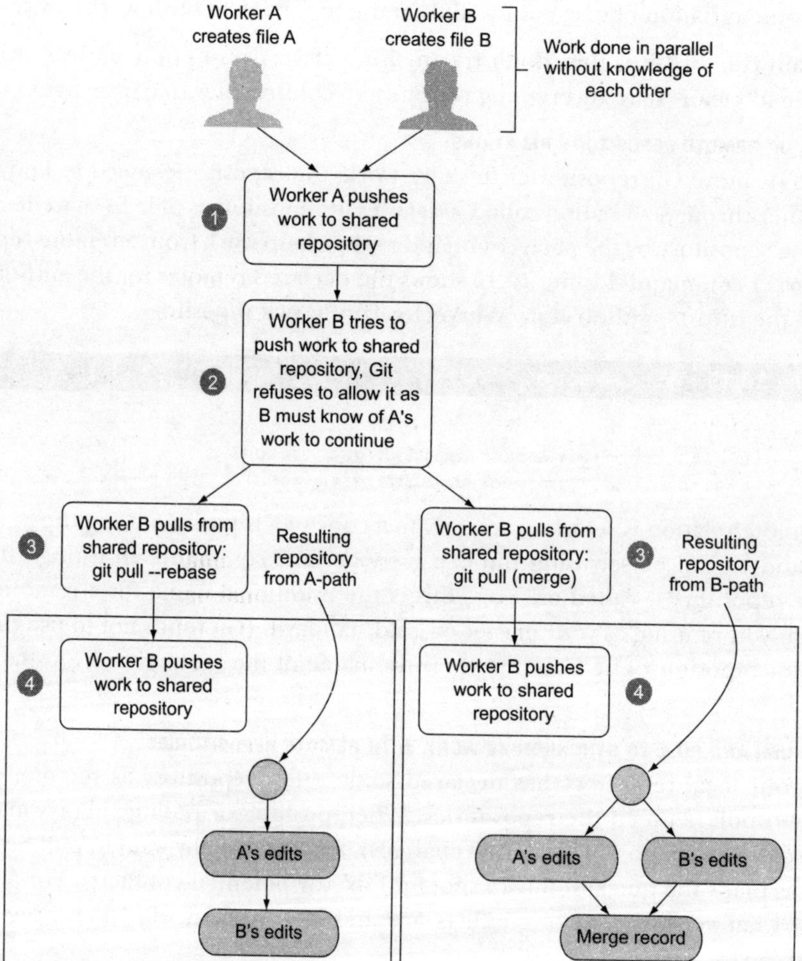

Figure 10.10 `git pull`: rebase versus merge

shared repository must decide how to specify the parallel work was performed. Either they can say the work was truly in parallel (represented by two branches being formed and then a merge record joining the work), or they can rebase their own work to claim their work was done "after" the other's work (preserving a linear edit history and avoiding the need for any merge records). Note: *before* and *after* are tracked in terms of arrows, not time.

Merging is what's really happening, but *rebase* is much simpler to read. The general rule is that you should only rebase work you haven't yet shared (in our example, Worker B should feel free to rebase their edits to appear to be after Worker A's edits, as Worker B hasn't yet successfully pushed their work anywhere). You should avoid rebasing records people have seen, as you're essentially hiding the edit steps they may be basing their work on (forcing them to merge or rebase in the future to catch up with your changed record keeping).

For most projects, we try to use a rebase-only strategy. For example, this book itself is maintained in a Git repository. We have only two authors who are in close proximity (so able to easily coordinate), and we're only trying to create one final copy of the book (we're not trying to maintain many branches for other uses). If we always rebase, the edit history will appear totally ordered (for each pair of edits, one is always recorded as having come before the other) and this makes talking about versions of the book much easier (again, *before* is determined by arrows in the edit history, not by time stamp).

> **DON'T CONFUSE VERSION CONTROL WITH BACKUP** Git keeps multiple copies and records of all of your work. But until you push to a remote destination, all of these copies are on your machine in the .git directory. So don't confuse basic version control with remote backups; they're complementary.

A bit on the Git philosophy

Git is interesting in that it automatically detects and manages so much of what you'd have to specify with other version control systems (for example, Git finds which files have changed instead of you having to specify them, and Git also decides which files are related). Because of the large degree of automation, beginners usually severely underestimate how much Git tracks for them. This makes Git fairly quick except when Git insists you help decide how a possible global inconsistency should be recorded in history (either as a rebase or a branch followed by a merge record). The point is this: Git suspects possible inconsistency based on global state (even when the user may not think there is such) and then forces the committer to decide how to annotate the issue *at the time of commit* (a great service to any possible readers in the future). Git automates so much of the record-keeping that it's always a shock when you have a conflict and have to express opinions on nuances you didn't know were being tracked. Git is also an "anything is possible, but nothing is obvious or convenient" system. This is hard on the user at first, but in the end is much better than an "everything is smooth, but little is possible" version control system (which can leave you stranded).

KEEP NOTES Git commands are confusing; you'll want to keep notes. One idea is to write a 3 x 5 card for each command you're regularly using. Ideally you can be at the top of your Git game with about seven cards.

10.4 Deploying models

Good data science shares a rule with good writing: show, don't tell. And a successful data science project should include at least a demonstration deployment of any techniques and models developed. Good documentation and presentation are vital, but at some point people have to see things working and be able to try their own tests. We strongly encourage partnering with a development group to produce the actual production-hardened version of your model, but a good demonstration helps recruit these collaborators.

We outline some deployment methods in table 10.7.

Table 10.7 Methods to demonstrate predictive model operation

Method	Description
Batch	Data is brought into R, scored, and then written back out. This is essentially an extension of what you're already doing with test data.
Cross-language linkage	R supplies answers to queries from another language (C, C++, Python, Java, and so on). R is designed with efficient cross-language calling in mind (in particular the Rcpp package), but this is a specialized topic we won't cover here.
Services	R can be set up as an HTTP service to take new data as an HTTP query and respond with results.
Export	Often model evaluation is simple compared to model construction. In this case, the data scientist can export the model and a specification for the code to evaluate the model, and the production engineers can implement (with tests) model evaluation in the language of their choice (SQL, Java, C++, and so on).
PMML	*PMML*, or *Predictive Model Markup Language*, is a shared XML format that many modeling packages can export to and import from. If the model you produce is covered by R's package `pmml`, you can export it without writing any additional code. Then any software stack that has an importer for the model in question can use your model.

We've already demonstrated batch operation of models each time we applied a model to a test set. We won't work through an R cross-language linkage example as it's very specialized and requires knowledge of the system you're trying to link to. We'll demonstrate service and export strategies.

10.4.1 Deploying models as R HTTP services

One easy way to demonstrate an R model in operation is to expose it as an HTTP service. In the following listing, we show how to do this for our buzz model (predicting discussion topic popularity).

Listing 10.16 Buzz model as an R-based HTTP service

```
library(Rook)                                  <-- Load the Rook HTTP server library.

load('thRS500.Rdata')                          <-- Load the saved buzz workspace (includes the random forest model).

library(randomForest)                          <-- Load the random forest library (loading the workspace doesn't load the library).

numericPositions <- sapply(buzztrain[,varslist],is.numeric)   <-- Determine which variables are numeric (in the Rook server, everything defaults to character).

modelFn <- function(env) {                     <-- Declare the modeling service.
   errors <- c()
   warnings <- c()
   val <- c()
   row <- c()

   tryCatch(
      {
         arg <- Multipart$parse(env)           <-- This block does the actual work: parse data and apply the model.
         row <- as.list(arg[varslist])
         names(row) <- varslist
         row[numericPositions] <- as.numeric(row[numericPositions])
         frame <- data.frame(row)
         val <- predict(fmodel,newdata=frame)
      },
      warning = function(w) { message(w)
         warnings <<- c(warnings,as.character(w)) },
      error = function(e) { message(e)
         errors <<- c(errors,as.character(e)) }
   )
   body <- paste(                              <-- Format results, place in a list, and return.
      'val=',val,'\n',
      'nerrors=',length(errors),'\n',
      'nwarnings=',length(warnings),'\n',
      'query=',env$QUERY_STRING,'\n',
      'errors=',paste(errors,collapse=' '),'\n',
      'warnings=',paste(warnings,collapse=' '),'\n',
      'data row','\n',
      paste(capture.output(print(row)),collapse='\n'),'\n',
      sep='')
   list(
      status=ifelse(length(errors)<=0,200L,400L),
      headers=list('Content-Type' = 'text/text'),
      body=body )
}

s <- Rhttpd$new()                              <-- Start a new Rook HTTP service.
s$add(name="modelFn",app=modelFn)              <-- Register our model function as an HTTP service.
s$start()                                      <-- Start the HTTP server.
print(s)
```

```
## Server started on 127.0.0.1:20714
## [1] modelFn http://127.0.0.1:20714/custom/modelFn
##
## Call browse() with an index number or name to run an application.
```

This is the URL where the service is running.

The next listing shows how to call the HTTP service.

Listing 10.17 Calling the buzz HTTP service

Function to convert a row of dataset into a huge HTML form that transmits all of the variable values to HTTP server on submit (when the Send button is clicked).

```
rowAsForm <- function(url,row) {
    s <- paste('<HTML><HEAD></HEAD><BODY><FORM action="',url,
       '" enctype="multipart/form-data" method="POST">\n',sep='')
    s <- paste(s,'<input type="submit" value="Send"/>',sep='\n')
    qpaste <- function(a,b) {
       paste('<p> ',a,' <input type="text" name="',a,
          '" value="',b,'"/> </p>',sep='') }
    assignments <- mapply('qpaste',varslist,as.list(row)[varslist])
    s <- paste(s,paste(assignments,collapse='\n'),sep='\n')
    s <- paste(s,'</FORM></BODY></HTML>',sep='\n')
    s
}

url <- 'http://127.0.0.1:20714/custom/modelFn'
cat(rowAsForm(url,buzztest[7,]),file='buzztest7.html')
```

Write the form representing the variables for the seventh test example to a file.

The URL we started the Rook HTTP server on; you'll have to copy the URL address and port from what's printed when you started the Rook service.

This produces the HTML form buzztest7.html, shown in figure 10.11 (also saved in our example GitHub repository).

The generated file buzztest7.html contains a form element that has an action of `"http://127.0.0.1:20714/custom/modelFn"` as a POST. So when the Send button on this page is clicked, all the filled-out features are submitted to our server, and (assuming the form's action is pointing to a valid server and port) we get a classification result from our model. This HTML query can be submitted from anywhere and doesn't require R. An example result is saved in GitHub as buzztest7res.txt. Here's an excerpt:

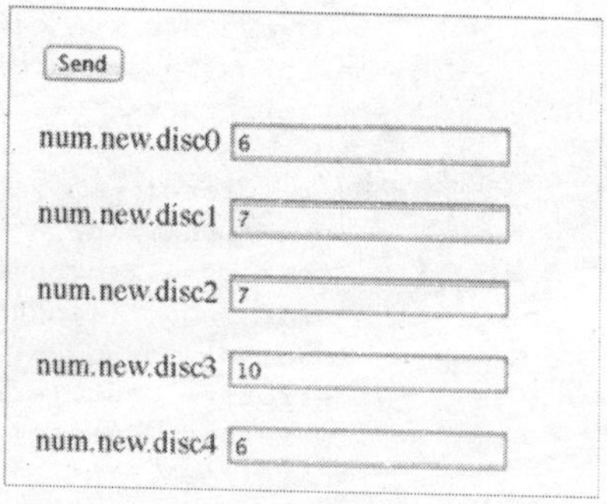

Figure 10.11 Top of HTML form that asks server for buzz classification on submit

```
val=1
nerrors=0
nwarnings=0
...
```

Note that the result is a prediction of `val=1`, which was what we'd expect for the seventh row of the test data. The point is that the copy of R running the Rook server is willing to classify examples from any source. Such a server can be used as part of a larger demonstration and can allow non-R users to enter example data. If you were pushing this further, you could move to more machine-friendly formats such as JSON, but this is far enough for an initial demonstration.

10.4.2 Deploying models by export

Because training is often the hard part of building a model, it often makes sense to export a finished model for use by other systems. For example, a lot of theory goes into how a random forest picks variables and builds its trees. The structure of our random forest model is large but simple: a big collection of decision trees. But the construction is time-consuming and technical. The idea is this: it can be easier to fax a friend a solved Sudoku puzzle than to teach them your entire solution strategy.

So it often makes sense to export a copy of the finished model from R, instead of attempting to reproduce all of the details of model construction. When exporting a model, you're depending on development partners to handle the hard parts of hardening a model for production (versioning, dealing with exceptional conditions, and so on). Software engineers tend to be good at project management and risk control, so export projects are also a good opportunity to learn.

The steps required depend a lot on the model and data treatment. For many models, you only need to save a few coefficients. For random forests, you need to export the trees. In all cases, you need to write code in your target system (be it SQL, Java, C, C++, Python, Ruby, and so on) to evaluate the model.[6]

One of the issues of exporting models is that you must repeat any data treatment. So part of exporting a model is producing a specification of the data treatment (so it can be reimplemented outside of R).

In listing 10.18, we show how to export the buzz random forest model. Some investigation of the random forest model and documentation showed that the underlying trees are accessible through a method called `getTree()`. In this listing, we combine the description of all of these trees into a single table.

Listing 10.18 Exporting the random forest model

Load the saved buzz workspace (includes the random forest model).

Load the random forest library (loading the workspace doesn't load the library).

```
load('thRS500.Rdata')
library(randomForest)
```

Define a function that joins the tree tables from the random forest getTree() method into one large table of trees.

```
extractTrees <- function(rfModel) {
   ei <- function(i) {
     ti <- getTree(rfModel,k=i,labelVar=T)
     ti$nodeid <- 1:dim(ti)[[1]]
```

6 A fun example is the Salford Systems Random Forests package that exports models as source code instead of data. The package creates a compilable file in your target language (often Java or C++) that implements the decision trees essentially as a series of `if` statements over class variables.

```
        ti$treeid <- i
        ti
     }
     nTrees <- rfModel$ntree
     do.call('rbind',sapply(1:nTrees,ei,simplify=F))
}

write.table(extractTrees(fmodel),
     file='rfmodel.tsv',row.names=F,sep='\t',quote=F)
```

Write the table of trees as a tab-separated values table (easy for other software to read).

A random forest model is a collection of decision trees, and figure 10.12 shows an extract of a single tree from the buzz random forest model. A decision tree is a series of tests traditionally visualized as a diagram of decision nodes, as shown in the top portion of the figure. The content of a decision tree is easy to store in a table where each table row represents the facts about the decision node (the variables being tested, the level of the test, and the IDs of the next nodes to go to, depending on the result of the test), as shown in the bottom part of the figure. To reimplement a random forest model, one just has to write code to accept the table representations of all the trees in the random forest model and trace through the specified tests.[7]

Your developer partners would then build tools to read the model trees and evaluate the trees on new data. Previous test results and demonstration servers become the basis of important acceptance tests.

10.4.3 What to take away

You should now be comfortable demonstrating R models to others. Of particular power is setting up a model as an HTTP service that can be experimented with by others, and also exporting models so model evaluation can be reimplemented in a production environment.

> **Always make sure your predictions in production are bounded**
>
> A secret trick of successful production deployments is to always make sure your predictions are bounded. This can prevent disasters in production. For a classification or probability problem (such as our buzz example), your predictions are automatically bounded between `0` and `1` (though there is some justification for adding code to tighten the allowed prediction region to between `1/n` and `1-1/n` for models built from `n` pieces of training data). For models that predict a value or score (such as linear regression), you almost always want to limit the predictions to be between the `min` and `max` values seen during training. This helps prevent a runaway input from driving your prediction to unprecedented (and unjustifiable) levels, possibly causing disastrous actions in production. You also want to signal when predictions have been so "touched up," as unnoticed corrections can also be dangerous.

[7] We've also saved the exported table here: https://github.com/WinVector/zmPDSwR/blob/master/Buzz/rfmodel.tsv.

Actual exported table representation of a decision tree from the random forest model

left daughter	right daughter	split var	split point	status	prediction	nodeid	treeid
2	3	num.displays6	2,517.5	1	NA	1	1
4	5	attention.level.author0	0.0004335	1	NA	2	1
6	7	number.total.disc5	3.5	1	NA	3	1
8	9	avg.disc.length4	127	1	NA	4	1
10	11	contribution.sparseness0	0.0037735	1	NA	5	1
12	13	num.displays7	3,948.5	1	NA	6	1
14	15	num.displays1	3,326	1	NA	7	1
16	17	num.authors.topic7	24.5	1	NA	8	1
0	0	NA	0	-1	0	9	1
18	19	avg.disc.length5	9	1	NA	10	1
20	21	num.displays2	959.5	1	NA	11	1
...							

Conceptual illustration of decision tree table

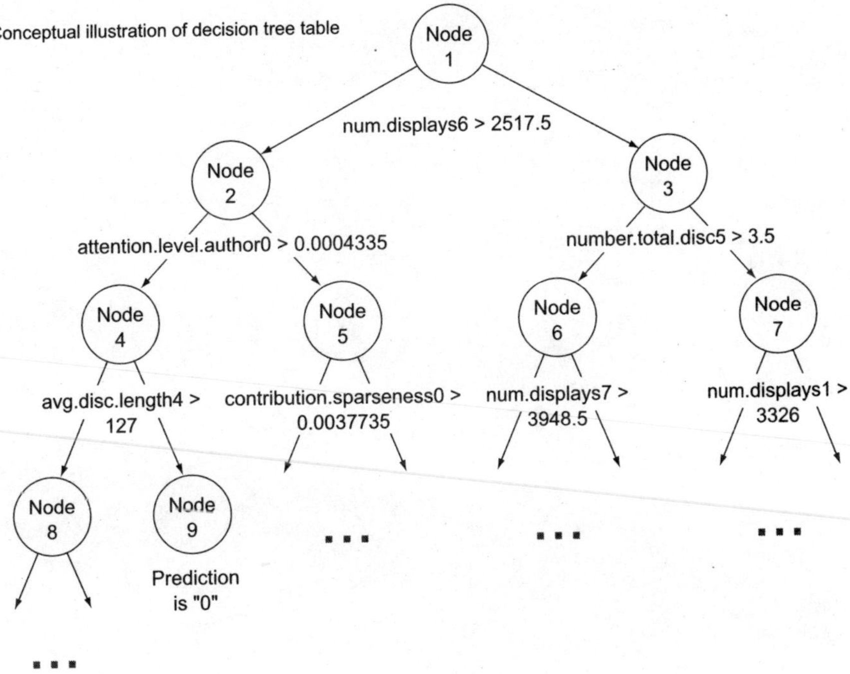

Figure 10.12 One tree from the buzz random forest model

10.5 Summary

This chapter shared options on how to manage and share your work. In addition, we showed some techniques to set up demonstration HTTP services and export models for use by other software (so you don't add R as a dependency in production).

Key takeaways

- Use knitr to produce significant reproducible milestone/checkpoint documentation.
- Write effective comments.
- Use version control to save your work history.
- Use version control to collaborate with others.
- Make your models available to your partners for experimentation and testing.

11 Producing effective presentations

This chapter covers

- Presenting your results to project sponsors
- Communicating with your model's end users
- Presenting your results to fellow data scientists

In the previous chapter, you saw how to effectively document your day-to-day project work and how to deploy your model into production. This included the additional documentation needed to support operations teams. In this chapter, we'll look at how to present the results of your project to other interested parties.

We'll continue with the example from last chapter: our company (let's call it WVCorp) makes and sells home electronic devices and associated software and apps. WVCorp wants to monitor topics on the company's product forums and discussion board to identify "about-to-buzz" issues: topics that are posed to generate a lot of interest and active discussion. This information can be used by product and marketing teams to proactively identify desired product features for future releases, and to quickly discover issues with existing product features. Once we've successfully built a model for identifying about-to-buzz topics on the forum, we'll want to explain the work to the project sponsor, and also to the product managers, marketing managers, and support engineering managers who will be using the results of our model.

Table 11.1 summarizes the relevant entities in our scenario, including products that are sold by our company and by competitors.

Table 11.1 Entities in the buzz model scenario

Entity	Description
WVCorp	The company you work for
eRead	WVCorp's e-book reader
TimeWrangler	WVCorp's time-management app
BookBits	A competitor's e-book reader
GCal	A third-party cloud-based calendar service that TimeWrangler can integrate with

A disclaimer about the data and the example project

The dataset that we used for the buzz model was collected from Tom's Hardware (tomshardware.com), an actual forum for discussing electronics and electronic devices. Tom's Hardware is not associated with any specific product vendor, and the dataset doesn't specify the topics that were recorded. The example scenario we're using in this chapter was chosen to present a situation that would produce data similar to the data in the Tom's Hardware dataset. All product names and forum topics in our example are fictitious.

Let's start with the presentation for the project sponsors.[1]

11.1 Presenting your results to the project sponsor

As we mentioned in chapter 1, the project sponsor is the person who wants the data science result—generally for the business need that it will fill. Though project sponsors may have technical or quantitative backgrounds and may enjoy hearing about technical details and nuances, their primary interest is business-oriented, so you should discuss your results in terms of the business problem, with a minimum of technical detail.

You should also remember that the sponsor will often be interested in "selling" your work to others in the organization, to drum up support and additional resources to keep the project going. Your presentation will be part of what the sponsor will share

1 We provide the PDF versions (with notes) of our example presentations at https://github.com/WinVector/zmPDSwR/tree/master/Buzz as ProjectSponsorPresentation.pdf, UserPresentation.pdf, and PeerPresentation.pdf.

with these other people, who may not be as familiar with the context of the project as you and your sponsor are.

To cover these considerations, we recommend a structure similar to the following:

1. Summarize the motivation behind the project, and its goals.
2. State the project's results.
3. Back up the results with details, as needed.
4. Discuss recommendations, outstanding issues, and possible future work.

Some people also recommend an "Executive Summary" slide: a one-slide synopsis of steps 1 and 2.

How you treat each step—how long, how much detail—depends on your audience and your situation. In general, we recommend keeping the presentation short. In this section, we'll offer some example slides in the context of our buzz model example.

Let's go through each step in detail.

We'll concentrate on content, not visuals

In our discussion, we'll concentrate on the content of the presentations, rather than the visual format of the slides. In an actual presentation, you'd likely prefer more visuals and less text than the slides that we provide here. If you're looking for guidance on presentation visuals, a good book is *The Craft of Scientific Presentations* by Michael Alley (Springer, 2003).

If you peruse that text, you'll notice that our bullet-laden example presentation violates all his suggestions. Think of our skeleton presentations as outlines that you'd flesh out into a more compelling visual format.

It's worth pointing out that a visually oriented, low-text format like Alley recommends is meant to be *presented*, not read. It's common for presentation decks to be passed around in lieu of reports or memos. If you're distributing your presentation to people who won't see you deliver it, make sure to include comprehensive speaker's notes. Otherwise, it may be more appropriate to go with a bullet-laden, text-heavy presentation format.

11.1.1 Summarizing the project's goals

This section of the presentation is intended to provide context for the rest of the talk, especially if it will be distributed to others in the company who weren't as closely involved as your project sponsor was. Let's put together the goal slides for the WVCorp buzz model example.

In figure 11.1, we provide background for the motivation behind the project by showing the business need and how the project will address that need. In our example, eRead is WVCorp's e-book reader, which led the market until our competitor released a new version of their e-book reader, BookBits. The new version of BookBits has a shared-bookshelves feature that eRead doesn't provide—though many eRead users expressed the desire for such functionality on the forums. Unfortunately, forum

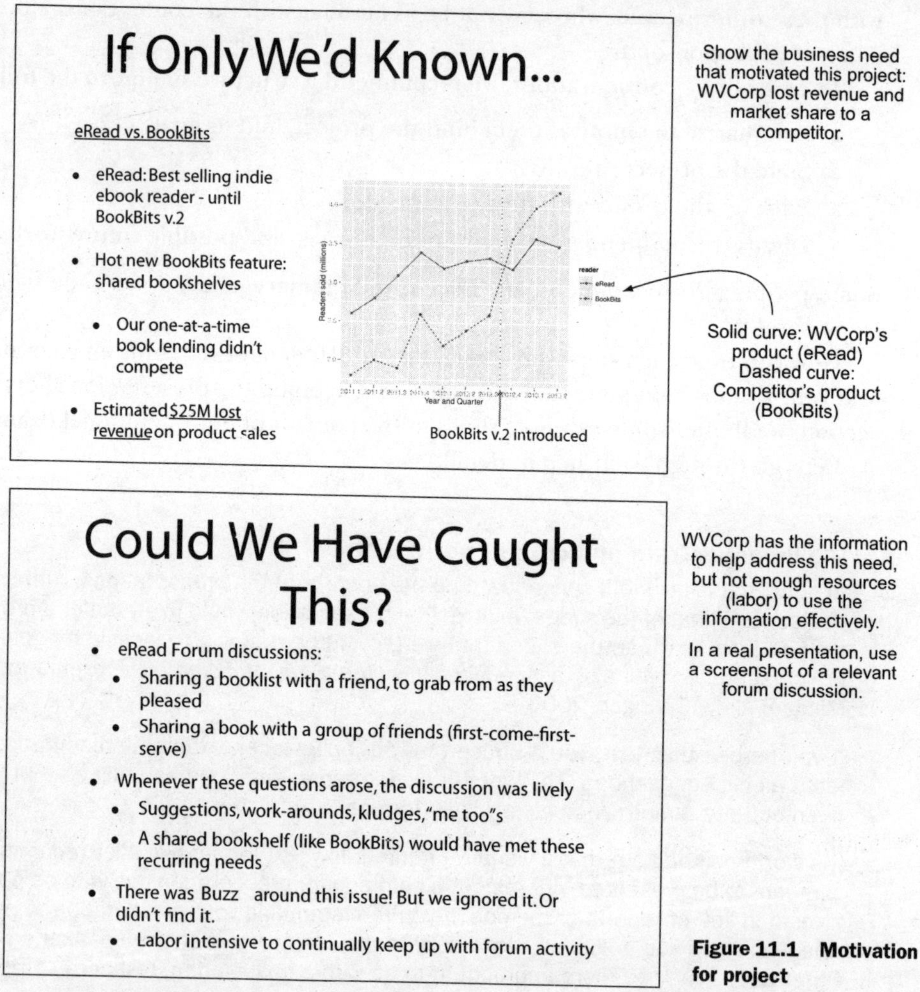

Figure 11.1 Motivation for project

traffic is so high that product managers have a hard time keeping up, and somehow missed detecting this expression of users' needs. Hence, WVCorp lost market share by not anticipating the demand for the shared-bookshelf feature.

In figure 11.2, we state the project's goal, in the context of the motivation that we set up in figure 11.1: we want to detect topics on the forum that are about to buzz so that product managers can find emerging issues early.

Once you've established the project's context, you should move directly to the project's results. Your presentation isn't a thriller movie—don't keep your audience in suspense!

11.1.2 Stating the project's results

This section of the presentation briefly describes what you did, and what the results were, in the context of the business need. Figure 11.3 describes the buzz model pilot study, and what we found.

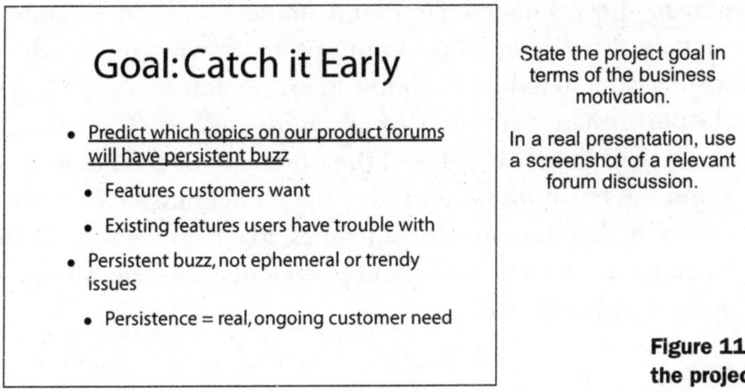

Figure 11.2 Stating the project goal

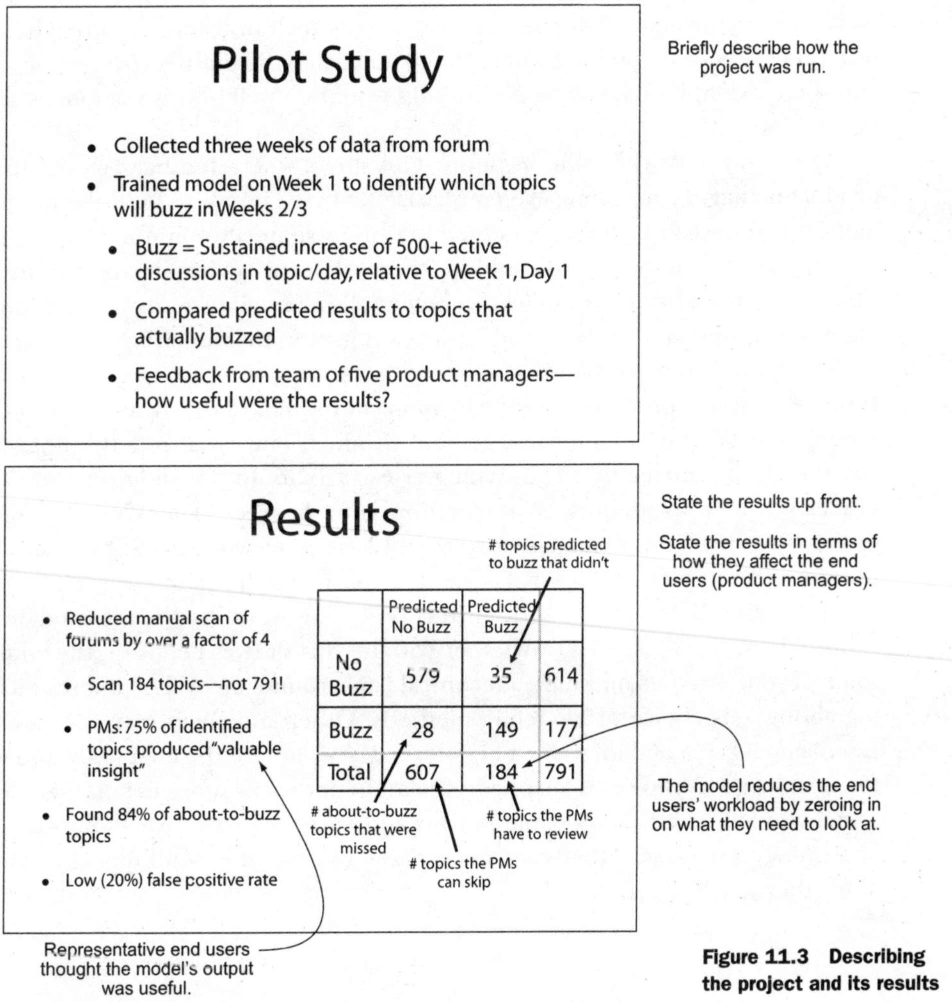

Figure 11.3 Describing the project and its results

Keep the discussion of the results concrete and nontechnical. Your audience isn't interested in the details of your model *per se*, but rather in why your model will help solve the problem that you stated in the motivation section of the talk. Don't talk about your model's performance in terms of precision and recall or other technical metrics, but rather in terms of how it reduced the workload for the model's end users, how useful they found the results to be, and what the model missed. In projects where the model is more closely tied to monetary outcomes, like loan default prediction, try to estimate how much money your model could potentially generate, whether as earnings or savings, for the company.

11.1.3 Filling in the details

Once your audience knows what you've done, why, and how well you've succeeded (from a business point of view), you can fill in details to help them understand more. As before, try to keep the discussion relatively nontechnical and grounded in the business process. A description of where the model fits in the business process or workflow and some examples of interesting findings would go well in this section, as shown in figure 11.4.

The "How it Works" slide in figure 11.4 shows where the buzz model fits into a product manager's workflow. We emphasize that (so far) we've built the model using metrics that were already implemented into the system (thus minimizing the number of new processes to be introduced into the workflow). We also introduce the ways in which the output from our model can potentially be used: to generate leads for potential new features, and to alert product support groups to impending problems.

The bottom slide of figure 11.4 presents an interesting finding from the project (in a real presentation, you'd want to show more than one). In this example, TimeWrangler is WVCorp's time-management product, and GCal is a third-party cloud-based calendar service that TimeWrangler can talk to. In this slide, we show how the model was able to identify an integration issue between TimeWrangler and GCal sooner than the TimeWrangler team would have otherwise (from the customer support logs). Examples like this make the value of the model concrete.

We've also included one slide in this presentation to discuss the modeling algorithm (shown in figure 11.5). Whether you use this slide depends on the audience—some of your listeners may have a technical background and will be interested in hearing about your choice of modeling methods. Other audiences may not care. In any case, keep it brief, and focus on a high-level description of the technique and why you felt it was a good choice. If anyone in the audience wants more detail, they can ask—and if you anticipate such people in your audience, you can have additional slides to cover likely questions. Otherwise, be prepared to cover this point quickly, or to skip it altogether.

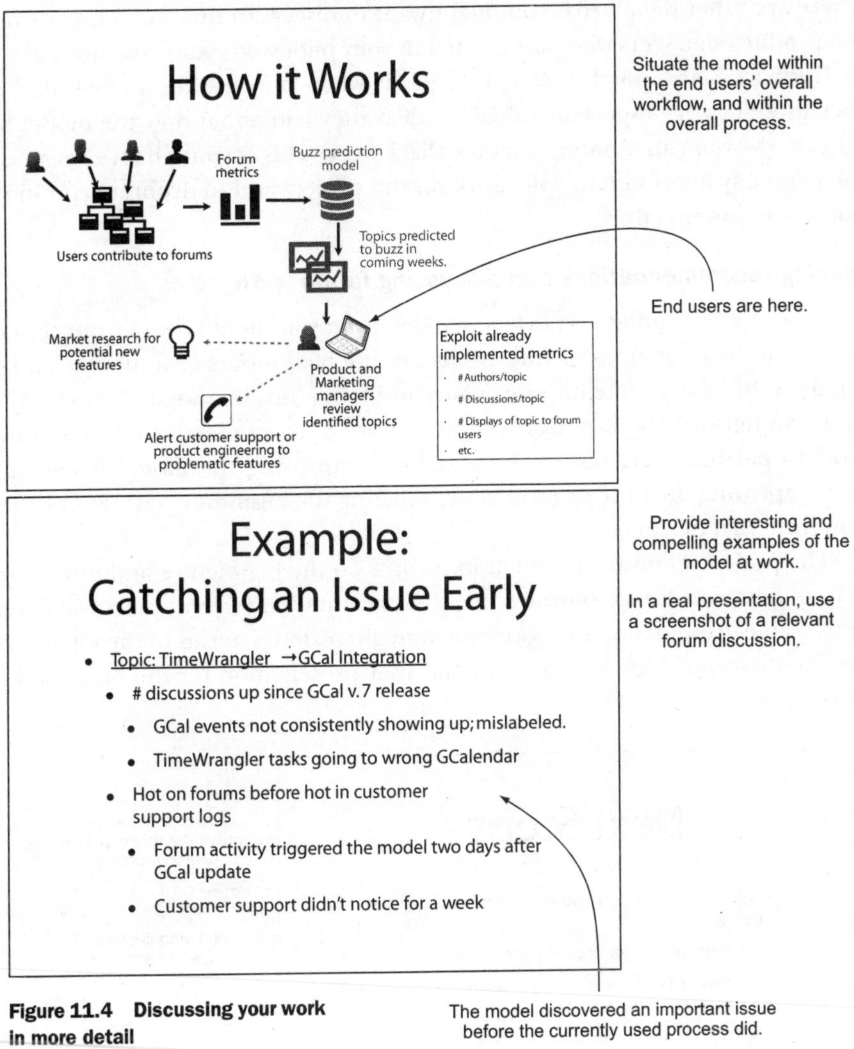

Figure 11.4 Discussing your work in more detail

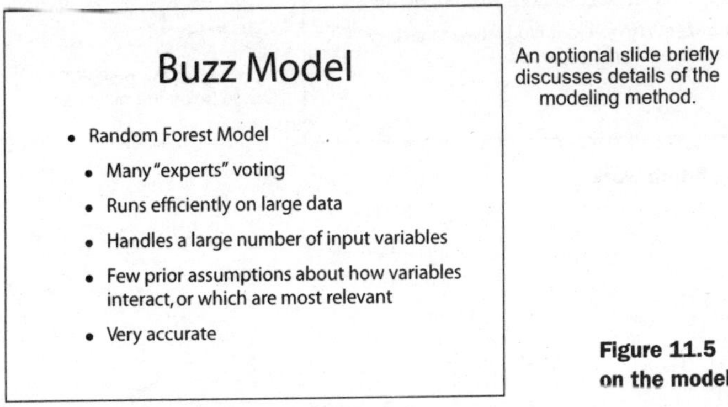

Figure 11.5 Optional slide on the modeling method

There are other details that you might want to discuss in this section. For example, if the product managers who participated in your pilot study gave you interesting quotes or feedback—how much easier their job is when they use the model, findings that they thought were especially valuable, ideas they had about how the model could be improved—you can mention that feedback here. This is your chance to get others in the company interested in your work on this project and to drum up continuing support for follow-up efforts.

11.1.4 Making recommendations and discussing future work

No project ever produces a perfect outcome, and you should be up-front (but optimistic) about the limitations of your results. In the buzz model example, we end the presentation by listing some improvements and follow-ups that we'd like to make. This is shown in figure 11.6. As a data scientist, you're of course interested in improving the model's performance, but to the audience, improving the model is less important than improving the process (and better meeting the business need). Frame the discussion from that perspective.

The project sponsor presentation focuses on the big picture and how your results help to better address a business need. A presentation for end users will cover much of the same ground, but now you frame the discussion in terms of the end users' workflow and concerns. We'll look at an end user presentation for the buzz model in the next section.

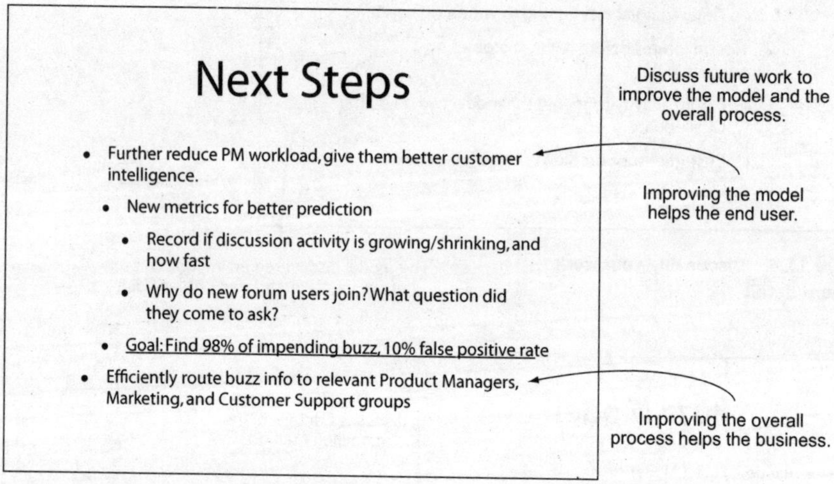

Figure 11.6 Discussing future work

11.1.5 Project sponsor presentation takeaways

Here's what you should remember about the project sponsor presentation:

- Keep it short.
- Keep it focused on the business issues, not the technical ones.
- Your project sponsor might use your presentation to help sell the project or its results to the rest of the organization. Keep that in mind when presenting background and motivation.
- Introduce your results early in the presentation, rather than building up to them.

11.2 Presenting your model to end users

No matter how well your model performs, it's important that the people who will actually be using it have confidence in its output and are willing to adopt it. Otherwise, the model won't be used, and your efforts will have been wasted. Hopefully, you had end users involved in the project—in our buzz model example, we had five product managers helping with the pilot study. End users can help you sell the benefits of the model to their peers.

In this section, we'll give an example of how you might present the results of your project to the end users. Depending on the situation, you may not always be giving an explicit presentation: you may be providing a user's manual or other documentation. However the information about your model is passed to the users, we believe that it's important to let them know how the model is intended to make their workflow easier, not more complicated. For the purposes of this chapter, we'll use a presentation format.

For an end user presentation, we recommend a structure similar to the following:

1. Summarize the motivation behind the project, and its goals.
2. Show how the model fits into the users' workflow (and how it improves that workflow).
3. Show how to use the model.

Let's explore each of these points in turn, starting with project goals.

11.2.1 Summarizing the project's goals

With the model's end users, it's less important to discuss business motivations and more important to focus on how the model affects them. In our example, product managers are already monitoring the forums to get a sense of customers' needs and issues. The goal of our project is to help them focus their attention on the "good stuff"—buzz. The example slide in figure 11.7 goes directly to this point. The users already know that they want to find buzz; our model will help them search more effectively.

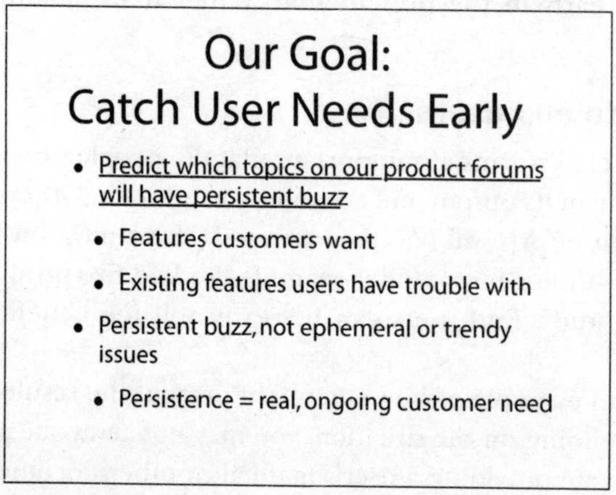

Provide motivation for the work from the end user's perspective: help them find useful buzz faster.

In a real presentation, you might use a screenshot of a relevant forum discussion.

Figure 11.7 Motivation for project

11.2.2 Showing how the model fits the users' workflow

In this section of the presentation, you explain how the model helps the users do their job. A good way to do this is to give before-and-after scenarios of a typical user workflow, as we show in figure 11.8.

Presumably, the before process and its minuses are already obvious to the users. The after slide emphasizes how the model will do some preliminary filtering of forum topics for them. The output of the model helps the users manage their already existing watchlists, and of course the users can still go directly to the forums as well.

The next slide (figure 11.9, top) uses the pilot study results to show that the model can reduce the effort it takes to monitor the forums, and does in fact provide useful information. We elaborate on this with a compelling example in the bottom slide of figure 11.9 (the TimeWrangler example that we also used in the project sponsor presentation).

You may also want to fill in more details about how the model operates. For example, users may want to know what the inputs to the model are (figure 11.10), so that they can compare those inputs with what they themselves consider when looking for interesting information on the forums manually.

Once you've shown how the model fits into the users' workflow, you can explain how the users will use it.

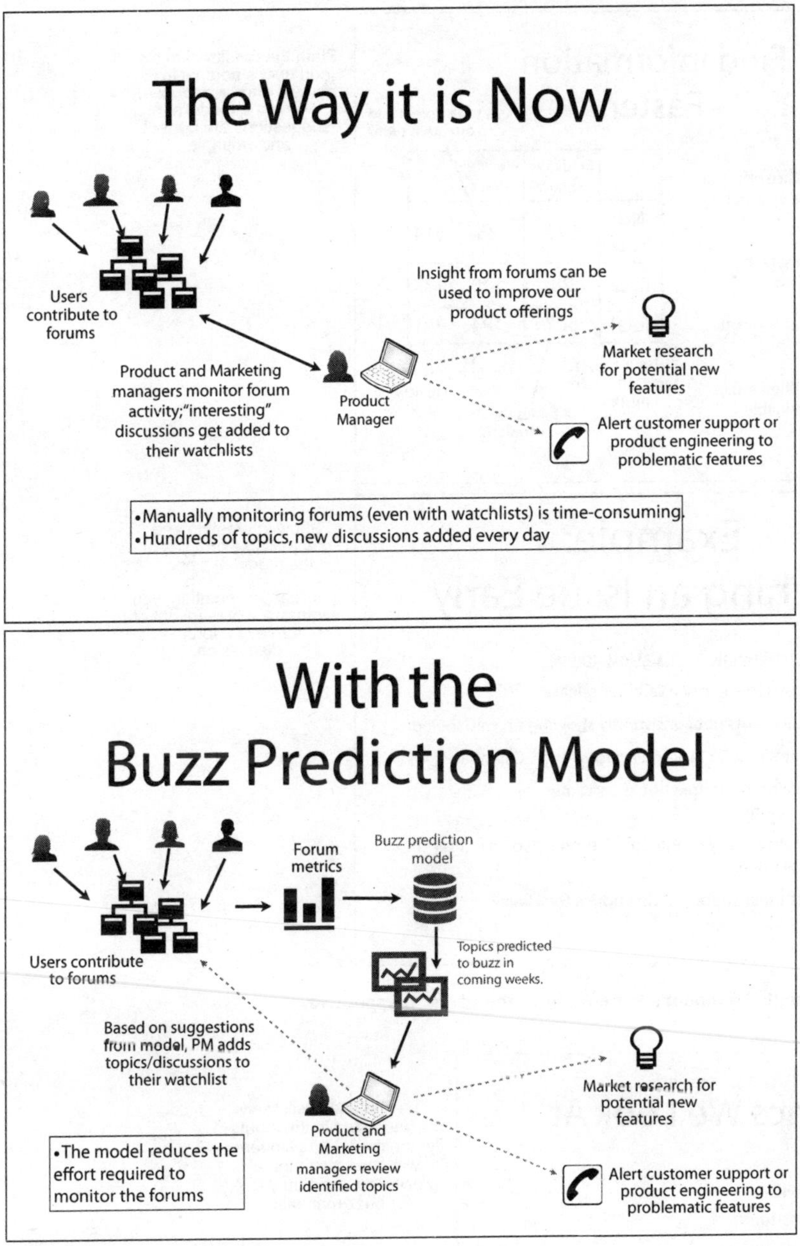

Compare the end users' day-to-day work process before and after the introduction of your model.

Before: time-consuming.

After: more focused, less time-consuming.

Figure 11.8 User workflow before and after the model

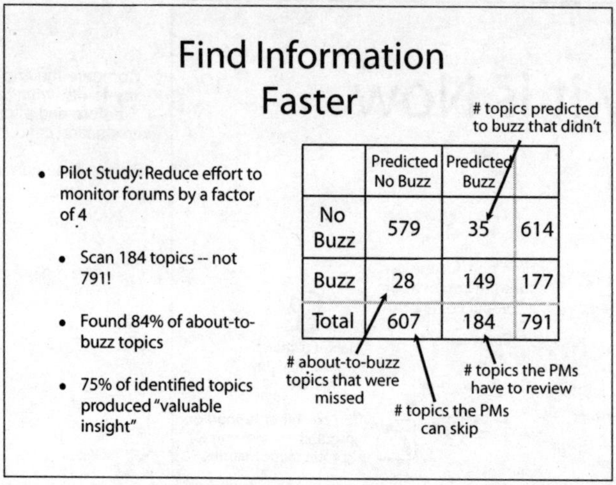

State the results from the end user's perspective: manual effort is reduced, and the model's suggestions are correct and valuable.

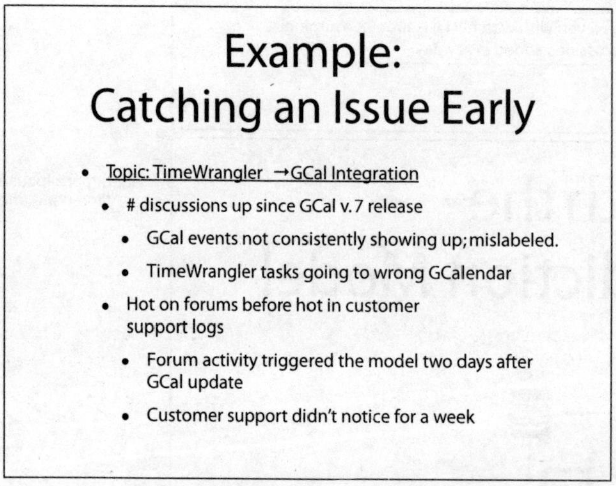

Show interesting and compelling examples of the model at work.

In a real presentation, you might use a screenshot of a relevant forum discussion.

Figure 11.9 Present the model's benefits from the users' perspective.

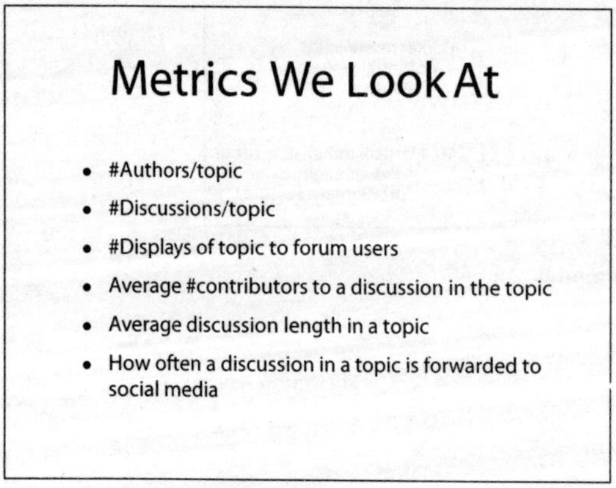

The end users will likely be interested in the inputs to the model (to compare with their own mental processes when they look for buzz manually).

Figure 11.10 Provide technical details that are relevant to the users.

11.2.3 Showing how to use the model

This section is likely the bulk of the presentation, where you'll teach the users how to use the model. The slide in figure 11.11 describes how a product manager will interact with the buzz model. In this example scenario, we're assuming that there's an existing mechanism for product managers to add topics and discussions from the forums to a watchlist, as well as a way for product managers to monitor that watchlist. The model will separately send the users notifications about impending buzz on topics they're interested in.

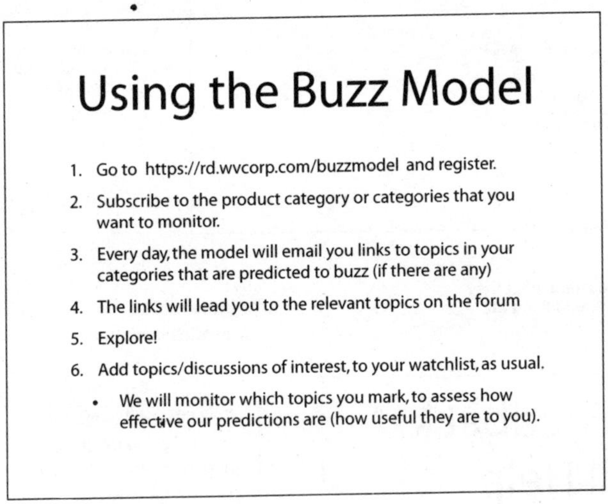

Show the users how to interact with the model.

In a real presentation, each point would be expanded with step-by-step detailed instructions and appropriate screenshots.

Figure 11.11 Describe how the users will interact with the model.

In a real presentation, you'd then expand each point to walk the users through how they use the model: screenshots of the GUIs that they use to interact with the model, and screenshots of model output. We give one example slide in figure 11.12: a screenshot of a notification email, annotated to explain the view to the user.

By the end of this section, the user should understand how to use the buzz model and what to do with the buzz model's output.

Finally, we've included a slide that asks the users for feedback on the model, once they've been using it in earnest. This is shown in figure 11.13. Feedback from the users can help you (and other teams that help to support the model once it's operational) to improve the experience for the users, making it more likely that the model will be accepted and widely adopted.

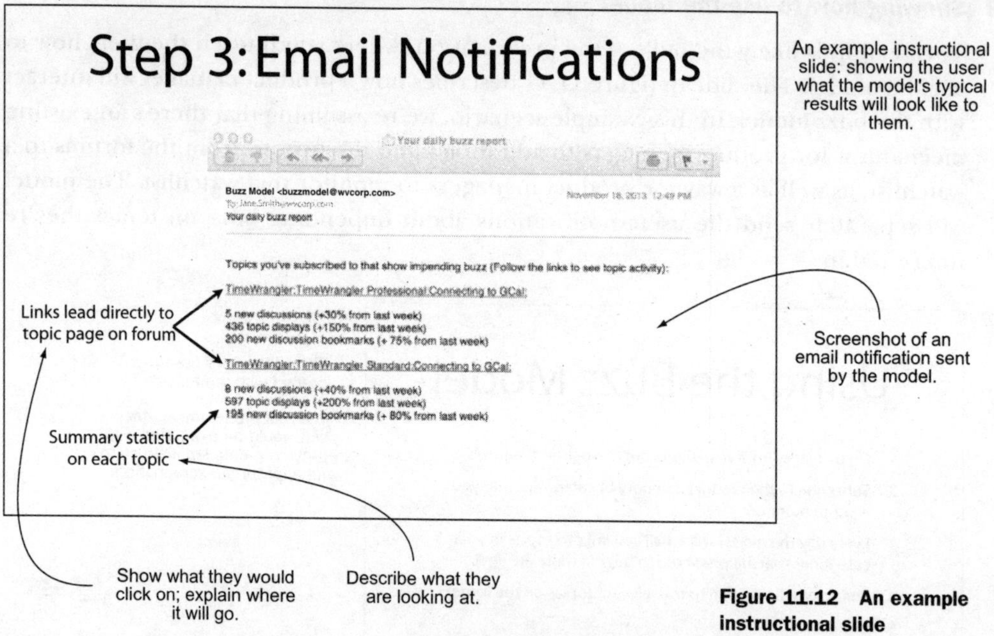

Figure 11.12 An example instructional slide

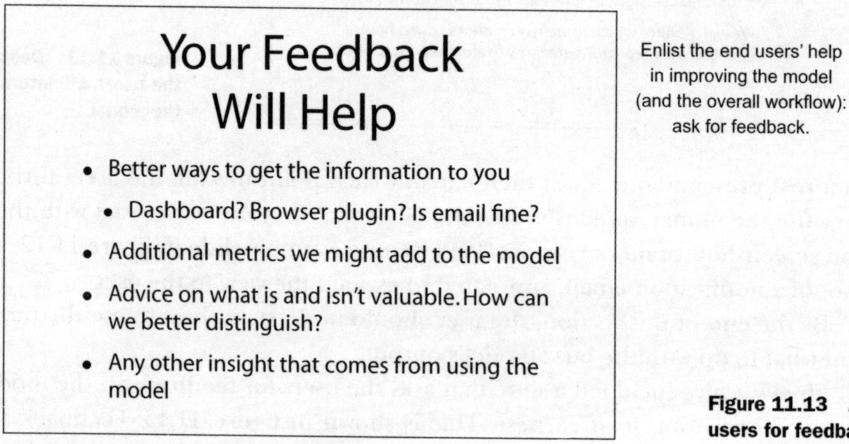

Figure 11.13 Ask the users for feedback.

In addition to presenting your model to the project sponsors and to end users, you may be presenting your work to other data scientists in your organization, or outside of it. We'll cover peer presentations in the next section.

11.2.4 End user presentation takeaways

Here's what you should remember about the end user presentation:

- Your primary goal is to convince the users that they want to use your model.
- Focus on how the model affects (improves) the end users' day-to-day processes.
- Describe how to use the model and how to interpret or use the model's outputs.

11.3 Presenting your work to other data scientists

Presenting to other data scientists gives them a chance to evaluate your work and gives you a chance to benefit from their insight. They may see something in the problem that you missed, and can suggest good variations to your approach or alternative approaches that you didn't think of.

Other data scientists will primarily be interested in the modeling approach that you used, any variations on the standard techniques that you tried, and interesting findings related to the modeling process. A presentation to your peers generally has the following structure:

1. Introduce the problem.
2. Discuss related work.
3. Discuss your approach.
4. Give results and findings.
5. Discuss future work.

Let's go through these steps in detail.

11.3.1 Introducing the problem

Your peers will generally be most interested in the prediction task (if that's what it is) that you're trying to solve, and don't need as much background about motivation as the project sponsors or the end users. In figure 11.14, we start off by introducing the concept of buzz and why it's important, then go straight into the prediction task.

This approach is best when you're presenting to other data scientists within your own organization, since you all share the context of the organization's needs. When you're presenting to peer groups outside your organization, you may want to lead with the business problem (for example, the first two slides of the project sponsor presentation, figures 11.1 and 11.2) to provide them with some context.

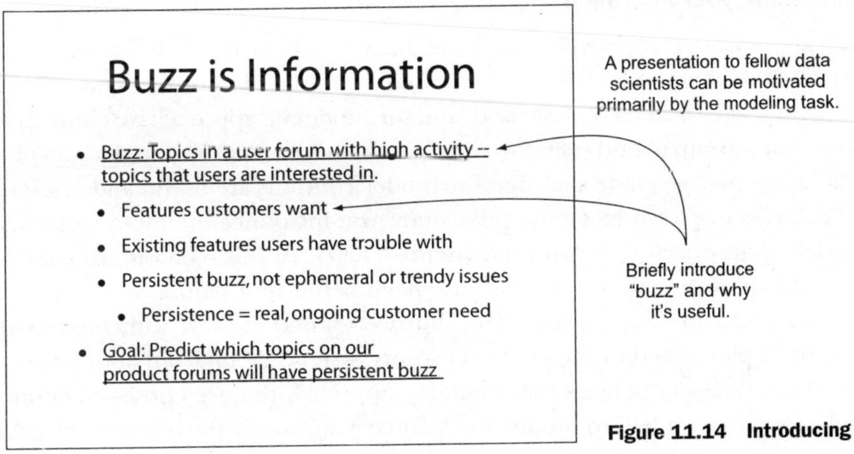

Figure 11.14 Introducing the project

11.3.2 Discussing related work

An academic presentation generally has a related work section, where you discuss others who have done research on problems related to your problem, what approach they took, and how their approach is similar to or different from yours. A related work slide for the buzz model project is shown in figure 11.15.

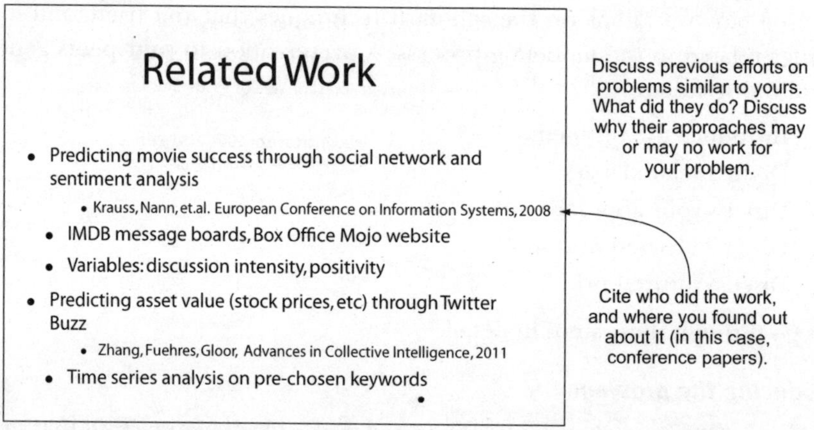

Figure 11.15 Discussing related work

You're not giving an academic presentation; it's more important to you that your approach succeeds than that it's novel. For you, a related work slide is an opportunity to discuss other approaches that you considered, and why they may not be completely appropriate for your specific problem.

After you've discussed approaches that you considered and rejected, you can then go on to discuss the approach that you did take.

11.3.3 Discussing your approach

Talk about what you did in lots of detail, including compromises that you had to make and setbacks that you had. For our example, figure 11.16 introduces the pilot study that we conducted, the data that we used, and the modeling approach we chose. It also mentions that a group of end users (five product managers) participated in the project; this establishes that we made sure that the model's outputs are useful and relevant.

After you've introduced the pilot study, you introduce the input variables and the modeling approach that you used (figure 11.17). In this scenario, the dataset didn't have the right variables—it would have been better to do more of a time-series analysis, if we had the appropriate data, but we wanted to start with metrics that were already implemented in the product forums' system. Be up-front about this.

The slide also discusses the modeling approach that we chose—random forest—and why. Since we had to modify the standard approach (by limiting the model complexity), we mention that, too.

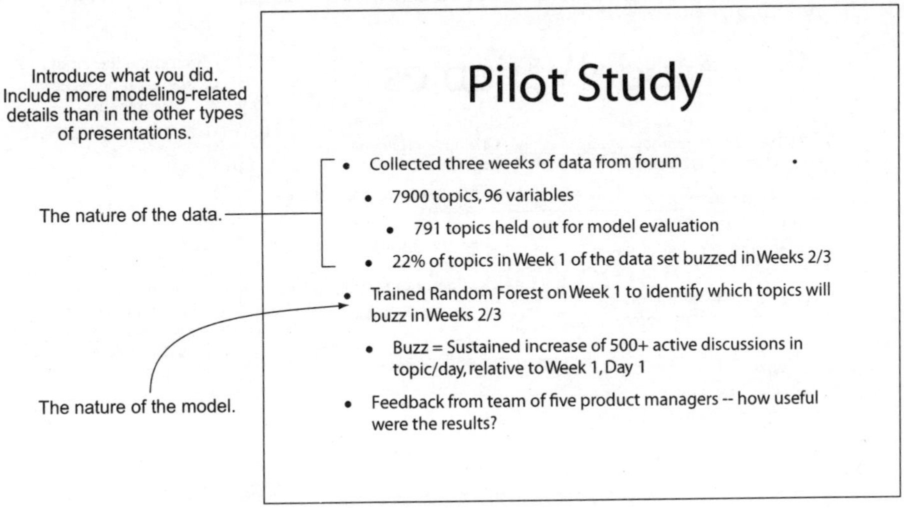

Figure 11.16 Introducing the pilot study

11.3.4 Discussing results and future work

Once you've discussed your approach, you can discuss your results. In figure 11.18, we discuss our model's performance (precision/recall) and also confirm that representative end users did find the model's output useful to their jobs.

The bottom slide of figure 11.18 shows which variables are most influential in the model (recall that the variable importance calculation is one side effect of building random forests). In this case, the most important variables are the number of times the topic is displayed on various days and how many authors are contributing to the topic. This suggests that time-series data for these two variables in particular might improve model performance.

You also want to add examples of compelling findings to this section of the talk—for example, the TimeWrangler integration issue that we showed in the other two presentations.

Once you've shown model performance and other results of your work, you can end the talk with a discussion of possible improvements and future work, as shown in figure 11.19.

Some of the points on the future work slide—in particular the need for velocity variables—come up naturally from the previous discussion of the work and findings. Others, like future work on model retraining schedules, aren't foreshadowed as strongly by the earlier part of the talk, but might occur to people in your audience and are worth elaborating on briefly here. Again, you want to be up-front, though optimistic, about the limitations of your model—especially because this audience is likely to see the limitations already.

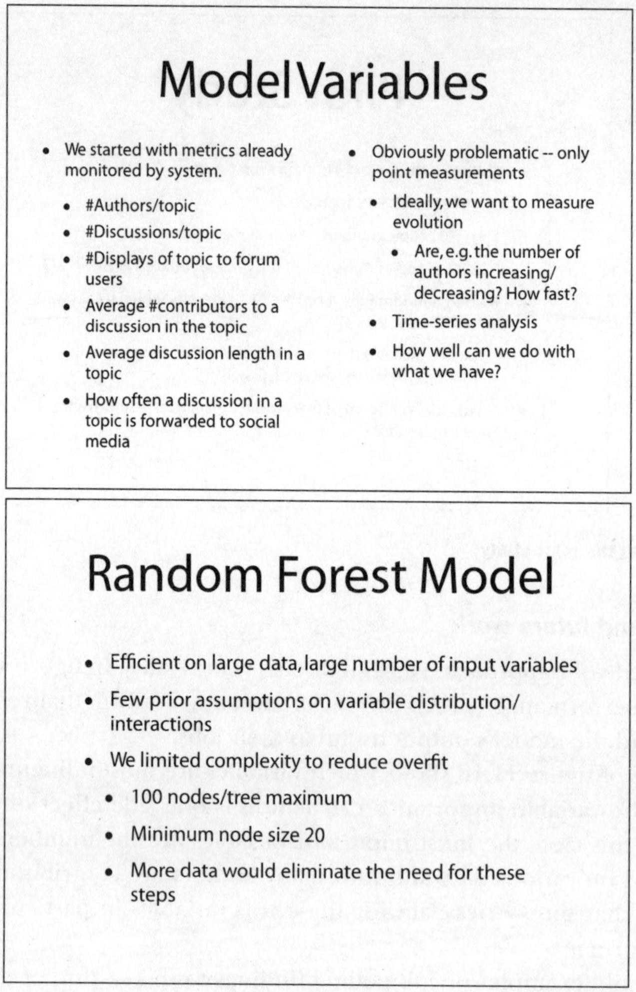

Figure 11.17 Discussing model inputs and modeling approach

11.3.5 Peer presentation takeaways

Here's what you should remember about your presentation to fellow data scientists:

- A peer presentation can be motivated primarily by the modeling task.
- Unlike the previous presentations, the peer presentation can (and should) be rich in technical details.
- Be up-front about limitations of the model and assumptions made while building it. Your audience can probably spot many of the limitations already.

11.4 Summary

In this chapter, you've seen how to present the results of your work to three different audiences. Each of these audiences has their own perspective and their own set of interests, and your talk should be tailored to match those interests. We've suggested

Results

- 84% recall, 83% precision
- Reduced manual scan of forums by over a factor of 4
  - From 791 to 184 topics to inspect
- PMs: 75% of identified topics produced "valuable insight"

	Predicted No Buzz	Predicted Buzz	
No Buzz	579	35	614
Buzz	28	149	177
Total	607	184	791

Show your results: model performance and other outcomes.

Variable Importance

- Key inputs:
  - # times topic is displayed to user (num.displays)
  - # authors contributing to topic (attention.level.author)
- Velocity variables for these two inputs could improve model

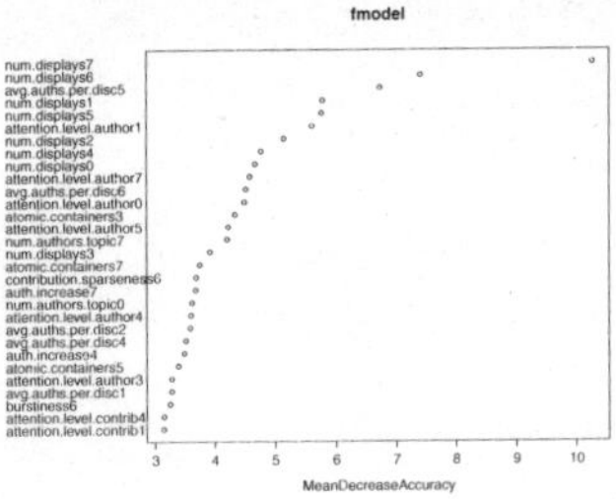

Discuss other key findings, like which variables were most influential on the model.

Figure 11.18 Showing model performance

Future Work

- Better input variables
  - Shape and velocity variables
    - How quickly #authors grows/shrinks
    - How much #topic displays increases/decreases
  - Information about new forum visitors
    - What questions do first-time visitors come to ask?
- Research optimal model retraining schedule

Discuss future work.

Figure 11.19 Discussing future work

ways to organize each type of talk that will help you to tailor your discussion appropriately. None of our suggestions are set in stone: you may have a project sponsor or other interested executives who want to dig down to the more technical details, or end users who are curious about how the internals of the model work. You can also have peer audiences who want to hear more about the business context. If you know this ahead of time (perhaps because you've presented to this audience before), then you should include the appropriate level of detail in your talk. If you're not sure, you can also prepare backup slides, to be used as needed. There's only one hard-and-fast rule: have empathy for your audience.

Key takeaways

- Presentations should be organized and written with a specific audience and purpose in mind.
- Organize your presentations to declare a shared goal and show how you're meeting that goal.
- Some presentations are more technical than others, but all should be honest and share convincing work and interesting results.

appendix A Working with R and other tools

In this appendix, we'll show how you can install tools and start working with R. We'll demonstrate some example concepts and steps, but you'll want to follow up with additional reading.

A.1 Installing the tools

The primary tool for working our examples will be R as run inside RStudio. But other tools (databases, version control) are also highly recommended. You may also need access to online documentation or other help to get all of these tools to work in your environment. The distribution sites we list are a good place to start.

RStudio and the database tools we suggest require Java. You can download Java from http://www.oracle.com/technetwork/java/javase/downloads/index.html. You won't need to enable Java in your web browser (Java enabled in the web browser is currently considered an unacceptable security risk).

A.1.1 Installing R

A precompiled version of R can be downloaded from CRAN (http://cran.r-project.org); we recommend picking up RStudio from http://rstudio.com. CRAN is also the central repository for the most popular R libraries. CRAN serves the central role for R, similar to the role that CPAN serves for Perl and CTAN serves for Tex. Follow the instructions given at CRAN to download and install R, and we suggest you install Git and RStudio before starting to use R.

A.1.2 The R package system

R is a broad and powerful language and analysis workbench in and of itself. But one of its real strengths is the depth of the package system and packages supplied through CRAN. To install a package from CRAN, just type `install.packages('nameofpackage')`. To use an installed package, type `library(nameofpackage)`.

Any time you type `library('nameofpackage')`[1] or `require('nameofpackage')`, you're assuming you're using a built-in package or you're able to run `install.packages('nameofpackage')` if needed. We'll return to the package system again and again in this book. To see what packages are present in your session, type `sessionInfo()`.

CHANGING YOUR CRAN MIRROR You can change your CRAN mirror at any time with the `chooseCRANmirror()` command. This is handy if the mirror you're working with is slow.

A.1.3 Installing Git

We advise installing Git version control before we show you how to use R and RStudio. This is because without Git, or a tool like it, you'll lose important work. Not just lose *your* work—you'll lose important *client* work. A lot of data science work (especially the analysis tasks) involves trying variations and learning things. Sometimes you learn something surprising and need to redo earlier experiments. Version control keeps earlier versions of all of your work, so it's exactly the right tool to recover code and settings used in earlier experiments. Git is available in precompiled packages from http://git-scm.com.

A.1.4 Installing RStudio

RStudio supplies a text editor (for editing R scripts) and an integrated development environment for R. Before picking up RStudio from http://rstudio.com, you should install both R and Git as we described earlier.

The RStudio product you initially want is called *RStudio Desktop* and is available precompiled for Windows, Linux, and OS X. RStudio is available in 64-bit and 32-bit versions—which version you want depends on whether your operating system is 32- or 64-bit. Use the 64-bit version if you can.

A.1.5 R resources

A lot of the power of R comes from the deep bench of freely available online resources. In this section, we'll touch on a few sources of code and documentation.

INSTALLING R VIEWS

R has an incredibly deep set of available libraries. Usually, R already has the package you want; it's just a matter of finding it. A powerful way to find R packages is using *views*: http://cran.r-project.org/web/views/.

---

[1] Actually, `library('nameofpackage')` also works with quotes. The unquoted form works in R because R has the ability to delay argument evaluation (so an undefined `nameofpackage` doesn't cause an error) as well as the ability to snoop the names of argument variables (most programming languages rely only on references or values of arguments). Given that a data scientist has to work with many tools and languages throughout the day, we prefer to not rely on features unique to one language unless we really need the feature. But the "official R style" is without the quotes.

You can also install all of the packages (with help documentation) from a view in a single command (though be warned: this can take an hour to finish). For example, here we're installing a huge set of time series libraries all at once:

```
install.packages('ctv')
library('ctv')
install.views('TimeSeries')
```

Once you've done this, you're ready to try examples and code.

ONLINE R RESOURCES

A lot of R help is available online. Some of our favorite resources include these:

- *CRAN*—The main R site: http://cran.r-project.org
- *Stack Overflow R section*—A question-and-answer site: http://stackoverflow.com/questions/tagged/r
- *Quick-R*—A great R resource: http://www.statmethods.net
- *LearnR*—A translation of all the plots from *Lattice: Multivariate Data Visualization with R (Use R!)* (by D. Sarker; Springer, 2008) into ggplot2: http://learnr.wordpress.com
- *R-bloggers*—A high-quality R blog aggregator: http://www.r-bloggers.com

A.2 Starting with R

R implements a dialect of a statistical programming language called *S*. The original implementation of S evolved into a commercial package called S+. So most of R's language design decisions are really facts about S. To avoid confusion, we'll mostly just say *R* when describing features. You might wonder what sort of command and programming environment S/R is. It's a pretty powerful one, with a nice command interpreter that we encourage you to type directly into.

Working with R and issuing commands to R is in fact scripting or programming. We assume you have some familiarity with scripting (be it Visual Basic, Bash, Perl, Python, Ruby, and so on) or programming (be it C, C#, C++, Java, Lisp, Scheme, and so on), or are willing to use one of our references to learn. We don't intend to write long programs in R, but we'll have to show how to issue R commands. R's programming, though powerful, is a bit different than many of the popular programming languages, but we feel that with a few pointers, anyone can use R. If you don't know how to use a command, try using the `help()` call to get at some documentation.

Throughout this book, we'll instruct you to run various commands in R. This will almost always mean typing the text or the text following the command prompt > into the RStudio console window, followed by pressing Return. For example, if we tell you to type `1/5`, you can type that into the console window, and when you press Enter you'll see a result such as `[1] 0.2`. The `[1]` portion of the result is just R's way of labeling result rows (and is to be ignored), and the `0.2` is the floating point representation of one-fifth, as requested.

HELP Always try calling `help()` to learn about commands. For example, `help('if')` will bring up help in R's `if` command.

Let's try a few commands to help you become familiar with R and its basic data types. R commands can be terminated with a line break or a semicolon (or both), but interactive content isn't executed until you press Return. The following listing shows a few experiments you should run in your copy of R.

Listing A.1 Trying a few R commands

```
> 1
[1] 1
> 1/2
[1] 0.5
> 'Joe'
[1] "Joe"
> "Joe"
[1] "Joe"
> "Joe"=='Joe'
[1] TRUE
> c()
NULL
> is.null(c())
[1] TRUE
> is.null(5)
[1] FALSE
> c(1)
[1] 1
> c(1,2)
[1] 1 2
> c("Apple",'Orange')
[1] "Apple"  "Orange"
> length(c(1,2))
[1] 2
> vec <- c(1,2)
> vec
[1] 1 2
```

MULTILINE COMMANDS IN R R is good with multiline commands. To enter a multiline command, just make sure it would be a syntax error to stop parsing where you break a line. For example, to enter `1+2` as two lines, add the line break after the plus sign and not before. To get out of R's multiline mode, press Escape. A lot of cryptic R errors are caused by either a statement ending earlier than you wanted (a line break that doesn't force a syntax error on early termination) or not ending where you expect (needing an additional line break or semicolon).

A.2.1 *Primary features of R*

R commands look like a typical procedural programming language. This is deceptive, as the S language (the language R implements) was actually inspired by functional programming and also has a lot of object-oriented features.

ASSIGNMENT

R has five common assignment operators: =, <-, ->, <<-, and ->>. Traditionally in R, <- is the preferred assignment operator and = is thought as a late addition and an amateurish alias for it.

The main advantage of the <- notation is that <- always means assignment, whereas = can mean assignment, list slot binding, function argument binding, or case statement, depending on context. One mistake to avoid is accidentally inserting a space in the assignment operator:

```
> x <- 2
> x < - 3
[1] FALSE
> print(x)
[1] 2
```

We actually like = assignment better because data scientists tend to work in more than one language at a time and more bugs are caught early with =. But this advice is too heterodox to burden others with (see http://mng.bz/hfug). We try to consistently use <- in this book, but some habits are hard to break.

The = operator is also used to bind values to function arguments (and <- can't be so used) as shown in the next listing.

Listing A.2 Binding values to function arguments

```
> divide <- function(numerator,denominator) { numerator/denominator }
> divide(1,2)
[1] 0.5
> divide(2,1)
[1] 2
> divide(denominator=2,numerator=1)
[1] 0.5
divide(denominator<-2,numerator<-1)  # yields 2, a wrong answer
[1] 2
```

The -> operator is just a right-to-left assignment that lets you write things like `x -> 5`. It's cute, but not game changing.

The <<- and ->> operators are to be avoided unless you actually need their special abilities. What they do is search through parent calling environments (usually associated with a stack of function calls) to find an unlocked existing definition they can alter; or, finding no previous definition, they create a definition in the global environment. The ability evades one of the important safety points about functions. When a variable is assigned inside a function, this assignment is local to the function. Nobody outside of the function ever sees the effect; the function can safely use variables to store intermediate calculations without clobbering same-named outside variables. The <<- and ->> operators reach outside of this protected scope and allow potentially troublesome side effects. Side effects seem great when you need them (often for error tracking and logging), but on the balance they make code maintenance, debugging, and documentation much harder. In the following listing, we show a good function that doesn't have a side effect and a bad function that does.

Listing A.3 Demonstrating side effects

```
> x<-1
> good <- function() { x <- 5}
> good()
> print(x)
[1] 1
> bad <- function() { x <<- 5}
> bad()
> print(x)
[1] 5
```

VECTORIZED OPERATIONS

Many R operations are called *vectorized*, which means they work on every element of a vector. These operators are convenient and to be preferred over explicit code like for loops. For example, the vectorized logic operators are `==`, `&`, and `|`. The next listing shows some examples using these operators on R's logical types `TRUE` and `FALSE` (which can also be written as `T` and `F`).

Listing A.4 R truth tables for Boolean operators

```
> c(T,T,F,F) == c(T,F,T,F)
[1]  TRUE FALSE FALSE  TRUE
> c(T,T,F,F) & c(T,F,T,F)
[1]  TRUE FALSE FALSE FALSE
> c(T,T,F,F) | c(T,F,T,F)
[1]  TRUE  TRUE  TRUE FALSE
```

NEVER USE && OR || IN R In many C-descended languages, the preferred logic operators are `&&` and `||`. R has such operators, but they're not vectorized, and there are few situations where you want what they do (so using them is almost always a typo or a bug).

To test if two vectors are a match, we'd use R's `identical()` or `all.equal()` methods.

R also supplies a vectorized sector called `ifelse(,,)` (the basic R-language `if` statement isn't vectorized).

R IS AN OBJECT-ORIENTED LANGUAGE

Every item in R is an object and has a type definition called a *class*. You can ask for the type of any item using the `class()` command. For example, `class(c(1,2))` is *numeric*. R in fact has two object-oriented systems. The first one is called *S3* and is closest to what a C++ or Java programmer would expect. In the S3 class system, you can have multiple commands with the same name. For example, there may be more than one command called `print()`. Which `print()` actually gets called when you type `print(x)` depends on what type `x` is at runtime. S3 is a bit of a "poor man's" object-oriented system, as it doesn't support the more common method notation `c(1,2).print()`

(instead using `print(c(1,2))`), and methods are just defined willy-nilly and not strongly associated with object definitions, prototypes, or interfaces. R also has a second object-oriented system called *S4*, which supports more detailed classes and allows methods to be picked based on the types of more than just the first argument. Unless you're planning on becoming a professional R programmer (versus a professional R user or data scientist), we advise not getting into the complexities of R's object-oriented systems. Mostly you just need to know that most R objects define useful common methods like `print()`, `summary()`, and `class()`. We also advise leaning heavily on the `help()` command. To get class-specific help, you use a notation *method.class*; for example, to get information on the `predict()` method associated with objects of class `glm`, you would type `help(predict.glm)`.

R IS A FUNCTIONAL LANGUAGE

Functions are first-class objects in R. You can define anonymous functions on the fly and store functions in variables. For example, here we're defining and using a function we call `add`. In fact, our function has no name (hence it's called *anonymous*), and we're just storing it in a variable named `add`:

```
> add <- function(a,b) { a + b}
> add(1,2)
[1] 3
```

To properly join strings in this example, we'd need to use the `paste()` function.

R IS A GENERIC LANGUAGE

R functions don't use type signatures (though methods do use them to determine the object class). So all R functions are what we call *generic*. For example, our addition function is generic in that it has no idea what types its two arguments may be or even if the + operator will work for them. We can feed any arguments into `add`, but sometimes this produces an error:

```
> add(1,'fred')
Error in a + b : non-numeric argument to binary operator
```

R IS A DYNAMIC LANGUAGE

R is a dynamic language, which means that only values have types, not variables. You can't know the type of a variable until you look at what value the variable is actually storing. R has the usual features of a dynamic language, such as on-the-fly variable creation. For example, the line `x=5` either replaces the value in variable `x` with a `5` or creates a new variable named `x` with a value of `5` (depending on whether `x` had been defined before). Variables are only created during assignment, so a line like `x=y` is an error if `y` hasn't already been defined. You can find all of your variables using the `ls()` command.

DON'T RELY ON IMPLICIT PRINT() A command that's just a variable name often is equivalent to calling `print()` on the variable. But this is only at the so-called "top level" of the R command interpreter. Inside a sourced script, function, or even a loop body, referring to a variable becomes a no-op instead of `print()`. This is especially important to know for packages like `ggplot2` that override the inbuilt `print()` command to produce desirable side effects like producing a plot.

R BEHAVES LIKE A CALL-BY-VALUE LANGUAGE

R behaves like what's known as a *call-by-value language*. That means, from the programmer's point of view, each argument of a function behaves as if it were a separate copy of what was passed to the function. Technically, R's calling semantics are actually a combination of references and what is called *lazy evaluation*. But until you start directly manipulating function argument references, you see what looks like call-by-value behavior.

Call-by-value is a great choice for analysis software: it makes for fewer side effects and bugs. But most programming languages aren't call-by-value, so call-by-value semantics often come as a surprise. For example, many professional programmers rely on changes made to values inside a function being visible outside the function. Here's an example of call-by-value at work.

Listing A.5 Call-by-value effect

```
> vec <- c(1,2)
> fun <- function(v) { v[[2]]<-5; print(v)}
> fun(vec)
[1] 1 5
> print(vec)
[1] 1 2
```

R ISN'T A DISCIPLINED LANGUAGE R isn't a disciplined language in that there's usually more than one way to do something. The good part is this allows R to be broad, and you can often find an operator that does what you want without requiring the user to jump through hoops. The bad part is you may find too many options and not feel confident in picking a best one.

A.2.2 Primary R data types

While the R language and its features are interesting, it's the R data types that are most responsible for R's style of analysis. In this section, we'll discuss the primary data types and how to work with them.

VECTORS

R's most basic data type is the *vector*, or array. In R, vectors are arrays of same-typed values. They can be built with the `c()` notation, which converts a comma-separated list of arguments into a vector (see `help(c)`). For example, `c(1,2)` is a vector whose first entry is `1` and second entry is `2`. Try typing `print(c(1,2))` into R's command prompt to see what vectors look like and notice that `print(class(1))` returns `numeric`, which is R's name for numeric vectors.

Numbers in R

Numbers in R are primarily represented in double-precision floating-point. This differs from some programming languages, such as C and Java, that default to integers. This means you don't have to write `1.0/5.0` to prevent `1/5` from being rounded down to `0`, as you would in C or Java. It also means that some fractions aren't represented perfectly. For example, `1/5` in R is actually (when formatted to 20 digits by `sprintf("%.20f",1/5)`) `0.20000000000000001110`, not the `0.2` it's usually displayed as. This isn't unique to R; this is the nature of floating-point numbers. A good example to keep in mind is `1/5!=3/5-2/5`, because `1/5-(3/5-2/5)` is equal to `5.55e-17`.

R doesn't generally expose any primitive or scalar types to the user. For example, the number `1.1` is actually converted into a numeric vector with a length of 1 whose first entry is `1.1`. Note that `print(class(1.1))` and `print(class(c(1.1,0)))` are identical. Note also that `length(1.1)` and `length(c(1.1))` are also identical. What we call scalars (or single numbers or strings) are in R just vectors with a length of 1. R's most common types of vectors are these:

- *Numeric*—Arrays of double-precision floating-point numbers.
- *Character*—Arrays of strings.
- *Factor*—Arrays of strings chosen from a fixed set of possibilities (called *enums* in many other languages).
- *Logical*—Arrays of `TRUE/FALSE`.
- *NULL*—The empty vector `c()` (which always has type `NULL`). Note that `length(NULL)` is `0` and `is.null(c())` is `TRUE`.

R uses the square-brace notation (and others) to refer to entries in vectors.[2] Unlike most modern program languages, R numbers vectors starting from 1 and not 0. Here's some example code showing the creation of a variable named vec holding a numeric vector. This code also shows that most R data types are *mutable*, in that we're allowed to change them:

```
> vec <- c(2,3)
> vec[[2]] <- 5
> print(vec)
[1] 2 5
```

NUMBER SEQUENCES Number sequences are easy to generate with commands like `1:10`. Watch out: the `:` operator doesn't bind very tightly, so you need to get in the habit of using extra parentheses. For example, `1:5*4 + 1` doesn't mean `1:21`. For sequences of constants, try using `rep()`.

[2] The most commonly used index notation is `[]`. When extracting single values, we prefer the double square-brace notation `[[]]` as it gives out-of-bounds warnings in situations where `[]` doesn't.

LISTS

In addition to vectors (created with the `c()` operator), R has two types of lists. Lists, unlike vectors, can store more than one type of object, so they're the preferred way to return more than one result from a function. The basic R list is created with the `list()` operator, as in `list(6,'fred')`. Basic lists aren't really that useful, so we'll skip over them to *named lists*. In named lists, each item has a name. An example of a named list would be created in `list('a'=6,'b'='fred')`. Usually the quotes on the list names are left out, but the list names are always constant strings (not variables or other types). In R, named lists are essentially the only convenient mapping structure (the other mapping structure being environments, which give you mutable lists). The ways to access items in lists are the `$` operator and the `[[]]` operator (see `help('[[')` in R's help system). Here's a quick example.

Listing A.6 Examples of R indexing operators

```
> x <- list('a'=6,b='fred')
> names(x)
[1] "a" "b"
> x$a
[1] 6
> x$b
[1] "fred"
> x[['a']]
$a
[1] 6

> x[c('a','a','b','b')]
$a
[1] 6

$a
[1] 6

$b
[1] "fred"

$b
[1] "fred"
```

Labels use case-sensitive partial match

The R list label operators (such as `$`) allow partial matches. For example, `list('abe'='lincoln')$a` returns `lincoln`, which is fine and dandy until you add a slot actually labeled `a` to such a list and your older code breaks. In general, it would be better if `list('abe'='lincoln')$a` was an error, so you have a chance of being signalled of a potential problem the first time you make such an error. You could try to disable this behavior with `options(warnPartialMatchDollar=T)`, but even if that worked in all contexts, it's likely to break any other code that's quietly depending on such shorthand notation.

As you see in our example, the `[]` operator is vectorized, which makes lists incredibly useful as translation maps.

> **Selection: [[]] versus []**
>
> `[[]]` is the strictly correct operator for selecting a single element from a list or vector. At first glance, `[]` appears to work as a convenient alias for `[[]]`, but this is not strictly correct for single-value (scalar) arguments. `[]` is actually an operator that can accept vectors as its argument (try `list(a='b')[c('a','a')]`) and return nontrivial vectors (vectors of length greater than 1, or vectors that don't look like scalars) or lists. The operator `[[]]` has different (and better) single-element semantics for both lists and vectors (though, unfortunately, `[[]]` has different semantics for lists than for vectors).
>
> Really you should *never* use `[]` when `[[]]` can be used (when you want only a single result). Everybody, including the authors, forgets this and uses `[]` way more often than is safe. For lists, the main issue is that `[[]]` usefully unwraps the returned values from the list type (as you'd want: compare `class(list(a='b')['a'])` to `class(list(a='b')[['a']])`). For vectors, the issue is that `[]` fails to signal out-of-bounds access (compare `c('a','b')[[7]]` to `c('a','b')[7]` or, even worse, `c('a','b')[NA]`).

DATA FRAMES

R's central data structure is called the *data frame.* A data frame is organized into rows and columns. A data frame is a list of columns of different types. Each row has a value for each column. An R data frame is much like a database table: the column types and names are the schema, and the rows are the data. In R, you can quickly create a data frame using the `data.frame()` command. For example, `d = data.frame(x=c(1,2), y=c('x','y'))` is a data frame.

The correct way to read a column out of a data frame is with the `[[]]` or `$` operators, as in `d[['x']]`, `d$x` or `d[[1]]`. Columns are also commonly read with the `d[,'x']` or `d['x']` notations. Note that not all of these operators return the same type (some return data frames, and some return arrays).

Sets of rows can be accessed from a data frame using the `d[rowSet,]` notation, where `rowSet` is a vector of Booleans with one entry per data row. We prefer to use `d[rowSet,,drop=F]` or `subset(d,rowSet)`, as they're guaranteed to always return a data frame and not some unexpected type like a vector (which doesn't support all of the same operations as a data frame).[3] Single rows can be accessed with the `d[k,]` notation, where `k` is a row index. Useful functions to call on a data frame include `dim()`, `summary()`, and `colnames()`. Finally, individual cells in the data frame can be addressed using a row-and-column notation, like `d[1,'x']`.

---

[3] To see the problem, type `class(data.frame(x=c(1,2))[c(T,F),])` or `class(data.frame(x=c(1,2))[1,])`, which, instead of returning single-row data frames, return numeric vectors.

From R's point of view, a data frame is a single table that has one row per example you're interested in and one column per feature you may want to work with. This is, of course, an idealized view. The data scientist doesn't expect to be so lucky as to find such a dataset ready for them to work with. In fact, 90% of the data scientist's job is figuring out how to transform data into this form. We call this task *data tubing*, and it involves joining data from multiple sources, finding new data sources, and working with business and technical partners. But the data frame is exactly the right abstraction. Think of a table of data as the ideal data scientist API. It represents a nice demarcation between preparatory steps that work to get data into this form and analysis steps that work with data in this form.

Data frames are essentially lists of columns. This makes operations like printing summaries or types of all columns especially easy, but makes applying batch operations to all rows less convenient. R matrices are organized as rows, so converting to/from matrices (and using transpose `t()`) is one way to perform batch operations on data frame rows. But be careful: converting a data frame to a matrix using something like the `model.matrix()` command (to change categorical variables into multiple columns of numeric level indicators) doesn't track how multiple columns may have been derived from a single variable and can potentially confuse algorithms that have per-variable heuristics (like stepwise regression and random forests).

Data frames would be useless if the only way to populate them was to type them in. The two primary ways to populate data frames are R's `read.table()` command and database connectors (which we'll cover in section A.3).

MATRICES

In addition to data frames, R supports matrices. Matrices are two-dimensional structures addressed by rows and columns. Matrices differ from data frames in that matrices are lists of rows, and every cell in a matrix has the same type. When indexing matrices, we advise using the `,drop=F` notation, as without this selections that should return single-row matrices instead return vectors. This would seem okay, except in R vectors aren't substitutable for matrices, so downstream code that's expecting a matrix will mysteriously crash at runtime. And the crash may be rare and hard to demonstrate or find, as it only happens if the selection happens to return exactly one row.

NULL AND NA

R has two special values: `NULL` and `NA`.

In R, `NULL` is just an alias for `c()`, the empty vector. It carries no type information, so an empty vector of numbers is the same type as an empty vector of strings (a design flaw, but consistent with how most programming languages handle so-called null pointers). `NULL` can only occur where a vector or list is expected; it can't represent missing scalar values (like a single number or string).

For missing scalar values, R uses a special symbol, `NA`, which indicates missing or unavailable data. In R, `NA` behaves like the not-a-number or `NaN` seen in most floating-point implementations (except `NA` can represent any scalar, not just a floating-point number). The value `NA` represents a nonsignalling error or missing value. *Nonsignalling* means you don't get a printed warning, and your code doesn't halt (not necessarily a good thing). NA is inconsistent if it reproduces. 2+NA is NA, as we'd hope, but paste(NA,'b') is a valid non-NA string.

Even though class(NA) claims to be logical, NAs can be present in any vector, list, slot, or data frame.

FACTORS

In addition to a string type called character, R also has a special "set of strings" type similar to what Java programmers would call an *enumerated type.* This type is called a *factor,* and a factor is just a string value guaranteed to be chosen from a specified set of values called *levels.* The value of factors is they are exactly the right data type to represent the different values or levels of categorical variables.

The following example shows the string red encoded as a factor (note how it carries around the list of all possible values) and a failing attempt to encode apple into the same set of factors (returning NA, R's special not-a-value symbol).

Listing A.7 R's treatment of unexpected factor levels

```
> factor('red',levels=c('red','orange'))
[1] red
Levels: red orange
> factor('apple',levels=c('red','orange'))
[1] <NA>
Levels: red orange
```

Factors are useful in statistics, and you'll want to convert most string values into factors at some point in your data science process.

Making sure factor levels are consistent

In this book, we often prepare training and test data separately (simulating the fact that new data will be usually prepared after the original training data). For factors, this introduced two fundamental issues: consistency of numbering of factor levels during training, and application and discovery of new factor level values during application. For the first issue, it's the responsibility of R code to make sure factor numbering is consistent. Listing A.8 demonstrates that lm() correctly handles factors as strings and is consistent even when a different set of factors is discovered during application (this is something you may want to double-check for noncore libraries). For the second issue, discovering a new factor during application is a modeling issue. The data scientist either needs to ensure this can't happen or develop a coping strategy (such as falling back to a model not using the variable in question).

Listing A.8 Confirm lm() encodes new strings correctly.

```
d <- data.frame(x=factor(c('a','b','c')),
                y=c(1,2,3))
m <- lm(y~0+x,data=d)
 print(predict(m,
   newdata=data.frame(x='b'))[[1]])
 # [1] 2
```

Build a data frame and linear model mapping a,b,c to 1,2,3.

Show that model gets correct prediction for b as a string.

```
print(predict(m,
   newdata=data.frame(x=factor('b',levels=c('b'))))[[1]])
 # [1] 2
```

Show that model gets correct prediction for b as a factor, encoded with a different number of levels. This shows that lm() is correctly treating factors as strings.

SLOTS

In addition to lists, R can store values by name in object slots. Object slots are addressed with the @ operator (see `help('@')`). To list all of the slots on an object, try `slotNames()`. Slots and objects (in particular the S3 and S4 object systems) are advanced topics we won't cover in this book. You need to know that R has object systems, as some packages will return them to you, but you shouldn't be creating your own objects early in your R career.

A.2.3 *Loading data from HTTPS sources*

In chapter 2, we showed how to use `read.table()` to read data directly from HTTP-style URLs. With so many of our examples hosted on GitHub, it would be convenient to be able to load examples into R directly from GitHub. The difficulties in loading directly from GitHub are these: first, finding the correct URL (to avoid any GitHub page redirects), and second, finding a library that will let you access data over an HTTPS connection.

With some digging, you can work out the structure of GitHub raw URLs. And you can load data from HTTPS sources as shown in the following listing.

Listing A.9 Loading UCI car data directly from GitHub using HTTPS

```
require(RCurl)
urlBase <-
  'https://raw.github.com/WinVector/zmPDSwR/master/'
mkCon <- function(nm) {
   textConnection(getURL(paste(urlBase,nm,sep='')))
}
cars <- read.table(mkCon('UCICar/car.data.csv'),
    sep=',',header=T,comment.char='')
```

Bring in the RCurl library for more connection methods.

Form a valid HTTPS base URL for raw access to the GitHub repository.

Define a function that wraps a URL path fragment into a usable HTTPS connection.

Load the car data from GitHub over HTTPS.

This method can be used for most of the examples in the book. But we think that cloning or downloading a zip file of the book repository is probably going to be more convenient for most readers.

A.3 *Using databases with R*

Some of our more significant examples require using R with a SQL database. In this section, we'll install one such database (H2) and work one example of using SQL to process data.

A.3.1 *Acquiring the H2 database engine*

The H2 database engine is a serverless relational database that supports queries in SQL. All you need to do to use H2 is download the "all platforms zip" from http://www.h2database.com. Just unpack the zip file in some directory you can remember. All you want from H2 is the Java JAR file found in the unzipped bin directory. In our case, the JAR is named h2-1.3.170.jar, or you can use what comes out of their supplied installer. The H2 database will allow us to show how R interacts with a SQL database without having to install a database server. If you have access to your own database such as PostgreSQL, MySQL, or Oracle, you likely won't need to use the H2 database and can skip it. We'll only use the H2 database a few times in this book, but you must anticipate that some production environments are entirely oriented around a database.

A.3.2 *Starting with SQuirreL SQL*

SQuirreL SQL is a database browser available from http://squirrel-sql.sourceforge.net. You can use it to inspect database contents before attempting to use R. It's also a good way to run long SQL scripts that you may write as part of your data preparation. SQuirreL SQL is also a good way to figure out database configuration before trying to connect with R. Both SQuirreL SQL and H2 depend on Java, so you'll need a current version of Java available on your workstation (but not necessarily in your web browser, as that's considered a security risk).

For example, we'll show how to use SQuirreL SQL to create an example H2 database that's visible to R. First start SQuirreL SQL, click on the Drivers pane on the right, and define a new database driver. This will bring up a panel as shown in figure A.1.

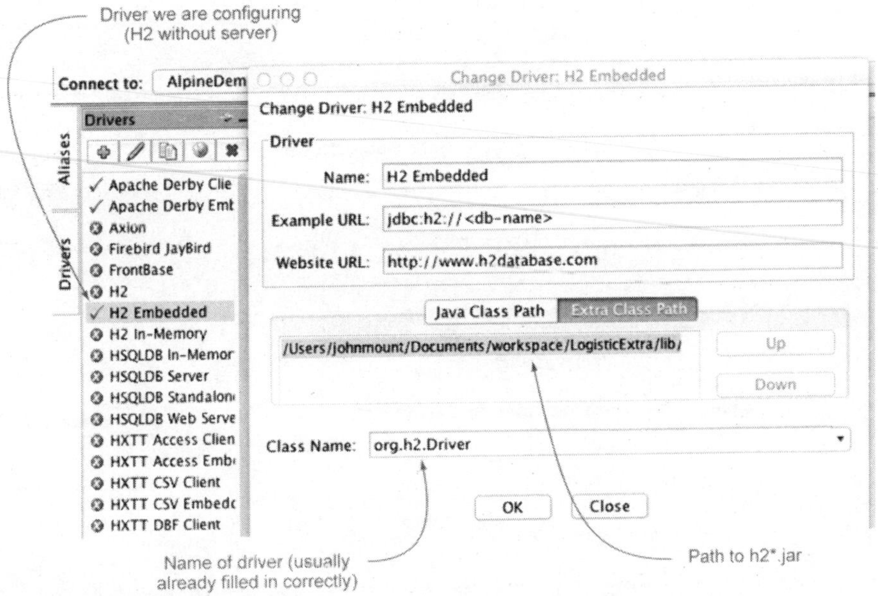

Figure A.1 SQuirreL SQL driver configuration

We've selected the H2 Embedded driver. In this case, the panel comes prepopulated with the class name of the H2 driver (something we'll need to copy to R) and what the typical structure of a URL referring to this type of database looks like. We only have to populate the Extra Class Path tab with a class path pointing to our h2-1.3.170.jar, and the driver is configured.

Then to connect to (and in this case create) the database, we go to the SQuirreL SQL Aliases panel and define a new connection alias, as shown in figure A.2. The important steps are to select the driver we just configured and to fill out the URL. For H2-embedded databases, the database will actually be stored as a set of files derived from the path in the specified URL.

Figure A.3 shows SQuirreL SQL in action. For our example, we're executing five lines of SQL code that create and populate a demonstration table. The point is that this same table can be easily accessed from R after we close the SQuirreL SQL connection to release the H2 exclusive lock.

To access any database from R, you can use R's JDBC package. In the next listing, we'll show how to do this. Each line beginning with a > prompt is a command we type into R (without copying the > prompt). Each line without the prompt is our copy of R's response. Throughout this book, for short listings we'll delete the prompts, and leave the prompts in when we want to demonstrate a mixture of input and output.

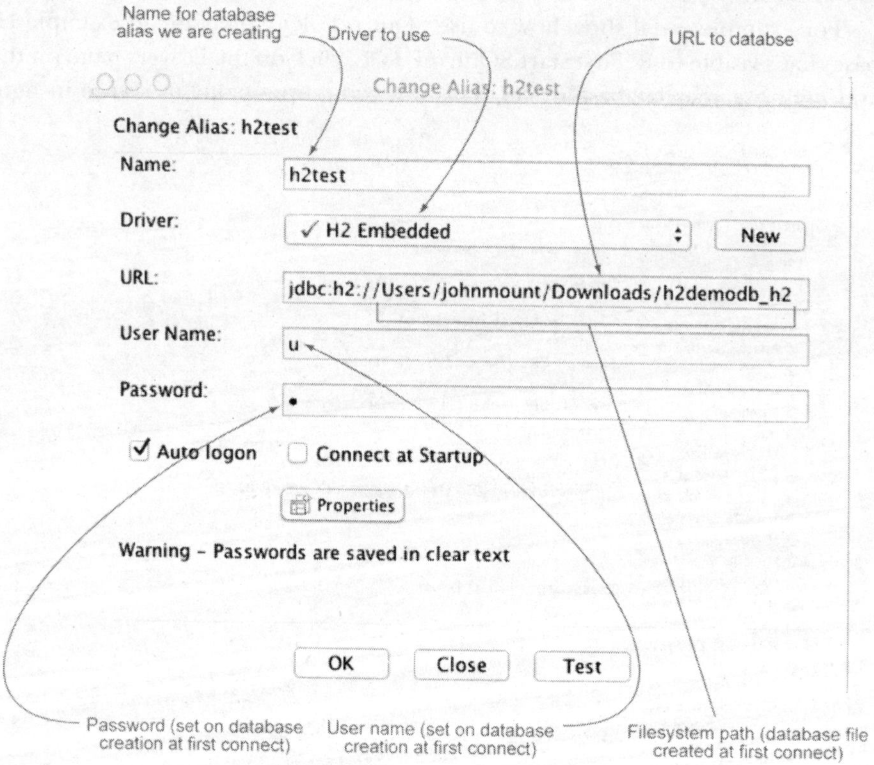

Figure A.2 SQuirreL SQL connection alias

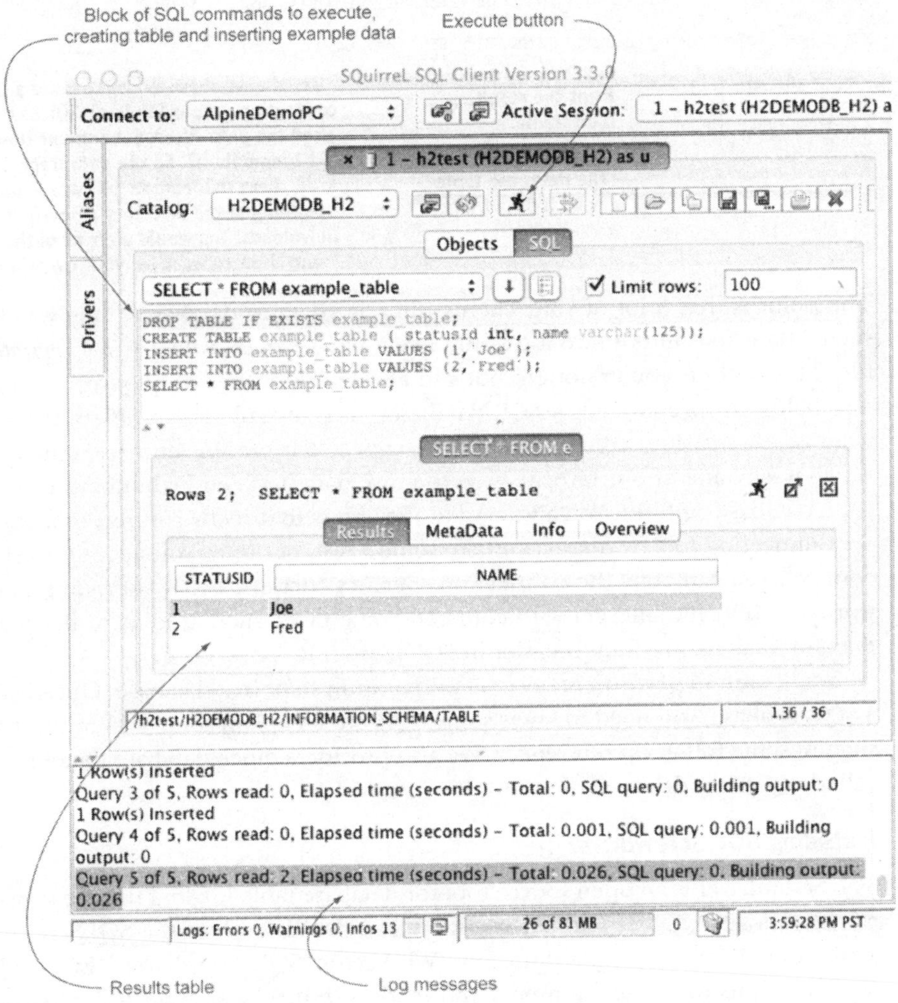

Figure A.3 SQuirreL SQL table commands

We'll define more of R's syntax and commands later, but first we want to show in the following listing how to read data from our example database.

Listing A.10 Reading database data into R

```
> install.packages('RJDBC')
 > library('RJDBC')
 > drv <- JDBC("org.h2.Driver","h2-
   1.3.170.jar",identifier.quote="'")
 > setwd('/Users/johnmount/Downloads')
```

Install the RJDBC package from the CRAN package repository.

Load the RJDBC library.

Use the RJDBC library to build a database driver.

```
> conn <- dbConnect(drv,"jdbc:h2://h2demodb_h2","u","u")
> d <- dbGetQuery(conn,"SELECT * FROM example_table")
> print(d)
  STATUSID NAME
1        1  Joe
2        2 Fred
```

Use the database driver to build a database connection. In our SQuirreL SQL example, we used the path /Users/johnmount/Downloads/h2demodb_h2. So the path fragment given here (h2demodb_h2) works only if R is working in the directory /Users/johnmount/Downloads. You would alter all of these paths and URLs to work for your own directories.

Run a SQL select query using the database connection to populate a data frame.

Print the result data frame.

The database table as an R data frame.

The point is this: a lot of your clients will have data in databases. One way to get at such data is to dump it into a text file like a *pipe-separated values* or *tab-separated values* file. This is often good enough, but can also lead to issues of quoting and parsing if text fields are present. Also, SQL databases carry useful *schema information* that provides types of various columns (not forcing you to represent numeric data as strings, which is why one of our favorite ways to move data between Python and R is the non-JDBC database SQLite). You always want the ability to directly connect to a database.

Connecting to a database can take some work, but once you get SQuirreL SQL to connect, you can copy the connection specifics (drivers, URLs, usernames, and passwords) into RJDBC and get R to connect. Some tasks, such as joins or denormalizing data for analysis, are frankly easier in SQL than in R.[4]

You'll want to perform many data preparation steps in a database. Obviously, to use a SQL database, you need to know some SQL. We'll explain some SQL in this book and suggest some follow-up references. We also provide a quick database data-loading tool called SQL Screwdriver.

A.3.3 Installing SQL Screwdriver

SQL Screwdriver is an open source tool for database table loading that we provide. You can download SQL Screwdriver by clicking on the *Raw* tab of the SQLScrewdriver.jar page found at https://github.com/WinVector/SQLScrewdriver. Every database comes with its own table dumpers and loaders, but they all tend to be idiosyncratic. SQL Screwdriver provides a single loader that can be used with any JDBC-compliant SQL database and builds a useful schema by inspecting the data in the columns of the tab- or comma-separated file it's loading from (a task most database loaders don't perform). We have some SQL Screwdriver documentation at http://mng.bz/bJ9B, and we'll demonstrate SQL Screwdriver on a substantial example in this section.

A.3.4 An example SQL data transformation task

We'll work through an artificial example of loading data that illustrates a number of R tools, including `gdata` (which reads Excel files) and `sqldf` (which implements SQL on top of R data frames). Our example problem is trying to plot the effect that room prices have on bookings for a small hotel client.

---

[4] Another option is to use R's `sqldf` package, which allows the use of SQL commands (including fairly complicated joins and aggregations) directly on R data frames.

Number of reservations on the book				
	reservations			
date	day of stay	1 before	2 before	3 before
7/1/13	105	98	95	96
7/2/13	103	100	98	95
7/3/13	105	95	90	80
7/4/13	105	105	107	98

Published price				
	prices			
date	day of stay	1 before	2 before	3 before
7/1/13	$250.00	$200.00	$280.00	$300.00
7/2/13	$200.00	$250.00	$290.00	$250.00
7/3/13	$200.00	$200.00	$250.00	$275.00
7/4/13	$250.00	$300.00	$300.00	$200.00

Figure A.4 Hotel data in spreadsheet form

LOADING DATA FROM EXCEL

Our data can be found in the file Workbook1.xlsx found at https://github.com/WinVector/zmPDSwR/tree/master/SQLExample. The contents of the Excel workbook look like figure A.4.

This data is typical of what you get from small Excel-oriented clients: it's formatted for compact appearance, not immediate manipulation. The extra header lines and formatting all make the data less regular. We directly load the data into R as shown in the next listing.

Listing A.11 Loading an Excel spreadsheet

```
library(gdata)
bookings <- read.xls('Workbook1.xlsx',sheet=1,pattern='date',
   stringsAsFactors=F,as.is=T)
prices <- read.xls('Workbook1.xlsx',sheet=2,pattern='date',
   stringsAsFactors=F,as.is=T)
```

We confirm we have the data correctly loaded by printing it out.

Listing A.12 The hotel reservation and price data

```
> print(bookings)
        date day.of.stay X1.before X2.before X3.before
1 2013-07-01         105        98        95        96
2 2013-07-02         103       100        98        95
3 2013-07-03         105        95        90        80
4 2013-07-04         105       105       107        98
> print(prices)
        date day.of.stay X1.before X2.before X3.before
1 2013-07-01     $250.00   $200.00   $280.00   $300.00
2 2013-07-02     $200.00   $250.00   $290.00   $250.00
3 2013-07-03     $200.00   $200.00   $250.00   $275.00
4 2013-07-04     $250.00   $300.00   $300.00   $200.00
```

For this hotel client, the record keeping is as follows. For each date, the hotel creates a row in each sheet of their workbook: one to record prices and one to record number of bookings or reservations. In each row, we have a column labeled `"day.of.stay"` and columns of the form `"Xn.before"`, which represent what was known a given number of days before the day of stay (published price and number of booked rooms). For example, the 95 bookings and $280 price recorded for the date 2013-07-01 in the column `X2 before` mean that for the stay date of July 1, 2013, they had 95 bookings two days before the date of stay (or on June 29, 2013) and the published price of the July 1, 2013, day of stay was quoted as $280 on June 29, 2013. The bookings would accumulate in a nondecreasing manner as we move toward the day of stay in the row, except the hotel also may receive cancellations. This *is* complicated, but clients often have detailed record-keeping conventions and procedures.

For our example, what the client actually wants to know is if there's an obvious relation between published price and number of bookings picked up.

RESHAPING DATA

For any dataset, you have keys and values. For our example of hotel booking and price data, the keys are the date (the day the customer will stay) and the number of days prior to the date the booking is made (`day.of.stay, X1.before, ...`). Right now, the date is a value column, but the number of days of stay is coded across many columns. The values are *number of bookings* and *quoted prices*. What we'd like to work with is a table where a specific set of columns holds keys and other columns hold values. The `reshape2` package supplies a function that performs exactly this transformation, which we illustrate in the next listing.

Listing A.13 Using `melt` to restructure data

```
library('reshape2')
bthin <- melt(bookings,id.vars=c('date'),
   variable.name='daysBefore',value.name='bookings')
pthin <- melt(prices,id.vars=c('date'),
   variable.name='daysBefore',value.name='price')
daysCodes <- c('day.of.stay', 'X1.before', 'X2.before', 'X3.before')
bthin$nDaysBefore <- match(bthin$daysBefore,daysCodes)-1
pthin$nDaysBefore <- match(pthin$daysBefore,daysCodes)-1
pthin$price <- as.numeric(gsub('\\$','',pthin$price))
```

Use melt to change columns that are not date (day.of.stay, Xn.before) to values stored in a new column called daysBefore. Each booking count becomes a new row (instead of having many different bookings in the same row).

Each price entry becomes a new row (instead of having many different prices in the same row).

Use match and dayCodes list to convert key strings to numeric nDaysBefore in our bookings data.

Use match and dayCodes list to convert key strings to numeric nDaysBefore in our price data.

Remove dollar sign and convert prices to numeric type.

```
> print(head(pthin))
        date  daysBefore price nDaysBefore
1 2013-07-01 day.of.stay   250           0
2 2013-07-02 day.of.stay   200           0
3 2013-07-03 day.of.stay   200           0
4 2013-07-04 day.of.stay   250           0
5 2013-07-01   X1.before   200           1
6 2013-07-02   X1.before   250           1
```

We now have our data in a much simpler and easier to manipulate form. All keys are values in rows; we no longer have to move from column to column to get different values.

LINING UP THE DATA FOR ANALYSIS

The bookings data is, as is typical in the hotel industry, the total number of bookings recorded for a given first day of stay. If we want to try to show the relation between price and new bookings, we need to work with change in bookings per day. To do any useful work, we have to match up three different data rows into a single new row:

- Item 1: a row from `bthin` supplying the total number of bookings by a given date (first day of stay) and a given number of days before the first day of stay.
- Item 2: a row from `bthin` supplying the total number of bookings for the same date as item 1 with `nDaysBefore` one larger than in item 1. This is so we can compare the two cumulative bookings and find how many new bookings were added on a given day.
- Item 3: a row from `pthin` supplying the price from the same date and number of days before stay as item 1. This represents what price was available at the time of booking (the decision to match this item to item 1 or item 2 depends on whether bookings are meant to record what is known at the end of the day or beginning of the day—something you need to confirm with your project sponsor).

To assemble the data, we need to use a fairly long SQL join to combine two references to `bthin` with one reference to `pthin`. While the join is complicated, notice that it specifies how we want rows to be matched up and not how to perform the matching.

Listing A.14 Assembling many rows using SQL

```
options(gsubfn.engine = "R")
library('sqldf')
joined <- sqldf('
  select
     bCurrent.date as StayDate,
     bCurrent.daysBefore as daysBefore,
     bCurrent.nDaysBefore as nDaysBefore,
     p.price as price,
     bCurrent.bookings as bookingsCurrent,
     bPrevious.bookings as bookingsPrevious,
     bCurrent.bookings - bPrevious.bookings as pickup
  from
     bthin bCurrent
  join
     bthin bPrevious
  on
     bCurrent.date=bPrevious.date
     and bCurrent.nDaysBefore+1=bPrevious.nDaysBefore
  join
     pthin p
```

- Prevent library(sqldf) from triggering a tcl/tk dependency which causes R to exit on OS X if XII isn't installed. See https://code.google.com/p/sqldf/ for troubleshooting details. (options / library lines)
- Create a new data frame of rows built out of triples of rows from pthin and bthin. (joined <- sqldf)
- SQL statements typically start with the word "select." (select)
- List of derived columns (and their new names) for our new data frame.
- First data frame we're pulling data from: bthin.
- Second pull from bthin.
- Conditions to match b1 rows to b2 rows.
- Third data frame we are pulling data from: pthin.

```
  on
    bCurrent.date=p.date
    and bCurrent.nDaysBefore=p.nDaysBefore
')
print(joined)
```

Conditions to match p to b2 (and implicitly bl).

In R, there are many ways to assemble data other than SQL. But SQL commands are powerful and can be used both inside R (through `sqldf`) and outside R (through `RJDBC`).

SQL commands can look intimidating. The key is to always think about them as compositions of smaller pieces. The fact that R allows actual line breaks in string literals lets us write a large SQL command in a comparatively legible format in listing A.14 (you could even add comments using SQL's comment mark `--` where we've added callouts). SQL is an important topic and we strongly recommend Joe Celko's *SQL for Smarties, Fourth Edition* (Morgan Kaufmann, 2011). Two concepts to become familiar with are `select` and `join`.

select

Every SQL command starts with the word `select`. Think of `select` as a scan or filter. A simple `select` example is `select date,bookings from bthin where nDaysBefore=0`. Conceptually, `select` scans through data from our given table (in our case `bthin`), and for each row matching the `where` clause (`nDaysBefore=0`) produces a new row with the named columns (`date,bookings`). We say conceptually because the `select` statement can often find all of the columns matching the `where` conditions much faster than a table scan (using precomputed indices). We already used simple `selects` when we loaded samples of data from a PUMS Census database into R.

join

`join` is SQL's Swiss army knife. It can be used to compute everything from simple intersections (finding rows common to two tables) to cross-products (building every combination of rows from two tables). Conceptually, for every row in the first table, each and every row in a second table is considered, and exactly the set of rows that match the `on` clause is retained. Again, we say conceptually because the `join` implementation tends to be much faster than actually considering every pair of rows. In our example, we used `joins` to match rows with different keys to each other from the `bthin` table (called a *self join*) and then match to the `pthin` table. We can write the composite join as a single SQL statement as we did here, or as two SQL statements by storing results in an intermediate table. Many complicated calculations can be written succinctly as a few joins (because the `join` concept is so powerful) and also run quickly (because `join` implementations tend to be smart).

The purpose of this section is to show how to reshape data. But now that we've used `select` and `join` to build a table that relates change in bookings to known price, we can finally plot the relation in figure A.5.

Listing A.15 Showing our hotel model results

```
library('ggplot2')
ggplot(data=joined,aes(x=price,y=pickup)) +
  geom_point() + geom_jitter() + geom_smooth(method='lm')
print(summary(lm(pickup~price,data=joined)))
#
#Call:
#lm(formula = pickup ~ price, data = joined)
#
#Residuals:
#    Min      1Q Median      3Q     Max
#-4.614 -2.812 -1.213  3.387  6.386
#
#Coefficients:
#              Estimate Std. Error t value Pr(>|t|)
#(Intercept) 11.00765    7.98736   1.378    0.198
#price       -0.02798    0.03190  -0.877    0.401
#
#Residual standard error: 4.21 on 10 degrees of freedom
#Multiple R-squared:  0.07144,  Adjusted R-squared:  -0.02142
#F-statistic: 0.7693 on 1 and 10 DF,  p-value: 0.401
```

The first thing to notice is the model coefficient p-value on *price* is way too large. At 0.4, the estimated relation between price and change in bookings can't be trusted. Part of the problem is we have very little data: the `joined` data frame only has 12 rows. Also, we're co-mingling data from different numbers of days before stay and different dates without introducing any features to model these effects. And this type of data is likely censored because hotels stop taking reservations as they fill up, independent of price. Finally, it's typical of this sort of problem for the historic price to actually depend on recent bookings (for example, managers drop prices when there are no bookings), which can also obscure an actual causal connection from price to bookings. For an actual client, the honest report would say that to find a relation more data is needed. We at least need to know more about hotel capacity, cancellations, and current pricing policy (so we can ensure some variation in price and eliminate confounding effects from our model). These are the sort of issues you'd need to address in experiment design and data collection.

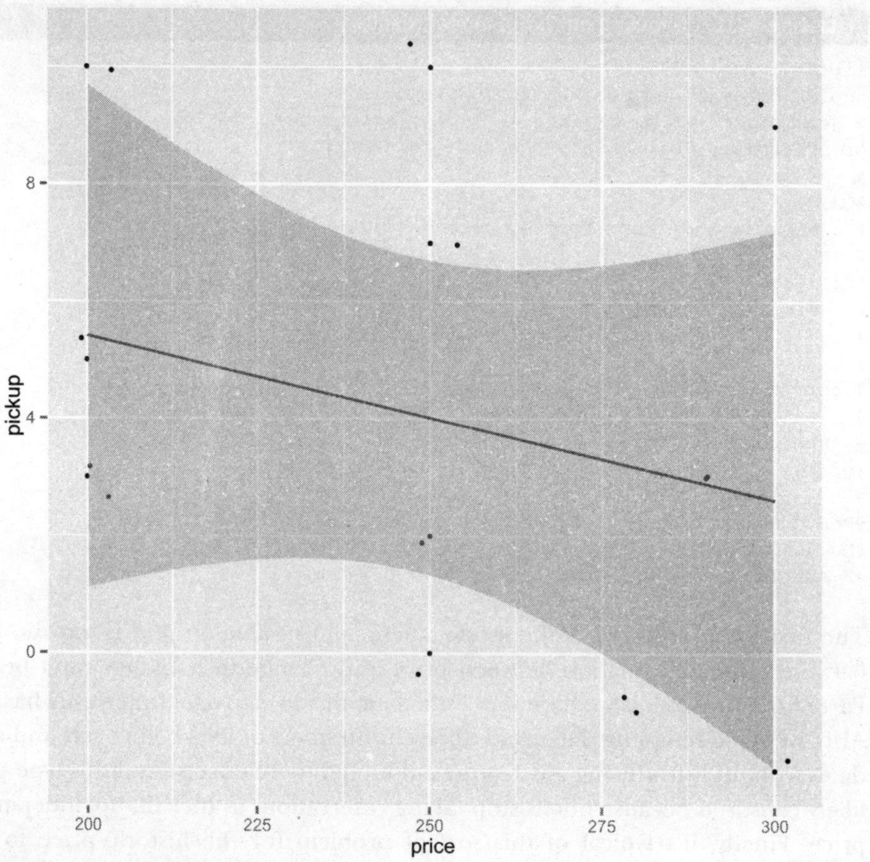

Figure A.5 Hotel data in spreadsheet form

A.3.5 *How to think in SQL*

The trick to thinking in SQL is this: for every table, classify the columns into a few important themes and work with the natural relations between these themes. One view of the major column themes is given in the table A.1.

Table A.1 Major SQL column themes

Column theme	Description	Common uses and treatments
Natural key columns	In many tables, one or more columns taken together form a natural key that uniquely identifies the row. In our hotel example (section A.3.4), for the original data, the only natural key was the date. After the reshaping steps, the natural keys were the pairs (date,daysBefore). The purpose of the reshaping steps was to get data organized so that it had key columns that anticipate how we were going to manipulate the data. Some data (such as running logs) doesn't have natural keys (many rows may correspond to a given timestamp).	Natural keys are used to sort data, control joins, and specify aggregations.

Table A.1 Major SQL column themes *(continued)*

Column theme	Description	Common uses and treatments
Surrogate key columns	Surrogate key columns are key columns (collections of columns that uniquely identify rows) that don't have a natural relation to the problem. Examples of surrogate keys include row numbers and hashes. In some cases (like analyzing time series), the row number can be a natural key, but usually it's a surrogate key.	Surrogate key columns can be used to simplify joins; they tend not to be useful for sorting and aggregation. Surrogate key columns must not be used as modeling features, as they don't represent useful measurements.
Provenance columns	Provenance columns are columns that contain facts about the row, such as when it was loaded. The `ORIGINSERTTIME`, `ORIGFILENAME`, and `ORIGFILEROWNUMBER` columns added in section 2.2.1 are examples of provenance columns.	Provenance columns shouldn't be used in analyses, except for confirming you're working on the right dataset, selecting a dataset (if different datasets are commingled in the same table), and comparing datasets.
Payload columns	Payload columns contain actual data. In section A.3.4, the payload columns are the various occupancy counts and room prices.	Payload columns are used for aggregation, grouping, and conditions. They can also sometimes be used to specify joins.
Experimental design columns	Experimental design columns include sample groupings like `ORIGRANDGROUP` from section 2.2.1, or data weights like the `PWGTP*` and `WGTP*` columns we mentioned in section 7.1.1.	Experiment design columns can be used to control an analysis (select subsets of data, used as weights in modeling operations), but they should never be used as features in an analysis.
Derived columns	Derived columns are columns that are functions of other columns or other groups of columns. An example would be the day of week (Monday through Sunday), which is a function of the date. Derived columns can be functions of keys (which means they're unchanging in many `GROUP BY` queries, even though SQL will insist on specifying an aggregator such as `MAX()`) or functions of payload columns.	Derived columns are useful in analysis. A *full normal form* database doesn't have such columns. In normal forms, the idea is to not store anything that can be derived, which eliminates certain types of inconsistency (such as a row with a date of February 1, 2014 and day of week of Wednesday, when the correct day of week is Saturday). But during analyses it's always a good idea to store intermediate calculations in tables and columns: it simplifies code and makes debugging much easier.

The point is that analysis is much easier if you have a good taxonomy of column themes for every supplied data source. You then design SQL command sequences to transform your data into a new table where the columns are just right for analysis (as we demonstrated in section A.3.4). In the end, you should have tables where every row is an event you're interested in and every needed fact is already available in a column. Building temporary tables and adding columns is much better than having complicated analysis code. These ideas may seem abstract, but they guide the analyses in this book.

appendix B
Important statistical concepts

Statistics is such a broad topic that we've only been able to pull pieces of it into our data science narrative. But it's an important field that has a lot to say about what happens when you attempt to infer from data. We've assumed in this book that you already know some statistical tools (in particular, summary statistics like the mean, mode, median, and variance). In this appendix, we'll demonstrate a few more important statistical concepts.

B.1 Distributions

In this section, we'll outline a few important distributions: the normal distribution, the lognormal distribution, and the binomial distribution. As you work further, you'll also want to learn many other key distributions (such as Poisson, beta, negative binomial, and many more), but the ideas we present here should be enough to get you started.

B.1.1 Normal distribution

The *normal* or *Gaussian distribution* is the classic symmetric bell-shaped curve, as shown in figure B.1. Many measured quantities such as test scores from a group of students, or the age or height of a particular population, can often be approximated by the normal. Repeated measurements will tend to fall into a normal distribution. For example, if a doctor weighs a patient multiple times, using a properly calibrated scale, the measurements (if enough of them are taken) will fall into a normal distribution around the patient's true weight. The variation will be due to measurement error (the variability of the scale). The normal distribution is defined over all real numbers.

In addition, the *central limit theorem* says that when you're observing the sum (or mean) of many independent, bounded variance random variables, the distribution of your observations will approach the normal as you collect more data. For example, suppose you want to measure how many people visit your website every day between 9 a.m. and 10 a.m. The proper distribution for modeling the number of visitors is the *Poisson distribution*; but if you have a high enough volume of traffic,

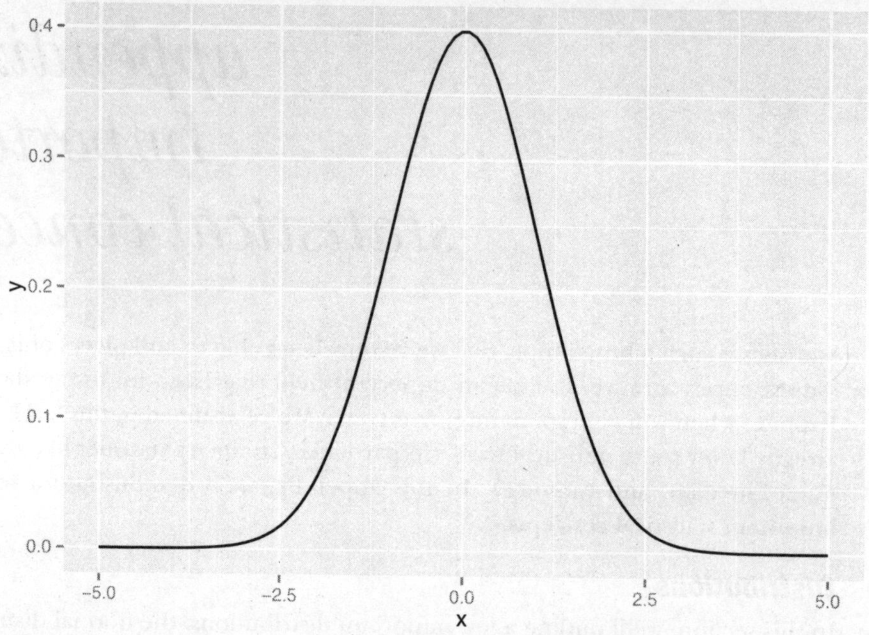

Figure B.1 The normal distribution with mean 0 and standard deviation 1

and you observe long enough, the distribution of observed visitors will approach the normal distribution, and you can make acceptable estimates about your traffic by treating the number of visitors as if it were normally distributed.

This is important; one reason that the normal is so popular is because it's relatively easy to calculate with. The normal is described by two parameters: the mean `m` and the standard deviation `s` (or alternatively, the variance, which is the square of `s`). The mean represents the distribution's center (and also its peak); the standard deviation represents the distribution's "natural unit of length"—you can estimate how rare an observation is by how many standard deviations it is from the mean. As we mention in chapter 4, for a normally distributed variable

- About 68% of the observations will fall in the interval `(m-s,m+s)`.
- About 95% of the observations will fall in the interval `(m-2*s,m+2*s)`.
- About 99.7% of the observations will fall in the interval `(m-3*s,m+3*s)`.

So an observation more than three standard deviations away from the mean can be considered quite rare, in most applications.

Many machine learning algorithms and statistical methods (for example, linear regression) assume that the unmodeled errors are distributed normally. Linear regression is fairly robust to violations of this assumption; still, for continuous variables, you should at least check if the variable distribution is unimodal and somewhat symmetric. When this isn't the case, consider some of the variable transformations that we discuss in chapter 4.

USING THE NORMAL DISTRIBUTION IN R

In R, the function dnorm(x, mean=m, sd=s) is the *normal distribution function*: it will return the probability of observing x when it's drawn from a normal distribution with mean m and standard deviation s. By default, dnorm assumes that mean=0 and sd=1 (as do all the functions related to the normal distribution that we discuss here). Let's use dnorm() to draw figure B.1.

Listing B.1 Plotting the theoretical normal density

```
library(ggplot2)

x <- seq(from=-5, to=5, length.out=100) # the interval [-5 5]
f <- dnorm(x)                           # normal with mean 0 and sd 1
ggplot(data.frame(x=x,y=f), aes(x=x,y=y)) + geom_line()
```

The function rnorm(n, mean=m, sd=s) will generate n points drawn from a normal distribution with mean m and standard deviation s.

Listing B.2 Plotting an empirical normal density

```
library(ggplot2)

# draw 1000 points from a normal with mean 0, sd 1
u <- rnorm(1000)

# plot the distribution of points,
# compared to normal curve as computed by dnorm() (dashed line)
ggplot(data.frame(x=u), aes(x=x)) + geom_density() +
   geom_line(data=data.frame(x=x,y=f), aes(x=x,y=y), linetype=2)
```

As you can see in figure B.2, the empirical distribution of the points produced by rnorm(1000) is quite close to the theoretical normal. Distributions observed from finite datasets can never exactly match theoretical continuous distributions like the normal; and, as with all things statistical, there is a well-defined distribution for how far off you expect to be for a given sample size.

The function pnorm(x, mean=m, sd=s) is what R calls the *normal probability function*, otherwise called the *normal cumulative distribution function*: it returns the probability of observing a data point of value less than x from a normal with mean m and standard deviation s. In other words, it's the area under the distribution curve that falls to the left of x (recall that a distribution has unit area under the curve). This is shown in the following listing.

Listing B.3 Working with the normal CDF

```
# --- estimate probabilities (areas) under the curve ---

# 50% of the observations will be less than the mean
pnorm(0)
# [1] 0.5
```

```
# about 2.3% of all observations are more than 2 standard
# deviations below the mean
pnorm(-2)
# [1] 0.02275013

# about 95.4% of all observations are within 2 standard deviations
# from the mean
pnorm(2) - pnorm(-2)
# [1] 0.9544997
```

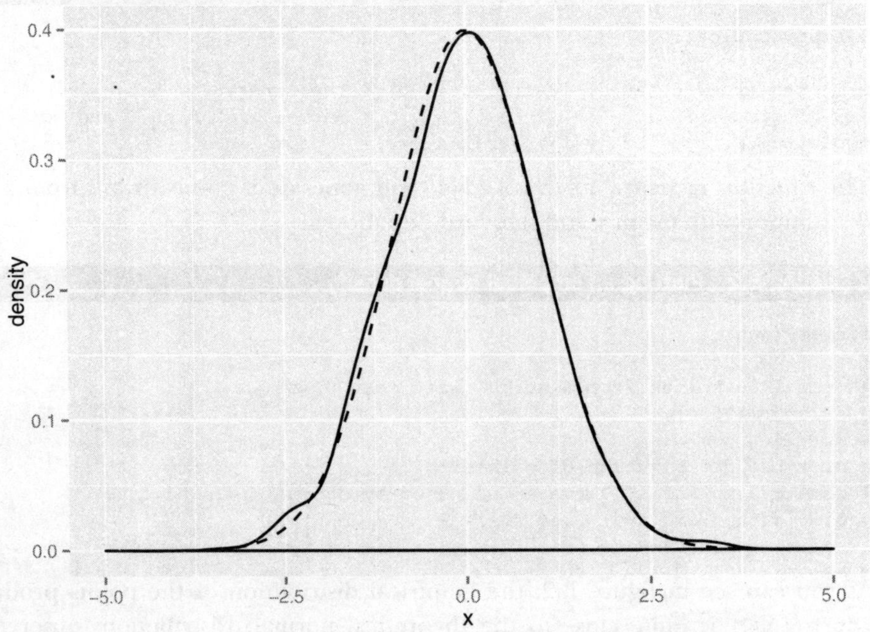

Figure B.2 The empirical distribution of points drawn from a normal with mean 0 and standard deviation 1. The dotted line represents the theoretical normal distribution.

The function `qnorm(p, mean=m, sd=s)` is the *quantile function* for the normal distribution with mean `m` and standard deviation `s`. It's the inverse of `pnorm()`, in that `qnorm(p, mean=m, sd=s)` returns the value x such that `pnorm(x, mean=m, sd=s) == p`.

Figure B.3 illustrates the use of `qnorm()`: the vertical line intercepts the x axis at `x = qnorm(0.75)`; the shaded area to the left of the vertical line represents the area 0.75, or 75% of the area under the normal curve.

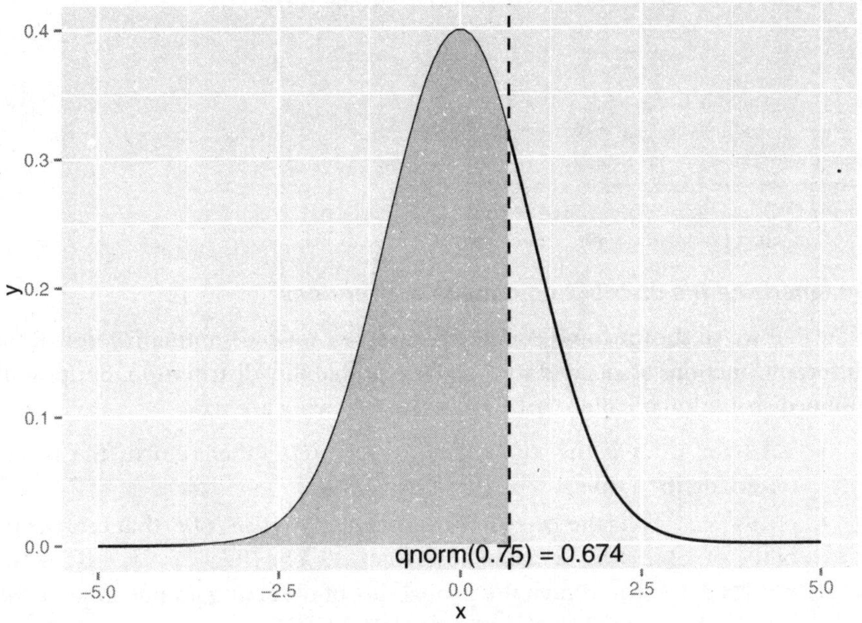

Figure B.3 Illustrating `x < qnorm(0.75)`

The code to create figure B.3 (along with a few other examples of using `qnorm()`) is shown in the following listing.

Listing B.4 Plotting `x < qnorm(0.75)`

```
# --- return the quantiles corresponding to specific probabilities ---

# the median (50th percentile) of a normal is also the mean
qnorm(0.5)
# [1] 0

# calculate the 75th percentile
qnorm(0.75)
# [1] 0.6744898
pnorm(0.6744898)
# [1] 0.75

# --- Illustrate the 75th percentile ---

# create a graph of the normal distribution with mean 0, sd 1
x <- seq(from=-5, to=5, length.out=100)
f <- dnorm(x)
nframe <- data.frame(x=x,y=f)

# calculate the 75th percentile
line <- qnorm(0.75)
xstr <- sprintf("qnorm(0.75) = %1.3f", line)
```

```
# the part of the normal distribution to the left
# of the 75th percentile
nframe75 <- subset(nframe, nframe$x < line)

# Plot it.
# The shaded area is 75% of the area under the normal curve
ggplot(nframe, aes(x=x,y=y)) + geom_line() +
  geom_area(data=nframe75, aes(x=x,y=y), fill="gray") +
  geom_vline(aes(xintercept=line), linetype=2) +
  geom_text(x=line, y=0, label=xstr, vjust=1)
```

B.1.2 Summarizing R's distribution naming conventions

Now that we've shown some concrete examples, we can summarize how R names the different functions associated with a given probability distribution. Suppose the probability distribution is called `DIST`. Then the following are true:

- `dDIST(x, ...)` is the *distribution function (PDF)* that returns the probability of observing the value `x`.
- `pDIST(x, ...)` is the *cumulative distribution function (CDF)* that returns the probability of observing a value less than `x`. The flag `lower.tail=F` will cause `pDIST(x, ...)` to return the probability of observing a value greater than `x` (the area under the right tail, rather than the left).
- `rDIST(n, ...)` is the random number generation function that returns `n` values drawn from the distribution `DIST`.
- `qDIST(p, ...)` is the quantile function that returns the `x` corresponding to the `p`th percentile of `DIST`. The flag `lower.tail=F` will cause `qDIST(p, ...)` to return the `x` that corresponds to the `1 - p`th percentile of `DIST`.

R'S BACKWARD NAMING CONVENTION For some reason, R refers to the cumulative distribution function (or CDF) as the *probability distribution function* (hence the convention `pDIST`). This drives us crazy, because most people use the term *probability distribution function* (or *PDF*) to refer to what R calls `dDIST`. Be aware of this.

B.1.3 Lognormal distribution

The *lognormal distribution* is the distribution of a random variable `X` whose natural log `log(X)` is normally distributed. The distribution of highly skewed positive data, like the value of profitable customers, incomes, sales, or stock prices, can often be modeled as a lognormal distribution. A lognormal distribution is defined over all non-negative real numbers; as shown in figure B.4 (top), it's asymmetric, with a long tail out toward positive infinity. The distribution of `log(X)` (figure B.4, bottom) is a normal distribution centered at `mean(log(X))`. For lognormal populations, the mean is generally much higher than the median, and the bulk of the contribution toward the mean value is due to a small population of highest-valued data points.

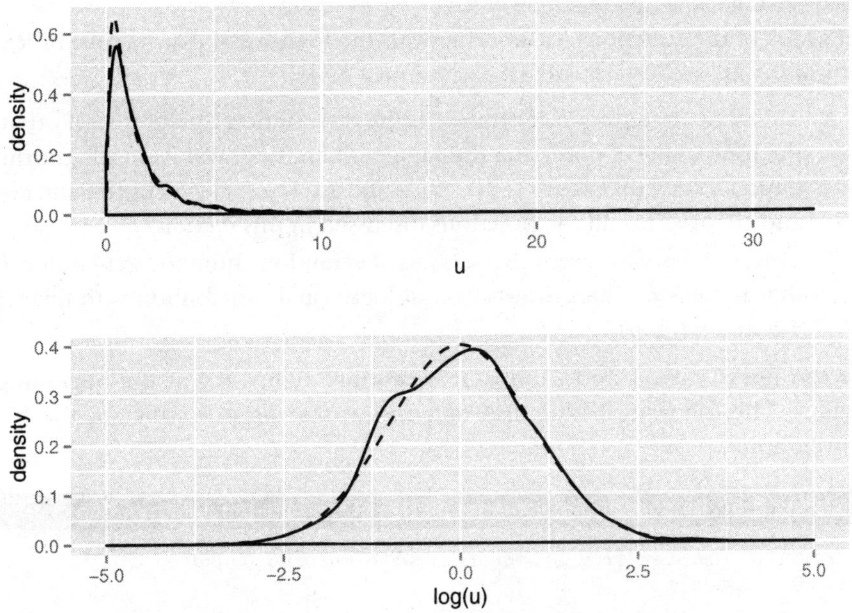

Figure B.4 Top: The lognormal distribution X such that `mean(log(X))=0` and `sd(log(X)=1`. The dashed line is the theoretical distribution, and the solid line is the distribution of a random lognormal sample. Bottom: The solid line is the distribution of `log(X)`.

> **DON'T USE THE MEAN AS A "TYPICAL" VALUE FOR A LOGNORMAL POPULATION** For a population that's approximately normally distributed, you can use the mean value of the population as a rough stand-in value for a typical member of the population. If you use the mean as a stand-in value for a lognormal population, you'll overstate the value of the majority of your data.

Intuitively, if variations in the data are expressed naturally as percentages or relative differences, rather than as absolute differences, then the data is a candidate to be modeled lognormally. For example, a typical sack of potatoes in your grocery store might weigh about five pounds, plus or minus half a pound. The length that a specific type of bullet will fly when fired from a specific type of handgun might be about 2,100 meters, plus or minus 100 meters. The variations in these observations are naturally represented in absolute units, and the distributions can be modeled as normals. On the other hand, differences in monetary quantities are often best expressed as percentages: a population of workers might all get a 5% increase in salary (not an increase of $5,000/year across the board); you might want to project next quarter's revenue to within 10% (not to within plus or minus $1,000). Hence, these quantities are often best modeled as having lognormal distributions.

USING THE LOGNORMAL DISTRIBUTION IN R

Let's look at the functions for working with the lognormal distribution in R (see also section B.1.2). We'll start with `dlnorm()` and `rlnorm()`:

- `dlnorm(x, meanlog=m, sdlog=s)` is the distribution function (PDF) that returns the probability of observing the value `x` when it's drawn from a lognormal distribution `X` such that `mean(log(X)) = m` and `sd(log(X)) = s`. By default, `meanlog=0` and `sdlog=1` for all the functions discussed in this section.
- `rlnorm(n, meanlog=m, sdlog=s)` is the random number generation function that returns `n` values drawn from a lognormal distribution with `mean(log(X)) = m` and `sd(log(X)) = s`.

We can use `dlnorm()` and `rlnorm()` to produce figure B.4 at the beginning of this section. The following listing also demonstrates some properties of the lognormal distribution.

Listing B:5 Demonstrating some properties of the lognormal distribution

```
# draw 1001 samples from a lognormal with meanlog 0, sdlog 1
u <- rlnorm(1001)

# the mean of u is higher than the median
mean(u)
# [1] 1.638628
median(u)
# [1] 1.001051

# the mean of log(u) is approx meanlog=0
mean(log(u))
# [1] -0.002942916

# the sd of log(u) is approx sdlog=1
sd(log(u))
# [1] 0.9820357

# generate the lognormal with meanlog=0, sdlog=1
x <- seq(from=0, to=25, length.out=500)
f <- dlnorm(x)

# generate a normal with mean=0, sd=1
x2 <- seq(from=-5,to=5, length.out=500)
f2 <- dnorm(x2)

# make data frames
lnormframe <- data.frame(x=x,y=f)
normframe <- data.frame(x=x2, y=f2)
dframe <- data.frame(u=u)

# plot densityplots with theoretical curves superimposed
p1 <- ggplot(dframe, aes(x=u)) + geom_density() +
  geom_line(data=lnormframe, aes(x=x,y=y), linetype=2)
```

```
p2 <- ggplot(dframe, aes(x=log(u))) + geom_density() +
  geom_line(data=normframe, aes(x=x,y=y), linetype=2)

# functions to plot multiple plots on one page
library(grid)
nplot <- function(plist) {
  n <- length(plist)
  grid.newpage()
  pushViewport(viewport(layout=grid.layout(n,1)))
  vplayout<-function(x,y) {viewport(layout.pos.row=x, layout.pos.col=y)}
  for(i in 1:n) {
    print(plist[[i]], vp=vplayout(i,1))
  }
}

# this is the plot that leads this section.
nplot(list(p1, p2))
```

The remaining two functions are the CDF `plnorm()` and the quantile function `qlnorm()`:

- `plnorm(x, meanlog=m, sdlog=s)` is the cumulative distribution function (CDF) that returns the probability of observing a value less than x from a lognormal distribution with `mean(log(X)) = m` and `sd(log(X)) = s`.
- `qlnorm(p, meanlog=m, sdlog=s)` is the quantile function that returns the x corresponding to the pth percentile of a lognormal distribution with `mean(log(X)) = m` and `sd(log(X)) = s`. It's the inverse of `plnorm()`.

The following listing demonstrates `plnorm()` and `qlnorm()`. It uses the data frame `lnormframe` from the previous listing.

Listing B.6 Plotting the lognormal distribution

```
# the 50th percentile (or median) of the lognormal with
# meanlog=0 and sdlog=10
qlnorm(0.5)
# [1] 1
# the probability of seeing a value x less than 1
plnorm(1)
# [1] 0.5

# the probability of observing a value x less than 10:
plnorm(10)
# [1] 0.9893489

# -- show the 75th percentile of the lognormal

# use lnormframe from previous example: the
# theoretical lognormal curve

line <- qlnorm(0.75)
xstr <- sprintf("qlnorm(0.75) = %1.3f", line)
```

```
lnormframe75 <- subset(lnormframe, lnormframe$x < line)

# Plot it
# The shaded area is 75% of the area under the lognormal curve
ggplot(lnormframe, aes(x=x,y=y)) + geom_line() +
  geom_area(data=lnormframe75, aes(x=x,y=y), fill="gray") +
  geom_vline(aes(xintercept=line), linetype=2) +
  geom_text(x=line, y=0, label=xstr, hjust= 0, vjust=1)
```

As you can see in figure B.5, the majority of the data is concentrated on the left side of the distribution, with the remaining quarter of the data spread out over a very long tail.

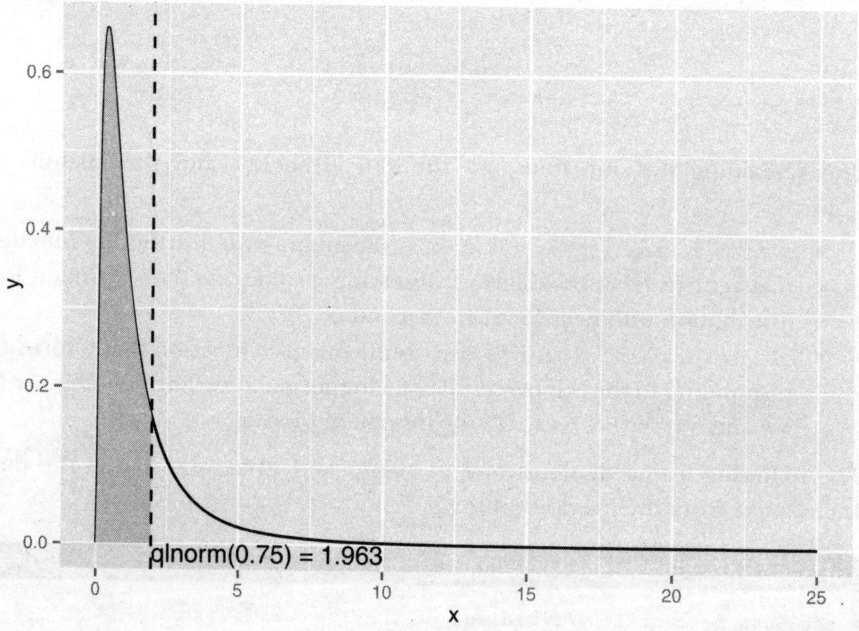

Figure B.5 The 75th percentile of the lognormal distribution with `meanlog=1, sdlog=0`

B.1.4 Binomial distribution

Suppose that you have a coin that has a probability `p` of landing on heads when you flip it (so for a fair coin, `p = 0.5`). In this case, the binomial distribution models the probability of observing `k` heads when you flip that coin `N` times. It's used to model binary classification problems (as we discuss in relation to logistic regression in chapter 7), where the positive examples can be considered "heads."

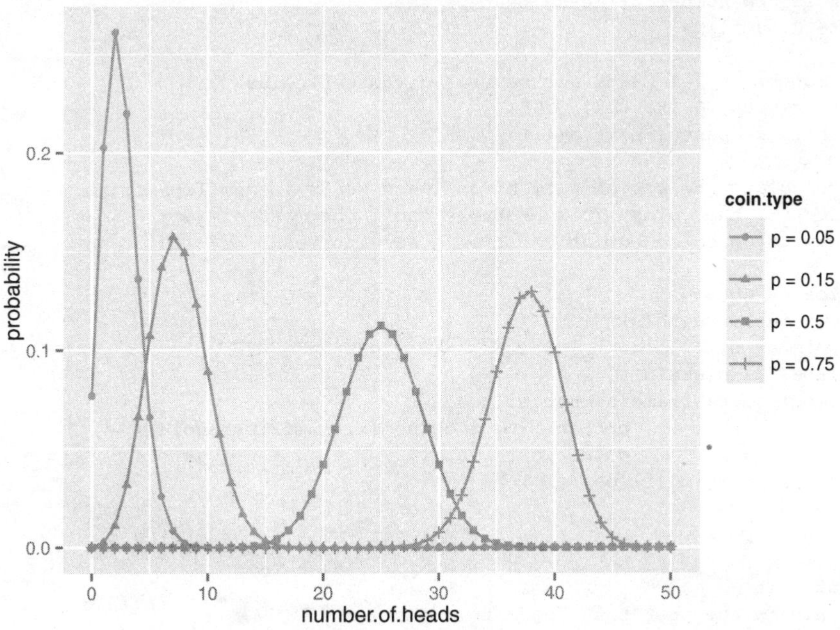

Figure B.6 The binomial distributions for 50 coin tosses, with coins of various fairnesses (probability of landing on heads)

Figure B.6 shows the shape of the binomial distribution for coins of different fairnesses, when flipped 50 times. Note that the binomial distribution is *discrete*; it's only defined for (non-negative) integer values of `k`.

USING THE BINOMIAL DISTRIBUTION IN R

Let's look at the functions for working with the binomial distribution in R (see also section B.1.2). We'll start with the PDF `dbinom()` and the random number generator `rbinom()`:

- `dbinom(k, nflips, p)` is the distribution function (PDF) that returns the probability of observing exactly `k` heads from `nflips` of a coin with heads probability `p`.
- `rbinom(N, nflips,p)` is the random number generation function that returns `N` values drawn from the binomial distribution corresponding to `nflips` of a coin with heads probability `p`.

You can use `dbinom()` (as in the following listing) to produce figure B.6.

Listing B.7 Plotting the binomial distribution

```
library(ggplot2)
#
# use dbinom to produce the theoretical curves
#

numflips <- 50
```

```
# x is the number of heads that we see
x <- 0:numflips

# probability of heads for several different coins
p <- c(0.05, 0.15, 0.5, 0.75)
plabels <- paste("p =", p)

# calculate the probability of seeing x heads in numflips flips
# for all the coins. This probably isn't the most elegant
# way to do this, but at least it's easy to read

flips <- NULL
for(i in 1:length(p)) {
  coin <- p[i]
  label <- plabels[i]
  tmp <- data.frame(number.of.heads=x,
                    probability = dbinom(x, numflips, coin),
                    coin.type = label)
  flips <- rbind(flips, tmp)
}


# plot it
# this is the plot that leads this section
ggplot(flips, aes(x=number.of.heads, y=probability)) +
  geom_point(aes(color=coin.type, shape=coin.type)) +
  geom_line(aes(color=coin.type))
```

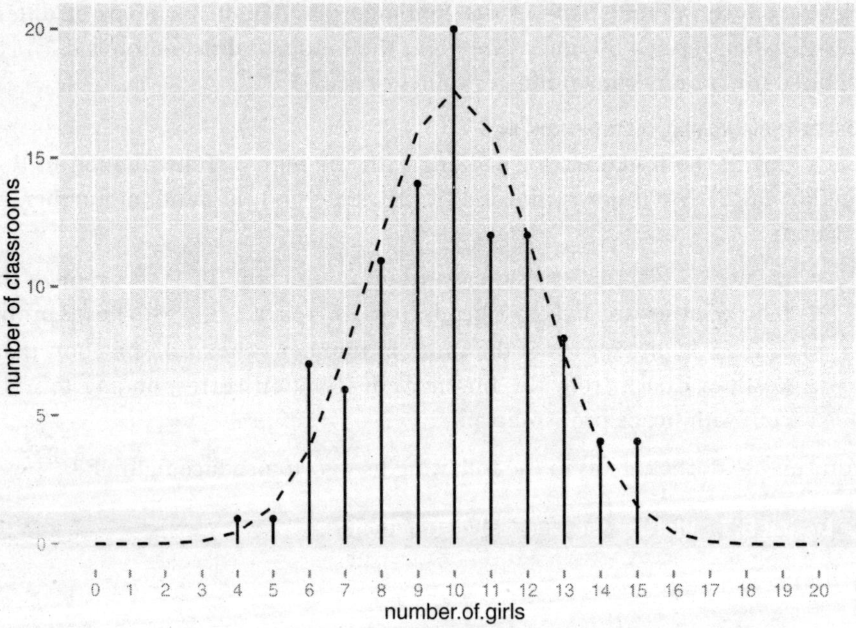

Figure B.7 The observed distribution of the count of girls in 100 classrooms of size 20, when the population is 50% female. The theoretical distribution is shown with the dashed line.

You can use rbinom() to simulate a coin-flipping-style experiment. For example, suppose you have a large population of students that's 50% female. If students are assigned to classrooms at random, and you visit 100 classrooms with 20 students each, then how many girls might you expect to see in each classroom? A plausible outcome is shown in figure B.7, with the theoretical distribution superimposed.

Let's write the code to produce figure B.7.

Listing B.8 Working with the theoretical binomial distribution

```
p = 0.5 # the percentage of females in this student population
class.size <- 20 # size of a classroom
numclasses <- 100 # how many classrooms we observe

# what might a typical outcome look like?
numFemales <-
      rbinom(numclasses, class.size, p)

# the theoretical counts (not necessarily integral)
probs <- dbinom(0:class.size, class.size, p)
tcount <- numclasses*probs

# the obvious way to plot this is with histogram or geom_bar
# but this might just look better

zero <- function(x) {0} # a dummy function that returns only 0

ggplot(data.frame(number.of.girls=numFemales, dummy=1),
  aes(x=number.of.girls, y=dummy)) +
  # count the number of times you see x heads
  stat_summary(fun.y="sum", geom="point", size=2) +
   stat_summary(fun.ymax="sum", fun.ymin="zero", geom="linerange") +
  # superimpose the theoretical number of times you see x heads
  geom_line(data=data.frame(x=0:class.size, y=probs),
            aes(x=x, y=tcount), linetype=2) +
  scale_x_continuous(breaks=0:class.size, labels=0:class.size) +
  scale_y_continuous("number of classrooms")
```

Because we didn't call set.seed, we expect different results each time we run this line.

stat_summary is one of the ways to control data aggregation during plotting. In this case, we're using it to place the dot and bar measured from the empirical data in with the theoretical density curve.

As you can see, even classrooms with as few as 4 or as many as 16 girls aren't completely unheard of when students from this population are randomly assigned to classrooms. But if you observe too many such classrooms—or if you observe classes with fewer than 4 or more than 16 girls—you'd want to investigate whether student selection for those classes is biased in some way.

You can also use rbinom() to simulate flipping a single coin.

Listing B.9 Simulating a binomial distribution

```
# use rbinom to simulate flipping a coin of probability p N times

p75 <- 0.75 # a very unfair coin (mostly heads)
N <- 1000  # flip it several times
flips_v1 <- rbinom(N, 1, p75)
```

```
# Another way to generat unfair flips is to use runif:
# the probability that a uniform random number from [0 1)
# is less than p is exactly p. So "less than p" is "heads".
flips_v2 <- as.numeric(runif(N) < p75)

prettyprint_flips <- function(flips) {
  outcome <- ifelse(flips==1, "heads", "tails")
  table(outcome)
}

prettyprint_flips(flips_v1)
# outcome
# heads tails
# 756   244
prettyprint_flips(flips_v2)
# outcome
# heads tails
# 743   257
```

The final two functions are the CDF `pbinom()` and the quantile function `qbinom()`:

- `pbinom(k, nflips, p)` is the cumulative distribution function (CDF) that returns the probability of observing `k` heads or fewer from `nflips` of a coin with heads probability `p`.

  `pbinom(k, nflips, p, lower.tail=F)` returns the probability of observing more than `k` heads from `nflips` of a coin with heads probability `p`.

  Note that the left tail probability is calculated over the inclusive interval `numheads <= k`, while the right tail probability is calculated over the exclusive interval `numheads > k`.
- `qbinom(q, nflips, p)` is the quantile function that returns the number of heads `k` that corresponds to the `q`th percentile of the binomial distribution corresponding to `nflips` of a coin with heads probability `p`.

The next listing shows some examples of using `pbinom()` and `qbinom()`.

Listing B.10 Working with the binomial distribution

```
# pbinom example

nflips <- 100
nheads <- c(25, 45, 50, 60)  # number of heads

# what are the probabilities of observing at most that
# number of heads on a fair coin?
left.tail <- pbinom(nheads, nflips, 0.5)
sprintf("%2.2f", left.tail)
# [1] "0.00" "0.18" "0.54" "0.98"

# the probabilities of observing more than that
# number of heads on a fair coin?
right.tail <- pbinom(nheads, nflips, 0.5, lower.tail=F)
sprintf("%2.2f", right.tail)
```

```
# [1] "1.00" "0.82" "0.46" "0.02"

# as expected:
left.tail+right.tail
#  [1] 1 1 1 1

# so if you flip a fair coin 100 times,
# you are guaranteed to see more than 10 heads,
# almost guaranteed to see fewer than 60, and
# probably more than 45.

# qbinom example

nflips <- 100

# what's the 95% "central" interval of heads that you
# would expect to observe on 100 flips of a fair coin?

left.edge <- qbinom(0.025, nflips, 0.5)
right.edge <- qbinom(0.025, nflips, 0.5, lower.tail=F)
c(left.edge, right.edge)
# [1] 40 60

# so with 95% probability you should see between 40 and 60 heads
```

One thing to keep in mind is that because the binomial distribution is discrete, `pbinom()` and `qbinom()` won't be perfect inverses of each other, as is the case with continuous distributions like the normal.

Listing B.11 Working with the binomial CDF

```
# because this is a discrete probability distribution,
# pbinom and qbinom are not exact inverses of each other

# this direction works
pbinom(45, nflips, 0.5)
# [1] 0.1841008
qbinom(0.1841008, nflips, 0.5)
# [1] 45

# this direction won't be exact
qbinom(0.75, nflips, 0.5)
# [1] 53
pbinom(53, nflips, 0.5)
# [1] 0.7579408
```

B.1.5 More R tools for distributions

R has many more tools for working with distributions beyond the PDF, CDF, and generation tools we've demonstrated. In particular, for fitting distributions, you may want to try the `fitdistr` method from the `MASS` package.

B.2 Statistical theory

In this book, we necessarily concentrate on (correctly) processing data, without stopping to explain a lot of the theory. The steps we use will be more obvious after we review a bit of statistical theory in this section.

B.2.1 Statistical philosophy

The predictive tools and machine learning methods we demonstrate in this book get their predictive power not from uncovering cause and effect (which would be a great thing to do), but by tracking and trying to eliminate differences in data and by reducing different sources of error. In this section, we'll outline a few of the key concepts that describe what's going on and why these techniques work.

EXCHANGEABILITY

Since basic statistical modeling isn't enough to reliably attribute predictions to true causes, we've been quietly relying on a concept called *exchangeability* to ensure we can build useful predictive models.

The formal definition of exchangeability is this: if all the data in the world is `x[i,],y[i]` (`i=1,...m`), we call the data *exchangeable* if for any permutation `j_1,...j_m` of `1,...m`, the joint probability of seeing `x[i,],y[i]` is equal to the joint probability of seeing `x[j_i,],y[j_i]`. The idea is that if all permutations of the data are equally likely, then when we draw subsets from the data using only indices (not snooping the `x[i,],y[i]`), the data in each subset, though different, can be considered as independent and identically distributed. We rely on this when we make train/test splits (or even train/calibrate/test splits), and we hope (and should take steps to ensure) this is true between our training data and future data we'll encounter in production.

Our hope in building a model is that the unknown future data the model will be applied to is exchangeable with our training data. If this is the case, then we'd expect good performance on training data to translate into good model performance in production. It's important to defend exchangeability from problems such as overfit and concept drift.

Once we start examining training data, we (unfortunately) break its exchangeability with future data. Subsets that contain a lot of training data are no longer indistinguishable from subsets that don't have training data (through the simple process of memorizing all of our training data). We attempt to measure the degree of damage by measuring performance on held-out test data. This is why generalization error is so important. Any data not looked at during model construction should be as exchangeable with future data as it ever was, so measuring performance on held-out data helps anticipate future performance. This is also why you don't use test data for calibration (instead, you should further split your training data to do this); once you look at your test data, it's less exchangeable with what will be seen in production in the future.

Another potential huge loss of exchangeability in prediction is summarized is what's called *Goodhart's law*: "When a measure becomes a target, it ceases to be a good measure." The point is this: factors that merely correlate with a prediction are good predictors ... until you go too far in optimizing for them or when others react to your use of them. For example, email spammers can try to defeat a spam detection system by using more of the features and phrases that correlate highly with legitimate email, and changing phrases that the spam filter believes correlate highly with spam. This is an essential difference between actual causes (which do have an effect on outcome when altered) and mere correlations (which may be co-occurring with an outcome and are good predictors only through exchangeability of examples).

BIAS VARIANCE DECOMPOSITION

Many of the modeling tasks in this book are what are called *regressions* where, for data of the form `y[i],x[i,]`, we try to find a model or function `f()` such that `f(x[i,])~E[y[j]|x[j,]~x[i,]]` (the expectation `E[]` being taken over all examples, where `x[j,]` is considered very close to `x[i,]`). Often this is done by picking `f()` to minimize `E[(y[i]-f(x[i,]))^2]`.[1] Notable methods that fit closely to this formulation include regression, KNN, and neural nets.

Obviously, minimizing square error is not always your direct modeling goal. But when you work in terms of square error, you have an explicit decomposition of error into meaningful components called the *bias/variance decomposition* (see *The Elements of Statistical Learning, Second Edition,* by T. Hastie, R. Tibshirani, and J. Friedman, Springer, 2009). The bias/variance decomposition says this:

```
E[(y[i]-f(x[i,]))^2] = bias^2 + variance + irreducibleError
```

Model bias is the portion of the error that your chosen modeling technique will never get right, often because some aspect of the true process isn't expressible within the assumptions of the chosen model. For example, if the relationship between the outcome and the input variables is curved or nonlinear, you can't fully model it with linear regression, which only considers linear relationships. You can often reduce bias by moving to more complicated modeling ideas: kernelizing, GAMs, adding interactions, and so on. Many modeling methods can increase model complexity (to try to reduce bias) on their own, for example, decision trees, KNN, support vector machines, and neural nets. But until you have a lot of data, increasing model complexity has a good chance of increasing model variance.

Model variance is the portion of the error that your modeling technique gets wrong due to incidental relations in the data. The idea is this: a retraining of the model on new data might make different errors (this is how variance differs from bias). An example would be running KNN with k=1. When you do this, each test example is scored by matching to a single nearest training example. If that example happened to be positive, your classification will be positive. This is one reason we tend to run KNN with a larger `k`: it gives us the chance to get more reliable estimates of the nature of neighborhood (by including more examples) at the expense of making

[1] The fact that minimizing the squared error gets expected values right is an important fact that gets used in method design again and again.

neighborhoods a bit less local or specific. More data and averaging ideas (like bagging) greatly reduce model variance.

Irreducible error is the truly unmodelable portion of the problem (given the current variables). If we have `i,j` such that `x[i,]=x[j,]`, then `(y[i]-y[j])^2` contributes to the irreducible error. What we've been calling a Bayes rate or error rate of a saturated model is an ideal model with no bias or variance term: its only source of error is the irreducible error. Again, we emphasize that irreducible error is measured with respect to a given set of variables; add more variables, and you have a new situation that may have its own lower irreducible error.

The point is that you can always think of modeling error as coming from three sources: bias, variance, and irreducible error. When you're trying to increase model performance, you can choose what to try based on which of these you are trying to reduce.

Averaging is a powerful tool

Under fairly mild assumptions, averaging reduces variance. For example, for data with identically distributed independent values, the variance of averages of groups of size `n` has a variance of `1/n` of the variance of individual values. This is one of the reasons why you can build models that accurately forecast population or group rates even when predicting individual events is difficult. So although it may be easy to forecast the number of murders per year in San Francisco, you can't predict who will be killed. In addition to shrinking variances, averaging also reshapes distributions to look more and more like the normal distribution (this is the central limit theorem and related to the law of large numbers).

STATISTICAL EFFICIENCY

The efficiency of an unbiased statistical procedure is defined as how much variance is in the procedure for a given dataset size. More efficient procedures require less data to get below a given amount of variance. This differs from computational efficiency, which is about how much work is needed to produce an estimate.

When you have a lot of data, statistical efficiency becomes less critical (which is why we haven't emphasized it in this book). But when it's expensive to produce more data (such as in drug trials), statistical efficiency is your primary concern. In this book, we take the approach that we usually have a lot of data, so we can prefer general methods that are somewhat statistically inefficient (such as using a test holdout set, using cross-validation for calibration, and so on) to more specialized statistically efficient methods (such as specific ready-made parametric tests like the Wald test and others).

Remember: it's a luxury, not a right, to ignore statistical efficiency. If your project has such a need, you'll want to consult with expert statisticians to get the advantages of best practices.

B.2.2 A/B tests

Hard statistical problems usually arise from poor experimental design. This section describes a simple, good statistical design philosophy called *A/B testing* that has very simple theory. The ideal experiment is one where you have two groups—control (A) and treatment (B)—and the following holds:

- Each group is big enough that you get a reliable measurement (this drives significance).
- Each group is (up to a single factor) distributed exactly like populations you expect in the future (this drives relevance). In particular, both samples are run in parallel at the same time.
- The two groups differ only with respect to the single factor you're trying to test.

A common way to set up such an ideal test situation is called an A/B test. In an A/B test, a new idea, treatment, or improvement is proposed and then tested for effect. A common example is a proposed change to a retail website that it is hoped will improve the rate of conversion from browsers to purchasers. Usually the treatment group is called *B* and an untreated or control group is called *A*. As a reference, we recommend "Practical Guide to Controlled Experiments on the Web" (R. Kohavi, R. Henne, and D. Sommerfield, KDD, 2007).

SETTING UP A/B TESTS

Some care must be taken in running an A/B test. It's important that the A and B groups be run at the same time. This helps defend the test from any potential confounding effects that might be driving their own changes in conversion rate (hourly effects, source-of-traffic effects, day-of-week effects, and so on). Also, you need to know that differences you're measuring are in fact due to the change you're proposing and not due to differences in the control and test infrastructures. To control for infrastructure, you should run a few A/A tests (tests where you run the same experiment in both A and B).

Randomization is the key tool in designing A/B tests. But the split into A and B needs to be made in a sensible manner. For example, for user testing, you don't want to split raw clicks from the same user session into A/B because then A/B would both have clicks from users that may have seen either treatment site. Instead, you'd maintain per-user records and assign users permanently to either the A or the B group when they arrive. One trick to avoid a lot of record-keeping between different servers is to compute a hash of the user information and assign a user to A or B depending on whether the hash comes out even or odd (thus all servers make the same decision without having to communicate).

EVALUATING A/B TESTS

The key measurements in an A/B test are the size of effect measured and the significance of the measurement. The natural alternative (or null hypothesis) to B being a good treatment is that B makes no difference, or B even makes things worse. Unfortunately, a typical failed A/B test often doesn't look like certain defeat. It usually looks like the positive effect you're looking for is there and you just need a slightly larger follow-up sample size to achieve significance. Because of issues like this, it's critical to reason through acceptance/rejection conditions before running tests.

Let's work an example A/B test. Suppose we've run an A/B test about conversion rate and collected the following data.

Listing B.12 Building simulated A/B test data

```
set.seed(123515)

d <- rbind(

    data.frame(group='A',converted=rbinom(100000,size=1,p=0.05)),

    data.frame(group='B',converted=rbinom(10000,size=1,p=0.055))

)
```

Build a data frame to store simulated examples.

Add 100,000 examples from the A group simulating a conversion rate of 5%.

Add 10,000 examples from the B group simulating a conversion rate of 5.5%.

Once we have the data, we summarize it into the essential counts using a data structure called a contingency table.[2]

Listing B.13 Summarizing the A/B test into a contingency table

```
tab <- table(d)
print(tab)
     converted
group     0     1
    A 94979  5021
    B  9398   602
```

The contingency table is what statisticians call a *sufficient statistic*: it contains all we need to know about the experiment. We can print the observed conversion rates of the A and B groups.

Listing B.14 Calculating the observed A and B rates

```
aConversionRate <- tab['A','1']/sum(tab['A',])
print(aConversionRate)
## [1] 0.05021
bConversionRate <- tab['B','1']/sum(tab['B',])
print(bConversionRate)
## [1] 0.0602
commonRate <- sum(tab[,'1'])/sum(tab)
print(commonRate)
## [1] 0.05111818
```

We see that the A group was measured at near 5% and the B group was measured near 6%. What we want to know is this: can we trust this difference? Could such a difference be likely for this sample size due to mere chance and measurement noise?

---

2 The confusion matrices we used in section 5.2.1 are also examples of contingency tables.

We need to calculate a significance to see if we ran a large enough experiment (obviously, we'd want to design an experiment that was large enough, what we call *test power,* which we'll discuss in section B.2.3). What follows are a few good tests that are quick to run.

Fisher's test for independence

The first test we can run is Fisher's contingency table test. In the Fisher test, the null hypothesis that we're hoping to reject is that conversion is independent of group, or that the A and B groups are exactly identical. The Fisher test gives a probability of seeing an independent dataset (A=B) show a departure from independence as large as what we observed. We run the test as shown in the next listing.

Listing B.15 Calculating the significance of the observed difference in rates

```
fisher.test(tab)

    Fisher's Exact Test for Count Data

data:  tab
p-value = 2.469e-05
alternative hypothesis: true odds ratio is not equal to 1
95 percent confidence interval:
 1.108716 1.322464
sample estimates:
odds ratio
  1.211706
```

This is a great result. The p-value (which in this case is the probability of observing a difference this large if we in fact had A=B) is 2.469e-05, which is very small. This is considered a significant result. The other thing to look for is the *odds ratio*: the practical importance of the claimed effect (sometimes also called *clinical significance,* which is not a statistical significance). An odds ratio of 1.2 says that we're measuring a 20% relative improvement in conversion rate between the A and B groups. Whether you consider this large or small (typically, 20% is considered large) is an important business question.

Frequentist significance test

Another way to estimate significance is to again temporarily assume that A and B come from an identical distribution with a common conversion rate, and see how likely it would be that the B group scores as high as it did by mere chance. If we consider a binomial distribution centered at the common conversion rate, we'd like to see that there's not a lot of probability mass for conversion rates at or above B's level. This would mean the observed difference is unlikely if A=B. We'll work through the calculation in the following listing.

Listing B.16 Computing frequentist significance

```
print(pbinom(                       <- Use the pbinom() call to calculate how likely different observed counts are.
    lower.tail=F,                   <- Signal we want the probability of being greater than a given q.
    q=tab['B','1']-1,               <- Ask for the probability of seeing at least as many conversions as our observed B groups did.
    size=sum(tab['B',]),            <- Specify the total number of trials as equal to what we saw in our B group.
    prob=commonRate                 <- Specify the conversion probability at the estimated common rate.
    ))

## [1] 3.153319e-05
```

This is again a great result. The calculated probability is small, meaning such a difference is hard to achieve by chance if A=B.

Bayesian posterior estimate

We can also find a Bayesian posterior estimate of what the B conversion rate is. To do this, we need to supply priors (in this case, centered around the common rate) and plot the posterior distribution for the B conversion rate. In a Bayesian analysis, the priors are supposed to be our guess at the distribution of the B conversion rate before looking at any data, so we pick something uninformative like the A conversion rate or some diffuse distribution. The posterior estimate is our estimate of the complete distribution of the B conversion rate after we've looked at the data. In a Bayesian analysis, uncertainty is measured as distributions of what we're trying to predict (as opposed to the more common frequentist analysis where uncertainty is modeled as noise or variations in alternate samples and measurements). For all this complexity, there's code that makes either analysis a one-line operation and it's clear what we're looking for in a good result. In a good result, we'd hope to see a posterior distribution centered around a high B rate that has little mass below the A rate.

The most common Bayesian analysis for binomial/Bernoulli experiments is to encode our priors and posteriors as a beta distribution and measure how much mass is in the left tail of the distribution, as shown in the next listing.

Listing B.17 Bayesian estimate of the posterior tail mass

```
print(pbeta(                        <- Use pbeta() to estimate how likely different observed conversion rates are.
    aConversionRate,                <- Ask for the probability of seeing a conversion rate no larger than aConversionRate.
```

```
shape1=commonRate+tab['B','1'],
shape2=(1-commonRate)+tab['B','0']))
## [1] 4.731817e-06
```

Estimate conversion count as prior commonRate plus the B observations.

Estimate nonconversion count as prior 1-commonRate plus the B observations.

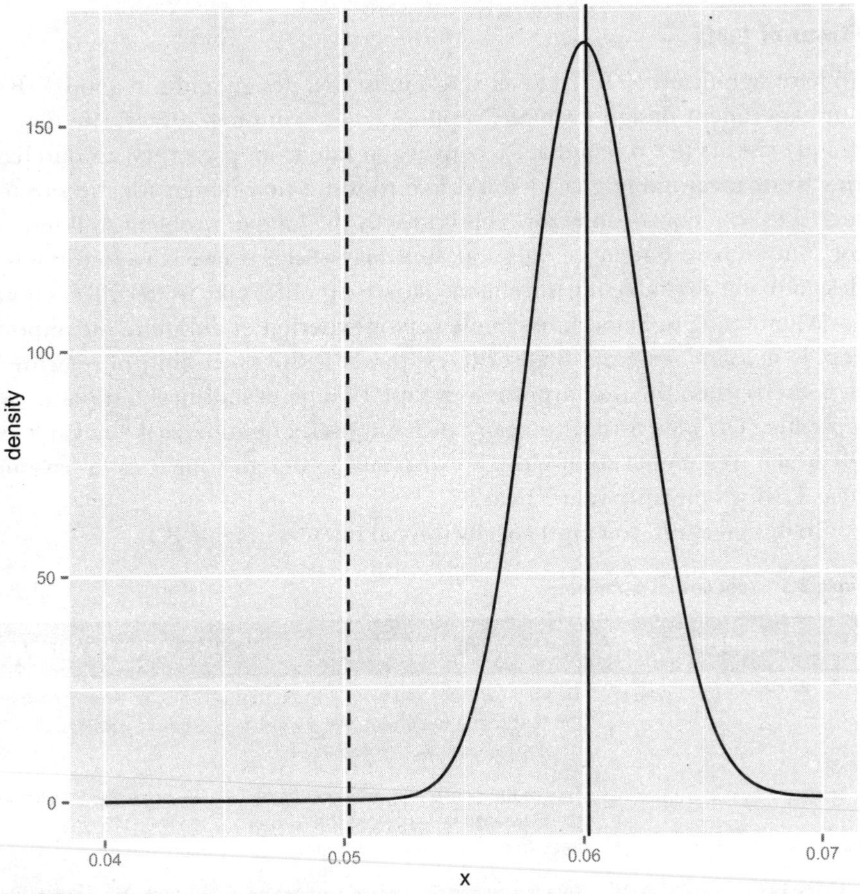

Figure B.8 Posterior distribution of the B conversion rate. The dashed line is the A conversion rate.

And again we have an excellent result. The number 4.731817e-06 is called the *posterior estimate* of the probability of seeing a conversion rate no higher than the A rate given the observed B data. This number being small means we estimate the unknown true B rate to likely be larger than the A rate. We can plot the entire posterior distribution (shown in figure B.8) as shown in the following listing.

Listing B.18 Plotting the posterior distribution of the B group

```
library('ggplot2')
plt <- data.frame(x=seq(from=0.04,to=0.07,length.out=301))
```

```
plt$density <- dbeta(plt$x,
    shape1=commonRate+tab['B','1'],
    shape2=(1-commonRate)+tab['B','0'])
ggplot(dat=plt) +
    geom_line(aes(x=x,y=density)) +
    geom_vline(aes(xintercept=bConversionRate)) +
    geom_vline(aes(xintercept=aConversionRate),linetype=2)
```

B.2.3 Power of tests

To have significant A/B test results, you must first design and run good A/B tests. For our experiment design example, suppose you're running a travel site that has 6,000 unique visitors per day and a 4% conversion rate from page views to purchase enquiries (your measurable goal).[3] You'd like to test a new design for the site to see if it increases your conversion rate. This is exactly the kind of problem A/B tests are made for! But we have one more question: how many users do we have to route to the new design to get a reliable measurement? How long will it take us to collect enough data?

When trying to determine sample size or experiment duration, the important concept is *statistical test power*. Statistical test power is the probability of rejecting the null hypothesis when the null hypothesis is false.[4] Think of statistical test power as 1 minus a p-value. The idea is this: you can't pick out useful treatments if you can't even identify which treatments are useless. So you want to design your tests to have test power near 1, which means p-values near 0.

To design a test, you must specify the parameters in table B.1.

Table B.1 Test design parameters

Parameter	Meaning	Value for our example
`confidence` (or `power`)	This is how likely you want it to be that the test result is correct. We'll write `confidence = 1 - errorProb`.	0.95 (or 95% confident), or `errorProb=0.05`.
`targetRate`	This is the conversion rate you hope the B treatment achieves: the further away from the A rate, the better.	We hope the B treatment is at least 0.045 or a 4.5% conversion rate.
`difference`	This is how big an error in conversion rate estimate we can tolerate.	We'll try to estimate the conversion rate to within plus/minus 0.4%, or 0.004, which is greater than the distance from our `targetRate` and our historical A conversion rate.

So the B part of our experimental design is to find out how many customers we'd have to route to the B treatment to have a very good chance of seeing a B conversion rate in the range of 4.1–4.9% if the true B conversion rate were in fact 4.5%. This would be a

[3] We're taking the 4% rate from http://mng.bz/7pT3.

[4] See B. S. Everitt, *The Cambridge Dictionary of Statistics, Second Edition*, Cambridge University Press, 2010.

useful experiment to run if we were trying to establish that the B conversion rate is in fact larger than the historic A conversion rate of 4%. In a complete experiment, we'd also work out how much traffic to send to the A group to get a reliable confirmation that the overall rate hasn't drifted (that the new B effect is due to being in group B, not just due to things changing over time).

The formula in listing B.19 gives a rule of thumb yielding an estimate of needed experiment sizes. Such a rule of thumb is important to know because it's simple enough that you can see how changes in requirements (rate we are assuming, difference in rates we are trying to detect, and confidence we require in the experiment) affect test size.

Listing B.19 Sample size estimate

```
estimate <- function(targetRate,difference,errorProb) {
   ceiling(-log(errorProb)*targetRate/(difference^2))
}

est <- estimate(0.045,0.004,0.05)
print(est)
## [1] 8426
```

We need about 8,426 visitors to have a 95% chance of observing a B conversion rate of at least 0.041 if the true unknown B conversion rate is at least 0.045. We'd also want to route a larger number of visitors to the A treatment to get a tight bound on the control conversion rate over the same period. The estimate is derived from what's called a *distribution tail bound* and is specialized for small probabilities (which is usually the case with conversion rates; see http:/mng.bz/Mj62).

More important than how the estimate is derived is what's said by its form. Reducing the probability of error (or increasing experimental power) is cheap, as error probability enters the formula through a logarithm. Measuring small differences in performance is expensive; the reciprocal of difference enters the formula as a square. So it's easy to design experiments that measure large performance differences with high confidence, but hard to design experiments that measure small performance differences with even moderate confidence. You should definitely not run A/B tests where the proposed improvements are very small and thus hard to measure (and also of low value).

R can easily calculate exact test power and propose test sizes without having to memorize any canned tables or test guides. All you have to do is model a precise question in terms of R's distribution functions, as in the next listing.

Listing B.20 Exact binomial sample size calculation

```
errorProb <- function(targetRate,difference,size) {
```

Define a function that calculates the probability of seeing a low number of conversions, assuming the actual conversion rate is targetRate and the size of the experiment is size. Low is considered be a count that's at least difference*size below the expected value targetRate*size.

```
  pbinom(ceiling((targetRate-difference)*size),
     size=size,prob=targetRate)
}

print(errorProb(0.045,0.004,est))
## [1] 0.04153646

binSearchNonPositive <- function(fEventuallyNegative) {
  low <- 1
  high <- low+1
  while(fEventuallyNegative(high)>0) {
    high <- 2*high
  }
  while(high>low+1) {
    m <- low + (high-low) %/% 2
    if(fEventuallyNegative(m)>0) {
       low <- m
    } else {
       high <- m
    }
  }
  high
}

actualSize <- function(targetRate,difference,errorProb) {
  binSearchNonPositive(function(n) {
      errorProb(targetRate,difference,n) - errorProb })
}

size <- actualSize(0.045,0.004,0.05)
print(size)
## [1] 7623
print(errorProb(0.045,0.004,size))
## [1] 0.04983659
```

Calculate probability of a bad experiment using estimated experiment size. The failure odds are around 4% (under the 5% we're designing for), which means the estimate size was slightly high.

Define a binary search that finds a non-positive value of a function that's guaranteed to be eventually negative. This search works around the minor non-monotonicity in errorProb() (due to rounding issues).

Calculate the required sample size for our B experiment.

So it's enough to route 7,623 visitors to the B treatment to expect a successful measurement. In running the experiment, it's important to use the precise population size estimate given by R's `pbinom()` distribution function. But for thinking and planning, it helps to have a simple expression in mind (such as the formula found in listing B.19).

Venue shopping reduces test power

We've discussed test power and significance under the assumption you're running one large test. In practice, you may run multiple tests trying many treatments to see if any treatment delivers an improvement. This reduces your test power. If you run 20 treatments, each with a p-value goal of 0.05, you would expect one test to appear to show significant improvement, even if all 20 treatments are useless. Testing multiple treatments or even reinspecting the same treatment many times is a form of "venue shopping" (you keep asking at different venues until you get a ruling in your favor). Calculating the loss of test power is formally called "applying the Bonferroni correction" and is as simple as multiplying your significance estimates by your number of tests (remember, large values are bad for significances or p-values). To compensate for this loss of test power, you can run each of the underlying tests at a tighter p cutoff: p divided by the number of tests you intend to run.

B.2.4 Specialized statistical tests

Throughout this book, we concentrate on building predictive models and evaluating significance, either through the modeling tool's built-in diagnostics or through empirical resampling (such as bootstrap tests or permutation tests). In statistics, there's an efficient correct test for the significance of just about anything you commonly calculate. Choosing the right standard test gives you a good implementation of the test and access to literature that explains the context and implications of the test. Let's work on calculating a simple correlation and finding the matching correct test.

We'll work with a simple synthetic example that should remind you a bit of our PUMS Census work in chapter 7. Suppose we've measured both earned income (money earned in the form of salary) and capital gains (money received from investments) for 100 individuals. Further suppose that there's no relation between the two for our individuals (in the real world, there's a correlation, but we need to make sure our tools don't report one even when there's none). We'll set up a simple dataset representing this situation with some lognormally distributed data.

Listing B.21 Building a synthetic uncorrelated income example

```
set.seed(235236)                                    <- Set the pseudo-random seed to a known value so the demonstration is repeatable.
d <- data.frame(EarnedIncome=100000*rlnorm(100),
                CapitalGains=100000*rlnorm(100))    <- Generate our synthetic data.
print(with(d,cor(EarnedIncome,CapitalGains)))
# [1] -0.01066116                                   <- The correlation is -0.01, which is very near 0—indicating (as designed) no relation.
```

We claim the observed correlation of -0.01 is statistically indistinguishable from 0 (or no effect). This is something we should quantify. A little research tells us the common correlation is called the *Pearson coefficient*, and the significance test for a Pearson coefficient for normally distributed data is a Student t-test (with the number of degrees of freedom equal to the number of items minus 2). We know our data is not normally distributed (it is, in fact, lognormally distributed), so we'd research further and find the preferred solution is to compare the data by rank (instead of by value) and use a test like Spearman's rho or Kendall's tau. We'll use Spearman's rho, as it can track both positive and negative correlations (whereas Kendall's tau tracks degree of agreement).

A fair question is, how do we know which is the exact right test to use? The answer is, by studying statistics. Be aware that there are a lot of tests, giving rise to books like *100 Statistical Tests: in R* by N. D. Lewis (Heather Hills Press, 2013). We also suggest that if you know the name of a test, consult Everitt's *The Cambridge Dictionary of Statistics*.

Another way to find the right test is using R's help system. `help(cor)` tells us that `cor()` implements three different calculations (Pearson, Spearman, and Kendall) and that there's a matching function called `cor.test()` that performs the appropriate significance test. Since we weren't too far off the beaten path, we only need to read up on these three tests and settle on the one we're interested in (in this case, Spearman). So let's redo our correlation with the correct test and check the significance.

Listing B.22 Calculating the (non)significance of the observed correlation

```
with(d,cor(EarnedIncome,CapitalGains,method='spearman'))
# [1] 0.03083108
with(d,cor.test(EarnedIncome,CapitalGains,method='spearman'))
#
#       Spearman's rank correlation rho
#
#data:  EarnedIncome and CapitalGains
#S = 161512, p-value = 0.7604
#alternative hypothesis: true rho is not equal to 0
#sample estimates:
#       rho
#0.03083108
```

We see the Spearman correlation is 0.03 with a p-value of 0.7604, which means truly uncorrelated data would show a coefficient this large about 76% of the time. So there's no significant effect (which is exactly how we designed our synthetic example).

B.3 Examples of the statistical view of data

Compared to statistics, machine learning and data science have an optimistic view of working with data. In data science, you quickly pounce on noncausal relations in the hope that they'll hold up and help with future prediction. Much of statistics is about how data can lie to you and how such relations can mislead you. We only have space for a couple of examples, so we'll concentrate on two of the most common issues: sampling bias and missing variable bias.

B.3.1 Sampling bias

Sampling bias is any process that systematically alters the distribution of observed data.[5] The data scientist must be aware of the possibility of sampling bias and be prepared to detect it and fix it. The most effective fix is to fix your data collection methodology.

For our sampling bias example, we'll continue with the income example we started in section B.2.4. Suppose through some happenstance we were studying only a high-earning subset of our original population (perhaps we polled them at some exclusive event). The following listing shows how, when we restrict to a high-earning set, it appears that earned income and capital gains are strongly anticorrelated. We get a correlation of -0.86 (so think of the anticorrelation as explaining about `(-0.86)^2 = 0.74 = 74%` of the variance; see http://mng.bz/ndYf) and a p-value very near 0 (so it's unlikely the unknown true correlation of more data produced in this manner is in fact 0). The following listing demonstrates the calculation.

[5] We would have liked to use the common term "censored" for this issue, but in statistics the phrase *censored observations* is reserved for variables that have only been recorded up to a limit or bound. So it would be potentially confusing to try to use the term to describe missing observations.

Listing B.23 Misleading significance result from biased observations

```
veryHighIncome <- subset(d, EarnedIncome+CapitalGains>=500000)
print(with(veryHighIncome,cor.test(EarnedIncome,CapitalGains,
    method='spearman')))
#
#       Spearman's rank correlation rho
#
#data:  EarnedIncome and CapitalGains
#S = 1046, p-value < 2.2e-16
#alternative hypothesis: true rho is not equal to 0
#sample estimates:
#       rho
#-0.8678571
```

Some plots help show what's going on. Figure B.9 shows the original dataset with the best linear relation line run through. Note that the line is nearly flat (indicating change in x doesn't predict change in y).

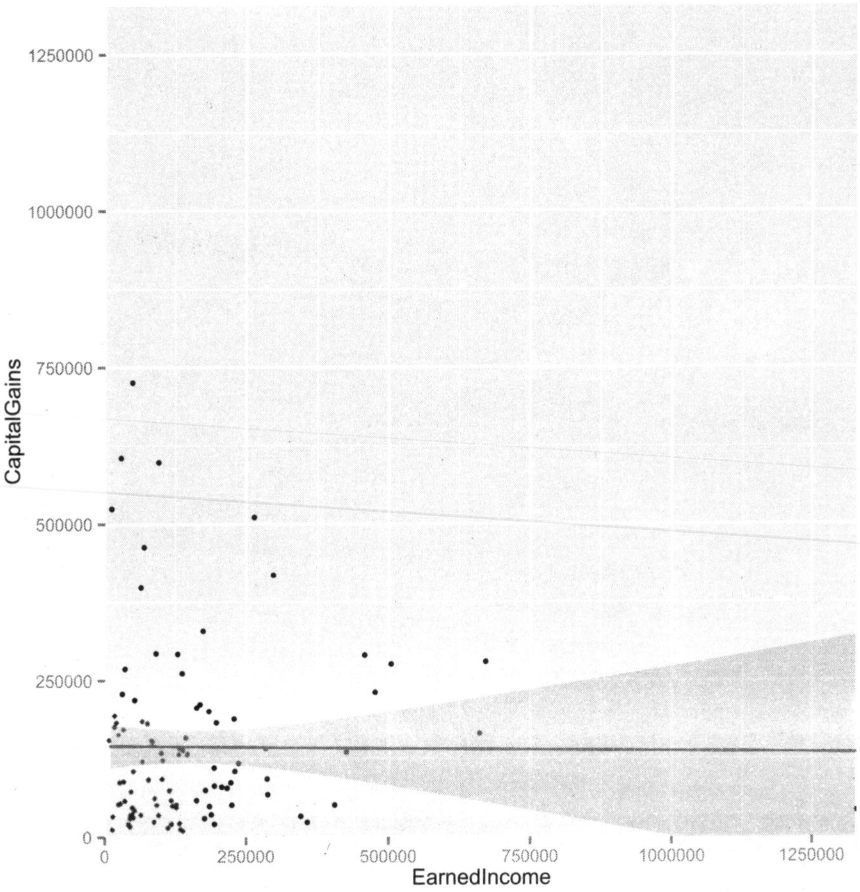

Figure B.9 Earned income versus capital gains

Figure B.10 shows the best trend line run through the high income dataset. It also shows how cutting out the points below the line `x+y=500000` leaves a smattering of rare high-value events arranged in a direction that crudely approximates the slope of our cut line (-0.8678571 being a crude approximation for -1). It's also interesting to note that the bits we suppressed aren't correlated among themselves, so the effect wasn't a matter of suppressing a correlated group out of an uncorrelated cloud to get a negative correlation.

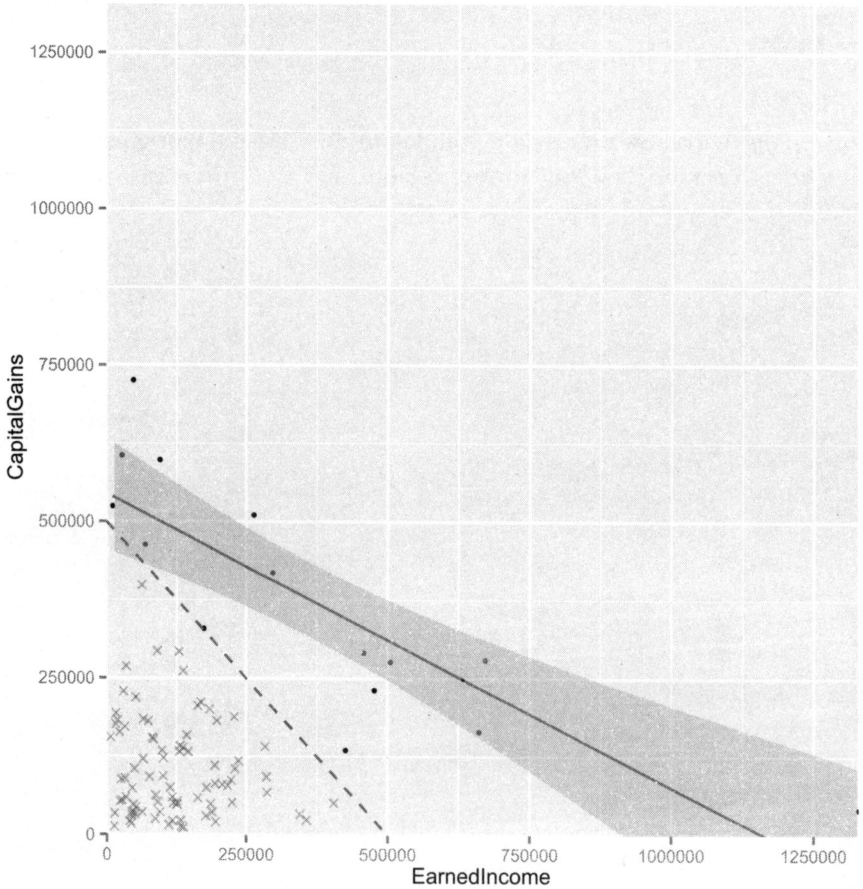

Figure B.10 Biased earned income versus capital gains

The code to produce figures B.9 and B.10 and calculate the correlation between suppressed points is shown in the following listing.

Listing B.24 Plotting biased view of income and capital gains

```
library(ggplot2)
ggplot(data=d,aes(x=EarnedIncome,y=CapitalGains)) +
   geom_point() + geom_smooth(method='lm') +
```

```
  coord_cartesian(xlim=c(0,max(d)),ylim=c(0,max(d)))
```

Plot all of the income data with linear trend line (and uncertainty band).

```
ggplot(data=veryHighIncome,aes(x=EarnedIncome,y=CapitalGains)) +
  geom_point() + geom_smooth(method='lm') +
  geom_point(data=subset(d,EarnedIncome+CapitalGains<500000),
        aes(x=EarnedIncome,y=CapitalGains),
     shape=4,alpha=0.5,color='red') +
  geom_segment(x=0,xend=500000,y=500000,yend=0,
     linetype=2,alpha=0.5,color='red') +
  coord_cartesian(xlim=c(0,max(d)),ylim=c(0,max(d)))
```

Plot the very high income data and linear trend line (also include cut-off and portrayal of suppressed data).

```
print(with(subset(d,EarnedIncome+CapitalGains<500000),
   cor.test(EarnedIncome,CapitalGains,method='spearman')))
#
#        Spearman's rank correlation rho
#
#data:  EarnedIncome and CapitalGains
#S = 107664, p-value = 0.6357
#alternative hypothesis: true rho is not equal to 0
#sample estimates:
#        rho
#-0.05202267
```

Compute correlation of suppressed data.

B.3.2 Omitted variable bias

Many data science clients expect data science to be a quick process, where every convenient variable is thrown in at once and a best possible result is quickly obtained. Statisticians are rightfully wary of such an approach due to various negative effects such as omitted variable bias, collinear variables, confounding variables, and nuisance variables. In this section, we'll discuss one of the more general issues: omitted variable bias.

WHAT IS OMITTED VARIABLE BIAS?

In its simplest form, omitted variable bias occurs when a variable that isn't included in the model is both correlated with what we're trying to predict and correlated with a variable that's included in our model. When this effect is strong, it causes problems, as the model-fitting procedure attempts to use the variables in the model to both directly predict the desired outcome and to stand in for the effects of the missing variable. This can introduce biases, create models that don't quite make sense, and result in poor generalization performance.

The effect of omitted variable bias is easiest to see in a regression example, but it can affect any type of model.

AN EXAMPLE OF OMITTED VARIABLE BIAS

We've prepared a synthetic dataset called `synth.RData` (download from https://github.com/WinVector/zmPDSwR/tree/master/bioavailability) that has an omitted variable problem typical for a data science project. To start, please download `synth.RData` and load it into R, as the next listing shows.

Listing B.25 Summarizing our synthetic biological data

```
> load('synth.RData')
> print(summary(s))
      week          Caco2A2BPapp         FractionHumanAbsorption
 Min.   :  1.00   Min.   :6.994e-08    Min.   :0.09347
 1st Qu.: 25.75   1st Qu.:7.312e-07    1st Qu.:0.50343
 Median : 50.50   Median :1.378e-05    Median :0.86937
 Mean   : 50.50   Mean   :2.006e-05    Mean   :0.71492
 3rd Qu.: 75.25   3rd Qu.:4.238e-05    3rd Qu.:0.93908
 Max.   :100.00   Max.   :6.062e-05    Max.   :0.99170
> head(s)
  week Caco2A2BPapp FractionHumanAbsorption
1    1 6.061924e-05              0.11568186
2    2 6.061924e-05              0.11732401
3    3 6.061924e-05              0.09347046
4    4 6.061924e-05              0.12893540
5    5 5.461941e-05              0.19021858
6    6 5.370623e-05              0.14892154
> View(s)
```

Display a date in spreadsheet-like window. View is one of the commands that has a much better implementation in RStudio than in basic R.

This loads synthetic data that's supposed to represent a simplified view of the kind of data that might be collected over the history of a pharmaceutical ADME[6] or bioavailability project. RStudio's `View()` spreadsheet is shown in figure B.11.

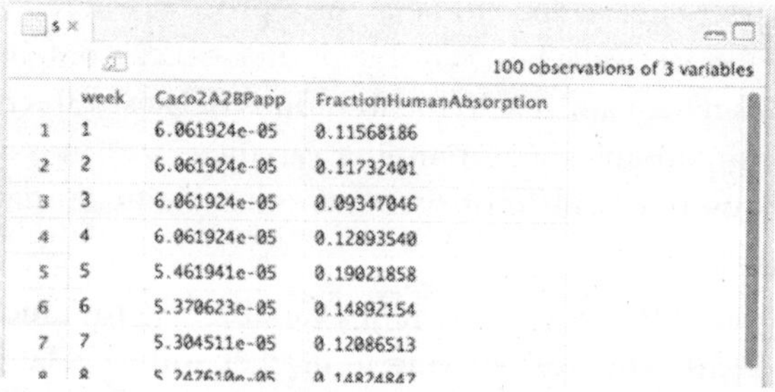

Figure B.11 View of rows from the bioavailability dataset

The columns of this dataset are described in table B.2.

Table B.2 Bioavailability columns

Column	Description
`week`	In this project, we suppose that a research group submits a new drug candidate molecule for assay each week. To keep things simple, we use the week number (in terms of weeks since the start of the project) as the identifier for the molecule and the data row. This is an optimization project, which means each proposed molecule is made using lessons learned from all of the previous molecules. This is typical of many projects, but it means the data rows aren't mutually exchangeable (an important assumption that we often use to justify statistical and machine learning techniques).

[6] ADME stands for absorption, distribution, metabolism, excretion; it helps determine which molecules make it into the human body through ingestion and thus could even be viable candidates for orally delivered drugs.

Table B.2 Bioavailability columns *(continued)*

Column	Description
Caco2A2BPapp	This is the first assay run (and the "cheap" one). The Caco2 test measures how fast the candidate molecule passes through a membrane of cells derived from a specific large intestine carcinoma (cancers are often used for tests, as noncancerous human cells usually can't be cultured indefinitely). The Caco2 test is a stand-in or analogy test. The test is thought to simulate one layer of the small intestine that it's morphologically similar to (though it lacks a number of forms and mechanisms found in the actual small intestine). Think of Caco2 as a cheap test to evaluate a factor that correlates with bioavailability (the actual goal of the project).
FractionHuman-Absorption	This is the second assay run and is what fraction of the drug candidate is absorbed by human test subjects. Obviously, these tests would be expensive to run and subject to a lot of safety protocols. For this example, optimizing absorption is the actual end goal of the project.

We've constructed this synthetic data to represent a project that's trying to optimize human absorption by working through small variations of a candidate drug molecule. At the start of the project, they have a molecule that's highly optimized for the stand-in criteria Caco2 (which does correlate with human absorption), and through the history of the project, actual human absorption is greatly increased by altering factors that we're not tracking in this simplistic model. During drug optimization, it's common to have formerly dominant stand-in criteria revert to ostensibly less desirable values as other inputs start to dominate the outcome. So for our example project, the human absorption rate is rising (as the scientists successfully optimize for it) and the Caco2 rate is falling (as it started high and we're no longer optimizing for it, even though it *is* a useful feature).

One of the advantages of using synthetic data for these problem examples is that we can design the data to have a given structure, and then we know the model is correct if it picks this up and incorrect if it misses it. In particular, this dataset was designed such that Caco2 is always a positive contribution to fraction of absorption throughout the entire dataset. This data was generated using a random non-increasing sequence of plausible Caco2 measurements and then generating fictional absorption numbers, as shown next (the data frame d is the published graph we base our synthetic example on). We produce our synthetic data that's known to improve over time in the next listing.

Listing B.26 Building data that improves over time

```
set.seed(2535251)
s <- data.frame(week=1:100)
s$Caco2A2BPapp <- sort(sample(d$Caco2A2BPapp,100,replace=T),
   decreasing=T)
sigmoid <- function(x) {1/(1+exp(-x))}
s$FractionHumanAbsorption <-
  sigmoid(
   7.5 + 0.5*log(s$Caco2A2BPapp) +
```

Build synthetic examples.

Add in Caco2 to absorption relation learned from original dataset. Note the relation is positive: better Caco2 always drives better absorption in our synthetic dataset. We're log transforming Caco2, as it has over 3 decades of range.

```
    s$week/10 - mean(s$week/10) +
    rnorm(100)/3
    )
write.table(s,'synth.csv',sep=',',
   quote=F,row.names=F)
```

Add in a mean-0 noise term.

Add in a mean-0 term that depends on time to simulate the effects of improvements as the project moves forward.

The design of this data is this: Caco2 always has a positive effect (identical to the source data we started with), but this gets hidden by the `week` factor (and Caco2 is negatively correlated with `week`, because `week` is increasing and Caco2 is sorted in decreasing order). Time is not a variable we at first wish to model (it isn't something we usefully control), but analyses that omit time suffer from omitted variable bias. For the complete details, consult our GitHub example documentation (https://github.com/WinVector/zmPDSwR/tree/master/bioavailability).

A SPOILED ANALYSIS

In some situations, the true relationship between Caco2 and `FractionHumanAbsorption` is hidden because the variable `week` is positively correlated with `FractionHumanAbsorption` (as the absorption is being improved over time) and negatively correlated with Caco2 (as Caco2 is falling over time). `week` is a stand-in variable for all the other molecular factors driving human absorption that we're not recording or modeling. Listing B.27 shows what happens when we try to model the relation between Caco2 and `FractionHumanAbsorption` without using the `week` variable or any other factors.

Listing B.27 A bad model (due to omitted variable bias)

```
print(summary(glm(data=s,
   FractionHumanAbsorption~log(Caco2A2BPapp),
   family=binomial(link='logit'))))
## Warning: non-integer #successes in a binomial glm!
##
## Call:
## glm(formula = FractionHumanAbsorption ~ log(Caco2A2BPapp),
##     family = binomial(link = "logit"),
##      data = s)
##
## Deviance Residuals:
##     Min       1Q  Median       3Q      Max
## -0.609  -0.246  -0.118    0.202    0.557
##
## Coefficients:
##                    Estimate Std. Error z value Pr(>|z|)
## (Intercept)         -10.003      2.752   -3.64  0.00028 ***
## log(Caco2A2BPapp)    -0.969      0.257   -3.77  0.00016 ***
## ---
## Signif. codes:  0 '***' 0.001 '**' 0.01 '*' 0.05 '.' 0.1 ' ' 1
##
## (Dispersion parameter for binomial family taken to be 1)
##
##     Null deviance: 43.7821  on 99  degrees of freedom
## Residual deviance:  9.4621  on 98  degrees of freedom
```

```
## AIC: 64.7
##
## Number of Fisher Scoring iterations: 6
```

For details on how to read the glm() summary, please see section 7.2. Note that the sign of the Caco2 coefficient is negative, not what's plausible or what we expected going in. This is because the Caco2 coefficient isn't just recording the relation of Caco2 to FractionHumanAbsorption, but also having to record any relations that come through omitted correlated variables.

WORKING AROUND OMITTED VARIABLE BIAS

There are a number of ways to deal with omitted variable bias, the best ways being better experimental design and more variables. Other methods include use of fixed-effects models and hierarchical models. We'll demonstrate one of the simplest methods: adding in possibly important omitted variables. In the following listing, we redo the analysis with week included.

Listing B.28 A better model

```
print(summary(glm(data=s,
   FractionHumanAbsorption~week+log(Caco2A2BPapp),
   family=binomial(link='logit'))))
## Warning: non-integer #successes in a binomial glm!
##
## Call:
## glm(formula = FractionHumanAbsorption ~ week + log(Caco2A2BPapp),
##     family = binomial(link = "logit"), data = s)
##
## Deviance Residuals:
##     Min        1Q    Median       3Q       Max
## -0.3474  -0.0568  -0.0010   0.0709   0.3038
##
## Coefficients:
##                    Estimate Std. Error z value Pr(>|z|)
## (Intercept)          3.1413     4.6837    0.67   0.5024
## week                 0.1033     0.0386    2.68   0.0074 **
## log(Caco2A2BPapp)    0.5689     0.5419    1.05   0.2938
## ---
## Signif. codes:  0 '***' 0.001 '**' 0.01 '*' 0.05 '.' 0.1 ' ' 1
##
## (Dispersion parameter for binomial family taken to be 1)
##
##     Null deviance: 43.7821  on 99  degrees of freedom
## Residual deviance:  1.2595  on 97  degrees of freedom
## AIC: 47.82
##
## Number of Fisher Scoring iterations: 6
```

We recovered decent estimates of both the Caco2 and week coefficients, but we didn't achieve statistical significance on the effect of Caco2. Note that fixing omitted variable bias requires (even in our synthetic example) some domain knowledge to propose important omitted variables and the ability to measure the additional variables (and try to remove their impact through the use of an offset; see `help('offset')`).

At this point, you should have a more detailed intentional view of variables. There are, at the least, variables you can control (explanatory variables), important variables you can't control (nuisance variables), and important variables you don't know (omitted variables). Your knowledge of all of these variable types should affect your experimental design and your analysis.

appendix C *More tools and ideas worth exploring*

In data science, you're betting on the data and the process, not betting on any one magic technique. We advise designing your projects to be the pursuit of quantifiable goals that have already been linked to important business needs. To concretely demonstrate this work style, we emphasize building predictive models using methods that are easily accessible from R. This is a good place to start, but shouldn't be the end.

There's always more to do in a data science project. At the least, you can

- Recruit new partners
- Research more profitable business goals
- Design new experiments
- Specify new variables
- Collect more data
- Explore new visualizations
- Design new presentations
- Test old assumptions
- Implement new methods
- Try new tools

The point being this: there's always more to try. Minimize confusion by keeping a running journal of your actual goals and of things you haven't yet had time to try. And don't let tools and techniques distract you away from your goals and data. Always work with "your hands in the data." That being said, we close with some useful topics for further research (please see the bibliography for publication details).

C.1 More tools

The type of tool you need depends on your problem. If you're being overwhelmed by data volume, you need to look into big data tools. If you're having to produce a lot of custom processing, you want to look into additional programming languages. And if you have too little data, you want to study more sophisticated statistical procedures (that offer more *statistically efficient inference* than the simple cross-validation ideas we emphasize in this book).

C.1.1 R itself

We've only been able to scratch the surface of R. Table C.1 shows some important further topics for study.

Table C.1 R topics for follow-up

R topic	Points of interest
R programming and debugging	Our current favorite R book is Kabacoff's *R in Action*, which presents a good mix of R and statistics. A good source for R programming and debugging is Matloff's *The Art of R Programming*, which includes parallelism, cross-language calling, object-oriented programming, step debugging, and performance profiling. Other avenues to explore are various IDEs such as RStudio and Revolution R Enterprise.
R packages and documentation	R packages are easy for clients and partners to install, so learning how to produce them is a valuable skill. Package documentation files also let you extend R's `help()` system to include details about your work. A starter lesson can be found at http://cran.r-project.org/doc/manuals/R-exts.html.

C.1.2 Other languages

R is designed to support statistical data analysis through its large environment of packages (over 5,000 packages are now available from CRAN). You always hope your task is close to a standard statistical procedure and you only need to write a small amount of adapting code. But if you're going to produce a lot of custom code, you may want to consider using something other than R. Many other programing languages and environments exist and have different relative advantages and disadvantages. The following table surveys some exciting systems.

Table C.2 Other programming languages

Language	Description
Python	Python is a good scripting language with useful tools and libraries. Python has been making strong strides in the data science world with IPython interactive computing notebooks, pandas data frames, and RPy integration.
Julia	Julia is an expressive high-level programming language that compiles to very fast code. The idea is to write concise code (as in R) but then achieve performance comparable to raw C. Claims of 20x speedup aren't uncommon. Julia also supports distributed parallelism and IJulia (an IPython-inspired notebook system).
J	J is a powerful data processing language inspired by APL and what's called *variable-free* or *function-level* programming. In J, most of the work is done by operators used in a compact mathematical composition notation. J supports powerful vector operations (operations that work over a lot of data in parallel). APL-derived languages (in particular, K) have historically been popular in financial and time-series applications.

With so many exciting possibilities, why did we ever advocate using R? For most mid-size data science applications, R is the best tool for the task. Each of these systems does something better than R does, but R can be thought of as a best compromise.

C.1.3 Big data tools

The practical definition of *big data* is data at a scale where storing and processing the data becomes an engineering problem unto itself. When you hit that scale, you'll need to move away from pure R (which performs all work in memory) to packages that store results out of memory (such as ff storage, RHadoop, and others). But at some point you may have to move your data preparation out of R. Big data tools tend to be more painful to use than moderate-size tools (data frames and databases), so you don't want to commit to them until you have an actual need. Table C.3 touches on some important big data tools.

Table C.3 Common big data tools

Tool	Description
Hadoop	The main open source implementation of Google's MapReduce. MapReduce is the most common way to manipulate very large data. MapReduce organizes big data tasks into jobs consisting of an initial scan and transformation (the map step), followed by sorting and distribution data to aggregators (the reduce step). MapReduce is particularly good for preprocessing, report generation, and tasks like indexing (its original applications). Other machine learning and data science tasks can require managing a large number of map-reduce steps.
Mahout	Mahout is a collection of large-scale machine-learning libraries, many of which are hosted on top of Hadoop.
Drill, Impala	Drill and Impala (and Google's Dremel) are large-scale data tools specializing in nested records (things like documents with content and attributes, or use records with annotations). They attempt to bring power and scale to so-called schemaless data stores and can interact with stores like Cassandra, HBase, and MongoDB.
Pig, Hive, Presto	Various tools to bring SQL or SQL-like data manipulation to the big data environment.
Storm	Storm (see http://storm-project.net) can be thought of as a complement for MapReduce. MapReduce does everything in batch jobs (very high latency, but good eventual throughput) and is suitable for tasks like model construction. Storm organizes everything into what it calls *topologies*, which represent a proposed flow of individual data records through many stages of processing. So Storm is an interesting candidate for deploying models into production.
HDF5	Hierarchical Data Format 5 is a method of storing and organizing large collections of numeric data (with support for sparse structures). You're not likely to see HDF5 outside of scientific work, but there are R and Python libraries for working with HDF5 resources. So for some problems you may consider HDF5 in place of a SQL database.

C.2 More ideas

Data science is an excellent introduction to a number of fields that can be rewarding avenues of further study. The fields overlap, but each has its own emphasis. You can't be expert in all of these fields, but you should be aware of them and consider collaborating with partners expert in some of these fields. Here are some fields we find fascinating, with a few references if you want to learn more.

C.2.1 Adaptive learning

In this book, we use data science in a fairly static manner. The data has already been collected and the model is static after training is finished. Breaking this rigid model gives you a lot more to think about: online learning, transductive learning, and adversarial learning. In online (and stream) learning, you work with models that adapt to new data, often in environments where there's too much data to store. With transductive learning, models are built after being told which test examples they will be used on (great for dealing with test examples that have missing variables). In adversarial learning, models have to deal with the world adapting against them (especially relevant in spam filtering and fraud detection). Adversarial learning has some exciting new material coming out soon in Joseph, Nelson, Rubinstein, and Tygar's *Adversarial Machine Learning* (Cambridge University Press, projected publishing date 2014).

C.2.2 Statistical learning

This is one of our favorite fields. In statistical learning, the primary goal is to build predictive models, and the main tools are statistics (for characterizing model performance) and optimization (for fitting parameters). Important concepts include ensemble methods, regularization, and principled dimension reduction.

The definitive book on the topic is Hastie, Tibshirani, and Friedman's *The Elements of Statistical Learning, Second Edition.* The book has a mathematical bent, but unlike most references, it separates the common learning procedures from the more important proofs of solution properties. If you want to understand the consequences of a method, this is the book to study.

C.2.3 Computer science machine learning

The nonstatistical (computer science) view of machine learning includes concepts like expert systems, pattern recognition, clustering, association rules, version spaces, VC dimension, boosting, and support vector machines. In the classic computer science view of machine learning, nonstatistical quantities such as model complexity (measured in terms of VC dimension, minimum description length, or other measures) are used to prove theorems about model generalization performance. This is in contrast to the statistical view, where generalization error is seen as a form of training bias that you simply test for.

In our opinion, the last great book on the topic was Mitchell's *Machine Learning* (1997), but it doesn't cover enough of the current topics. Overall, we prefer the statistical learning treatment of topics, but there are some excellent books on specific topics. One such is Cristianini and Shawe-Taylor's *An Introduction to Support Vector Machines and Other Kernel-based Learning Methods.*

C.2.4 Bayesian methods

One of the big sins of common data science is using "point estimates" for everything. Unknowns are often modeled as single values, estimates are often single values, and even algorithm performance is often reported on a single test set (or even worse, just on the training set). Bayesian methods overcome these issues by working with explicit distributions before (prior) and after (posterior) learning.

Of particular interest are Bayesian hierarchical models, which are a great formal alternative to important tricks we use in the book (tricks like regularization, dimension reduction, and smoothing). Good books on the topic include Gelman, Carlin, Stern, Dunson, Vehtari, and Rubin's *Bayesian Data Analysis, Third Edition,* and Koller and Friedman's *Probabilistic Graphical Models: Principles and Techniques.*

C.2.5 Statistics

Statistics is a fascinating field in and of itself. Statistics covers a lot more about inference (trying to find the causes that are driving relations) than data science, and has a number of cool tools we aren't able to get to in this book (such as ready-made significance tests and laws of large numbers).

There are a number of good books; for a good introductory text, we recommend Freedman, Pisani, and Purves's *Statistics, Fourth Edition.*

C.2.6 Boosting

Boosting is a clever technique for reweighting training data to find submodels that are complementary to each other. You can think of boosting as a complement to bagging: bagging averages ensembles to reduce variance, and boosting manipulates weights to find more diverse models (good when you feel important effects may be hidden as interactions of variables). These ideas about data reweighting are interesting generalizations of the statistical ideas of offsets and orthogonality, but take some time to work through. We recommend trying the R package gbm (Generalized Boosted Regression Models): http://cran.r-project.org/web/packages/gbm/gbm.pdf.

C.2.7 Time series

Time series analysis can be a topic to itself. Part of the issue is the need to ensure that non-useful correlations between time steps don't interfere with inferring useful relations to external parameters. The obvious fix (differencing) introduces its own issues (root testing) and needs some care.

Good books on the topic include Shumway and Stoffer's *Time Series Analysis and Its Applications, Third Edition,* and Tsay's *Analysis of Financial Time Series, 2nd Edition.*

C.2.8 Domain knowledge

The big fixes for hard data science problems are (in order): better variables, better experimental design, more data, and better machine learning algorithms. The main way to get better variables is through intuition and picking up some domain knowledge. You don't have to work in the field to develop good domain knowledge, but you need partners who do and to spend some time thinking about the actual problem (taking a break from thinking about procedures and algorithms). A very good example of this comes from the famous "Sears catalogue problem" (see John F. Magee, "Operations Research at Arthur D. Little, Inc.: The Early Years") where clever consultants figured out the variable most predictive of future customer value was past purchase frequency (outperforming measures like order size). The lesson is: you can build tools to try and automatically propose new features, but effective data science is more often done by having people propose potential features and letting the statistics work out their relative utility.

bibliography

Adler, Joseph. *R in a Nutshell, Second Edition.* O'Reilly Media, 2012.

Agresti, Alan. *Categorical Data Analysis, Third Edition.* Wiley Publications, 2012.

Alley, Michael. *The Craft of Scientific Presentations.* Springer, 2003.

Brooks, Jr., Frederick P. *The Mythical Man-Month: Essays on Software Engineering.* Addison-Wesley, 1995.

Casella, George and Roger L. Berger. *Statistical Inference.* Duxbury, 1990.

Celko, Joe. *SQL for Smarties, Fourth Edition.* Morgan Kauffman, 2011.

Chakrabarti, Soumen. *Mining the Web.* Morgan Kauffman, 2003.

Chambers, John M. *Software for Data Analysis.* Springer, 2008.

Chang, Winston. *R Graphics Cookbook.* O'Reilly Media, 2013.

Charniak, Eugene. *Statistical Language Learning.* MIT Press, 1993.

Cleveland, William S. *The Elements of Graphing Data.* Hobart Press, 1994.

Cover, Thomas M. and Joy A. Thomas. *Elements of Information Theory.* Wiley, 1991.

Cristianini, Nello and John Shawe-Taylor. *An Introduction to Support Vector Machines and Other Kernel-based Learning Methods.* Cambridge Press, 2000.

Dalgaard, Peter. *Introductory Statistics with R, Second Edition.* Springer, 2008.

Dimiduk, Nick and Amandeep Khurana. *HBase in Action.* Manning Publications, 2013.

Efron, Bradley and Robert Tibshirani. *An Introduction to the Bootstrap.* Chapman and Hall, 1993.

Everitt, B. S. *The Cambridge Dictionary of Statistics, Third Edition.* Cambridge Press, 2006.

Freedman, David. *Statistical Models: Theory and Practice.* Cambridge Press, 2009.

Freedman, David; Robert Pisani; and Roger Purves. *Statistics, Fourth Edition.* Norton, 2007.

Gandrud, Christopher. *Reproducible Research with R and RStudio.* CRC Press, 2014.

Gelman, Andrew; John B. Carlin; Hal S. Stern; David B. Dunson; Aki Vehtari; and Donald B. Rubin. *Bayesian Data Analysis, Third Edition.* CRC Press, 2013.

Gentle, James E. *Elements of Computational Statistics.* Springer, 2002.

Good, Philip. *Permutation Tests.* Springer, 2000.

Hastie, Trevor; Robert Tibshirani; and Jerome Friedman. *The Elements of Statistical Learning, Second Edition.* Springer, 2009.

James, Gareth; Daniela Witten; Trevor Hastie; and Robert Tibshirani. *An Introduction to Statistical Learning.* Springer, 2013.

Kabacoff, Robert. *R in Action, Second Edition.* Manning Publications, 2014.

Kennedy, Peter. *A Guide to Econometrics, Fifth Edition.* MIT Press, 2003.

Koller, Daphne and Nir Friedman. *Probabilistic Graphical Models: Principles and Techniques.* MIT Press, 2009.

Kuhn, Max and Kjell Johnson. *Applied Predictive Modeling.* Springer, 2013.

Loeliger, Jon and Matthew McCullough. *Version Control with Git, Second Edition.* O'Reilly Media, 2012.

Magee, John. "Operations Research at Arthur D. Little, Inc.: The Early Years." *Operations Research,* 2002. 50 (1), pp. 149-153.

Marz, Nathan and James Warren. *Big Data.* Manning Publications, 2014.

Matloff, Norman. *The Art of R Programming: A Tour of Statistical Software Design.* No Starch Press, 2011.

Mitchell, Tom M. *Machine Learning.* McGraw-Hill, 1997.

Provost, Foster and Tom Fawcett. *Data Science for Business.* O'Reilly Media, 2013.

Sachs, Lothar. *Applied Statistics, Second Edition.* Springer, 1984.

Seni, Giovanni and John Elder. *Ensemble Methods in Data Mining.* Morgan & Claypool, 2010.

Shawe-Taylor, John and Nello Cristianini. *Kernel Methods for Pattern Analysis.* Cambridge Press, 2004.

Shumway, Robert, and David Stoffer. *Time Series Analysis and Its Applications, Third Edition.* Springer, 2013.

Spector, Phil. *Data Manipulation with R.* Springer, 2008.

Spiegel, Murray R. and Larry J. Stephens. *Schaum's Outlines Statistics (Fourth Edition).* McGraw-Hill, 2011.

Tsay, Ruey S. *Analysis of Financial Time Series, 2nd Edition.* Wiley, 2005.

Tukey, John W. *Exploratory Data Analysis.* Pearson, 1977.

Wasserman, Larry. *All of Nonparametric Statistics.* Springer, 2006.

Wickham, Hadley. *ggplot2: Elegant Graphics for Data Analysis (Use R!).* Springer, 2009.

Xie, Yihui. *Dynamic Documents with R and knitr.* CRC Press, 2013.

index

Symbols

A

B

D

P

Q

R

S

T

W

X